# Gutting Mysticism

## Explaining the Roots of All Supernatural Beliefs

By

Endall Beall

First Edition



ISBN 13: 978-1984046550
ISBN 10: 1984046551

# Dedication

This book is dedicated to every person who can defeat the inner fear of changing their deep-rooted belief systems and exchange them for a higher truth that leads to wisdom and understanding, rather than living in a world of continual mystical mysteries.

# Table of Contents

# ACKNOWLEDGEMENTS

I want to acknowledge and express my gratitude to Richard Redhawk for allowing me to use his artwork for the cover of this book. I also want to express thanks to my friends and associates who served as sounding boards and helped in providing research assistance, insights and help in editing the final product while I worked to compile this book. You all know who you are, and you are not forgotten. My deepest thanks to all of you.

# INTRODUCTION

As I contemplated writing this introduction it occurred to me that many will come into this work cold and have no familiarity with the previous works of this Author. And since his other books address with vivid detail the same topics, how could he possibly Gut Mysticism any more than he already had?

But considering that I had made it my mission to find an error in the Author's works, unbeknownst to him, to disprove one of his assertions, and hold fast to my particular area of belief that contradicts his teachings, I made certain that I had access to all his previous published work, YouTube video productions, Patreon platform presentation, etc., because that's just what I do when I find something with so many pieces to the puzzle. And yet there's always something that doesn't fit in similar presentations and is only forced into the picture which raises a red flag for me. If that faulty piece was there, I was going to find it as I had done so many times before with other authors.

Perhaps he did know on some level why I was so interested and participated wherever possible, and perhaps even knew that by allowing my attempt to disprove it, I would gain the necessary freedom to advance my cognition in the process by default.

Mr. Beall does suggest throughout all his books his willingness to be corrected, so long as it's not just your denial or your belief that is the mechanism of protest and provide the evidence to show him his error and he'll consider it. I painstakingly attempted to disprove his chapter on the *Virus Vector*. I failed to do so.

Finding what isn't true is not so difficult. Finding what *is* true is where the rubber meets the road. And although I was primed for the information, I was in no way prepared for what was shown to me. The pieces that had always been missing were handed to me this time and I saw the rendering and not just a rendition of the original.

It is no wonder why academics and bible scholars suffer so intensely and ultimately fail in their attempts to describe the original. They are working with faulty renditions by those who wish to conceal the original and can only speculate on what they have been shown and heard, never looking below the surface for the intent of the original author.

What I did manage to do studying this new release, was to come away with an amazing amount of information that I would never have gotten otherwise and cannot dispute. Information I never cared to know that has realigned my perceptions completely and taken me on a journey out of first cognition thinking and placed me into a whole new arena of awareness.

After completing the book, I finally realized just how critical it is to know how the canvas was prepared by the original artist, what the intent was in the creation and why it was so easy to manipulate humanity for so long. Until you see exactly what the original artist's/creator's vision was prior to the brush ever laying the first stroke to the canvas, you'll only ever see what has been covered up with paint and never know what's hidden within and beneath it.

Ancient historical detail always bored me, as it was meant to, but I finally disciplined myself to the study of every word and suffering through the extensive details, I began to see what lay beneath the illusory depiction of this reality and it was nothing I had ever imagined.

Coming from a place of having studied much of Beall's material, I asked myself what would keep me interested in finishing this book if I had come into it cold? What would keep my "Spiritual" friends and acquaintances reading enough to see the whole picture? What would Christian friends and family do with this much knowledge? Could they handle it? How about all those folks I'd made acquaintance with online over the years who believed they'd finally come to the "Divine" truth by adopting all the various Gnostic teachings, Astrology, Numerology, mastering the Art of Meditation, Remote Viewing, Astral travel as well as channeling, even going so far as to proclaim they "Finally got it this time!".... only to find they hadn't when disappointment reared its ugly head once again, as it always does.

Christians would initially gobble this book up based on the title alone as a way to prove their doctrines against Mysticism, only to eventually find their own place within the chapters and then throw the baby out with the bathwater without caring to find out how they too have been deceived in the worst way. They are just the bottom of the rung.

Energy healers, Tarot experts, Astrologists, Channelers and all other Mystery School adherents gaining a sense of ability with their own traits would reject it outright as an attack against their own Sovereignty or connection to Source, Creator or "The Divine".

Feminists and Goddess worshippers will balk at the fact that the author is male and reject the material outright as simply his bias against the Divine Feminine.....thinking he probably just hates women. If they *only knew* what was within all his work and what the priesthoods and priestesses actually were...

How do you tell someone that reading this book would finally put to rest to all their old belief systems? All their sacred cows, would soon be dumped into the ever-expanding quagmire of long forgotten foolishness such as Santa Claus and the Easter Bunny? And worse, how do you tell them that everything they currently believe, information they feel *must* hold some validity since it obviously superseded their prior religious indoctrination, was nothing but *more of the same* clothed in another cleverer disguise?

How do you tell them that, if they could see it, it would destroy everything they've built their lives around, and even threaten to dissolve their daily 15 minutes of fame on YouTube to stroke the needy virus-infected ego and possibly eliminate any monetary rewards from selling what they themselves have really never understood because well, it's a mystery...you know?

And finally...how do you tell people exactly how easy it is to know when a self-proclaimed "Teacher of The Mysteries" is nothing more than just another adept who sold themselves out to the mind virus hive for profit, and wants you to become an adept too so they won't feel so desperately lonely in their presumed position of authority? I've already seen how quickly people run back to their Gurus when the truth is exposed, when the only other alternative is to become responsible for themselves.

Many who have been programmed into studying only that which supports their already held "Sacred Cows" will be shocked to know where that term originates. You'll have no doubt where and why after digesting all the evidence provided within the first 12 chapters showing that Mr. Beall has done all the homework for you this time.

If you aren't one who has the self-discipline to read a very detailed layout of all the evidence to prove the assertions made in this book right out of the gate, and/or you fall into any one of the aforementioned categories, I suggest you go right to chapters 13-15 for the slam dunk and then, and only then, return to the first several chapters for all the actual evidence to support those 3 chapters. It will make the final chapters easier to assimilate once you have the case all laid out for you. This is provided you have the strength to get past the cognitive dissonance that will no doubt create an internal psychological disturbance resulting from facing this information.

If you *are* disciplined, I suggest starting at the beginning and allowing Mr. Beall to present a sound argument first before having to see the painful reality that you will find yourself in by the end of this book.

There is a way out. It's up to you to decide whether the Red Pill and the Blue Pill are one and the same. Don't be fooled into believing that they make purple and therefore you have solved the mystery. You have only just begun. Save yourself the trouble of discovering the monstrosity of having to swallow the Purple Pill the hard way. A spoonful of sugar won't help with this one.

It's all here in this book and the author has not only GUTTED MYSTICISM, but the entire illusion of your reality.

Kris Monet

June 2018

# 1. The Saga of Humanity

Humanity stands in the shadow of thousands of years of beliefs in the supernatural. The concept of magical, mystical or miraculous occurrences so poisons the mind of most of humanity that it has become a multibillion dollar industry in our world today. From religions preaching about their gods and prophets, to the beliefs in divine prophecies and endless pursuits of mystical spiritualism, humanity is hooked on the supernatural, and it has only been since the advent of the Age of Reason and the birth of modern science that some members of our species have transcended this reliance on the supernatural. Yet, even as science and technology advances at an exponential pace, more than 2/3 of the world's population still embraces some belief in the supernatural, magic or spiritual mysticism. This runs the gamut of Theosophy, New Age thinking, magical religions like Wicca, many varieties of Occultism and Kabbalah, Hinduism, Tibetan Buddhism, neo-Shamanism, and the supernatural religions of the mainstream variety like Christianity and Islam in their many varied offshoots whose adherents keep their eyes ever lifted heavenward waiting for the return of Jesus, the Jewish Messiah, or desire to ascend to heaven and live in the eternal afterlife in the presence of their individual gods.

Darwin posited a theory of linear human evolution from where our presumed ancestors climbed down from the trees as apes and magically evolved the human species into what it is today. Naturally, there is no smoking-gun evidence for how these evolutionary changes actually took place, and there is even less evidence of any other species on this planet morphing into another species in a similar manner, but it gives science its own mystical theory to answer from a secular position why the creationist theory of God creating everything is wrong. In essence, it is only trading one magical belief system for another more acceptable belief system to the mind of a materialist scientist. Both camps holding these ideologies are as rigid and unbending to any new idea that might explain things better than their beliefs, and all sides will pillory anyone who challenges their belief system with all the self-righteous indignation they can muster to defend how right their belief is above all others. Nowhere in this equation do we find anyone with a genuinely open mind to consider possibilities that go beyond their own worldview predicated solely on their personal belief system and the human 5-sense perception of reality. Anything that stands outside this 5-sense measuring stick is considered 'supernatural'.

This book is being written, as have all my books, to challenge the standard and accepted beliefs of the world. A belief is only a wish or hope that something is true. With all beliefs, when challenged honestly, one will discover that the belief is usually based on nothing more than handed-down traditions and cultural hearsay. Once any belief system gets created, it isn't long before it becomes rigid and starts to ossify and become stagnant.

The belief and human desire for supernatural intervention in their lives is probably the most long-lasting and pernicious of fallacious beliefs. Despite the scientific bluster defending Darwin's theory of evolution, there is nothing that indicates that life can spring from inanimate material into life without some element of magical thinking involved, even if they hide behind the mask of calling it science.

It doesn't really matter what the foundations of these beliefs in the supernatural are, whether they are founded in occult magical practices, praying and giving homage to one god or another, or the belief in one's ability to connect with the idea of some kind of cosmic Oneness, this book is going to prove that all such mystical beliefs are predicated on a single core element of deception. As with all things, humans have a tragic tendency to ignore the truth in favor of embracing their perceptual illusions, so there are probably only going to be a few people who are open-minded enough to take the information in this volume and reassess their perception of reality. The illusions are much easier to digest than the truth, for the illusions we embrace as our reality bring us a sense of cognitive psychological comfort. In the illusionary supernatural perception of reality, humans are always lesser beings to some presumed higher cosmic authority, whose guiding hand we believe is at the helm of the universe, providing one's destiny and reason for existence. In other words, we were only created to pay homage to the infinite divine, which is usually perceived as some singular Source/God or another.

From ancient times into the present era, the endless pursuit for seeking either the approval of, or communion with this presumed divine intelligence, has left humanity in a state of arrested cognitive development. We have given up our heritage as a species to beliefs which have rarely been investigated objectively, and the avoidance of challenging such beliefs only results in denial and the sustained beliefs in these supernatural elements perceived as God. Denial and blind acceptance have left the solution to this ages-old enigma sitting on the shelf, and neither the scientists nor the believers in the mystical are willing or able to move beyond their own superficial perceptions to think large enough to solve the riddle of supernaturalism by doing a thorough investigation. Protecting the turf of their own belief system is more important than winnowing out the truth, let alone facing such truth.

Regardless of the claim that people only want to know the truth, humanity is only willing to accept what they *think* is truth that supports their own beliefs. This is called confirmation bias, and with this programmed mindset, there is no actual pursuit of genuine truth, only the pursuit of whatever presumed truth we find that supports our individual beliefs and world perceptions. Anything that disrupts this perception of truth is immediately denied for the very simple reason that it just makes us to psychologically uncomfortable to come to terms with. This resistance to the truth runs across the spectrum of human beliefs, and there is no one on this planet, no matter their station or status in life, that is not guilty of this practice. It is nothing more than a form of cognitively lying to ourselves, all so we can protect our illusionary reality.

This book is going to take the reader on a historical tour of mystical and supernatural religious beliefs throughout the ages. It is not the journey through our past that we have been taught, and it has been avoided at all costs by our authorities, both secular and religious, for to reveal and accept this past, it will require a total reassessment of who we are as a species, what we have been psychologically subjected to, and taking responsibility to overcome these circumstances of our past. I am not going to pull any punches in this volume. I will no longer apologize for the ignorance of our intellectual and academic classes in denying these truths, for they are equally as lost in living their own illusions as the rest of humanity that they have sought to control throughout the centuries since the rise of materialist scientism during the so-called Age of Reason. If the reader has not read any of my previous work, then they are coming into this volume clueless in regard to what they will encounter within these pages. Coming to this material cold is going to be a very rough ride that is going to challenge everything you think you know about your reality. This is not an idle statement.

Humanity was created by an offworld race of beings roughly 200,000 years ago. Our species was created as both a slave work force and as a food supply. Even Egyptian texts, such as the *Instruction for Merikare,* plainly states: "*Well tended is* ***mankind - god's cattle***". You are going to discover the truth in this book that humans on this planet have always been viewed as cattle, and even the Jewish word *goyim*, translates directly to mean "cattle". There is more at play with the human species on this planet than meets the public eye, and this book is one of the 24 books I have authored or co-authored designed to set the record straight once and for all. Whether the reader has the guts to accept this resetting of human history into the correct context or not depends solely on the reader.

For over 100,000 years humans on this planet lived short and brutal lives at the hands of these offworld overlords. The creators of this species hailed from a planet orbiting around the star Betelgeuse in the Orion constellation. The name of this particular human species is unknown, so I refer to them simply as the Orioners. In ancient Greek texts they were referred to as the Titans, and in ancient Sumerian texts, this race of beings was referred to as the Elder Gods. Of these Elder Gods you find the ruler god An, or Anu, and his alleged son, Enlil. Anu was the chief god or chief of the Orioner race who 'lived in heaven', while Enlil served as the magistrate overseer on this planet. Although there is much fascination and disinformation about the ancient Anunna gods, or Anunnaki from Mesopotamia (Sumeria) since Zechariah Sitchin produced his *Earth Chronicles* series of books; it was not the Anunnaki god EA, or Enki, who created humans on this planet with the assistance of his sister Ninmah or Ninhursag. The Sumerian texts report that even the Anunna gods were created by the Elder Gods long before humans were created. Unfortunately, all too many people take Sitchin at his word and never venture into reading the scholarly translations of the ancient Sumerian texts to discover that Sitchin was wrong on so many points.

The modern near-religion that has arisen around the propagandized tales concocted by the Anunnaki gods, (truly the world's first literary propagandists), based on Sitchin's conjectural hypothesis, can be equated to the rise of any popular religion of the past, or other modern quasi-religions like the belief in the flat Earth. Just follow some of the comment threads on Youtube or social networking sites and you will see the Sitchinites parroting everything he wrote as if it were gospel. To these staunch believers in Sitchin's writing, it has become a form of gospel, promoting end-times fear fascination about the return of Planet X, or Nibiru, the home world of the Anunnaki, no different than the end-times prophecies of other world religions.

Modern academia is stuck in the myth of Darwinism and only sees what it wants to see through its own form of scientific tunnel vision. Anything that is disruptive of the Darwinian theory is scorned just as vehemently by academics and science as religionists scorn anything that challenges their beliefs. To academia, ancient paganism is all about the worship of statues or as allegorical references to the stars and planets as gods. They will not remotely accept the idea that the gods that people paid homage to, worshipped and feared, actually walked among is. They can't understand the idea of what a personal god was in a pagan context. I am going to try and simplify this so even an intellectual academic can understand it. There will be no speculative blurring of the lines, no metaphorical innuendo and no allegory for these intellectuals to ponder over the meaning of what I am writing. This is going to be clear, concise and to the point.

At some point in our past about 30,000-40,000 years ago, give or take a few millennia, other races of human or humanoid beings were 'invited' here by the Orioners to work on a collective project, whose immediate goal is unknown. Possibly, it may have been the first experiment in multiculturalism. The Orioners were the landlords of the planet and most of the races who came here had already been subjugated to Orioner domination in their own star systems. We had participants from a conquered civilization from a planet orbiting Rigel, represented by some of the Egyptian gods of old, to wit, Isis, Osiris, Sekhmet, Bastet, Thoth and some others whose names survive from the most ancient records of Egypt. In India, we have races from Andromeda (your blue-skinned beings in Indian legends) and the smaller-statured race from Arcturus, usually illustrated in Hindu artwork as orange-skinned, although their natural skin color more closely mirrors the skin tones of modern Indians.

In the more northerly climes we had races of beings who survive in legend like Odin and Thor, who originated from a planet in the Pleiadian star system, and stories of the women warriors known as the Valkyries whose home world orbits Vega is the constellation Lyra. Native Americans claim that many of their progenitor races, the Hopi in particular, also originated in the Pleaides, and the Sioux people have a keen affinity with the star Sirius. In some African peoples we also find legends of origins from Sirius, and this doesn't count the potentially unknown hundreds of other races who interfaced on this planet in the prehistoric ages of humanity on this planet.

The Anunnaki were designated the region of Mesopotamia as they were a hybrid race genetically crossed from different fish species on Nibiru with the genetics of the Orioners. The Orioners took up habitation high in the mountains, where the temperatures were cold, especially during the last ice age, partly because, as overlords, they had little to do with the projects of the other offworld tenants on the planet, and partly because the cold climate served as a protective barrier and deterrent against intrusion from the Anunnaki, who were numerous at earlier ages and whose species grew torpid and slow in colder climes. This is one reason Enlil was called Lord of the Mountain.

For thousands of years humans were bred as cattle, literally for food for some of these gods, and more often as a distraction in blood sports. In time, certain offworlders trained their human cattle in the art of war, and one faction would send their human army against another faction's human army, often for little more reason than the entertainment value of the bloody spectacles. These wars were not over territorial expansion because Enlil ruled over all the other offworld enclaves and made sure boundaries to these enclaves stayed secure between these other factions. So, the wars were more for sport or distraction than why humans fight wars today, although countless humans today still go to war over the beliefs in their gods. There was no territorial gain in these ancient conflicts, just warfare. In time, after so many generations of trained, and an almost inbred nature for fighting by human warriors, the human cattle started to become unmanageable, so a plan was designed to come up with a 'god' concept in an attempt to settle these human warrior cattle down into something more civilized. This was the era that began the idea of god as a ruler, and each offworld civilization here partook of this god plan, structuring their own hierarchy of gods within their own territories.

This god program spread through all the inhabitable enclaves, from Egypt to India and beyond. The concept was basically the same everywhere, the only difference was in how certain regional doctrines were shaped by the various offworld gods to best subdue and better domesticate their own human herds. In time, some of this warring slowed down, but through the introduction of the god concept, humans were soon sent off into battles to protect their gods. Now move that forward into the modern eras of religious wars and tell me how much you think humanity has really advanced in the last 30,000 years or more beyond developing more devious means and technologies to destroy ourselves on a larger scale.

Along with using humans here as food and armies, they were also used as a labor force once they were domesticated enough to follow instructions beyond just killing other humans. Since they were considered as nothing more than beasts of burden, certain offworld races did a lot of genetic experimentation on their human herds. If you want to understand the origins of the different races here, then blame the offworld geneticists who toyed with the Orioner template human design, and who then genetically modified their human cattle into their 'image and likeness'. This is the ignominious origin of the human race on this planet. Contrary to modern ancient alien theories, humans on this planet were not 'visited' by the gods. The gods owned the planet from the start, and humans were simply a byproduct slave race created to meet their needs. Humanity was made to 'serve god' and that is what we have done for close to 200,000 years without fail.

In ancient times, the human cattle had to take on the name of their gods, like Mary Jo Inanna, which signified that Mary Jo was the property of Inanna, her personal goddess. You will find this naming convention highly prevalent, particularly with Sumerian and later Babylonian naming conventions. Other gods tattooed or marked their human cattle with brands. They were not, as modern scholars believe, names taken on just as dedication to the gods or goddesses, but as a designation of property ownership. It utterly baffles me how our academic elite are not only unwilling to admit but can barely grasp what the evidence from these ancient cultures tell us about the gods walking among us, managing all human affairs. Their minds default to the later practices of erecting statues in memory of these gods after they left the planet and feel that our ancestors were only superstitious believers and that stone idols had the ability to reach into their lives like the former living gods once had.

The fact is that the gods came from the heavens, just like every tradition about them planet-wide states, and that they appeared when they chose to, and our ancestors never knew when they would return, so they kept honoring them in the best manner they knew how so the gods wouldn't be pissed off if they returned and their human cattle weren't toeing the line in their temple and taxation practices. All the gods were feared in the ancient world, particularly after the Anunnaki took control of the planet. They were vindictive and judgmental, and meted out punishment whenever their human cattle got out of line. Even the staunchest Bible believers have a record of this, yet totally refuse to see the truth that lies before their eyes in their holy book in the stories of their neurotic and vengeful God.

The tales of the wars between the gods populate every ancient written tradition in existence, no matter how fanciful the tales may have been embellished over the millennia. The Hindu texts are rife with the stories about the wars between the Devas and the Asuras (demons), and the stories from the Middle East and the incessant wars between their gods are no different, although the conflicts are more individualized to national gods than between competing factions of gods as with the Hindu renderings. The biblical God mandated that there should be no other gods before him, which is indicative that there were other gods competing for control of human herds just like the God of the Old Testament. If the God of the Bible was as powerful as the religious followers of the book believe, would this all-powerful God really be threatened, have his power challenged by a bunch of stone idols? I mean, think about this seriously and tell me that you can't see the failure in logic that must be applied when this is looked at objectively.

I have covered this offworld god thing in other books, and for more comprehensive evidence in the matter I point the reader to my books *We Are Not Alone – parts 1-3 (WANA)*, and *No Trespassing: Transcending the Psychology of the Gods*. As I have stated repeatedly in my prior works, humanity on this planet has an all too high opinion of itself, whether that self-image is garnered through creationist mythology or Darwinian mythology. There is not one offworld race that ever took this species under its wing to openly nurture us and educate us in mystical or magical practices without harboring their own personal, selfish agenda. All the modern hype about our space buddies where humanity holds center stage in the equation is utter hogwash. These ideas are all based on the human concept that this race is somehow special and deserves to sit center stage in the cosmos. We may have been created to serve the gods, but that is because we were created *special*. At least that is the psychotic, egotistical image humanity holds of itself, particularly in every religion on this planet.

The alien abduction phenomenon at the hands of the alleged Greys, is nothing more than a continuation of genetic experimentation on this species that was a hallmark of our species' past. As horrified as we may be over such occurrences with our high opinions of ourselves as a species, other races out there still see us as dumb, undeveloped cattle, and therefore nothing more than experimental fodder. We cringe in horror over the idea that any other race of beings could be so callous as to perform such experimentation on our species, yet we do the same thing with lab animals without giving any thought to what the animals we experiment on may think or feel in the process. To some of these other races, we have always been viewed as experimental lab rats, and what we may think or feel as a result of such experimentation makes them no more difference than the concern we give the animals we experiment with. I hate to be the bearer of this bad news, but as they say, reality bites.

There was massive genetic experimentation taking place on this planet for thousands of years before written language was introduced to our species. Many of the stories about mythological hybrid monsters like the Minotaur and Medusa, have some foundation in fact. We have to ask what would lead our ancient ancestors to concoct such stories unless there was something in the real world that could support such notions. Granted, in our modern scientific era such stories may seem impossible, but our geneticists are already mixing human and animal genetics in their experimentation seeking to create such hybrid creatures themselves. This idea is not new, and goes back almost a century, and there have been those who have actively promoted such ideas, such as J.B.S. Haldane in is paper, *Daedalus, or, Science and the Future*, written in 1923. In a potential forecast of humanity's future, Haldane theorized the idea:

> *"If reproduction is once completely separated from sexual love mankind will be free in an altogether new sense. At present the national character is changing slowly according to quite unknown laws. The problem of politics is to find institutions suitable to it. In the future perhaps it may be possible by selective breeding to change character as quickly as institutions. I can foresee the election placards of 300 years hence, if such quaint political methods survive, which is perhaps improbable, "Vote for Smith and more musicians", "Vote for O'Leary and more girls", or perhaps finally "Vote for Macpherson and a prehensile tail for your great-grandchildren". We can already alter animal species to an enormous extent, and it*

*seems only a question of time before we shall be able to apply the same principles to our own.*

*I suggest then that biology will probably be applied on lines roughly resembling the above. There are perhaps equally great possibilities in the way of direct improvement of the individual, as we come to know more of the physiological obstacles to the development of different faculties. But at present we can only guess at the nature of these obstacles, and the line of attack suggested in the myth is the one which seems most obvious to a Darwinian. We already know however that many of our spiritual faculties can only be manifested if certain glands, notably the thyroid and sex-glands, are functioning properly, and that very minute changes in such glands affect the character greatly. As our knowledge of this subject increases we may be able, for example, to control our passions by some more direct method than fasting and flagellation, to stimulate our imagination by some reagent with less after-effects than alcohol, to deal with perverted instincts by physiology rather than prison. Conversely there will inevitably arise possibilities of new vices similar to but even more profound than those opened up by the pharmacological discoveries of the 19th century."*

Haldane was a Fabian Marxist ideologue. Much of what he forecasted in the *Daedalus* paper, if not yet fulfilled as his 'prophetic meanderings', is already in the works where gene-splicing and combining human and animal genetics is concerned. For us to sit back and deny that the all too real ancient gods did not function in the same fashion is merely a form of cavalier denial that only brings us a sense of cognitive comfort living in a world of illusion. Human geneticists are only following in the footsteps of the ancient so-called gods.

The cosmos is a vast unknown, and human science is a laughably thin coat of paint when seeking to describe that unknown vastness. While materialist Newtonian scientists laud their accomplishments of science in the material world, they spurn the concepts of quantum science because it offers no material empiricism that material science demands in the world of the 5-sense illusion. This capricious focus on pure materialism leaves modern science as blind to reality as much as religious superstition and mystical enchantments do with the supernatural gods. Just as our ancestors spurned the idea of invisible agents called germs, modern science and psychology, in their sublime ignorance, refuse to acknowledge anything other than the world that presents itself to us through the five primary senses. If there is something that doesn't present itself to these primary five senses in our material world, or that can't be seen, tested and measured through similar materialist means, then it simply doesn't exist in their minds. It is all considered 'supernatural' or 'paranormal' and therefore worthy of immediate scorn to the religion of scientism.

We have more than enough substantive evidence of beings that were not fully human found with elongated skulls unearthed all around the world, and science refuses to do any genetic testing on these skulls, for they are going to prove that humans are not alone in this universe. Science would rather fabricate a convenient lie that all of these hundreds of skulls found around the world are the result of human head binding to emulate the gods, than investigate the truth which would expose the Darwinian lie. To do such investigative analysis would not only destroy the sciences of archaeology and Darwinian theory, it would also destroy every religion as well, for humanity would finally have to own up to the truth that we are not, and never have been alone as a species in this universe, and more especially, not alone even on this planet!

Aside from the physical evidence that challenges this comfortable reality based in denial, just as we have hidden bacteria and germs that can infect human populations with illness, there are also invisible viruses that came from the stars that have invaded human consciousness, which will be the primary focus of the rest of this book. As much as you may protest what is provided in the chapters to follow, absent the explanations I will provide, science, psychology and religions are all at a loss to explain the phenomena I will present, with thousands of years of evidence that has remained undiagnosed as the symptomatology of an infectious mind virus that I refer to as the hapiym virus, an acronym for HAcker Program In Your Mind.

Not only has humanity been infected with the hapiym virus, but the gods themselves fell prey to the same mind virus, and that is why humans on this planet exhibit the same egotistical neuroses as the fickle and selfish gods who shaped our species in all its varied racial forms. The story that is to follow will read like a horror story or some sort of convoluted science fiction fantasy, but human understanding is so stunted at this point of our evolution that it cannot perceive beyond the comfortable illusion of reality that humanity lives with at only a superficial and rudimentary level of consciousness. This is going to be a story about a form of tyranny unimaginable to how we perceive reality, but the evidence for which has been in our purview for millennia. Our species tunnel vision has blinded us to what the evidence has tried to tell us, and our modern scientific culture is no less blind than our ancestors were in discovering what has taken place. Worst of all is the field of Psychology, which has no genuine understanding of consciousness, that is only plying its trade diagnosing the symptoms of the hapiym mind virus thinking that these symptoms are the 'human norm' where our consciousness is concerned.

You are about to embark on a journey deep into the rabbit hole of a reality that you would rather ignore and deny than face as truth. If you proceed in reading the rest of this volume, expect to have everything you think you know about reality turned on its head. I do not make this claim lightly, nor as form of sensationalist braggadocio. I am fully aware of what this information can do to a mind lost in illusion and denial, for I have had to face this reality myself. As uncomfortable and unbelievable as it all might sound, before you discount it in whole, you are challenged to come up with any other viable explanations for what is about to be revealed other than the constrained ideas about science and religion you have been fed your entire life. Accepting this challenge, you are only going to find your explanations fitting with those insufficient excuses already offered by science, psychology and religion; all of which have been pure speculation and misinterpretation of the data for thousands of years.

As will be shown in the pages ahead, humanity and its concept of god went through an alteration from dealing with genuine physical offworlders passing themselves off as gods, to a more metaphysical and mystical view of the invisible concept of god. The exact date of this transition is unknown, for the dates we use to count our history as a species since the invention of the written word, are still questionable and under fierce debate. I am going to do my best to at least point out the indicators of where and how this transition started taking place, and at least one offworld entity who was greatly responsible for this transition where religious thinking is concerned. The reader is asked to prepare themselves to feel confused, angry, incredulous and unbelieving as this story unfolds, for it truly is a huge pill to swallow, but I think the evidence offered will make my case if you can stay with me through this presentation to look at and weigh all the evidence objectively. Objectivity is required in reading this material, and the demand to protect your current perceptions and beliefs will only lead to reader down the road to the denial that this species currently supports its illusion of reality with. Denial doesn't make the truth untrue, it is only a refusal to admit the truth.

This being the first volume of the *Beyond the Second Cognition* series of books, brings with it an opportunity for expanding human consciousness from our limited material world perception, and invites the reader to see the greater reality that has been hidden from our species since we were created. I stated in the *No Trespassing* book that I am no longer going to justify the information we present to a species that demands to live in illusionary denial of what it is and what it can become as a mature species. I will provide all the evidence necessary that I feel supports my conclusions in the matter at hand, but I am also not going to pull any punches on what has occurred just to bring the deniers some sense of cognitive psychological comfort. Humanity needs to be shaken from the dream, and at this point of our evolution as a species, it is only going to be a hard shaking of our sensibilities that is liable to make the change our species needs to endure to advance itself beyond the illusions we call reality. This series is for truly open-minded individuals that want to grow themselves and help humanity advance as a species. It is not written for the deniers or the naysayers who are wholly content to live their lives lost in illusions dictated to them by others. If you demand to live in your status quo reality, then don't read this book, for I do not support static, status quo limited thinking or perceptions. I am a heretic to that reality, and after reading this book, you may well become a heretic too. If so, then I have met my objective in presenting this material.

# 2. The Ancient Gods – A Recap

I covered much of the material presented in this chapter in the three *WANA* books which were part of the *Evolution of Consciousness* series that launched this enterprise. I am not going to rehash all that material in this chapter but will provide an overview recap of that information for the new reader, as well as provide more information that was not offered in that subset of books to more completely fill out the picture of our past and why we are in the situation we are as a species in the present.

Science has always operated from the assumption that our planet originated and always resided in this solar system. I provided comprehensive evidence in *WANA – Part 1* that should prove to the critical reader that this planet originated in the constellation Sirius and originally orbited a now-collapsed star, Sirius B. Granted, there is nothing in the historical accounting of human history that tells is this fact directly, but there is more than enough allegorical information in ancient creation myths that provide the evidence to extrapolate what the allegorical stories truly tell us. Modern Newtonian physics will argue this premise, but as will be shown throughout this book, our science is still fumbling around in the dark where truly understanding the cosmos is concerned, i.e. the universe doesn't always function according to humanity's limited materialist perceptions or beliefs, whether scientific or otherwise.

I put forth the idea in the *WANA* books that the star Sirius B was artificially induced to go supernova about half a million years ago as a result of a territorial war for planetary domination by the Orioner race of beings who fought against the indigenous inhabits of this planet at that time. As a result of Sirius B being artificially forced to explode, either by the introduction of nuclear weapons or other technology we have no concept of, this planet was relocated from the Sirius star system and captured or placed here orbiting our present sun. Despite our modern physicists arguing that it defies the laws of science, our science doesn't possess all knowledge, nor does it really know how things work beyond our 3D comprehension of the universe with materialist theories formulated strictly by living on this planet.

All arguments to the contrary notwithstanding, there is enigmatic physical evidence of this cataclysm on our planet which science still can't account for, and the one key factor is what is known as the 'iridium anomaly'. I wrote about this in *WANA – Part 1* as follows:

> *"To further expand on my contentions that this planet once orbited Sirius B and that it was artificially induced to go supernova, we need to examine whether there is any evidence on this planet that might scientifically support this. I think we need look no further than what is known as the 'iridium anomaly', which is a layer of iridium*

*deposit found everywhere on the planet. Since iridium is an extremely rare element found on Earth, there is no real reason for this band of iridium deposits to be on this planet unless there was some external event that brought that iridium here.*

*Science theorizes that the existence of this enigmatic layer of iridium that surrounds the planet provides the explanation for the extinction of the dinosaurs some 66 million years ago, and they theorize that this iridium came in when a large asteroid hit our planet, thereby releasing iridium into the planet's atmosphere. Overall, this is not a bad theory so long as you are only considering such a possibility as the only solution. I will put forth another theory based on the destruction of Sirius B scenario.*

*When Sirius B collapsed, the force of the explosion caused the supercontinent of Pangaea on this planet to split, thereby resulting in the eastern and western hemispheric continents today. Not only was the blast of the sun going supernova the cause of the breaking up of the supercontinent, the tremendous amount of radiation that this planet was bombarded with before the shock wave also saturated the atmosphere with iridium and other radioactive waves like gamma rays and xrays, thereby creating the iridium anomaly which is found in a layer of iridium present everywhere on the planet.*

*Initially, scientists and geologists may protest at such an idea, especially since I project this event occurred only 500,000 years ago. Scientists are firmly convinced that it was 66 million years ago that the iridium deposit occurred, but here is where scientists and geologists make their error. Every science on this planet operates from the incorrect assumption that this planet has always been in this solar system since its beginning. All of their theories of geology and evolution are predicated on the foundation of this assumed uninterrupted linearity and stability of this planet always residing in this orbit around our present sun. Any scientific theory developed on a false foundation will always, always, deliver false conclusions. This is where we find ourselves today with the vast majority of scientific theoretical conjecture. It is all predicated on a false presumption of an uninterrupted linearity of events that shaped this planet. With this primary assumption as the foundation of their theories, they also rely on the approach that these things all occurred gradually, over millions of years. It is through this assumption of evolutionary gradualism, that everything has always been the same as it is now where this planet's assumed unchanging stability is concerned, that they miss other possibilities. In light of that, I challenge all scientists with this question. If what I am relating is true, then where does that leave Darwinism and the linear progression of evolution of the species when every species on this planet was destroyed from a supernova event in another star system that destroyed all life on this planet a mere 500,000 years ago? Where does that leave the science of geology and its theories of the gradual geological formation of this planet?"*

Another thing that must be considered with the iridium anomaly is that it was a major *extinction* event. Science conjectures that it killed off the dinosaurs and about 70% of other life. My challenge to science is that, if it was an extinction event, why science feels *any* percentage of life should survive? Naturally, science must keep that 30% of surviving life or else Darwin would have no place to hang his hat and his evolutionary theory goes right down the drain and collapses upon itself for the mythical conjecture that it is. This is but one example of the scientific mental gymnastics involved in perpetuating their own mystical belief in Darwin's theory.

Given the premise I propose, then all scientific conjecture would have to be reanalyzed, just as science will have to reanalyze Darwin's theories in the presence of those elongated skulls found round the world, which mainstream scientists still refuse to do genetic testing on. If all life on this planet was destroyed, then that only leaves the explanation about life regenerating on this planet as a result of a terraforming operation which created or brought in new plant and animal life, the last element of which I propose was the human species. By offering this suggestion, I am not talking about some mystical God waving his magic wand to make this happen, but that it came about by intervention of technologically advanced beings who not only had the capability to neutralize the highly radioactive iridium anomaly, but also introduced all the life that we know existed in our current planetary knowledge.

If we can accept Zechariah Sitchin's projected timetable based on Sumerian records as sound, then the Anunnaki and their Orioner overlords arrived on this planet some 400,000 years ago. I will assert here that it wasn't until after most of this terraforming had taken place by unknown races that the Orioners and Anunnaki decided to inhabit this planet for their own exploitation of minerals. One thing the Orioners were never into was hard labor. They were exploiters and tyrants, not laborers.

The oldest known structures on this planet that we know of, and which science is again ignoring, are thousands of square miles of stone structures that pepper the landscape all over South Africa. Michael Tellinger is the foremost proponent pushing acknowledgment of these structures as ancient Anunnaki habitation sites. With this theoretical conjecture, I have to agree, Where Tellinger and I part ways is in the belief that these stone edifices were in any way 'temples'. Humanity has this god psychosis so drilled into its brain that any ancient site that gets unearthed, like the ruins at Gobekli Tepe in Turkey, are automatically designated a *temple*. Gobekli Tepe is a total enigma to science and archaeologists because it shouldn't be where it is, or more accurately 'when' it is, because it casts Darwin's progression of man into the gutter. The Gobekli Tepe site is more ancient than alleged hunter-gatherer tribes could have built or fabricated if we are to believe Darwinian conjecture. Of course, science is already bending the evidence of the site to fit the Darwinian narrative, but it doesn't alter the antiquity of the site or how it threatens Darwinian theory. Can you hear the sound of the toilet flushing Darwin down the drain?

Once again, if we can take some of the Sumerian records as being at least partially truthful, the creation of humans on this planet came about due to a revolt of the Anunnaki workers who were tired of laboring for their Orioner overlords and demanded that they create a new species to take the workload off their backs. Where Sitchin failed in his interpretations of the Sumerian texts is that he took them more literally than they deserved in all cases. He failed to recognize that the alleged history of the Anunnaki gods, in particularly Enki and Ninhursag, contained a lot of self-glorifying propaganda. I will give credence to the idea that Ninhursag was a master geneticist, and she was personally responsible for creating many of the hybrid monstrosities we hear about in some ancient legends, but neither she nor Enki created humans on this planet. That was all strictly the doing of Orioner geneticists. After the later wars of the gods on this planet, the Anunnaki become sole rulers of the planet, therefore they were the victors who got to write history the way they wanted it presented and the way they wanted themselves perceived in writing that history. Subsequent books in this series will go into greater detail on some of these matters, but that goes beyond the scope of this presentation.

At some unknown point between about 50,000-30,000 years ago, other stellar races were 'invited' to this recently terraformed planet to offer their own contributions to it. All of these other offworld races had already been subjugated to the tyranny of the Orioners, so their 'invitation' was superficial at best. Regardless of how they got here, they were all mandated that if they wanted to use and experiment with the human livestock, they had to use the Orioner genetic human template as the foundation for their experimentation. Through the introduction of the genetics of these other races from different parts of the universe, the human livestock was diversified into all the racial variants of humans that inhabit the planet today. I have never found the elements of Darwin's theory sound enough to account for the diversity of racial types present on this planet. It doesn't make logical sense. I do, however, think that the idea I presented in my works logically accounts for our planetary racial diversity. I leave it to the reader to decide which concept makes more logical sense.

All the races that came to this planet were not genetically manipulated into being by the Orioners. They were races that had developed through natural evolutionary means on their own home worlds or migrated there from other human-inhabited planets, with the primary exception of the Anunnaki, who I assert, were created from breeds of intelligent telepathic fish that inhabited the planet Nibiru, and whose genes were combined with the Orioner gene pool to create the species we know as the Anunnaki. Sadly, the two breeds were near mirror reflections of one another where avarice and the quest for power was concerned. In the final wars between the gods, which I covered in *WANA – Part 2*, the Orioners left this planet and left all the other offworld races to fend for themselves against an invading army created by Ninhursag. That genetically-created race of beings who was that invading army is commonly referred to as the Aryans.

I realize that this chapter probably creates more questions than it answers, but many of these questions cannot be answered, and the ones we do have some information to answer will be presented in later books in this series. The primary information that our species needs to acknowledge first and foremost is that our history as a species has been a complete and utter lie, and the further removed we are from our past, the less we know about it and the more the propagandized 'official story' becomes perceived truth to the masses, i.e. the illusion of reality just keeps expanding. Much of what is revealed in this chapter is known by 'the elite Aryan controllers on this planet.' More evidence of these ancient alien races has been intentionally swept under the rug or outright destroyed in order to perpetuate the myths of science and religion to keep our species as far removed from the truth as they want to keep us. They cannot continue to control humanity once the truth comes to light, which is why they have a vested interest in keeping that truth out of the public's purview and knowledge, and why they continue in perpetuating their lies, selling the world mythology and calling it historical fact.

# 3. The Aryan Enigma

Now we come to another area of mystery, and that is the origins of the enigmatic race known as the Aryans. Contrary to popular opinion based on Hitlerian ideas about the alleged White Aryan race, the ideas for this concept go back as far as 1785 with a volume entitled *The Outline of History of Mankind* by the German anthropologist Christoph Meiners, This volume was the first attempt to classify and justify scientific racism, using white-skinned Aryans as the foundation of European culture, in particular the "venerable….German race."

The next salvo in this form of White supremacist scientific Aryanism was fired by a French aristocrat named Arthur de Gobineau in an 1853 essay entitled, *Essay on the Inequality of the Human Races,* where Gobineau elevated Whites above the Black and Yellow races as inferior humans. When philologist Max Müller did his research into the commonality of languages, the core elements of what are now referred to as the Indo-European languages, theoretically sealed the deal on the idea of Aryan racial superiority, once again erroneously applying the Aryan moniker to European White races. From this historical context, Hitler was just the latest in a series of individuals to buy into this White Aryan racial theory. Hitler didn't invent the idea.

What is notable about the root word for Aryan, *arya* in Sanskrit, was noted by philosopher Friedrich Nietzsche, stating that the root word meant 'noble', or more accurately, 'owner'. I must agree with Nietzsche's assessment based on my own research into the alleged Aryan phenomenon, for it is Aryan elitists who have ruled the world since very soon after their arrival on this planet roughly 6,000 years ago.

I stated in *We Are Not Alone – Part 2 (WANA)*, that the Aryan invaders were landed here roughly 3760 BC, using the start date of the Jewish calendar as the benchmark date for their arrival. I also used the projected orbital cycle of the planet Nibiru, referenced in ancient Sumerian texts, and interpreted by Zechariah Sitchin to orbit in and out of our solar system roughly every 3,600 years. His speculated date of Nibiru's entrance into our solar system circa 3800 BC correlates not only with the start date of the Jewish calendar, but also cross-foots with modern archaeological conjecture about the time period in which the Aryan culture arose in the steppes of southern Russia ca. 4000-3000 BC.

In *WANA – Part 2,* I asserted that the Aryans, who had no known predecessors, appeared out of nowhere onto the stage of human history during this timeframe, and that the reason they had no evolutionary predecessors is because they did not originate on this planet, but were in fact artificially produced and developed in a genetic laboratory on the planet Nibiru by the Anunnaki geneticist Ninhursag, the ancient Sumerian Mother Goddess. As much as this idea may challenge how you think the world operates, and that it is only human beings from this planet that have been in control of our destiny, I think I provided more than enough evidence in all the *WANA* books to substantiate my position.

The Aryan peoples were as diverse racially as the human race on this planet is today on this planet. They were designed and manufactured to match the human racial types on this planet, so they could blend in to any culture they invaded without detection. They were not, as the racial theories presented by Meiners, Gobineau and Müller, all White people, but were a composite variety of all the different human racial types. As I reported in *WANA – Part 2*, the Aryans were created as an invading army to intervene in a war seeking the systematic destruction of the Anunnaki race on this planet, initiated by an order issued by the Orioner overlord/governor of this planet, Enlil. The story of the order given by Enlil for the destruction of the Anunnaki can be found in numerous Lamentation texts from Sumeria and Babylon and is not a wild assertion on my part based on no textual evidence to back it up. (See *Lamentation over the Destruction of Sumer and Ur*, and *Ur Lament* through a Google lookup).

Ninhursag, known as the Queen of Heaven, since she was in charge of the Anunnaki home planet Nibiru, got word of this war of eradication while Nibiru was out on the far swing of its orbital cycle, at an estimate of possibly 1,800 years away from Earth. This estimate gave her more than enough time to genetically fabricate her Aryan armies in preparation for her invasion in response to Enlil's order to destroy the Anunnaki. When Nibiru arrived in our solar system roughly 3800 BC, her Aryan invading army was staged in a region formerly uninhabited by any other offworld race from which to launch their counterassault, which is the southern steppes of Russia near the Caucasus mountains.

Although the Aryan people these days go by many other identifiers in the archaeological community as they continually reclassify their discoveries, Indo-European is the more politically correct manner they are described since Hitler did what he did to give the word Aryan such a distaste in people's minds. Regardless of this linguistic softening of the term, the Sanskrit word *arya* still applies to describe these people, and I will use the term Aryan with the qualifier that it signifies many different racial types and not just White people.

Through specific linguistic and philological comparisons, there are root words that are found in all the Indo-European languages, pointing to a common ancestor in these languages. The Aryans are that common key, as most scholarly assessment acknowledges. It is a generally accepted premise that is was the appearance of the Aryan races on the scene which initiated the use of written language, and why their expansionist policies carried with them the roots of all the Indo-European languages. This is not to say that they invented the many and varied human languages, only that it was the Aryans who put those languages into written form as the elitist administrators over their conquered peoples.

I covered in *WANA – Part 2* how writing burst on the scene just prior to 3000 BC in both Sumeria and Egypt, and how it gradually worked its way into the East based on the war scenario between the offworld races inhabiting this planet at that time. Once again, this is another correlation to the timeframe of the

Aryan invasion which modern scholarship is finding agreement with based on their own discoveries.

Wherever the invading Aryan armies set up housekeeping, it took little time to prop themselves up as the ruling classes over their conquered adversaries. It will be found through a close examination of history's conquerors that the tactics never vary with Aryan warfare, whether it was from the first Aryans who were landed here, through the Alexanders, Rameses, Huns, Mongol hordes, Romans, Assyrians or any other conquering overlords. There is a repeating and noticeable sameness in their tactics that never changes, through which we find a hallmark of their control over humanity on this planet for almost 6,000 years. Because of the European misdirection about all Aryans being White, historians have overlooked the obvious sameness in Aryan tactics throughout history, regardless of their racial characteristics. Scholars are too lost in emphasizing differences to see these profound commonalities.

What gave the first invading Aryan armies their edge over other armies of the time was the development of the spoked wheel and the two-wheeled chariot, which gave them speed and mobility to serve as a shock-force army of invaders over more infantry-based cultures. Their use of horses and chariots made them storm troopers to all their adversaries and delivered a tactical superiority which allowed them such great success in their early rise to power. Modern scholarship suggests that the Aryans were the first to domesticate horses, but this is based on the limited use of them elsewhere in present archaeological knowledge. Regardless of whether the Aryans were the first to domesticate horses or not, they did develop, or arrived here with the concept of the spoke-wheeled chariot as a weapon, and were all equipped to facilitate creating written language to correlate with the varying human oral languages that already existed before their invasion of this planet.

This short recap on the Aryans is a necessary element to the story that follows, for it will be shown that it is the Aryans themselves, working in collusion with the ancient Anunnaki gods, and ultimately the hapiym hive collective, who have set the tone for world history since their arrival on this planet. Whether you are willing to accept this premise or not matters little, for our world is in the condition it is due to the Aryan global elite and their agenda for total global domination, regardless of their difference in racial appearance. I have spared no ink in my books to reveal this 6,000-year-old perfidy, and this book is only the latest installment in that revealing. The reader is strongly advised to do their own research into the matter and reach their own conclusions in regard to the Aryans. Examine the data for yourself and connect the dots.

# 4. The Physical Gods

We are now going to cover ground that I also covered in the *WANA* books, and that is the controversial idea about physical offworlders serving in the roles of gods to our ancient ancestors. The modern ancient alien conjecture has the picture backwards when it airs the belief that humans already existed on this planet and the ancient alien gods came to 'visit' our species or did some kind of genetic experimentation elevating humanity from available simian raw material by genetically manipulating apes into humans. This is a safe scenario because it leaves the Darwinian premise intact and uses the enigmatic 'missing link' concept of Darwinism as the foundation upon which to build and sell such ideas to the public. Unfortunately, it is totally false and presents an inverted picture of the past.

The ancient physical gods, collectively, were not and never claimed to be the creators of the universe and all creation. This was later mythology developed by Enki and Ninhursag through their over-inflated psychopathic and egotistical views of themselves when they became the last surviving 'supreme' gods on this planet after the wars between the offworlders. It was these two Anunnaki in particular, along with their Aryan scribes, who wrote the religious propaganda that has been handed down to humanity as our presumed religious history in its many various forms. The term god never took on a serious metaphysical meaning until very late in the god game perpetrated against the human race. The tyrant Orioner race never used the term 'god' to designate itself in such a manner, and it was only late in the Anunnaki propaganda mill that the distinction between the Gods and the Elder Gods was invented.

The fact that humanity on this planet was created as a subservient slave race to these offworld races left humans with no uncertainty as to who was boss. A goodly percentage of these races were of greater stature than our species, so determining who was who didn't take a lot of brain power to make the distinction. The Orioner race measured in, as a general rule, at about 12 feet in stature. The other subjugated races ranged in size from your smaller species of Greys, to the 8-to-10 feet height range for many of other races. As a standard, most humans were smaller in stature than their offworld managers. There were a few exceptions such as the Arcturans, who were not a race of 'giants' like many of the other offworlders, but who had allied with the taller blue-skinned race from Andromeda as a form of mutual protection.

There is no shortage of stories in ancient myths and holy books about the existence of giants that inhabited our planet in the past, although many of these tales have been blown way out of practical acceptance with stories of giants running thousands of feet in height. Much of this impossible embellishment was designed as propaganda to obscure the truth I am sharing here. In the Western religions, the Bible has become the most accepted book of religious mythology, and it is a concatenation of stories stolen from other peoples around the Middle East and consolidated into the religious mythology that it has become, no different than the tales of the gods in other places around the world.

Aside from the story of Goliath and his race in the Old Testament, other giants grace the pages of the Bible in the form of the Nephilim, who were purportedly the 'sons of God' who bred with humans. Let's remove all the supernatural connotations from the whole God equation and take the information for what it tells us in a more reasonable light. The Nephilim were only representative of other human-like races that came here from the stars. Their genetics closely matched our genetics enough that they could, and did, breed with us whether physically or allegorically through genetic experimentation, which I assert is the primary reason for the diversity of racial types on this planet. Our species bears the 'likeness and image' of the gods, as I explained in *WANA – Part 1*. Without all the supernatural creator of the universe God mythology, this explanation makes perfectly reasonable and logical sense, and we don't have to twist logic half an inch to see the rationality of this conclusions. To arrive at such a conclusion requires that we move our simplistic thinking beyond all the supernatural hocus pocus that is all religions, and simply face the facts. Granted, this requires that we remove ourselves from that pedestal of being a special and unique species for which God created the entire universe, but with the progression of science, that should not be such a hard thing to do. To continue to believe that we are the only form of human life in this vast universe exhibits a species arrogance that defies logic.

When we can remove the mythical mystique from these ancient stories and read between the lines without religious and mystical embellishment to blind us from what these stories tell us, no matter how corrupted they have been passed down to us, then what I am sharing here makes the most logical sense. If what I present were not the case, then we have to ask why these supernatural gods all seemed to demand physical temples, or shall we simply call them Beverly Hills mansions, in which to dwell. Why did they demand physical tribute? Why did their temple treasuries accumulate gold, silver, precious gems, and the 'first fruit' of all crops planted if they didn't have physical needs and were only holy ghost-like beings living beyond our perception? Even illiterate humans would question such practices were it not for some type of enforcement mechanism to make them build these temples and literally sacrifice their labor and livelihood, and that enforcement mechanism, I assert, was the physical presence of these offworld entities we call gods. It was their physical presence here that served as the primary foundation for all early religions and mythical legends. The Darwinian conjecture that the beliefs in the gods and spirits arose out of an evolving species' fear of lightning and the elements just doesn't have the feel of genuineness in light of this alternative explanation.

I will readily admit that the first generations of the human species on this planet were not particularly well-gifted with intelligence, and more than likely functioned just above the level of dumb beasts, and that it was only through the cross-breeding experiments by these offworld races that begat higher levels of intelligence in the Earth human beast stock. The first humans were unruly animals. As much as such an idea makes you rebel in protest, once again logic would point to this as the primary truth of the matter. As a simple comparison, just look at the opening stages of artificial intelligence (AI) and look at the difficulty faced in begetting consciousness into a created being. Granted humans are more biological rather than technological machines, but we would be unwise to assume that the first models of humans to roll of the Orioner genetic cloning assembly line were top of the line products. Even the propagandized stories of the creation of humans handed down through Enki and Ninhursag's Sumerian tales tell stories of these early failures in creating Earth humans, although they were telling the stories secondhand to glorify themselves.

Archaeologists and Darwinists fail the public when they demand that their theories are correct, with no more foundation in truth than the evidence presents. The recent unearthing of the site of Gobekli Tepe has sent the Darwinists scrambling to reassess their theories, just as much as archaeology has challenged the historical veracity of the Bible, the timetable from which early archaeologists utilized to establish their tentative guidelines in determining the reigns of the Egyptian pharaohs. In both cases, archaeology casts suspicion on both Darwin's theory of linear evolution and the historicity of the Bible as any kind of accurate measure of our past. Yet it is these two competing theories which have ruled archaeological projections for generations. Whenever a hole is found in either mode of determining archaeological antiquity of things, the apologists are trotted out to provide numerous explanations to wipe away the faultiness in their theories.

With the excavation of the sites in Iraq, (ancient Mesopotamia), and the unearthing of hundreds of thousands of Sumerian tablets, it was discovered that the stories in the Old Testament in the Bible originated from earlier stories in Sumeria. The Bible is only the Reader's Digest version of much more lengthy and older Sumerian tales of their gods. There is little of originality in the Bible except the production of the myth about the people of Israel.

From the ancient world into modern society, people sought to claim an antiquity to their race, where peoples from different regions tried to lay claim to direct genetic heritage from their gods. We see this claim in many ancient kings, most notably Alexander the Great who, unwilling to believe his father was Phillip of Macedon, consulted an oracle of the Egyptian god Amun, and was told 'in a dream', that he was the son of the god Amun. Naturally, Alexander's ego inflated over this elevation in status from being human to that of a demigod and it drove his quest for world conquest all the way to India.

I bring up Alexander's dream because dreams and visions are going to play a seminal role in what is revealed in the rest of this volume where shaping and interpreting mystical and religious traditions is concerned. There is a sound, albeit highly controversial aspect that resides hidden behind all these visionary states and the answer is not going to be one that most readers are going to be willing to accept, especially those whose religious beliefs are founded on visions received by their religion makers.

To understand these visionary states, which I covered in overview in *Revamping Psychology* as well as in *The Energetic War Against Humanity*, one must have the working knowledge of the space-borne hapiym virus which infected the consciousness of every human species everywhere across the cosmos. The next chapter is going to provide some of the basics for understanding this virus and how it has controlled the human psyche since humans on this planet were created.

# 5. The Hapiym Virus

At this late stage of cosmic evolution, determining what or who created the hapiym virus would only be speculative at best. As much as we are fascinated with origins as a species, there are some things that are so timeless that finding a point of origin becomes meaningless and we are left dealing with understanding things from our present circumstances without the necessity to understand the origin of things. We don't always have the answer to why things occur, only that they have occurred, and in light of these occurrences, what we are going to do about them in the present.

Every scientific postulate starts with a premise of a 'given' set of ideas. With Darwinism, for instance, the presumed given is that life evolved in a linear fashion with an ever-increasing modification and mutation from very simple single-celled creatures that over millions of years lead to the mutation called humans. Granted, this particular 'given' is an assumption and bears no more weight than the 'given' that a singular God or creator designed the entire multiverse, yet this presumed given is what drives the theory.

To fully understand what is to follow in this book, the foundational 'given' is the existence of an invisible mind virus (the hapiym), which functions in a hive structure, that is hierarchal in nature, and that all humanity has been infected with this virus. The presence of this virus inside us all is the basis for beliefs in the soul, the afterlife, and the false *persona* referred to as the ego in our works. The two definitions of ego will follow for the sake of greater understanding.

Under the control and infection of the hapiym mind virus, each of us is at least two people on the inside. One person is that of our waking state, which is meant to be the governor of our lives to navigate in the world around us. This is what psychology works from as the basis of the ego self. There is, however, a secondary false ego persona, which is the fabricated persona of the hapiym virus, which models itself on our waking personality, mimics that personality, and eventually overshadows that primary self by creating a false illusion of who we are, a false ego.

The hapiym virus is so masterful in this overlaying of our primary self that we are completely unaware of the hidden tyranny that usurps our consciousness and through which the virus uses our minds and our emotions to become nothing more than the generator of its food supply, which is the energies generated by our emotions. The more this internal virus cell can spark you into emotional reactions of all kinds, the better able it is to manipulate your mind and body to produce its food supply, which is the energy of your emotions.

Aside from manipulating your personal emotions, the food supply the virus produced in large groups of people is even more powerful, and this is exhibited through the group-think mentality of a mob running on fear or anger. The reason that people so easily fall prey to the mob mentality has to do with the hive nature of the virus itself. For the sake of clarification, a mob doesn't necessarily have to be running rampant in the streets, political and religious ideologies create a similar form of mob mentality where those who adhere to these varying group beliefs are driven by their emotions and zealotry to produce emotions in mass through righteous indignation, fear, and the demand to eradicate all those who disagree with their own herd mentality. There is really very little difference between an assumed 'civilized' mob and an undisciplined mob running out of control except the appearance of 'civility'. A mob mentality is a mob mentality, no matter the mask of civility or righteous indignation it may wear to justify the actions of the mob or herd.

Because all the hapiym hive virus cells are connected through the nature of its existence, there is a form of resonance that exists between all these individual hive cells that have a mandate to cluster into hives, or herds. This is why a riot can seem to spark from very little in the form of a catalyst to turn a tense situation into an out of control mob. Each virus cell triggers on the collective hive consciousness of the cells around them to turn from individual hive beasts into a collective herd beast in virtually an instant. Psychology has been abused as a soft-science to prod human herds into channels of controlled behavior since its inception as a science, primarily based on the observations of Gustave le Bon in his book *The Crowd* published in 1895. This abuse has occurred with the advice and consent of the Aryan ruling elite on this planet and it has all been designed to sow chaos in an attempt to create so much chaos that humanity will finally submit to a global new world order, or as more ancient texts refer to it, “a reformation of the whole wide world”. This reformation of the whole wide world will be one of the major focuses of this volume and I will provide the explanations behind the drive to reform the world into a homogenous whole and how it has been a designed agenda of the overall hapiym hive intelligence to conquer humanity.

Until we can understand the machinations of the hapiym virus in our own psyche, we can’t comprehend the tyranny involved in an ages old agenda for domination over this species and this planet. Most of this tyranny has revolved around teaching our species about a presumed eternal afterlife and communion with the mystical concepts of God, Source or Creator that permeates every spiritual and religious teaching on the planet. Until we can grasp and accept the idea that all these visions and promises for the hereafter are nothing more than contrived doctrines formulated by the hapiym virus hive itself, our species will continue to be deluded into ignoring the life they can live in exchange for a perpetual yearning for something beyond what life presents to us. Too much of humanity is involved in escapist ideas about the afterlife and communion with some concept of God to be able to live their lives fully without this dependency on winning the favor of these God concepts. At least two-thirds of this species spend years of their lives studying doctrines on how to attain the afterlife that they give up the life the could be leading in favor of the mystical alternative. It will be shown in this volume how this quest for the afterlife is nothing more than an instinctual need of the individual virus cell embedded in every human being to join with the mother hive collective. This is the basis for the God syndrome present in humanity, the incessant quest for God and the Divine.

It is virtually impossible for individual human beings to discern what it is like to be part of a hive collective, particularly when we all think we are individuals with free will to choose what we want to do with our lives. But the fact remains, when you look at it with total honesty and objectivism, humans have become herd beasts. As much as our psyche screams to us that we are individuals, our actions betray this lip-service claim to being free and autonomous consciousnesses. Everything we do, except in the rarest individuals, is predicated on being part of one herd or another, whether that is the herd of our religions, spiritual beliefs, political ideologies or our social circles. While we bluster about being autonomous individuals, even our perceptions about ourselves are dictated through the eyes of others. The measure of our own sense of self-worth is gauged by the opinions of others, whether they be family members, social friends and acquaintances, our authority figures (including our holy books), and the standards dictated to us by our cultures. Everyone is a slave to one herd perception or another. The entire foundation of your false ego personality is a product of such herd indoctrination, whether you are willing to admit this or not.

The infectious hapiym hive cell has no identity of its own. It is no different than an amoeba which simply duplicates itself over and over again. Through a similar process of amoebic cell splitting, the hapiym virus replicated itself in a similar manner, Being part of a hive collective, it has access to certain hive memories, and the psychologist Carl Jung made the astute observation in his theory of the collective unconscious, that the language of this collective unconscious was the language of symbols. Jung's collective unconscious is the hapiym hive collective of consciousness. It is the root database with controls all hive cells in its infected human host population.

Once one becomes infected with the virus, usually at birth, then the new cell starts to adapt itself to its human host, taking on the personality and mannerisms of that host personality, eventually overlaying the true personality with the false virus persona that I refer to as the ego. Don Juan noted that we are all independent consciousnesses until such time as we have been indoctrinated enough with the mind of the 'predator', as he referred to the virus, that we become a full-fledged 'member' of the hive associative culture. At this point, usually around age 6 or a bit older, the virus takes control and starts ruling our psyche. When we attain this level of membership within our cultural milieu, we have become herd animals and are no longer autonomous consciousnesses. Our psyche is driven by the needs and mandates of our selective cultural herds and we lose all personal autonomy of consciousness except the false perception that we are cognitively free. It is this illusion of freedom that the virus feeds us to keep us subdued into the hive/herd animal it has turned us into. Its deception is so profound that everyone will deny that they are controlled by this seductive and deceptive mind virus and the habits it creates in us to make us nothing more than emotion generators, so it could feed upon our very existence.

The cosmic hive itself had the utter conquest of the multiverse as its ultimate design. Earth humans, basically being a 'new' race on the cosmic stage, have made the conquest of our species very important in these designs of cosmic dictatorship. I realize how troubling such information may be to you, and I also know the resistance that such ideas beget in people who can't face the magnitude of such a horrible truth. While Hollywood pumps out movies with themes like *The Invasion of the Body Snatchers*, such an invasion has already taken place and our species is blissfully unaware of this conquest of our consciousness by the hapiym hive mind virus.

The greatest tool the hive virus has used in its deception against our species has been the lure of the supernatural and the mystical to entice us to give up what's left of our genuine selves to doctrines and beliefs formulated by the hive that invite us to give up the last of our humanity and exchange it for mystical promises of magical powers and eternity in a false afterlife. Every mystical tradition on this planet that promotes such ideas is a hidden tool for tyranny that create within our psyche a dependency syndrome of a magnitude that most followers of religious or spiritual traditions are willing to acknowledge. They would rather die defending these false beliefs than step into the light of the truth that will free their consciousness from this tyranny masquerading as Divine Love or the Love of God.

Because we are material beings living in a material world, totally governed by our primary five senses, anything that goes beyond these five senses is considered supernatural or paranormal. Science has utterly failed humanity by refusing to investigate these paranormal experiences out of fear of being tarnished by being called superstitious, so materialist scientism is worthless where seeking understanding of the mind virus and its tactics are concerned. The religionists and the mystical believers in the hive doctrines have also failed because they insist on embracing these supernatural doctrines and yearn for the false promises created by the virus hive to lead all humanity into a cognitive trap of a magnitude that truly boggles the mind. Being deceived by these doctrines, they do not question what they desire, nor what some of them experience, they only know that their desire for magical powers or mystical experiences count more than asking probing questions to discover what may lie beyond their perceptions.

In both cases of science and religion, we are faced with different versions of selective blindness and a grave insufficiency and profound unwillingness to investigate what has really taken place with our species. We are faced with either dismissal through denial by science, or denial through faith by those who believe these hive ideologies without question. In neither arena do we find anyone willing to critically question or analyze any of this, and as a result of this species denial, the virus has gone undiscovered for thousands of years of recorded human history by the intellectual classes of every era. What I will provide in the rest of this volume is the historical examples with references, where possible, to clarify this picture for the reader's greater understanding.

# 6. The Lure of the Supernatural

As humans, we have a bad habit of desiring magical abilities, and much of this is founded on all too many hero stories, and this includes hero stories attributed to our holy men, messiahs and saviors throughout time. With stories of miraculous healing, walking on water, feeding thousands with a few fish and a few loaves of bread in the Christian context, the desire to be a miracle healer is present in the ego desires with many people. For those who doubt this fascination with miraculous hands-on healing, we only have to look at the practice of Reiki that has really burgeoned in the New Age arena since the 1980s. Millions of people have gravitated to becoming attuned to the practice of reiki without having any concept of what reiki actually is or what it really does.

Throughout human history people have flocked to purported magical healers, usually part of the priesthoods of old, to heal their ailments or to seek protection from angry gods or demons through purchasing magical talismans to protect them from both. Reiki is just a modern-day continuation of this human fascination with miraculous healing powers of one sort or another.

Also, throughout these same annals of history we have a long record of shamans and other occultists who seek power over others through learning how to cast spells for love potions or performing curses for pay to the magical practitioner. Witch shops still line the streets in New Orleans and other places around the world where 'magical herbs' can be purchased for spellcasting for religions like Voudun (voodoo) as just one example. Another aspect of occult magic that draws people into its clutches is the secret nature of most occult traditions. What motivates people to pursue any of these practices, even into newly organized religions like Wicca, will vary from person to person. Some want to learn to have power over others to do harm or to influence their own love affairs. Others, like in the practice of reiki, feel a compulsion based on their compassion to heal the world with their magical, energetic reiki powers. Wicca is a religion based in witchcraft where meetings and rituals are often performed nude on nights of the moon phases where they invoke the names of their gods and goddess to imbue the practitioners with power, so they can use these powers to manipulate their life or the lives of others. These are just three basic examples of how the human fascination with supernatural powers is a draw to millions of people all around the planet.

Aside from the ego's desire to become a hands-on healer or spellcaster in occult religions and traditions, we have the alleged holy men all around the planet who teach about the paradise of the Divine and how one can, through meditation, tantric practices, praying, reciting mantras, fasting or psychedelic drug use lead to a mystical ecstatic experience, what modern psychologists call a 'peak experience'. The recent field of Transpersonal Psychology is one of the most recent offshoots of these mystical traditions which has permeated the public fascination through over a century's promotion by the

Theosophical Society and other secret society organizations like Freemasonry, which has worked in collusion with the Theosophists since the mystic Madame Helena Blavatsky created the Theosophical Society in 1875.

Any deep study into these organizations will reveal a heavy influence of Gnosticism as well as occult Kabalistic traditions from Jewish mysticism, with correlative links that tie into certain Hindu religious practices, Tibetan Buddhism, and can be traced back to the original religion of dualism, Zoroastrianism, which was the primary influence for all three major western religions. Along with these occult traditions, outside the apparent venue of religion, we find similar elements in Greek Philosophy, which itself served as a masquerade to religion coupled with scientific inquiry.

As will be illustrated as this volume continues, the reader is going to find a historical thread of consistency that spans thousands of years hiding an agenda that, had it been allowed to come to fruition, would have made humanity on this planet nothing more than vessels for the hapiym hive mind virus. Through the alleged mystery schools of ancient and modern times, the reader is going to come face to face with this agenda as the mystery is revealed for the dastardly deception is represents. You will be confronted with a conspiracy that has been going on so long that its very existence defies rationality in our limited lifespan view of who we think we are as a species.

What will also be illustrated will be two integral players in this cosmic drama, two self-proclaimed Anunnaki gods who were both vying for supremacy over this planet and our species, and how one of them eventually allied with the hapiym hive in an effort to take control of this planet once and for all. What follows is going to be a very convoluted story of a deception that defies description in the dastardliness of its scope, with humanity on this planet being nothing but pawns in the game to these sinister machinations hiding behind the mask of the Divine, Love and Spirituality. The reader is going to have to exhibit patience as I seek to weave these pieces together in order to present this story in the most comprehensive light I can offer. The first step on this journey is in accepting the idea that the human fascination with the supernatural has been the greatest weakness our species has provided to these tyrants, and it has been played upon mercilessly throughout the ages. Through this fascination with magical powers and indoctrinated hero mentalities, we have made ourselves easy prey to these 'Divine' deceptions, and we are still doing the same thing to this very day.

Our short lifespans have also been used against us because our ancestors witnessed the longevity of these offworld races who seemed to live forever while humanity on this planet lived short and miserable lives as slaves to these races with greater longevity than our own. The quest for immortality goes back at least as far as the Sumerian *Epic of Gilgamesh*, a Sumerian demigod who went on a hero's quest for a plant that would allegedly give him the same eternal life as the gods. This idea about seeking immortality, as ancient as it may be, was not lost on future generations of humanity as in 1513, the explorer Ponce de Leon was mythologized in search of the Fountain of Youth. Humanity can't shake the idea of becoming immortal, and much of the scientific research into genetics is a continuing quest for immortality. The late advent of cybernetics and robotics now offers a new lure for immortality by fusing man with machine in the Transhumanist agenda. Make no mistake, despite all the talk of how robots are supposedly going to make our lives easier, the ultimate quest for artificial intelligence and merging humans with machines is being funded by Aryan elitists who have gathered the wealth of this planet into their coffers and are investing that money to find any workable solution to solve the immortality issue so they can ideally rule the world forever. This, I assert, is the agenda behind the publicly proclaimed agenda that is driving not only the Transhumanist agenda but cracking the human genome code. Immortality is the sought-after prize.

With all these factors at play, it is little wonder that humanity is so readily seduced by the lure of immortality, whether in this life or in the presumed afterlife. Every major religion, as will be shown, is an escapist quest for immortality, finding how one can be a presumed savior or hero of humanity, and being lifted up to Heaven to be with one's god, or being whisked away to some $5^{th}$ Dimensional space paradise, which idea also originated within the doctrines of Theosophy and pervade New Age spiritual thinking. With these varied doctrines, anything is better than being human. We are taught to hate our humanness and seek refuge in the arms of the alleged Divine, which we have been told for thousands of years is the only refuge worth aspiring to as lowly humans. It has created an insecurity complex of gigantic proportions, and our species is so blinded by the quest for the supernatural that we hate being human. What a sad testimony for a species that has such great potential on its own without all this Divine dependency.

Through these false spiritual doctrines perpetuated by the hapiym hive hierarchy, our very existence has been cheapened as all these religions teach that we are all lesser beings, have all come short of the glory of God, and that the only way we can 'redeem' ourselves is to submit to the 'Divine Will' of God, Source, Creator or the Universe. We are told that we are inept as a species and only the 'enlightened ones' of the heavenly hierarchy and their earthly 'servants' are suited to lead us into these spiritual lands of milk and honey. Sadly, all too many humans on this planet buy this spiritual swill and sell their very existence short standing in the shadows of these Divine scams and these presumed gods and alleged divine representatives of the hapiym hive. It has all been a cosmic con game with humanity being the target of the sting. Until humanity is willing to remove itself from this fascination with the supernatural and stop chasing mystical rainbows, their consciousness will continue to be controlled by priestly con artists selling salvation to anyone who believes they are unworthy as a human being and require salvation from being who they are.

# 7. The Bible – A Starting Point

The approach to exposing this massive fraud may at first seem haphazard as there are so many diverse threads that must be sewn into this tapestry before the full picture can be revealed. Since the Western world has been slave to the stories in the Bible, I am going to use that book as a launching point and expand from there as I weave this picture together.

Those who have studied history, particularly the history of comparative religions, and who are not simply apologists for their own faith seeking to bolster their beliefs by using selective blindness to avoid the truth, know that what became Christianity in Rome was a blending and careful concatenation of many religious traditions that preceded the birth of Immanuel. Out of the many gods who walked the Earth in ancient times, there was a slow and steady consolidation of the many gods into basically two primary elements of godhead. We find the foundations of the Christian trinity in the ancient religion of Egypt with the father god Osiris, his sister wife, Isis, and her alleged son Horus. In Christian iconography this trinity is represented in one of two forms, God the Father, the Son and the Holy Spirit; or God, the Son and the Mother Mary. In many traditional translations, the holy spirit is symbolized by the dove and has female attributes.

I am not concerned with Christian arguments in defending their faith denying these things, as their beliefs bear no relevance on the truth that will be revealed herein. The Jewish god of the Old Testament (OT) was a patriarchal god whose attributes matched other roles played by Enki in other lands under other names, like Ea in Sumeria, Babylon and Akkad; Zeus in Greece; Osiris and Amun in Egypt; and Jupiter in Rome. He always played the role of Father God. Reading some of the stories about Zeus, although fanciful in many cases, illustrates Enki as a magician and deceiver on many occasions.

Christians have been sold the idea through the centuries that their God was the god of the Hebrews, who only believed in one God. Yet the concept for monotheism predates the idea presented in the OT back as far the 14th century BC with the heretic pharaoh Akhenaten and his cult of sun worship, the Aten disk. This solar iconography is going to play a major role in solving these puzzles down through the ages. So, the idea of a singular God was not specifically a Hebrew or Jewish invention, it was grafted in from other cultures.

Another aspect of the religion of the Jews was the presence of Yahweh's female consort, his Asherah. The existence of Asherah has been intentionally excluded and whitewashed from biblical storytelling because it doesn't fit the narrative as the one supreme male God. In the OT, Asherah has been diminished to the role of a competing cult to Yahweh's system of monotheism. Asherah was Ninhursag and was also known by other names such as Ashtoreth, Ishtar, Inanna, Isis and a plethora of other goddess identifiers like Juno, Hera, Minerva, Cybele, Allat as well as certain male gods, such as Horus, Ra, Ashur, and Ahura Mazda. It is important to remember these variations as this story unfolds for they play a very important role in this deception.

Enki and Ninhursag on occasion worked together when a project suited both their agendas, and the rest of the time they competed with each other for the domination over this planet and this species. Most of the time it was a game of one-upmanship between the two with a rivalry that spanned thousands of years. Despite the biblical whitewashing and demonizing of Ninhursag as Asherah/Ishtar, when the Yahweh temple cult started, they were working side by side as God and his consort. Archaeological evidence bears this out and the book by Raphael Patai, *The Hebrew Goddess* provides an excellent evidentiary study of this.

Enki was what one could call a sexual prig, whereas Ninhursag was a hedonistic sexual libertine, as the cults that grew up around her varied roles proved over time. Enki's priggishness is patently evident in how he exhibited his misogynistic mandates as the God of the Hebrews in the Bible. Virtually everything he mandated as a sin against him were the very things that Ninhursag endorsed in her own religions. These mandates for destruction of Ninhursag's aspects of worship are illustrated in the following verses from the OT:

> *Exodus 34:13 -"But rather, you are to tear down their altars and smash their sacred pillars and cut down their Asherim.*

*Leviticus 26:30 - 'I then will destroy your **high places**, and cut down your incense altars, and heap your remains on the remains of your idols, for My soul shall abhor you.*

*Micah 1:7*

*All of **her** idols will be smashed, All of **her** earnings will be burned with fire And all of **her** images I will make desolate, For she collected them from a harlot's earnings, And to the earnings of a harlot they will return.*

[Bold emphasis mine]

What should be noted in these passages is that Nin had built her temples on high places, and in particular, that of Mt, Zion as noted in the following verse:

*Lamentations 2:8-10 - The LORD determined to destroy **the wall of the daughter of Zion**. He has stretched out a line, He has not restrained His hand from destroying, And He has caused rampart and wall to lament; They have languished together.*

[Bold emphasis mine]

Although there has been much masking in the Bible about what Zion was, this verse illustrates that the temple or city built atop Mt, Zion was in fact one of Ninhursag's cult centers. For further evidence of this nature of the 'daughters of Zion' being associated with Nin's goddess cults, the following verse should remove any doubt:

> *Isaiah 3:16-26 - The Lord said: Because the daughters of Zion are haughty and walk with outstretched necks, glancing wantonly with their eyes, mincing along as they go, tinkling with their feet, therefore the Lord will strike with a scab the heads of the daughters of Zion, and the Lord will lay bare their secret parts. In that day the Lord will take away the finery of the anklets, the headbands, and the crescents; the pendants, the bracelets, and the scarves; the headdresses, the armlets, the sashes, the perfume boxes, and the amulets; ...*

What needs to be noticed in this passage is not only the finery and wearing bells on their toes, which is reminiscent of the Isis cult, but the reference to the crescent. The upside-down crescent was one of the primary symbolic motifs in goddess worship and Nin was often featured wearing this symbol in headdresses from Egypt all the way to India. This crescent motif is also present in many images of the Mother Mary in Catholic iconography. These two passages should leave absolutely no doubt that references to Zion in the biblical context refer to Ninhursag's goddess cult. In the same light, modern day Zionism, it will be shown, is nothing more than a hidden aspect of Nin's worship through the Kabbalah in secret societies to this day.

Another passage from the OT illustrates the ire exhibited by Enki when vanquishing Nin's cult center:

> *Lamentations 1:1-22 - How lonely sits the city that was full of people! How like a widow has she become, she who was great among the nations! She who was a princess among the provinces has become a slave. She weeps bitterly in the night, with tears on her cheeks; among all her lovers she has none to comfort her; all her friends have dealt treacherously with her; they have become her enemies. Judah has gone into exile because of affliction and hard servitude; she dwells now among the nations, but finds no resting place; her pursuers have all overtaken her in the midst of her distress. The roads to Zion mourn, for none come to the festival; all her gates are desolate; her priests groan; her virgins have been afflicted, and she herself suffers bitterly. Her foes have become the head; her enemies prosper, because the Lord has afflicted her for the multitude of her transgressions; her children have gone away, captives before the foe. ..."*

This scattering of Nin's acolytes and believers followed her wherever Enki could shut them down. Her followers and her cults were continuously run underground to escape the patriarchal persecution wrought by Enki's patriarchal priesthoods, and eventually this turned into the so-called underground stream of knowledge that the secret societies throughout the ages have kept alive. Despite the whitewash that Zion represents the city of Jerusalem and the alleged sinful ways of Israel, these verses verify in no uncertain terms that it was a war of elimination for Nin's goddess cults at the hands of Enki's patriarchal zealots. Taken all together, the verses present a substantially different picture than the biblical illusion sold to later generations of Jews and Christians alike. They illustrate a competition between two separate forces vying for supremacy with the human followers of either 'faith' being nothing but the prize on the poker table.

This pattern of cutting down sacred groves dedicated to Ninhursag in any number of her goddess roles became a *modus operandi* for Enki's priestly step-and-fetch-its, as illustrated by Rome's conquest of Athens in 85 BC, where a grove dedicated to Athena, a Greek goddess of wisdom was cut down, so the Romans could build siege engines to attack the city. The grove had existed for 300 years before its destruction. And this brings us to another key element in solving these riddles, and that is Ninhursag's claim to be the goddess of wisdom in her many and varied identities. This wisdom motif is going to bear profound relevance as this volume continues to unfold, so I ask the reader to not lose sight of this wisdom connection where Nin is concerned.

As I have stated in a number of my other books, the Bible, particularly the Old Testament, is a concatenated collection of stories stolen from other lands. I have referred to the biblical synopsized storytelling as a *Reader's Digest* version of more ancient and lengthy tales from other lands. In many respects, it is

Enki's brag book and little more, although there are more obfuscated references to some of Nin's ideas contained within the book. Despite the claimed hoary age of the book, we have no extant copies of any of it existing prior to the discovery of the Dead Sea Scrolls (DSS). There is not, for instance, a surviving copy of the Septuagint, the legendary compilation of the Hebrew scriptures that allegedly took place in Alexandria, Egypt in about the 3rd century BC. All that survives of this legendary book are much later renditions of it that post-date the DSS. There are not even any fragments of the Septuagint that evidence the early compilation and translation of the book in Alexandria, so to this author, it is only an unsubstantiated religious legend – another myth in the catalog of Jewish and Christian deceptions.

To return to the verse provided above from Isaiah, it should be noted that pagan priests often wore bells in their religions processions to ward off evil spirits. Dionysus, also known as Bacchus in Rome, was another male role played by Ninhursag in her varied disguises, and the followers of Dionysus wore headbands tied in bows in their religious processions. The wearing of headdresses, particularly masks of the jackal-headed God Anubis, were worn by the priests of Isis in their religious processions as well. With all of these varied cults associated with Ninhursag, we find virtually every element criticized and scorned as sinful by the self-righteous God of the OT, Enki.

Other aspects of Nin's cults were drunken revelry and sexual orgies, particularly in the cult of Dionysus and reportedly in the Eleusian Mysteries, where the worshippers drank a substance known a *kykeon*, which had known hallucinogenic properties. Through the cult of Demeter and her daughter Persephone (also known as Kore), the religious myth held that Persephone was kidnapped by Hades and taken to the dark underworld. Through the dramatic ritualization of this story, the kidnapping of Kore and Demeter's search for her, the followers of the Eleusian Mysteries followed a procession from Athens to Eleusis, considered the dramatic search in the dark underworld for Kore, progressing along the Sacred Way, to finally arrive at the place of the mysteries where they would 'emerge from the dark', and into the 'light' where the goddess Demeter herself provided visions to the initiates. Such visionary experiences are also reportedly associated with the initiates who could pay for the right to sleep in the Temples of Isis, where the goddess would bestow on the initiates divine visions. Isis was also known as the goddess of wisdom.

Among these wisdom traditions, early on we find the Egyptian god Thoth (Tehuti), who in later traditions was equated with the sage of wisdom Hermes Trismegistus, which translates to mean Hermes the Thrice Great. There is some basis for this correlation between the Egyptian god Thoth and the thrice great Hermes as there survives in Egyptian texts, references to the "great, great, great Thoth." Thoth, I will assert, was another Ninhursag personality overlay and was the Egyptian god of writing and wisdom. In tracking Enki, and especially Ninhursag, one has to follow the appellations and symbols associated with them to solve these riddles. Although there are some scholars who do see parallels in many of these beliefs, they are more likely to attribute these things to a form of cultural appropriation than accept the idea that it was the same entities moving about and playing these different roles, with their symbols and claims to fame following them wherever they went.

Within the biblical narrative, then, we find a competition between Nin's goddess cults, which Enki was continually seeking to quash into non-existence, and Nin working to undermine Enki's systems of patriarchy wherever possible. They often collaborated in certain projects, even Christianity, yet they both had their own hidden agendas and power plays hidden from one another when they did so. The motif of the Mother and Son aspect present in Christianity is only a variant of the same theme present with the cult of Isis and the fictional son Horus. The name Jesus was a fabrication, a tool to harness the power given up by the believers and invokers of the name. It was just another cognitive and energetic trap sowing dependency and insecurity on the part of the believers who were always less than their perception of God. The mythical name Jesus became the epitome of perfection to which no human could ever hope to aspire, and it kept the followers of the name ever subservient to standing in the shadow of such perfection, always unworthy and serving as lesser beings to an agenda that humanity in all its sordid history never perceived.

Another aspect of the biblical religion of Yahweh is that of the mandate for his priests to sacrifice a red heifer without blemish on his altars. From the earliest times in Egypt, Hathor was the cow goddess, and the sacred cow was symbolized by the cow goddess Kamadhenu in India. The direct correlation between Hathor, another alleged mother goddess, either mother or wife of Horus, mother of Isis and a daughter of Ra, can be found in

Kamadhenu in India, represented as the subsummation of all gods and goddesses. Wikipedia reports this way about Kamadhenu:

> *"...also known as Surabhi, is a divine bovine-goddess described in Hinduism as the mother of all cows. She is a miraculous "cow of plenty" who provides her owner whatever he desires and is often portrayed as the* ***mother of other cattle*** *as well as the eleven Rudras. In iconography, she is generally depicted as a white cow with a female head and breasts, the wings of a bird, and the tail of a peafowl or as a white cow* ***containing various deities within her body****."*

> *"According to the Monier Williams Sanskrit–English Dictionary (1899), Surabhi means fragrant, charming, pleasing, as well as cow and earth. It can specifically refer to the divine cow Kamadhenu,* ***the mother of cattle who is also sometimes described as a Matrika ("mother") goddess.*** *Other proper names attributed to Kamadhenu are Sabala ("the spotted one") and Kapila ("****the red one****")."*

> *"****All the gods are believed to reside in the body of Kamadhenu—the generic cow****. Her four legs are the scriptural Vedas; her horns are the* ***triune*** *gods Brahma (tip), Vishnu (middle) and*

*Shiva (base); **her eyes are the sun and moon gods**, her shoulders the **fire-god Agni** and the wind-god Vayu and her legs the Himalayas. Kamadhenu is often depicted in this form in poster art."*

*"The Matsya Purana notes two conflicting descriptions of Surabhi. In one chapter, it describes Surabhi as the **consort of Brahma** and their union produced the cow Yogishvari, the eleven Rudras, "lower animals", goats, swans and **"high class drugs"**. She is then described as the **mother of cows and quadrupeds**. In another instance, she is described as a daughter of Daksha, wife of Kashyapa and the mother of cows. The Harivamsa, an appendix of the Mahabharata, calls Surabhi the mother of Amrita (ambrosia), **Brahmins**, cows and Rudras."*

[Bold emphasis mine]

A few things must be taken away from these passages. First is the reference to her being the "mother of other cattle" and the reference in the last section about her being the "mother of cows and quadrupeds." The natural assumption from the last passage would lead one to think that the cows referenced are themselves quadrupeds, yet I will assert that her being the "mother of all cattle" is a subliminal reference to humans as cattle, and not strictly bovine quadrupeds. When dealing with these ancient Anunnaki allegories, things can't be taken at superficial face value, for as we will discover as we move forward, there is much that lies hidden in allegory and metaphor. Nothing is as it seems.

We should also pay attention to the fact that as Kapila, or 'the red one,' Nin was symbolized by a red cow. We have to wonder exactly why Enki mandated the sacrifice of a red heifer to his Jewish priests? Was it just another shot at being vindictive to Ninhursag and her cow goddess roles? Along with her role as the cow mother goddess, we once again find that consort motif as found with Yahweh and Asherah through Kamadhenu and Brahma. We also find that triune aspect of Nin, along with her affiliation with the sun and moon as we find with Hathor, Isis and the Mother Mary in Catholicism. As stated previously, following the symbology we finally start to unravel the puzzle pieces and the mysteries clear up, even if we don't like the picture it paints.

It should also be noted that through the alleged union with Brahma that she created "high class drugs". This is most likely a reference to the hallucinogenic psilocybin mushroom that grows in cow manure and will have serious implications as these mysteries unfold.

Although we have wandered afield of purely biblical references in this chapter, it is a necessary journey before we can start to weave the overall tapestry of tyranny together that these mystical traditions present to our species. We have a very bad habit of breaking things down and compartmentalizing them as separate, when in fact they are not as separate as they appear. There has been a concerted effort by the controlling elite of this planet to make things appear to be separated so this massive cognitive fraud can continue unchallenged and unrevealed to most of Earth's human population. The con game can only work through deception, and when the truth is known, it must necessarily fall apart once revealed for what it is. This is why these traditions were called 'mysteries'. Once exposed, there is no mystery whatsoever, only a manipulated fraud against human consciousness to keep us as a slave race, serving false gods, false spiritual and religious doctrines, and false ideologies that all profess collectivism and the superiority of the herd over the individual. We will revisit other aspects of the Bible in later chapters in a different context, but one which ties into these ancient traditions and the war between Enki and Ninhursag, and ultimately to the hapiym hive collective.

# 8. Horus and Ahura Mazda

As noted in the last chapter, as well as in a number of my other books, we can track Enki and Ninhursag through their varied roles by the symbols they chose to use to identify themselves through their cults. Unfortunately, our history has been so intentionally corrupted over time that we will never have a full true accounting in a linear fashion of events in our prehistoric past. There are pieces of truth from which we must try and cobble a picture together in an attempt to make sense of it all. One thing is for certain, our species has been left with intentionally corrupted myths and legends to keep us from discovering the full truth of our past, but there is enough evidence that survives in more ancient myths that can give us some foundation from which to try and reconstruct pieces of our past.

As I stated in my previous works, Egypt was the stronghold of forces aligned with the Orioner god Enlil and was governed by the original god Osiris and his wife Isis. When Ninhursag returned to Earth with her Aryan armies, the primary objective was to retake Mesopotamia, and the secondary objective was to usurp Osiris and his armies who had followed the orders of the planetary overlord, Enlil, to try and eradicate the Anunnaki. What modern scholarship shows in both Mesopotamia and in Egypt at virtually the same time, is the appearance of civilizations with fully develop systems of writing without having a linear historical predecessor for these civilizations. By scholarly assessment, they are enigmas that appeared out of nowhere.

There are legends that tell of invading armies, who are referred to as the Followers of Horus, alternately named the Shemsu Hor, that invaded Upper Egypt (southern Egypt) and usurped the armies of the resident god Seth or Set. This invasion is what brought this civilization of writing and architecture to Egypt in predynastic times in Egypt. Because the Horus myth has been tampered with so much over the millennia, the Horus that invaded Upper Egypt in those ancient times is erroneously referred to as Horus the Elder, who is often coupled with being the husband of Hathor, another ancient Egyptian deity who lived before Ninhursag claimed her attributes and took her place in the Egyptian pantheon. Later legends, through corrupted mythology, has Horus being born to Isis after Set allegedly tricked Osiris into a coffin and threw him into the river Nile, only later to retrieve the body and cut it up into 14 pieces before Isis could find him. This later rendition of Horus is referred to as Horus the Younger. For the sake of clarity, both Horuses represent the same entity, Ninhursag, in one of her male roles. The deliberate obfuscation of these two entities, which were in fact one and the same personage as the hermaphrodite Ninhursag, has left scholars baffled for generations.

The Followers of Horus, I will assert, were the Aryan armies led by Ninhursag playing the role as Horus, the conqueror of Set, the alleged ruler of Upper Egypt, when the Aryan army invaded Upper Egypt around 3500-3400 BC. Egyptian legend is very sparse in reporting where Horus originated and where his army of followers came from except "the sky". This information cross-foots with all the information I shared in a previous chapter and also in my *WANA* books.

The symbol of Horus was the winged solar disc, which was first found in Behedet in Upper Egypt, and represents the midday sun and is called Horus Behdety in Edfu in Upper Egypt, the primary cult center of Horus in ancient Egypt. It goes beyond the scope of this presentation to try and make sense out of nonsensical Egyptian religious mythology, but what is important is the symbolism of the winged solar disk and its association with Horus, also called Horus the Mezer, in what is known as the *Inventory Stele* found at the Giza Plateau in 1858. Although the Inventory Stele may be a priestly piece of propaganda from the 26$^{th}$ Dynasty (ca. 670 BC), the reference to Horus the Mezer doesn't seem to be in question as an appellation for Horus.

The importance of this appellation and the symbolism of the winged disc associated with Horus is directly translatable to a similar symbol for the god of Zoroaster, Ahura Mazda, the only difference being the insertion of a male deity 'riding' within the disc. This same symbol came to be associated with the national god of the Assyrians, Assur or Ashur and is called the fravahar. Where Zoroaster makes his distinction in the realm of religious practices is that he is one of the first notable 'prophets' who declared his religion based on alleged Divine visions and conversations with, and tutelage by the equivalent of angels. The name Ahura Mazda translates to mean Lord Wisdom. Following the traces of Ninhursag through her many name transitions, the association with Wisdom follows her virtually everywhere.

In the Mazdaean religion, we do not find an entity proclaiming itself to be god as in the previous ages when the physical gods walked the Earth. Instead we find a transition point between the material gods and the alleged immaterial god of the hapiym virus hive posturing as the one supreme god with his bevy of angels to reinforce the belief system. We move from the concept of the physical gods to the singular metaphysical god, or metaphysical monotheism with Ahura Mazda being the One True God. Along with Ahura Mazda, we find two compatriots in the trinity attributed to him, Mithra and the goddess Anahita – the latter two both being considered as 'divinity of the waters'. Mithra is also considered a 'Guardian of the Cattle'. With Ahura Mazda, Mithra and Anahita, we find the holy trinity of Zoroastrianism. They are not gods (or angels) that walked the Earth but were instead visionary 'emanations' of a higher manifestation of an invisible creator of souls. This transition to the metaphysical set the stage for all spiritual teachings over the last 3,500 years or more and is still the active element in religions and spiritual traditions to this day.

Unfortunately, no one knows when Zoroaster was born, and the estimates of the origin of his religion vary from as early as 1850 BC to the 6th century BC. I have a tendency to lean toward the older date as the religion of Ahura Mazda is an Aryan religion, equally as much as the Vedic religion is in India. Although it is still hotly contested by Indian nationalists, the Aryan invaders intruded themselves into virtually every culture after their arrival and became the elite ruling classes of kings and priests, and from my research, because of the extreme similarities in the Vedic religion and that of Zoroaster, I feel that they spawned from the same root. I'm sure there are those who would contest this position.

It is through Zoroastrianism that the dualistic concept of a good god and a bad god emerged, with the bad god, Angra Mainyu, or Ahriman, eventually being turned into the Christian concept of the Devil. Although Christians want to believe that their religion is unique, there are too many similar characteristics between Zoroastrianism and all three major western religions to accept such a notion any longer. The Jewish concept of *sheol*, which was taken singularly from Zoroastrian doctrine, was later turned into the concept of the fiery Hell in Christian traditions. There are far too many similarities in all of these other religions to discount Zoroastrianism as the most likely source, in both Eastern as well as Western religions.

Although there are stories of the worshippers of Isis having visions in her temples, the Anunnaki were a telepathic species which could create illusions in the minds of others. The ancient stories of the wars between the gods in India attest to these gods creating illusions, what is referred to as *maya*, in fighting these wars. Many of these tales of visions from Isis were from later centuries, so there is every likelihood that these visions were provided by the hive version of Nin's personality after her virus cell vacated her form.

There is no solid foundation of evidence to pinpoint when the event I am about to share occurred, somewhere along the line with all of her own experimentation, Ninhursag discovered the hive and made an arrangement with the hive proper to establish herself as a god/goddess amongst the hapiym hive hierarchy. As much as she competed with Enki over the ages, he always seemed to best her at any game she could devise. I will conjecture at this point that once she discovered the hive, then she started working in earnest to establish her religious, spiritual and philosophical ideologies in order to establish her power base within the hive. Once she felt she had all her bases covered, she simply gave up the ghost, let her form die, and then moved the hapiym hive cell personality to the cosmic hive proper. If this is all correct, then it was most likely Nin in one of her metaphysical male guises that appeared in the visions to Zoroaster as the god Ahura Mazda. The trinity of Ahura Mazda, Mithra and Anahita should serve as conformation of her tripartite Hermaphroditic nature, especially considering the fact that a hapiym hive cell could only imitate the personality and characteristics of its host's body. From this foundation, she then started spreading the metaphysical religions in collusion with the hive that set the stage for human spiritual desires over the last 3,000-4,000 years.

Another aspect that Ninhursag played in collusion with the hive hierarchy was that of the Spenta Armaiti. A Spenta in Zoroastrian religion is an 'emanation' or alternative aspect of the Divine. Armaiti is one of the divine intelligences associated with Ahura Mazda and amongst the highest archangels of the Mazdaean religion. Armaiti is a feminine aspect of godhead who is allegedly all-seeing and was vested with all the vision and manifesting power of the divine. She is associated with spiritual/mental energies and translates to mean "perfect contemplation". This focus on the intellect as the source of spirituality will bear particular relevance as the evidence unfolds. This contemplative aspect of the alleged divine is evident today with the varying methods of meditation hawked in many spiritual traditions around the world. There is a profound basis for these practices and all is not as it seems once their purpose is revealed.

Before discounting these ideas out of hand, one must look at Ninhursag's fingerprints in all these traditions, and as this story unfolds, you are going to see more and more of her influence through Greek Philosophy, Gnosticism, Hermeticism, Marxism, Zionism, Hinduism, Christianity, Islam, Theosophy and into the modern New Age. By the time you finish this book, the trail of evidence should be overwhelming enough to convince even the staunchest open-minded denier of her personal agenda for this planet. I am not here to say that Nin was singularly responsible for providing humanity with access to the hive, for there is a long legendary history of shamanism and necromancy to attest to hive interference from the ages of prehistory. I will, however, suggest that her involvement with the hive opened the doors to a more subversive and refined form of invading human consciousness through the active hive cells when the hive was alive, and turned it into metaphysical spirituality.

Although there is a lot of nonsense about necromancy with stories about people raising dead bodies and all, the primary root of necromancy is speaking with the 'spirits' of the dead. In the 19th century, this was all the craze and it was called Spiritism, and mediums were sought out to speak with their clients' dead relatives, ofttimes with the idea that they could predict the future. These presumed spirits of the dead were the stolen personalities of dead humans mimicked by the hapiym hive virus cells that inhabited the human form of the deceased and survived the form after death. They were never the actual dead relatives living in the afterlife but were merely stolen hive replicas of their personalities and nothing more.

With Madame Blavatsky and Alice Bailey serving as mediums to talk to their alleged Tibetan Ascended Masters, they were doing exactly the same type of necromancy prohibited in the Bible, except they changed the word and called it 'channeling', or 'mediumship' to make it more acceptable to the public. Every alleged spiritual medium who ever talked to the spirits who crossed over was only communicating with hapiym hive cells masquerading as their dead human hosts. Every New Age channeler is only a facilitator to the hive with all its nonsensical Love and Light doctrines of compassion and serving the world, as with Alice Bailey's Group of World Servers. Every unwitting member of these associations and others like them have only been useful idiots to the hive agenda, masquerading tyranny and the design to take over all humanity, as spirituality.

This formalized type of communication between the hive and the religion makers who came after, all started with Zoroaster and his visions with Ahura Mazda and the purported seven angels, the Amesha Spentas as they are referred to in the Zoroastrian *Gathas*, the Mazdaean scriptures. From this foundation began all metaphysical and mystical spirituality on this planet in the form of mystical religions, and *every bit of it* without exception was hive deception in one form or another.

Another association within Mazdaism is that of the Eternal Flame, which is representative of the power of Ahura as the Solar Logos, the Word of God. The Eternal Flame is an earthly representation of the Light of Ahura Mazda, or the overlord of the hive. It is from this concept of the Light of the Eternal God, represented by the sun and fire, that all the modern spiritual twaddle about the 'Divine Spark Within' originates. Given that humans were all infected with the hive virus, the alleged Divine Spark Within was only the virus cell that dwelled inside every human host. It was the 'little soul' that connected to the overall hive collective 'soul'. The alleged Divine Spark is the Hindu *Atman* to the hive overlord's *Brahman*.

Although there is competition to this day between these varied religious ideologies as to which one is the ultimate source of these teachings, it is only through Zoroaster that we find the singular source for these doctrines, no matter how much Brahmanic Hinduism seeks to lay claim to these ideological origins. There may have been hints of it in ancient Egyptian religion when referencing the *ka* and the *ba,* but it wasn't until Zoroaster that the teachings became the formalized intellectual mystical spirituality that has been handed down through the ages. Prior to Zoroaster, everything came from the gods and was originated by the gods. Only Zoroaster was the first human to knowingly connect with the hive and his concept of god as Ahura Mazda, where the ancient physical gods were circumvented and altered into metaphysical 'emanations' of the supreme hive god, that humanity gained its first direct access *en masse* to the hive in alternative to literally serving as servants, the physical gods of old.

Despite the furor that this attestation may cause in certain religious circles, there is no other human that can be directly attributed to performing this act other than Zoroaster. I have already vindicated Immanuel and Buddha as providing teachings about advancing psoyca sentient consciousness in my book, *From Belief to Truth – From Truth to Wisdom*, so anyone claiming Buddha as the source of these teachings can be ruled out. Even the Vedic traditions about Agni and his Eternal Flame hold a physical Anunnaki god as the predecessor, not a human like Zoroaster. It was the Oracles of the Zoroastrians of Chaldea, the *Magi* from Babylon within ancient Persia, which drove the Greek philosophers like Pythagoras, Socrates and Plato to posit their philosophical ideologies, not a human Indian scholar. Zarathustra was the sage supreme in Greek philosophy as well as through later Gnostic and Hermetic traditions; into the secret societies like the Rosicrucians and Freemasons through Hermeticism; into modern Theosophy and the New Age; with the same traditions creeping into Psychology today through Transpersonal Psychology and the schools of 'Spiritual Psychology', which are only now expanding in our universities. There will be more on this in the following chapters.

To connect the dots laid out in this chapter with Ninhursag and the hive, we only need to turn to the Chaldean Oracles themselves to see the syncretism involved in homogenizing the many roles Ninhursag hid behind and her mergence with the hive in formulating these metaphysical and mystical doctrines. There are questions about the Zoroastrian veracity of some of these ideas, as with all things, because of counterfeiting and attributing ideas to the Chaldeans that may not have originated with the Zoroastrian mystical teachings. Later-era religious syncretism brought a lot of disparate elements into the Neoplatonist teachings of the first to fourth centuries AD. Be that as it may, I am going to offer those sayings that are questionable as well and those that aren't so questioned so the reader can reach their own conclusions on the matter in determining whether my assertions stand on their own merit or not. This first passage appears in *The Chaldaick Oracles* printed in 1661, translated by Thomas Stanley.

*"MONAD. DUAD. TRIAD.*

*Where the Paternal Monad is.*

*The Monad is enlarged, which generates two.*

*For the Duad sits by him, and glitters with* ***Intellectual Sections****.*

*And to govern all Things, and to Order every thing not Ordered,*

***For in the whole World shineth the Triad, over which the Monad Rules****.*

*This Order is the beginning of all Section.*

*For the Mind of the Father said, that All things be cut into three,*

*Whose Will assented, and then All things were divided.*

*For the Mind of the Eternal Father said* ***into three,***

*Governing all things by the Mind.*

***And there appeared in it [the Triad]*** *Virtue and wisdome,*

*And Multiscient Verity.*

***This Way floweth the shape of the Triad, being præ-existent.***

*Not the first [Essence] but where they are measured.*

*For thou must conceive that all things serve these* ***three*** *Principles.*

***The first Course is sacred, but in the middle,***

***Another the third, aërial; which cherisheth the Earth in fire.***

*And fountain of fountains, and of all fountains.*

***The Matrix containing all things.***

*Thence abundantly springs forth the Generation of multivarious Matter.*

***Thence extracted a prester the flower of glowing fire,***

*Flashing into the Cavities of the Worlds: for all things from thence*

*Begin to extend downwards their admirable Beams."*

[Bold emphasis mine]

What the reader should take away from the highlighted sections is that the 'triad' lies 'below' as a part of the Monad. From the Monad (hive central), divides the individual cells that infected every human being, the Duad. This vast cosmic hive infection is the 'Matrix' referred to in this passage. The Triad is representational of Ninhursag in her tripartite sexual role as a hermaphroditic male-female-androgyne who stands as the intercessor to the hive Monad. This triune aspect is mirrored in the torch-bearing three-faced Greek goddess Hecate, who is also referenced in the Chaldean Oracles, sometimes as Hecate, sometimes as Isis, Psyche; or *the Magna Mater*, the Great Mother goddess. Ninhursag is represented in many varied forms in Hinduism as the Great Mother Goddess Durga, whose many aspects are simply different 'emanations', similar to Zoroaster's *Amesha Spentas*, of the co-opted personalities of other goddesses that preceded her, or simply names she made up to gather worshippers. You can't separate the Mother Goddess from the hive metaphysical doctrines, despite the patriarchal nature of the Monad hive 'Father', Brahman or Ahura Mazda. They are all incestuously linked together.

Prior to Alexander the Great's mandate to syncretize all the religions of the conquered Greek territories into a unified religion, such a process of syncretism was already in motion through the earliest Greek philosophers like Pythagoras and others as early as the 6$^{th}$ century BC, which will be discussed in more depth in the next chapter. The basis for this syncretism and harmonization of these doctrines was initially sought with the

*Oracles of Zoroaster*, or *Chaldean Oracles*. At roughly the same time that we started to see this religious innovation in Greece, India was also going through a similar type of religious and cultural upheaval during the same period with the rise of Jainism, which contains many similar foundational beliefs as those of Zoroaster. The primary similarity between the religion of Ahura Mazda, as with Jainism, is the dualistic conflict between the material form and the 'soul', and presents a similarity to later Gnosticism. In like kind, the homogenization of the early Greek gods and the move toward the concept of a 'Divine Oneness' started to intrude into Greek philosophical thinking. The doctrines of Zoroaster were very far reaching.

As an example, I am going to provide some of the most well-known and surviving *Oracles of Zoroaster* and then offer my commentary to further explain what they mean without all the mystical overtones. These tenets appeared in the book *The Chaldæn Oracles of Zoroaster* by William Wynn Westcott in 1895. Westcott himself was known as a magician, a Theosophist and a Freemason. What will be noted in these sayings is that they are passed down through the Greek philosophers who will be covered more extensively in chapter 9.

---

**OF ZOROASTER.**

CAUSE. GOD.
FATHER. MIND. FIRE.
MONAD. DYAD. TRIAD.

1. But God is He **having the head of the Hawk**. The same is the first, incorruptible, eternal, unbegotten, indivisible, dissimilar: the dispenser of all good; indestructible; the best of the good, the Wisest of the wise; He is the Father of Equity and Justice, self-taught, physical, perfect, and wise--He who inspires the Sacred Philosophy.

Eusebius. *Præparatio Evangelica*, liber. I., chap. X. – *This Oracle does not appear in either of the ancient collections, nor in the group of oracles given by any of the mediæval occultists. Cory seems to have been the first to discover it in the voluminous writings of Eusebius, who attributes the authorship to the Persian Zoroaster*

2. Theurgists assert that He is a God and celebrate him as both **older and younger**, as a circulating and eternal God, as understanding the whole number of all things moving in the World, and moreover infinite through his power and energizing a spiral force.

Proclus on the *Timæus* of Plato, 244. Z. or T. p.24 - *The Egyptian Pantheon had an Elder and a Younger Horus--a God--son of Osiris and Isis. Taylor suggests that He refers to Kronos, Time, or Chronos, as the later Platonists wrote the name. Kronos, or Saturnus, of the Romans, was son of Uranos and Gaia, husband of Rhea, father of Zeus.*

3. The God of the Universe, eternal, limitless, **both young and old**, having a spiral force.

*Cory includes this Oracle in his collection, but he gives no authority for it. Lobeck doubted its authenticity.*

4. For the Eternal Æon *--according to the Oracle--is the cause of never failing life, of unwearied power and unsluggish energy. Taylor.--T.

5. Hence the inscrutable God is called silent by the divine ones, and is said to consent with **Mind**, and to be known to human souls through the **power of the Mind alone**.

Proclus in *Theologiam Platonis*, 321. T. – *Inscrutable. Taylor gives "stable;" perhaps "incomprehensible" is better.*

6. The Chaldæans call the God Dionysos (or Bacchus), Iao in the Phoenician tongue (instead of the Intelligible Light), and he is also called Sabaoth, * signifying that he is above the Seven poles, that is the Demiurgos.

Lydus, *De Mensibus*, 83. T.

7. Containing all things in the one summit of his own Hyparxis, He Himself subsists wholly beyond.

Proclus in *Theologiam Platonis*, 212. T. *Hyparxis, is generally deemed to mean "Subsistence." Hupar is* Reality *as distinct from* appearance; *Huparche is a* Beginning.

8. Measuring and bounding all things.

Proclus in *Theologiam Platonis*, 386. T. *"Thus he speaks the words," is omitted by Taylor and Cory, but present in the Greek.*

9. For nothing imperfect emanates from the Paternal Principle, *Psellus*, 38; *Pletho*. Z.

*This implies--but only from a succedent emanation.*

10. The Father effused not Fear, **but He infused persuasion**.

*Pletho*. Z.

11. The Father hath apprehended Himself, and hath not restricted his **Fire** to his own intellectual power.

*Psellus*, 30; *Pletho*, 33. Z.

Taylor gives: --The Father hath hastily withdrawn Himself, but hath not shut up his own **Fire** in his **intellectual** power.

*The Greek text has no word "hastily," and as to withdrawn--Arpazo means, grasp or*
*snatch, but also "apprehend with the mind."*

12. Such is the Mind which is energized before energy, while yet it had not gone forth, but abode in the Paternal Depth, and in the Adytum of God nourished silence.

Proc. in *Tim.*, 167. T.

13. All things have issued from that **one Fire**. The Father perfected all things, and delivered them over to the **Second Mind, whom all Nations of Men call the First.**
*Psellus*, 24; *Pletho*, 30. Z.

14. The Second Mind conducts the Empyrean World.
Damascius, *De Principiis*. T.

15. What the Intelligible saith, it saith by understanding.
*Psellus*, 35. Z.

16. Power is with them, but **Mind is from Him**.
Proclus in *Platonis Theologiam*, 365. T.

17. The Mind of the Father riding on the subtle Guiders, which glitter with the tracings of inflexible and relentless **Fire.**
Proclus on the *Cratylus of Plato*. T.

18. . . . . After the Paternal Conception
I the Soul reside, a heat animating all things.
. . . . For he placed
The Intelligible in the Soul, and the **Soul in dull body**,
Even so **the Father of Gods and Men placed them in us**.
Proclus in *Tim. Plat.*, 124.. Z. or T.

19. Natural works co-exist with the intellectual light of the Father. For it is the Soul which adorned the vast Heaven, and which adorneth it after the Father, but **her** dominion is established on high.
Proclus in Tim., 106. Z. or T.
*Dominion, krata: some copies give kerata, horns.*

20. The **Soul**, being a brilliant **Fire**, by the power of the Father remaineth immortal, and is Mistress of Life, and filleth up the many recesses of the bosom of the World.
*Psellus*, 28; *Pletho*, 11. Z.

21. The channels being intermixed, therein **she** performeth the works of incorruptible Fire.
Proclus in *Politico*, p. 399. Z. or T.

22. For not in Matter did the Fire which is in the first beyond enclose His active Power, **but in Mind**; for the framer of **the Fiery World is the Mind of Mind.**
Proclus in *Theologian*, 333, and *Tim*., 157. T.

23. Who first sprang **from Mind, clothing the one Fire with the other Fire, binding them together**, that he might mingle the fountainous craters, while preserving unsullied the brilliance of His own Fire.
Proclus in *Parm. Platonis*. T.

24. And thence a Fiery Whirlwind drawing down the brilliance of the flashing flame, penetrating the abysses of the Universe; for from thence downwards do extend their wondrous rays.
Proclus in *Theologian Platonis*, 171 and 172. T.

25. The Monad first existed, and the Paternal Monad still subsists.
Proclus in *Euclidem*, 27. T.

26. **When the Monad is extended, the Dyad is generated**.
Proclus in *Euclidemi*, 27. T.

*Note that" What the Pythagoreans signify by Monad, Duad and Triad, or Plato by Bound, Infinite and Mixed; that the Oracles of the Gods intend by Hyparxis, Power and Energy."*
Damascius *De Principiis*. Taylor.

27. And beside Him is seated **the Dyad which glitters with intellectual sections, to govern all things and to order everything not ordered.**
Proclus in *Platonis Theologiam*, 376. T.

28. The Mind of the Father said that all things should be cut **into Three**, whose Will assented, and immediately all things were so divided.
Proclus in *Parmen*. T.

29. The Mind of the Eternal Father said into **Three, governing all things by Mind.**
Proclus, *Timæus of Plato*. T.

30. The Father **mingled every Spirit from this Triad**.
Lydus, *De Mensibus*, 20. Taylor.

31. **All things are supplied from the bosom of this Triad**.
Lydus, *De Mensibus*, 20. Taylor.

32. All things are governed and subsist **in this Triad**.
Proclus in I. *Alcibiades*. T.

33. For thou must know that **all things bow before the Three Supernals**.
Damascius, *De Principiis*. T.

34. From thence floweth forth the **Form of the Triad**, being preëxistent; not the first Essence, but that whereby all things are measured.
Anon. Z. or T.

35. And there appeared in it Virtue and Wisdom, and multiscient Truth.
Anon. Z. or T.

36. For in each World shineth the **Triad, over which the Monad ruleth.**
Damascius in *Parmenidem*. T.

37. The First Course is Sacred, in the middle place courses the Sun, * in the third the Earth is heated by the internal fire.
Anon. Z. or T.

38. Exalted upon High and animating **Light, Fire** Ether and Worlds.

Simplicius in his *Physica*, 143. Z. or T."

[Bold emphasis mine]

To solve all the seeming mysterious meandering in these sayings, one only has to view the hapiym hive mind virus as the epicenter of all these teachings, i.e. the Father, the Monad, the One, or the Fire. When we remove the mystical elements of it all and bring it down to the level of pragmatic understanding, all the mystery and philosophical gobble-de-gook disappears, and we realize that we have been told the truth the whole time yet lacked the understanding to realize the tyranny it represented to our species. When we see the Light of God as a mere representation of the hive core, and all these alleged angels, Ascended Masters, subsumed gods and goddesses as nothing but individuated cells within the anything-but-divine hierarchy, then we start to see through the massive con game that has been perpetrated against our species at the hands of *intellectuals* and mystics throughout recorded human history.

To further my assertion that the Anunnaki hermaphrodite Ninhursag, or at least her infected hive cell, did in fact 'ascend' to the hive after her death, the following quote should more than validate my claim in reference to Hecate and her role with the hive.

> *"Among the immortal gods Hecate has never said to the wise spokesmen of the gods anything vain or unfulfilled; but* ***descending out of the domain of the Father from the omnipotent***

*__Intellect__, she is always irradiated by Truth, and about her stays firm Understanding striding with irrefragable words. Now, call me with a __binding spell__. For thou leadest such a __mighty goddess as was able to ensoul the highest world of all.__"*

[Bold emphasis mine]

As much as your mind may rebel at such ideas, the documentary trail of evidence as well as humanity's perpetual fascination with mysticism, supernaturalism and the afterlife of their presumed 'soul' has left an indelible mark on the human psyche. As will be observed as this book unfolds, the reader is going to discover that there was nothing Divine about any of these teachings; that the hive collective was comprised of every type of human personality that ever lived, and that the collective was not above lying to push forth its agenda to control the human form and our entire species.

When you read the works of Madame Blavatsky and Alice Bailey and their collaborative corps of Ascended Masters and sundry controllers of their spiritual Seven Rays, you are taking the words of dead humans whose personalities survive in the hive cells who stole them. These two pinnacles of the Theosophical Society were necromancers, despite calling themselves mediums or channelers, and the hive collective has been leading the Theosophists and secret societies around by the nose for thousands of years masquerading as the occult and the divine, just as they did Zoroaster and every mystic throughout the ages. Our 'local' planetary overlord was the stolen personality of the

Anunnaki goddess Ninhursag in her tripartite manifestation as a god, goddess or androgyne. This is the basis for all the spiritual boojum about the male joining with the female, the mergence of the two into one, the modern revival of goddess cults, Feminism, the gay agenda and the transgender agenda. It has all been contrived and produced through the hive virus infection and the programming of the human psyche through the infectious agent of the hapiym hive cell that lived in every human until only about two years ago, when the virus was finally eradicated everywhere across the cosmos. Humanity is now left with the residual programming of our psyches that the virus left in its wake, and this includes the belief in every mystical tradition on the planet and every belief in the supernatural. Until we can rid our minds of all this virus programming as a species, we will never advance into an autonomous civilization, but will only live in the shadow of the hapiym mind virus, perpetuating its curse from generation to generation through repetitive psychological programming and the demand to embrace false supernatural beliefs.

# 9. The Greek Philosophers

Using the last chapter as the launching point for what shaped the thinking of the foremost Greek philosophers, we must turn to the word theurgy to understand their thinking and practices. Theurgy is defined as "the operation or effect of a supernatural or divine agency in human affairs"; alternatively, as "a system of white magic practiced by the early Neoplatonists." Given the nature of the hive virus infection, we must look at the times of those eras. The physical gods had all but disappeared from the radar of humanity's perceptions. The worship of the gods in statuary form had mostly become a state-controlled function and many had become disenchanted with the myths of the gods and the required sacrifices to those cults.

It doesn't take much imagination to see how people who were merely pawns of the gods and their perfidy throughout the ages would gravitate to a new idea where humans were not simple slaves to the whims of capricious gods and were faced with a new alternative where they could become 'Divine' themselves. The concept of Zoroaster's 'Divine Spark Within' would have been mighty seductive just as it holds the same seductive qualities in spiritual teachings today. Finally, humanity could aspire to be like the gods, or even become gods themselves if they could only ignite that divine spark within themselves and connect with the presumption of the cosmic Divinity!

In the Rigveda, it is the two-faced Anunnaki god Agni who represented the Eternal Flame with imported Hinduism brought in by the Aryans from the west (the Persian region of the Fertile Crescent). The name of the god Agni as the god of fire and sacrifice is where we get the Latin word for ignite, *ignire* or *ignis*. As noted in the passages offered in the last chapter, it is this concept of the Flame of the Eternal One that was symbolized by the sun as the physical representation to humanity of that Divine Fire. Scholarly assessment makes a big deal about solar cult worship where the sun was considered the 'life-giver' in ancient cultures. There is probably some validity to this idea, but since the advent of Zoroaster and Ninhursag's hive doctrines about the sun simply being a symbolic physical representation of the invisible Flame of the Divine, they overlook the true meaning of it. It did not amount to simply worshipping the sun as an object but revering the sun as the physical representation of the Divine Cosmic presence. In other words, the sun was a living idol signifying the immortality of spirit. The sun was *not* that spirit, it was only a symbolic physical representation of that spirit which served to remind its followers of the 'Light' that it was. This was the allegory of solar cultism within the mystical traditions. It was not so much the worship of the sun *as* the sun, but reverence for the sun as a *symbol* of the hive and the Eternal Flame representing the hive collective.

Once these ideas of the divine spark within started to spread, where any man or woman could allegedly attain communion with this godhead by getting in touch with their own internal divine spark, then the age of mysticism really started to grow and expand. In the past, these abilities were relegated to shamans, priests, priestesses and Divine Oracles such as Pythia, who was the High Priestess of the Temple of Apollo and also the chief Oracle for that sun god at Delphi. For greater understanding as this presentation proceeds, further information is required to pull all the seemingly disparate pieces together before completion. Wikipedia informs us in regard to Pythia:

> *"The name Pythia is derived from Pytho, which in myth was the original name of Delphi. In etymology, the Greeks derived this place name from the verb, πύθειν (púthein) "to rot", which refers to the sickly sweet smell of the decomposition of the body of the monstrous Python after she was slain by Apollo.* ***Pythia was the House of Snakes.***
>
> *The Pythia was established at the latest in the 8th century BC, and was widely credited for her prophecies inspired by being filled by the spirit of the god (or enthusiasmos), in this case Apollo. The Pythian priestess emerged pre-eminent by the end of 7th century BC and would continue to be consulted until the 4th century AD. During this period the Delphic Oracle was the most prestigious and authoritative oracle among the*

*Greeks, and she was without doubt the most powerful woman of the classical world. The oracle is one of the best-documented religious institutions of the classical Greeks. Authors who mention the oracle include Aeschylus, Aristotle, Clement of Alexandria, Diodorus, Diogenes, Euripides, Herodotus, Julian, Justin, Livy, Lucan, Nepos, Ovid, Pausanias, Pindar, Plato, Plutarch, Sophocles, Strabo, Thucydides and Xenophon."*

The Oracle at Delphi looks to have been established as early as 1400 BC and started by Cretan priests. It was on the island of Crete that the Minoan civilization was centered as early as 1700 BC or before, and the legend of the Minotaur, surviving pictures of 'bull-jumping' and some statues of a goddess holding two serpents survive in the archaeological record. As Wikipedia reports further under Pythia:

*"The earliest account of the origin of the Delphic oracle is provided in the Homeric Hymn to Delphic Apollo, which recent scholarship dates within a narrow range, c. 580–570 BC. It describes in detail how Apollo chose his first priests, whom he selected in their "swift ship"; they were "Cretans from Minos' city of Knossos" who were voyaging to sandy Pylos. But Apollo, who had Delphinios as one of his cult epithets, leapt into the ship in the form of a dolphin (delphys", gen.*

*"delphinos). Dolphin-Apollo revealed himself to the terrified Cretans, and bade them follow him up to the "place where you will have rich offerings". The Cretans "danced in time and followed, singing Iē Paiēon, like the paeans of the Cretans in whose breasts the divine Muse has placed "honey-voiced singing". "Paean" seems to have been the name by which Apollo was known in Mycenaean times."*

There are several important reasons I am focusing on the Oracle at Delphi. One of those reasons is the connection with the Minoan civilization probably being the originating the cult center, presumed to be 'the navel of the Earth' during its heyday. The association with serpents is going to have high relevance as this chapter proceeds as well, so take note of the snake factor in what has been presented in these passages. The other major factor is how the Oracles functioned and that, like virtually all cases with religions and mystics, there is always a monetary bottom line that figures into these cults. Continuing with part of what Wikipedia offers:

*"According to earlier myths, the office of the oracle was initially possessed by the goddesses Themis and Phoebe, and the site was initially sacred to Gaia. Subsequently, it was believed to be sacred to Poseidon, the "Earth-shaker" god of earthquakes. During the Greek Dark Age, from the 11th to the 9th century BC, a new god of prophecy,*

*Apollo, allegedly seized the temple and expelled the twin guardian serpents of Gaia,* ***whose bodies he wrapped around the caduceus****. Later myths stated that Phoebe or Themis had "given" the site to Apollo, rationalizing its seizure by priests of the new god, but presumably, having to retain the priestesses of the original oracle because of the long tradition."*

*"Diodorus also explained how, initially, the Pythia was an appropriately clad young virgin, for great emphasis was placed on the Oracle's chastity and purity to be reserved for union with the god Apollo. But he reports one story as follows:*

*Echecrates the Thessalian, having arrived at the shrine and beheld the virgin who uttered the oracle, became enamoured of her because of her beauty, carried her away and violated her; and that the Delphians because of this deplorable occurrence passed a law that in the future a virgin should no longer prophesy but that an elderly woman of fifty would declare the Oracles and that she would be dressed in the costume of a virgin, as a sort of reminder of the prophetess of olden times.*

*The scholar Martin Litchfield West writes that the Pythia shows many traits of shamanistic practices, likely inherited or influenced from Central Asian practices, although there is no evidence of any Central Asian association at this time. He cites the Pythia sitting in a cauldron on a tripod, while making her prophecies in an ecstatic trance state, like shamans, and her unintelligible utterings."*

In later 'incarnations', Ninhursag played the role of Hermes, or Mercury in Rome, who was symbolized by the caduceus, the symbol for modern medical practices. We must remember that Apollo is a sun god, or one who was symbolized by the sun, just as Horus was symbolized by the sun, as well as Ahura Mazda. As separate and confusing as tracking Ninhursag through her many roles may be, the symbols tell the story of what she did before she joined the hive. The fact that the Oracles were allegedly predictors of the future, (for a fee of course), is also indicative of trance channeling, which will become even more important as we proceed into the mystical workings of the Greek philosophers.

As for the Oracle priestess sitting in the cauldron with vapors around her, scientists have recently discovered that the oracular cave sits atop two fault lines, which are mostly inactive now, but when active in the past, did produce vapors. They have discovered a chemical called ethylene, which produces a sweet-smelling narcotic hallucinogenic gas, which would be perfectly suitable for putting the Oracle into a cognitively compromised state of awareness that would allow the inner hapiym virus cell to connect with other aspects of the hive collective and receive 'channeled' messages by those who purported to be gods. These hallucinogenic properties would produce the same state of mind as psilocybin mushrooms or other similar substances used by other mystical cults to reach a state of 'visionary' enlightenment and access the collective of the hive.

As a correlative side note, I want to bring up an ancient Anunnaki 'god' called Ningishzida. The curious thing about Ningishzida is that in Sumerian hierarchal traditions, the male gods were represented with the designator of En, meaning 'lord', such as En-ki or En-lil. The goddesses' names were preceded by the designator 'Nin', meaning 'lady'. The curious factor about Ningishzida is that he was considered a god, not a goddess, yet his determinate, 'Nin', in all other cases represented female goddesses or 'ladies'. Ningishzida is pictorially represented with two serpents wrapped around him that cross at the mid-section of the god's body. In later representations, the caduceus also represents Ningishzida, which presents a correlative tie-in with the later Greek Apollo and Hermes. When we understand the hermaphroditic nature of Ninhursag, then the 'Nin' determinate in Ningishzida's name is no longer a mystery.

In Babylonian traditions, according to the research of A.L Frothingham in his 1916 paper, *Babylonian Origin of Hermes the Snake God, and of the Caduceus,* Frothingham reports:

> *"I expect to show that the prototype of Hermes was an Oriental deity of Babylonian extraction; whose character was that of a god of*

*spring; whose function it was to preside over fertilization; whose position was not that of a primal deity, but that of* ***agent and messenger of the Great Mother****, in whose domain he brought life to light in the springtime of each year, and so became also associated with* ***the spring sun.***

*This proto-Hermes was always a snake-god, and before the era of complete anthropomorphism he was thought of in snake form. But it is an essential element of his function* ***that he was not a single snake - for the great single Earth Snake was the Mother Goddess-but the double snake, male and female,*** *the most prolific form of copulation in the animal kingdom.*

*For this reason the emblem of the god was the Kerykeion or caduceus, a pair of snakes wound around a wand or sceptre. But before it became the god's emblem, the caduceus had been, in the pre-anthropomorphic era,* ***the god himself****; and continued to be so regarded long after the prevalence of anthropomorphism.*

*The Caduceus-god was, therefore, the predecessor of the Priapic herm-god. The* ***two-sex snakes*** *conveyed the same idea as the phallus."*

[Bold emphasis mine]

With the highlighted sections above, we find that the double-serpent of the caduceus represents the male and female intertwined together, and also that the snake represented the Mother Goddess, no different than Python in the Delphic mythology above. This double-serpent symbolism wholly typifies the hermaphroditic traits of Ninhursag as I have stated, as well as considering the unspoken third aspect of this hermaphroditism where the male and female combine to form the androgyne. In another passage from the same article, Frothingham reports:

> *"The only Babylonian ruler who mentions Ningishzida is the above-mentioned Gudea; and he, while naming this god as his patron, enumerates him at the end of his list of eighteen gods adored at Lagash (Shirpurla). Gudea has a dream which he asks the goddess NinA to interpret. She tells him that he has seen the supreme god, of colossal size, Ningirsu, crowned and with the sacred eagle, Im-gig, in his hand, the storm-wind at his feet and a lion crouching on either side: also a woman with a tablet and a man marking the plan of a temple on another tablet, showing that he should build a temple to Ningirsu. Then came a figure* ***representing the rising sun, which the goddess identifies****--after naming the others--****as Ningishzida****, saying:* ***"The Sun which lifted itself up from the earth before thee, is thy god Ningishzida. Like the Sun he goes forth from the earth."*** *In another passage Ningishzida is described as leading Gudea forth to battle and as*

*his king. A separate temple was dedicated to his worship by Gudea."*

[Bold emphasis mine]

Gudea was the king (*ensi*) of the state of Lagash in southern Mesopotamia ca. 2144–2124 BC. This dating shows that the traditions of Ninhursag/Hermes in one of her earliest guises predates all Hellenic occupation with the later traditions of Hermes. The entwined double-serpent of the caduceus associated with Ningishzida with its bisexual role is also associated, as noted above, with the sun god. Here again, following Ninhursag's symbols tells the tale of her reputation-building for over 4,000 years. There is more going on here than just cultural appropriation, despite what many scholars errantly presume.

Coupled with this serpent/solar association with Ningishzida, we find a direct correlation with the ancient Egyptian winged disc which has twin serpents (*uraeus*) draping down on either side of the solar disc appearing roughly in the 26$^{th}$ century BC, where as I reported earlier, it was associated with the sun god Horus, or Re. We have now firmly established a trail of evidence linking the sun god Horus to the Babylonian sun god Ningishzida, into the Persian Ahura Mazda and the triple goddess Hecate and the Greek god Hermes. For further elucidation on the male-female aspects of Ningishzida, Frothingham reveals:

*"In some magical texts where Ningishzida is among the minor* ***solar deities*** *invoked, it is not as a male* ***but as a female deity and as the wife or***

***consort of the sun-gods** Nusku or Ninib or even of Gibil the primitive **Fire-god**.*

*In Jastrow's opinion Ningishzida was one of the insignificant secondary deities that tended to disappear and to be absorbed in the more powerful deities. In this case the absorber would be Ninib. This was natural because Ninib is called "the first-born of Ea" and also as the rising sun or the spring sun, the offspring of the Earth (or "E Kur"), because he ascended from below the earth surface. The association with Nusku, on the other hand, is due to Nusku's character as a messenger of Anu, the supreme god of heaven, and of all the gods. In this sense, perhaps, Ningishzida is called in one of Gudea's texts the "Son" of Anu (Cyl. B 23, 5) and bracketed with **Bau**, the daughter of Anu (Cyl. E 8, 12-13), who is the consort of Ningirsu, the supreme god of Lagash**, and is the Mother Goddess who gives birth to mankind**."*

[Bold emphasis mine]

This passage reveals a number of things to the observant reader who is familiar with the facts surrounding the competitive warfare between Enki and Ninhursag. Enki's name in Sumeria and Babylon was Ea. The fact that Ningishzida is usurped by an alleged 'first born son of Ea' is indicative of this conflict between Enki and Ninhursag and how Ninhursag's role as Ningishzida was eventually usurped and overthrown by Enki in just another one of their battles for power on this planet. Seeing as how the Anunnaki, like Earth humans, were created by the Orioner gods, over whom Anu was the primary leader, the claim to be a 'Son of Anu' also falls in line with my contentions in this book. Again, the mysteries start to unravel when we are in possession of the facts and not the mythical propaganda.

Ningishzida's association with the ancient Fire God should also come as no surprise given the evidence I have presented in regard to the Eternal Flame of Zoroastrianism and its correlation to the center of the hive collective, 'the Light'. All the elements of these myths and legends now start to dovetail into a cohesive picture that the propagandized mystical stories of the ancient past have conspired to remove from our eyes as our ancient history.

Before moving on to the ideologies of the Greek philosophers I want to offer one more lengthy passage from Frothingham's paper:

> *"The most important proof of caduceus-cult among the Hittites: the group of three gods worshipped at Hierapolis in North Syria. This was one of the most sacred centres in Western Asia down to a late Roman period and was extraordinarily conservative in its cult and liturgy. It has had the advantage of a fuller exposition by an ancient author than was given of any other sacred fane. It is in the treatise De Dea Syria by Lucian, which can be supplemented by the*

*Saturnalia of Macrobius.' The Hierapolis triad consisted of the Mother Goddess, who was supreme, of a coordinate yet subordinate male deity, the son-husband, and of a mysterious youth or nondescript emblem. The goddess was Atargatis and she was attended by lions: the god was Hadad and his attendants were two bulls. Lucian calls them Zeus and Hera simply to make them conform as far as possible to Hellenic ideas, but he admits that the Goddess has attributes of several other goddesses. I quote the most pregnant passages of Lucian from the translation given in Strong and Garstang, The Syrian Goddess (London, 1913). "There is in Syria a city not far from the river Euphrates: it is called 'The Sacred City' and is sacred to the Assyrian Hera [i.e. Atargatis], (p. 41). The great temple is open to all; the sacred shrine to the priests alone and not to all even of these, but only to those who are deemed nearest to the gods and who have the charge of the entire administration of the sacred rites. In this shrine are placed the statues, one of which is Hera, the other Zeus, though they call him by another name. Both of these are golden, both are sitting; Hera is supported by lions, Zeus is sitting on bulls. The effigy of Zeus recalls Zeus in all its details-his head, his robes, his throne; nor even if you wished it could you take him for another deity. Hera, however, as you look at her will recall to you a variety of forms. Speaking generally she is undoubtedly Hera, but she has something of the attributes of Athene, and of Aphrodite, and of Selene, and of Rhea, and of Artemis, and of Nemesis, and of the Fates. In one of her hands she holds a sceptre, in the other a distaff; on her head she bears rays and a tower and she has a girdle wherewith they adorn none but Aphrodite of the Sky. And without she is gilt with gold, and gems of great price adorn her, some white, some sea-green, others wine-dark, others flashing like fire. Besides these there are many onyxes from Sardinia and the jacinth and emeralds, the offerings of the Egyptians and of the Indians, Ethiopians, Medes, Armenians, and Babylonians. But the greatest wonder . . . she bears a gem on her head called a Lychnis . . . From this stone flashes a great light in the night-time, so that the whole temple gleams brightly as by the light of myriads of candles. . . .*

*"Between the two [gods] there stands another image of gold, no part of it resembling the others. This possesses no special form of its own, but recalls the characteristics of the other gods. The Assyrians themselves speak of it as a symbol [o~7u'ov, "semeion"], but they have assigned to it no definite name. They have nothing to tell us*

*about its origin, nor its form: some refer it to Dionysus; others to Deucalion; others to Semiramis; for its summit is crowned by a golden pigeon, and is why they allege that it is the effigy of Semiramis. It is taken down to the sea twice in every year to bring up the water of which I have spoken." This attempted description by Lucian of the third image of the group of cult statues in the temple is a descriptive failure, so that the form of it has remained a mystery, for what he says is merely negative. It occupied a central position between the enthroned pair, but it was not a human figure. It was called by the Syrians "Semeion"; had no resemblance to either of the other figures but represented some of their characteristics. His last sentence is interesting as it shows that the image could hold water and was the means of reconsecration of the temple.*

*Six quotes the Syrian writer Melito as making Simo the daughter of Hadad, who draws water in the sea [i.e. Euphrates] and throws it into the sacred temple chasm. Another legend makes the daughter of Atargatis and Hadad to be Semiramis. On the other hand Diodorus (II, 4) turns "Semeion" into "Simios," a youth who was the lover of Atargatis. Dussaud has proposed to see in Simios* ***the Son-lover of the goddess*** *and compares the Hierapolitan triad Hadad-Atargatis-*

*Simios with the Heliopolitan triad, Jupiter-Venus-Mercury.*

*The passage of Macrobius is more specific, both as to the original names of the two gods and as to* ***their solar characteristics*** *(Sat. ch. 23): "The Syrians give the name Adad to the god, which they revere as first and greatest of all; his name signifies* ***"The One."*** *They honour this god as all powerful, but they associate with him the goddess named Adargatis, and* ***assign to these two divinities supreme power over everything****, recognizing in them the Sun and the Earth. Without expressing by numerous names the different aspects of their power, their predominance is implied by the different attributes assigned to the two divinities. For* ***the statue of Adad is encircled by descending rays, which indicate that the force of heaven resides in the rays which the sun sends down to earth: the rays of the statue of Adargatis rise upward, a sign that the power of the ascending rays brings to life everything that the earth produces****. Below this statue are the figures of lions, emblematic of the earth; for the same reason that the Phrygians so represent the Mother of the Gods, that is to say, the earth, borne by lions."*

*Cumont, in discussing the formation of triads in the evolution of oriental local cults, especially in Syria, says: "To the primitive couple of the Baal and the Baalat a third member was added in order to form one of those triads dear to Chaldean theology. This took place at Hierapolis as well as at Heliopolis, and the three gods of the latter city, Hadad, Atargatis and Simios, became Jupiter, Venus and Mercury in Latin inscriptions."*

*We have, then* ***as the third figure of the Hierapolitan triad, a youthful person, sometimes thought of as male, sometimes as female, offspring and lover of one or both of the principal deities****."*

[Bold emphasis mine]

Within these passages we find all the elements of Ninhursag, the divine hermaphrodite goddess; the elements of the overarching 'One' of the hive illustrated in the god Hadad (or Ahura Mazda) and the solar rays bestowing their 'power' onto humanity, these same rays reflected back by the goddess signifying the intercessor to the hive One god over Earth, and the androgyne unidentifiable figure between them that is neither male nor female but offers attributes of both. Once more we find the alleged divine trinity symbolized as three characters representing Ninhursag the hermaphrodite as the holy trinity. Without understanding Ninhursag's hermaphrodite characteristics, scholars have been unable to figure out the true meaning of this symbology.

It matters not that Ninhursag presented herself as the three-faced Hecate, the Thrice Great Hermes, the holy triad of Osiris, Isis and Horus; the Heliopolitan Zeus, Aphrodite, and Hermes; or the Christian trinity of Father, Son and Holy Spirit (female), the indelible stamp of Ninhursag's distinctive fingerprint resides in all these concepts. Regardless of the contention that may arise from this with religionists and their beliefs in their faiths, the evidence all points this direction to the unbiased and objective observer of the evidence. Without this key element of understanding, then the continual trinities that appear in religions around the world have no foundation through which the truth can be gleaned.

With the foregoing information now in hand, we can start to disassemble the 'mysteries' of the Greek philosophers and their concepts of Monotheism, their Divine Monad. I established in the last chapter that the Monad or One True God concept that permeates so many religions, is in fact a truthful representation of the singular intelligence that oversaw the hapiym hive hierarchy. I have provided more than enough information in this volume, and in a number of my other works (the *WANA* trilogy and *The Energetic War Against Humanity*), about the existence of the hapiym hive virus as an invasive mind virus that serves as a 'secondary' consciousness to our normal waking state of awareness. I feel I have provided enough preliminary evidence in this volume for the reader to understand the nature and circumstances of the ancient Anunnaki hermaphrodite 'goddess' Ninhursag and how she was either killed or allowed herself to die so her residual hapiym hive mimic personality could join the cosmic hive, and who served as the intercessor between human hive consciousness and the immortal 'One' of the cosmic hive. With all these facts in mind, then it is time to look at the ideologies of Pythagoras, Socrates, Plato and the later Neoplatonists and their hidden mystical doctrines. I will leave it up to the scholars to agonize over every last detail of their mystical ideologies as they have for centuries, but for the purpose of this volume, the primary keys to unraveling the mysteries are all I am concerned with.

Using the basis of communication established through the trance state illustrated with Zoroaster and the Oracles of old, the existence of hive communication is ancient indeed, and as stated earlier, goes far back into human antiquity and tribal shamanic practices, which will be covered in a later chapter. What the Pythagoreans and other Monotheists were seeking to achieve was that alleged direct communion with the Divine, which was nothing more than the hive cell within themselves being able to overcome their waking consciousness through varied disciplines, so the inner hive cell could talk to the cosmic hive, whether that was communication with the presumed spirits of the dead, or to other presumed 'Masters' of the hive hierarchy who often masqueraded as gods or angels. In our modern era, this type of hive chicanery had morphed into the hive masquerading as offworld aliens delivering these channeled messages in the New Age bailiwick.

These otherworldly consciousnesses were classified by the Greek philosophers either as gods or goddesses, daemons, geniuses or spirits of the dead. Their objectives in these communications were many and varied. Many wanted to inquire into what life was like in the presumed afterlife, the Elysian Fields; to contact the spirits of dead teachers and/or relatives; or to make contact with this discarnate hive entities who they felt could educated them in alleged wisdom of the universe or prophesy the future.

Many of the early philosophers created their own mystery schools through which they managed their initiation rites to guide others into this alleged communion with the Divine. As noted previously in the Zoroastrian Oracles, when we remove the blinders of the mystical from this equation, then we discover that any initiations into these mystery schools were designed to lead the acolyte to discover the hive cell within themselves, what they mistakenly thought was the soul, and form an alliance with what they also mistakenly presumed to be the Divine. This was all a game of cognitive deception predicated on preconceived notions about gods and divinity. With such beliefs already in place in the consciousness of the human hosts, and the incessant drive by the hapiym virus to herd with others of its kind, the inner desire for this communion with the Divine became the driving force of power hungry egos worldwide seeking presumed spiritual enlightenment.

This human desire, based primarily on the desires of the hapiym virus itself, to be more than what one is, to gain and possess great supernatural power, is what has driven mystical and occult traditions throughout human history. If you look at all these alleged spiritual pursuits, they are only a quest for power, for the human to gain abilities that are more than human, to access the supernatural. It doesn't matter if this quest for power is found through philosophical or religious beliefs and ideologies, or whether it is the pursuit of mystical occult powers through magical practices, it has all been the quest of the hive-infected human ego to be more than what it is. The interactions with the hapiym hive cosmic collective has fed these notions of the supernatural from the start, and in the end, there has never been any genuine payoff for human cognitive advancement. Through these misplaced desires, human consciousness has been held in a mystical trap, with the lure of supernatural or mystical powers ever being the basis of this selfish quest to be more than human. This is also what is behind Joseph Campbell's 'Hero's Quest' ideology.

Through Zoroastrian teachings, and the known use of psychedelic substances to allegedly reach that state of 'divine awareness', the search for supernatural powers took root in humanity's psyche, and to this day, our species refuses to let go of these illusions fostered by the hapiym hive collective consciousness. Where all of humanity's spiritual and philosophical predecessors have failed is in their desire for supernatural powers and their utter lack of discernment to see through the illusions formulated by the hive collective. Their own personal quests for supernatural abilities, driven by the virus infection itself, blinded them all from seeing through the charade and every one of them fell for the lie, even those who worked in active collusion with the hive over the centuries.

The intellectual classes have been the primary focus of the hive over the ages for it could only make the hive collective 'smarter' through the harvested consciousnesses of its human hosts. The hapiym virus was a data miner, and all the knowledge it professed to possess was knowledge stolen from its human hosts. As such, the hive collective had always leaned toward focusing on and currying the intellectual elite, which it worked in collusion with to establish its own kingdom on this planet, ultimately seeking to bring 'Heaven on Earth', meaning turning all of humanity into nothing more than repositories for hive consciousness. Had this occurred, humanity as a species would have only been empty vessels filled with hapiym hive cells, replicating the cosmic hive on the material plane of existence. As far-fetched as this may sound, evidence will be presented further along in this book that will remove any doubt about this assertion.

At this juncture, I personally wonder how much of what has been handed down to this species in our modern age actually originated with human genius, and how much may have originated with recycled hive personalities invading human forms. For generations the standard of education was the teaching of the classics, the seven principles embodied in Greek philosophy. We have to wonder how many of these seven aspects of classical education may be influenced by the seven rays found within the mystical teachings of Zoroaster and these early philosophers. In our sanitized and sterile academic world of today, all the mystical elements of the origin of these sciences has been removed from curriculum that is primarily based in materialist thinking. As a preliminary look into Pythagoras, I will rely on some of Wikipedia's information about him:

> *"The teaching most securely identified with Pythagoras is* ***metempsychosis, or the "transmigration of souls", which holds that every soul is immortal and, upon death, enters into a***

***new body***. *He may have also devised the doctrine of musica universalis, which holds that the planets move according to mathematical equations and thus resonate to produce an inaudible symphony of music. Scholars debate whether Pythagoras himself developed the numerological and musical teachings attributed to him, or if those teachings were developed by his later followers, particularly Philolaus of Croton. He probably prohibited his followers from eating beans, but he may or may not have advocated a strictly vegetarian diet."*

*"...the Egyptians are said to have taught him geometry, the Phoenicians arithmetic, the Chaldeans astronomy, and the Magi the principles of religion and practical maxims for the conduct of life. According to Diogenes Laërtius, Pythagoras not only visited Egypt and learnt the Egyptian language (as reported by Antiphon in his On Men of Outstanding Merit), but* ***also "journeyed among the Chaldaeans and Magi."***

*"Although the exact details of Pythagoras's teachings are uncertain, it is possible to reconstruct a general outline of his main ideas. Aristotle writes at length about the teachings of the Pythagoreans, but without mentioning Pythagoras directly. One of Pythagoras's main doctrines*

*appears to have been* ***metempsychosis, the belief that all souls are immortal and that, after death, a soul is transferred into a new body****. This teaching is referenced by Xenophanes, Ion of Chios, and Herodotus.*

*Empedocles alludes in one of his poems that Pythagoras may have claimed to possess the ability* ***to recall his former incarnations****. Diogenes Laërtius reports an account from Heraclides Ponticus that Pythagoras told people that* ***he had lived four previous lives that he could remember in detail.*** *The first of these lives was as Aethalides the son of Hermes, who granted him the ability to remember all his past incarnations. Next, he was incarnated as Euphorbus, a minor hero from the Trojan War briefly mentioned in the Iliad. He then became the philosopher Hermotimus, who recognized the shield of Euphorbus in the temple of Apollo. His final incarnation was as Pyrrhus, a fisherman from Delos. One of his past lives, as reported by Dicaearchus, was as a beautiful courtesan"*

[Bold emphasis mine]

With these revelatory passages, if they are in fact true, then it becomes obvious that Pythagoras was influenced by all of the elements presented thus far in this book. If he did in fact study in these schools of thought, then it is little wonder that his philosophies were bent toward the mystical. If he did have specific recall of previous lives, then that is another aspect of the hive infection that will be addressed as well with his doctrine of *metempsychosis*.

In later eras, others of his followers have been designated as Neopythagoreans, and of them Wikipedia reports this:

> *"Central to Neopythagorean thought was the concept* ***of a soul and its <u>inherent desire</u> for a unio mystica with the divine****."*

> *"Neopythagoreanism was an attempt* ***to re-introduce a mystical religious element into Hellenistic philosophy*** *(dominated by the Stoics) in place of what had come to be regarded as an arid formalism. The founders of the school sought to invest their doctrines with the halo of tradition by ascribing them to Pythagoras and Plato. They went back to the later period of Plato's thought, the period when Plato endeavoured to combine his doctrine of Ideas with Pythagorean number theory,* ***and identified the Good with the Monad (which would give rise to the Neoplatonic concept of the One), the source of the duality of the Infinite and the Measured with the resultant scale of realities from the One down to the objects of the material world.***

***They emphasized the fundamental distinction between the soul and the body. God must be worshipped spiritually by prayer and the will to be good, not in outward action. The soul must be freed from its material surrounding, the "muddy vesture of decay," by an ascetic habit of life. Bodily pleasures and all sensuous impulses must be abandoned as detrimental to the spiritual purity of the soul. God is the principle of good, Matter the groundwork of Evil.*** *In this system can be distinguished not only the asceticism of Pythagoras* ***and the later mysticism of Plato****, but also the influence of the Orphic mysteries and of Oriental philosophy. The Ideas of Plato are no longer self-subsistent entities but are the elements which constitute the content of spiritual activity.* ***The non-material universe is regarded as the sphere of mind or spirit****."*

[Bold emphasis mine]

The highlighted portions present the hive doctrines in all its splendent glory, the primary thread being to detest your humanity and only embrace the hive virus cell within you. The Pythagorean philosophy contains all the elements of the hive structure, the individual hive cell's desire to be in union with its cosmic hive brotherhood in the immaterial realms of mind (intellect) and promoting the hive false spirit, or soul. One's humanness is to be forsaken in favor of this mystical lie and everything that makes us human should be spurned as filth and rubbish. This is the hatefulness of these Divine ideologies, the hidden tyranny throughout the ages that has deceived humanity with doctrines of Goodness, Love and Light which, when viewed through the lens of perception offered in this book, shows itself to be a mere replica of a human being.

Just as the mystical elements for the foundation of modern science pushed forth through the Renaissance and Hermeticism have been conveniently glossed over and swept under the rug, the mystical aspect and potential influence of the hive doctrines have also been whitewashed in favor of presenting these Greek philosophers as materialist scientists and mathematicians. The mystical elements are looked at as more an aberration in modern academia rather than the driving force behind their intellectual contributions to the world. Their studies into music and numbers were launched from the platform of seeking to explain the Divine through these avenues of discovery, not as the sterile materialistic scientific practices as they have been turned into. With materialist scientism only focusing on the mundane 3D human material aspects of these innovations and trashing the mystical elements, they do not understand what the motivational force was that drove these philosophers into their theories in geometry, astronomy, mathematics, music, rhetoric, grammar or anything else they produced. Academics also blithely accept that these earlier philosophers were just human geniuses, but we must wonder just how much of their genius was solely theirs and how much may have come about through hive interference and influence.

As for Plato, he was the first professed 'Statist' as exhibited in his writing *The Republic*, yet even his ideologies on Statism are only a reflection of the hive collective whereby he professed that the State should be managed by philosopher-rulers "who are capable of apprehending what is eternal and unchanging". People who do not apprehend the "Divine", Plato says, are "those who are incapable of this [and] lose themselves and wander amid the multiplicities of multifarious things." The Platonic concept of hive Statism, ruled by a philosophical elite is present in our modern world through Marxist ideologies being pushed forward by the Fabian Society, which is an incestuous cousin to the Theosophical Society as I have reported in my earlier works. With this comprehensive understanding of the hive now in hand, and Plato's mystical association with the hive collective, then his Statist ideology takes on a more sinister meaning in our present world, with hive mysticism at its root. This thread of hive interference winds its way down the path of all human history via prophets, visionaries, revolutionaries and religion-makers throughout the ages. Through the annals of time it has been *their* names in whose shadows of intellect we should stand, *their* operatives pushing the hive's tyrannical collectivist agenda inexorably forward, and humanity as a whole has only been unwitting slaves, mere footnotes to the history of the elite and their devices.

Within the Chaldean Oracles we find the scorn for "herd-animals" and the "conceit of puny humans". This is not only the mindset of these glorified philosophers and self-appointed elite, but is also a clear reflection of the hive mentality itself and how it viewed humanity. The teachings of these earliest philosophers drip with the venom and hatred the hive virus felt for humanity as a whole, all the while peddling false doctrines of Love, Light and Harmony through its lying doctrines from which it only sought acolytes who were willing to give up their humanity and trade it for the false 'heavenly' promises of this hive virus illusion. Supernaturalism and mysticism was the lure, and sadly, most of humanity bought the lie hook, line and sinker. These early hive doctrines are filled with what some mistakenly call magic in their ignorance, and the philosophies are rife with spells to invoke and bind hive cells from the cosmic collective, such spells which were naturally provided by the hive itself to woo humans into thinking they had supernatural abilities.

In time, the Greek *daemons* and *geniuses*, all of which were hive cell replicas of humans (or gods) that once lived, were turned into the modern-day concept of demons. Through these invocations and binding spells from the philosophers and mystics of old, the concept of demon possession took hold and the business of exorcism burgeoned. These philosophers, the Greeks in particular, wrote their spells in hexameter poems, which I will suggest is the origination point for the concept of magical hexes. Recent discoveries of 44 magical spells from the 5th century BC, written on lead tablets in Greek hexametric form are presented in *The Getty Hexameters: Poetry, Magic, and Mystery in Ancient Selinous* by Christopher A. Faraone, Dirk Obbink. These early Greek philosophers were well-steeped in what in modern times would be called witchcraft with their magical invocations and binding spells. This is one reason that the hive magical traditions throughout time have been called heresy and witchcraft by the more mundane mainstream perceptions of religion.

This summary is by no means inclusive of every Greek philosopher of old, but the ones held up for the most respect and highest esteem, such as Plato, Aristotle, Pythagoras and later philosophers like Iamblichus, Porphyry, Plotinus and others, were all eyeball deep in these hive mystical traditions. These same traditions threaded their way into Gnosticism, which itself was not a homogenized set of beliefs but which contained many varied offshoots of these philosophies as well, which happened to focus substantially on the personage of Jesus. I will provide an overview of the Gnostics in a later chapter.

Amidst all these doctrines we are going to find Ninhursag in one role or another, holding a hidden supremacy of respect and adoration in all these mystical traditions. Her professing to be the Goddess of Wisdom traces through all these traditions and her fingerprints are everywhere as a prime mover for the hive agenda. Before moving this hive agenda forward in time, we will regress further back in history to ancient shamanic traditions and show the hive influences far into our prehistoric past.

# 10. Shamanism

We are now going to embark on a journey into the dark recesses of humanity's unknown history. Even though many of these practices had prehistoric origins, the rigid adherence to traditionalism has served in many cases to preserve glimmerings of ancient shamanic practices. Naturally, much of this is based on a type of speculative reverse-engineering in regard to determining when and where it all started, but that is basically what all history is at best, especially given the fact of how much of human history has been intentionally sanitized and expunged at the hands of the Aryan elite controllers.

In researching into these mystical traditions, we must often rely on those who have studied them and who, in many cases, have been involved in pushing the mystical hive agenda forward through their writings, for they have been the ones 'in the know' on these matters. This chapter will rely somewhat on Mircea Eliade and his book, *Shamanism: Archaic Techniques in Ecstasy*, originally published in French in 1946. As Eliade observes in the Foreword of the book, the shamanic state, to a modern psychologist, will appear as a form of madness. This is not an unfair observation on at least two counts, the first being that of the ecstatic state usually brought about through the use of hallucinogenic substances or other practices to assist one in detaching their consciousness from their waking state and connecting with the hive collective intelligence, and the fact that one who can or has achieved this 'ecstatic' state can progress into a state referred to as 'divine madness', which Wikipedia explains as:

> *"Divine madness, also known as theia mania and crazy wisdom, refers to unconventional, outrageous, unexpected, or unpredictable antinomian behavior linked to religious or spiritual pursuits. Examples of divine madness can be found in Christianity, Hinduism, Buddhism, Sufism, and Shamanism.*
>
> *It is usually explained as* ***a manifestation of enlightened behavior*** *by persons who have transcended societal norms, or as a means of spiritual practice or teaching among mendicants and teachers. These behaviors may seem to be symptoms of mental illness to mainstream society, but* ***are a form of religious ecstasy****, or deliberate "strategic, purposeful activity," "by highly self-aware individuals making strategic use of the theme of madness in the construction of their public personas."*
>
> *"According to June McDaniel and other scholars, divine madness is found in the history*

*and practices of many cultures and may reflect religious ecstasy or expression of* ***divine love****. Plato in his Phaedrus and his ideas on theia mania, the Hasidic Jews, Eastern Orthodoxy, Western Christianity, Sufism along with Indian religions all bear witness to the phenomenon of divine madness. It is not the ordinary form of madness, but a behavior that is consistent with the premises of a spiritual path or a form of complete absorption in God."*

*"Theia mania (Ancient Greek: θεία μανία) is a term used by Plato and his protagonist Socrates to describe a condition of "divine madness" (unusual behavior attributed to the intervention of a god) in the Platonic dialogue Phaedrus. In this work, dating from around 370 BC, Socrates' character describes this state of divine inspiration as follows:*

*"In such families that accumulated vast wealth were found dire plagues and afflictions of the soul, for which mania devised a remedy, inasmuch as the same was a gift from God, if only to be rightly frenzied and possessed, using proper atonement rituals."*

*Plato further described Divine Madness as a gift of god, with Socrates stating in Phaedrus, "in fact the best things we have comes from madness", and expounds upon the concept in Plato's Ion. In eastern cultures, it has been deployed as a catalyst and means for the deeper understanding of spiritual concepts.*

*The poet Virgil, in his Aeneid, describes the Delphian priestess (Pythia) as prophesying in a frenzied state:*

*"...neither her face nor hue went untransformed; Her breast heaved; her wild heart grew large with passion. Taller to their eyes, sounding no longer mortal, she prophesied what was inspired from The God breathing near, uttering words not to be ignored. [citation needed]"*

*In the classical world, the phenomenon of "love at first sight" was understood within the context of a more general conception of passionate love, a kind of madness or, as the Greeks put it, theia mania ("madness from the gods")."*

In light of the information shared in the last chapter about the hive and its manipulation of human consciousness, then it takes no imagination whatsoever to understand what the alleged 'ecstatic state' of divine madness represents. This ecstatic state, or 'peak experience' as it is referred to in Transpersonal Psychology, is the sought-after state of awareness when one allegedly connects with the divine through whatever means one can use to achieve this altered stated of awareness. The use of hallucinogenic substances weakens the cognitive threshold between our normal waking state and opens the door to the virus-controlled subconscious mind. Eliade's preliminary assessment is that "shamanism = technique of ecstasy" which, given the foundational framework already laid, puts shamanism in bed with the later traditions of seeking altered states of ecstatic experiences such as those enumerated and practiced in the mysteries by the Greek philosophers and other mystics of their ilk throughout the ages.

Eliade also notes that the shaman should be viewed as a psychopomp, which is defined as "a guide of souls to the place of the dead", or "the spiritual guide of a living person's soul". The Catholic Church's practice of giving Last Rites would make every priest a psychopomp in a similar manner, just as every guru, preacher, shaman and priest has been serving in the role of psychopomp 'spiritual consultants' to their acolytes, students and congregations. With the late advancements in developing Spiritual Psychology as a legitimate field of study and practice, the intent is to move this type of mystical psychopompery onto the therapist's couch.

Along with what the mystical Greek philosophers taught in their mystery schools about helpful daemons and geniuses, a shaman's stock in trade is also reliant on his helper spirits who, it is assumed, knows how to control them, versus an unskilled magical practitioner who doesn't. Too many people figure that shamans are all medicine men or women and can provide cures for what ails you, and there are shamans that are multi-talented in these areas of bone-setting and herbal cures, but the shaman is primarily a 'soul healer' by nature, despite any other medical specialties they may possess. All medicine people are not automatically shamans based on this evaluation, and all shamans are not necessarily inclined to be considered a medicine man or woman of the herbalist variety. The shaman's specialty is reaching into the spiritual realm, whether that is heaven or hell, to perform their work while in these ecstatic states. This places the shaman's practice of caring for 'souls' at hive central, particularly given the misperception that the hapiym virus cell represented the soul. The modern practice of Psychology is a form of mainstream shamanism where the therapist fills the role of healing the hive-infected egos of their clients, working to help them fit back into their cultural environments. With the expansion of Psychology now turning to Transpersonal Psychology and Spiritual Psychology, each practitioner of these schools of thought will be bringing ancient shamanism onto the therapist's couch, where the psychologist takes on the role of guru or spiritual advisor, thereby perpetuating the same hive mystical doctrines in a professional setting. For those who may want to contradict this idea, I refer you to the book by two Jungian psychologists, Marion Woodman and Elinor Dickson, entitled *Dancing in the Flames: The Dark Goddess in the Transformation of Consciousness.* These two women are merely professional doctrinaires using Jungian psychology as the platform to peddle the goddess doctrine in their practices. They are not unique in the field and mysticism in the field of Psychology is only seeking to expand itself.

Although the word shaman itself is of Central Russian or Siberian origin, the concept has been spread worldwide with the study of anthropologists who have categorized these varied functions under one overarching umbrella definition. Unfortunately, this has created a milieu for almost anyone who has done ayahuasca, magic mushrooms, DMT, LSD or other psychedelic substances to claim to be a shaman, particularly in the Theosophy-spawned Western New Age arena. As with the Greek philosophers, one only has to learn the mystical 'script' well enough to impress the gullible, uninformed, spiritually-hungry rubes and convince them that doing drugs or performing in sweat lodge ceremonies, for instance, will lead them to enlightenment. As with all things magical, there are always opportunists willing to cash in with mystical chicanery. But then, given the deceptive nature of the hive virus, it has all been self-serving chicanery from the start where the hive agenda is concerned, and collecting high fees from initiates has been practiced for thousands of years.

As with the mystagogues of the past and present, shamans are the 'elect' according to Eliade, and with this assessment, I have to totally agree, for the same reasons already elucidated in this book. The shamans are those seemingly 'chosen' amongst us who have access to the divine and whom humanity has foolishly relied upon throughout the ages to guide us in matters spiritual. Every religion around the planet possesses certain elements of this mystique in their priestly hierarchy and their rituals without exception. With the reliance and utter dependency on the divine in our perception that we are 'lesser beings', primarily out of fear of going to Hell or not cutting it in the eyes of our perceptions of God, humanity has fallen prey to these divine intercessors worldwide throughout time. Fear and lack of understanding the true nature of things is what places these mystical adepts on their pedestals of power, bringing both respect and fear due to their mysterious talents.

As with later mystical and religious traditions, many of these ancient peoples believed in an overarching celestial god, often portrayed as 'high, lofty and luminous' coupled with attendant ideas about the Great God having spiritual 'sons' and 'daughters' at varying levels of a celestial hierarchy through whom the shaman maintains his or her connection with the Divine Realm. Are we starting to see a repeating pattern in all this?

Eliade also makes note of the fact that there are stark similarities in the proto-Indo-Europeans and their concept of the sky god, who was patriarchal, in many of these ancient shamanic traditions. Read Indo-Europeans to mean Aryans, as they were called before political correctness altered the use of the word after Hitler tarnished the word Aryan with his political ideologies. The root word for divine comes from the Aryan *dyeu*, meaning 'to shine', also in relation to 'heaven, sky and god'. More accurately 'sky father'. From this root comes the Latin *deus*, and *divinus* meaning 'of a god'. I covered in *WANA – Part 2* how the Anunnaki gods were referred to as the *devas* or 'shining ones' in Hindu mythology in their ancient stories about the wars between the gods. From this it is easy to transliterate the physical 'shining ones' to the hive metaphysical shining god concept of the Light. The Anunnaki had a presence on this planet well before humans were invented, and in the end, became their primary gods. As Eliade also notes, there is no such thing as a primordial religion as the complexion of history keeps changing, just as I have shared so far in the book with the transition from the physical gods of old to the metaphysical ideas of the hive as god. Through Ninhursag, these traditions have altered to a certain degree from the Aryan patriarchal system to ones who competed with it to elevate the goddess above the patriarchal god of old, found first with the misogynistic Orioners (Greek Titans), and passed down to Enki once they left the planet.

In many cultures the role of a shaman becomes a form of hereditary elitism, requiring certain rights of passage through ecstatic dreams or visions, and instruction which could be equated with a form of initiation into the spirit realm, and learning secret languages that are passed down through the generational bloodlines of shamans. Similar initiatory rites are found in other Aryan religions and ideologies and have threaded their way through history via means of mystery schools and secret societies. It will be shown that this is all part and parcel of the hapiym hive's mystical construct to keep a specific form of elitism in place for its human initiates to maintain their control over the rest of the human 'herd' rabble.

The hive collective was predatory, and it was never averse to capitalizing on any opportunity to draft a human who possessed inherent latent capabilities into their mystical ranks. I reported in

*Revamping Psychology* about how hive-induced visionary states could be brought on when someone's consciousness was compromised through illness, trauma, drug ingestion, driving oneself into a trance state through hive-contrived meditation practices like Transcendental Meditation (TM) and other similar practices. The alleged kundalini experience symbolized by a serpent coiled at the root chakra and having it elevate through the spine to bring on a powerful ecstatic experience was one of Ninhursag's specifically designed programs to induce this hive state of awareness. The serpent association with the practice is the hallmark of her type of hive cell manipulation.

Eliade also observes that these visionary states are often brought on under physical duress of illness or fever and have served as a form of personal initiation when one is 'chosen' by the gods. Near Death Experiences (NDEs) have also been a great foundation for visionary states that leave the victim substantially altered after the fact. As stated, the hive collective was ever opportunistic when it came to finding ways to deceive humans into buying into their mystical ideologies, usually when our cognitive guard is down. This fact alone should illustrate the lack of integrity the composite hive collective intelligence possessed.

Many times, during these ecstatic trance states, the body of the shaman is taken over or 'possessed' by the god or angelic representative. According to Eliade's research, based on a broad spectrum of research by others, after a frenzied bout of divine madness, shaman candidates often fall unconscious, at which point their 'soul' is carried away to the land of the 'spirits' to begin their divine tutelage. The hidden nature of the Greek mystery schools carries echoes of similar happenings when the philosophical writings allude to being possessed by their daemons or geniuses. Such 'holy' possessions also took place in early Christian traditions when the religion's followers were 'overcome by the power of the Holy Spirit' and started speaking the gibberish of divine madness reported as speaking in tongues. The Pentecostal Church is filled with avid believers seeking similar direct divine ecstatic experiences and revelations from God, with many members claiming to be talking in tongues when the spirit overcomes them, and the act of snake handling is also an exhibition of their faith. We can only surmise at this juncture where handling poisonous serpents entered into this belief system, although there is a verse in the New Testament at Mark 16: 17-18 that seems to justify the practice which reads:

> *"And these signs shall follow them that believe: In my name shall they cast out devils; they shall speak with new tongues. They shall take up serpents; and if they drink any deadly thing, it shall not hurt them; they shall lay hands on the sick, and they shall recover."*

Although there is not a lot of surviving evidence other than texts of the church fathers writing against heresies, there are references to a Gnostic sect called Ophites in a few texts that bear looking into as a possible source of this Pentecostal tradition, Wikipedia shares:

*"Pseudo-Tertullian (probably the Latin translation of the lost work Syntagma of Hippolytus, written c. 220) is the earliest source to mention Ophites, and the first source to discuss the connection with serpents. He claims (Haer. 2.1-4) that the Ophites taught that:*

*Christ did not exist in the flesh (Christum autem non in substantia carnis fuisse; 2.4); that they extolled the serpent and preferred it to Christ (serpentem magnificant in tantum, ut ilium etiam ipsi Christo praeferant; 2.1); and that Christ imitated (imitor) Moses' serpent's sacred power (Num 21:6-9) saying, "And just as Moses lifted up the serpent in the wilderness, so must the Son of Man be lifted up (John 3:14)" (Haer. 2:1). In addition, Eve is said to have believed the serpent, as if it had been God the Son (Eua quasi filio deo crediredat; 2.4).*

*The name "Jesus" is not mentioned in the account. Epiphanius' account differs from that of Pseudo-Tertullian only in a few places. According to the former,* ***the Ophites did not actually prefer the snake to Christ, but thought them identical*** *(Pan. 37.1.2; 2.6; 6.5-6; 8.1)."*

[Bold emphasis mine]

Given the information I have shared about Ninhursag and her many roles within trinities, I find it particularly interesting that the Ophites allegedly equated the serpent with Christ. If what I have presented this far is the truth, and I assert that it is, then the association between Christ and the serpent within the Ophite ideology correlates fully with Nin's association with the serpent in many other roles in other lands.

I have sidetracked a bit on the aspect of shamanism somewhat with these last passages, but the correlation between ecstatic experiences and the human demand to gain a direct connection to the alleged divine traces through time, and that lure for the supernatural experience has not waned over the millennia but has merely changed doctrinal clothing from culture to culture. It doesn't really matter what colors you use to paint the picture, the canvas is always the same at its root, and that is why this chapter is a necessary inclusion for this body of work. While many scholars over the generations have seen these commonalities, they also focus entirely too much on the superficial differences, and as such, they have utterly failed to stand far enough away from the painting to see the full picture that all this evidence presents.

What has been illustrated thus far constitutes what is known as the *perennial philosophy.* I want to offer a couple of short passages from Wikipedia on this philosophy for the reader's greater understanding:

> *"Perennial philosophy (Latin: philosophia perennis), also referred to as Perennialism and perennial wisdom, is a perspective in modern*

*spirituality that views* ***each of the world's religious traditions as sharing a single, metaphysical truth or origin from which all esoteric and exoteric knowledge and doctrine has grown****.*

*Perennialism has its roots in the Renaissance interest in neo-Platonism and its idea of* ***The One****, from which all existence emanates. Marsilio Ficino (1433–1499) sought to integrate Hermeticism with Greek and Jewish-Christian thought. discerning a Prisca theologia which could be found in all ages. Giovanni Pico della Mirandola (1463–94) suggested that truth could be found in many, rather than just two, traditions. He proposed a harmony between the thought of Plato and Aristotle, and saw aspects of the Prisca theologia in Averroes, the Koran, the Cabala and other sources. Agostino Steuco (1497–1548) coined the term philosophia perennis.*

*A more popular interpretation argues for universalism, the idea that all* ***religions, underneath seeming differences point to the same Truth****. In the early 19th century the Transcendentalists propagated the idea of a metaphysical Truth and universalism, which inspired the Unitarians, who proselytized among Indian elites. Towards the end of the 19th century,* *the* ***Theosophical Society*** *further popularized universalism, not only in the western world, but also in western colonies. In the 20th century universalism was further popularized in the English-speaking world through the neo-Vedanta inspired Traditionalist School, which argues for a metaphysical, single origin of the orthodox religions, and by Aldous Huxley and his book* ***The Perennial Philosophy****, which was inspired by neo-Vedanta and the Traditionalist School."*

*"One such universalist was Aldous Huxley, who propagated a universalist interpretation of the world religions, inspired by Vivekananda's neo-Vedanta. According to Aldous Huxley, who popularized the idea of a Perennial philosophy with a larger audience,*

*The Perennial Philosophy is expressed most succinctly in the Sanskrit formula, tat tvam asi ('That thou art');* ***the Atman, or immanent eternal Self, is one with Brahman, the Absolute Principle of all existence****; and the last end of every human being, is to discover the fact for himself,* ***to find out who he really is****.*

*In Huxley's 1944 essay in* Vedanta and the West, *he describes The Minimum Working*

*Hypothesis; the basic outline of the Perennial Philosophy found in all the mystic branches of the religions of the world:*

*That there is a Godhead or Ground, which is the unmanifested principle of all manifestation.*

*That the Ground is transcendent and immanent.*

*That it is possible for human beings to love, know and, from virtually, to become actually identified with the Ground.*

*That to achieve this unitive knowledge, to realize this supreme identity, is the final end and purpose of human existence.*

*That there is a Law or Dharma, which must be obeyed, a Tao or Way, which must be followed, if men are to achieve their final end."*

[Bold emphasis mine]

What we find in everything revealed in this chapter is an unending thread weaving its way through history with the ultimate goal of subduing all human consciousness with the desire that we all find this mystical communion with the hive collective's 'Oneness'. Aldous Huxley was a member of the Fabian Society as well as a member of the Theosophical Society. It is not accidental that these self-appointed elitists laud their own and promote the ideologies of a world government given the nature and agenda of the hive intelligence itself, which was to subdue and enslave all human consciousness and activate the hapiym hive cell replicas in all humanity, thereby making our planet nothing but a material playground for the hive infection to thrive and grow.

It must also be remembered that Huxley authored the dystopian fantasy novel *Brave New World* wherein a future world existed where the populace was genetically manipulated by class to know their place within that society and were constantly controlled through a substance called soma. A free-thinking human being was anathema within this Fabian nightmare of a future and considered a 'beast', no different than any other hive ideology presented thus far in this presentation. The perennial philosophy is the hapiym mind virus itself and nothing more. The virus infection lies at the root of every religious tradition on this planet, just as the tenets of the perennial philosophy fully acknowledge. We human beings in our material form with our waking consciousness are the 'herd' to elitists the likes of Huxley and his Fabian and Theosophical fellow travelers. This attitude has been evidenced throughout time where the minority elite classes hold superiority over the masses of humanity. It has been shown from Greek philosophy forward that it is the hapiym mind virus which has controlled the destiny of humanity with its mystical illusions over the last 5,000-6,000 years. We may wish to deny this, but I am still not finished with providing evidence to make my case and put the final nails in the coffin of mysticism.

Shamanism was only the start of what became a more organized institutional effort since the disappearance of the physical gods, and therefore plays a necessary part in understanding the terrible agenda of tyranny perpetrated against humanity on this planet.

# 11. Gnosticism

This chapter is not going to be an exhaustive study of all the facets of Gnosticism as the Gnostic traditions were in fact rather wide and varied in their doctrinal divergences. Unfortunately, in modern spiritual vernacular, particularly within the Theosophy-spawned New Age arena, Gnosticism has become a general catch-all phrase that most New Agers bandy around loosely without having any understanding of what it was nor its origins. It is simply a doctrinal buzzword within this arena, and I can attest to this fact because many years ago I also bought into many of these superficial beliefs with no understanding of their origin or meaning. I have been there and done that, so I am more than qualified to know about which I speak in this regard.

The word *gnosis* is the Greek word for knowledge, particularly the knowledge about spiritual mysteries or 'knowing'. At this juncture, the root of these alleged 'spiritual mysteries' should be quite clear to the reader. In the historical sequence of events, Gnosticism preceded later Neoplatonism by about a century, arising primarily from Jewish philosophical schools in Alexandria, Egypt and thriving in the late 1$^{st}$ to 2$^{nd}$ century AD, paralleling what scholars refer to as the Middle Platonism timeframe. The Gnostics were influenced by the Middle Platonist ideologies, although the later Neoplatonists rejected the Gnostic doctrines and ideologies.

For a full understanding Gnosticism, ideally a 'direct' form of knowledge of God, we have to comprehend the Greek word Sophia, which translates to mean wisdom. Looking up *Sophia (wisdom)* on Wikipedia we discover:

> *"Sophia (Greek: σοφία sophía 'wisdom') is a central idea in Hellenistic philosophy and religion, Platonism, Gnosticism, and Christian theology.*
>
> *In Orthodox and Roman Catholic Christianity,* ***Holy Wisdom (Hagia Sophia) is an expression for God the Son (Jesus Christ) in the Trinity (as in the dedication of the church of Hagia Sophia in Constantinople) and, rarely, for the Holy Spirit.*** *References to "Wisdom" (Sophia) in the Old Testament translate to the Hebrew term Chokhmah.*
>
> *The Ancient Greek word sophia (σοφία, sophía) is the abstract noun of σοφός (sophós), which variously translates to* ***"clever, skillful, intelligent, wise"****. These words share the same* ***Proto-Indo-European root*** *as the Latin verb sapere (lit. "to taste; discern"), whence sapientia. The noun σοφία as "skill in handicraft and art" is*

*Homeric and in Pindar is used to describe both Hephaistos and Athena."*

[Bold emphasis mine]

With the understanding of Sophia being a core element of Hellenistic philosophical teachings, as well as Gnosticism, Platonism and Christianity, we once again encounter the triune aspect of Ninhursag already illustrated thus far in this volume. We also find the root word from the Aryan (Indo-European) language group. The concepts of being 'clever, skillful and intelligent' within this definition will have more relevance as we proceed into later chapters.

To further elucidate Sophia where Gnosticism is concerned, we have to look at a separate definition in Wikipedia, and that is Sophia (Gnosticism), where we find:

*"Sophia (Greek Σοφία, meaning "wisdom," Coptic* ⲧⲥⲟⲫⲓⲁ *tsophia) is a major theme, along with Knowledge (Greek γνῶσις gnosis, Coptic sooun), among many of the early Christian knowledge-theologies grouped by the heresiologist Irenaeus as gnostikos,* ***"learned."*** *Gnosticism is a 17th-century term expanding the definition of Irenaeus' groups to include other syncretic and mystery religions.*

*In Gnostic tradition,* ***Sophia is a feminine figure****, analogous to the* ***human soul*** *but also* *simultaneously* ***one of the feminine aspects of God****. Gnostics held that* ***she was the syzygy of Jesus Christ (i.e. the Bride of Christ), and Holy Spirit of the Trinity.*** *She is occasionally referred to by the Hebrew equivalent of Achamōth (Ἀχαμώθ, Hebrew חכמה chokhmah) and as Prunikos (Προύνικος). In the Nag Hammadi texts,* ***Sophia is the lowest Aeon****, or anthropic expression of the* ***emanation of the light of God****. She is considered to have fallen from grace in some way, in so doing* ***creating or helping to create the material world.****"*

[Bold emphasis mine]

Within this passage we once again find reference to the feminine aspect of God, the emanations, providing echoes of Platonic mysticism and Zoroastrianism, the Light of God and the trinitarian aspects of Christianity. The references to the 'Bride of Christ' and 'creating or helping create the material world' are going to have a relevance that one's immediate perceptions may overlook. Both of these latter aspects will be discussed in later chapters.

A further passage in the same look-up, under the sub-header *Christology*, reveals this:

*"At times the Church Fathers named* ***Christ as "Wisdom".*** *Therefore, when rebutting claims about Christ's ignorance, Gregory of*

*Nazianzus insisted that, inasmuch as he was divine, Christ knew everything: "How can he be ignorant of anything that is, when he is Wisdom, the maker of the worlds, who brings all things to fulfilment and recreates all things, who is the end of all that has come into being?" (Orationes, 30.15). Irenaeus represents another, minor patristic tradition* ***which identified the Spirit of God, and not Christ himself, as "Wisdom"*** *(Adversus haereses, 4.20.1–3; cf. 3.24.2; 4.7.3; 4.20.3). He could appeal to Paul's teaching about* ***wisdom being one of the gifts of the Holy Spirit*** *(1 Cor. 12:8). However, the majority* ***applied to Christ the title/name of "Wisdom"****.*

*Emperor Constantine set a pattern for Eastern Christians by dedicating a church to* ***Christ as the personification of Divine Wisdom****. In Constantinople, under Emperor Justinian, Hagia Sophia ("Holy Wisdom") was rebuilt, consecrated in 538, and became a model for many other Byzantine churches. In the Latin Church, however, "the Word" or Logos came through more clearly than "the Wisdom" of God as a central, high title of Christ."*

[Bold emphasis mine]

Here again, we find all the same elements already highlighted with Wisdom equated with both Jesus and the Holy Spirit. At this juncture, there should be little confusion as to what these references truly represent, despite Christian apologists going through a mental juggling act to make sense of the agenda.

Another aspect of Gnosticism I want to cover in this presentation to support my contentions about the war between the followers of Enki in competition with the followers of Ninhursag, Wikipedia reports under *Gnosticism*:

> *"Gnosticism originated in the late first century CE in nonrabbinical Jewish sects and early Christian sects, and many of the Nag Hammadi texts make reference to Judaism,* ***in some cases with a violent rejection of the Jewish God.****"*
>
> [Bold emphasis mine]

As with all the mystery religions out of Greece and elsewhere, the Gnostic treatises were top-heavy with philosophy and were primarily focused on proselytizing to an elite and educated class of individuals. Most of the illiterate world at that time would have had a hard time comprehending the highly philosophical doctrines, so Gnosticism itself was a Jewish spinoff of Pythagorean and Platonic philosophies without the scientific research of the Greek philosophers added to the mix. The focus was primarily spiritual as within the Hellenistic mystery schools, but the Gnostics were working hard at weaving Jesus into this new mystery school mythology. As will be shown by certain passages from the *Nag Hammadi Library* of works unearthed in 1947, we are going to find the same hive doctrines and those of Ninhursag as the female aspect of Divine Wisdom sewn into the Gnostic tapestry, referred to throughout those works by the Greek word *Sophia*.

For the direct correlation with what I have shared so far, Wikipedia provides this overview under the sub-header of **Philosophical Relations** within the lookup on *Gnosticism*:

> *"Gnostics borrow a lot of ideas and terms from Platonism. They exhibit a keen understanding of Greek philosophical terms and the Greek Koine language in general, and use Greek philosophical concepts throughout their text, including such concepts as hypostasis (reality, existence), ousia (essence, substance, being), and demiurge (creator God). Good examples include texts such as the* Hypostasis of the Archons *(Reality of the Rulers) or* Trimorphic Protennoia ***(The first thought in three forms)****.*
>
> *Gnostics structured their world of* ***transcendent being*** *by ontological distinctions. The plenitude of the divine world emerges from a* ***sole high deity by emanation, radiation, unfolding and mental self-reflection****. The technique of self-performable* **contemplative**

***mystical ascent towards and beyond a realm of pure being**, which is rooted in Plato's* Symposium *and was common in Gnostic thought, was also expressed by Plotinus.*

> ***Divine triads**, tetrads, and ogdoads in Gnostic thought often are closely related to Neo-Pythagorean arithmology. **The trinity of the "triple-powered one"** (with the powers consisting of the modalities of existence, life and mind) in* Allogenes ***mirrors quite closely the Neoplatonic doctrine of the Intellect differentiating itself from the One in three phases**, called Existence or reality (hypostasis), Life, and Intellect (nous). Both traditions heavily emphasize the role of negative theology or apophasis, and Gnostic emphasis on the ineffability of God often echoes Platonic (and Neoplatonic) formulations of **the ineffability of the One** or the Good."*

[Bold emphasis mine]

I have taken the liberty to highlight the portions relevant to this presentation, and that is the direct correlation with the single Monadic concept of God, or 'the One', as well as showing the continuing theme within Jewish philosophical thought about the 'triple-powered one', which I assert is the same pattern of the hive's and Ninhursag's fingerprints we find resident in all these doctrines.

The first place we will look for some of this evidence is in a Gnostic document entitled *The Thunder, Perfect Mind*, found with the buried scrolls found in Nag Hammadi Egypt:

*"**For I am the first and the last**.*
*I am the honored one and the scorned one.*
*I am the whore and the holy one.*
*I am the wife and the virgin.*
*I am <the mother> and the daughter.*
*I am the members of my mother.*
*I am the barren one*
*and many are her sons.*
*I am she whose wedding is great,*
*and I have not taken a husband.*
*I am the midwife and she who does not bear.*
*I am the solace of my labor pains.*
*I am the bride and the bridegroom,*
*and it is my husband who begot me.*
*I am the mother of my father*
*and the sister of my husband*
*and he is my offspring."*

Within this seemingly confusing passage we find Ninhursag's stamp in many of the claims made in this passage. To show the intimate association with Jesus in the Bible where he claims to be the Alpha and the Omega, we find the female personage in this passage claiming to be the 'first and the last.' She admits that she is the 'whore' as well as the 'virgin', which is found in many of the goddess roles Ninhursag hid behind. She is the 'mother and the daughter' echoing the story of Demeter and Persephone, and she is both bride and bridegroom, once again illustrating her hermaphroditism. Ninhursag never bore children so she was the 'barren one' yet who had many 'sons', which covers her invented sons, Horus, Dionysus and Jesus, whose fictitious roles she also played and harvested worshipful energy from their names.

The rest of the treatise is a confusing list of brags where the female speaker basically claims to be all things and creates a 'mystery' through the intentional confusion wrought in the document. There is no genuine understanding expected to be gleaned from the treatise because it is all *supposed* to be a mystery. It is designed to be an intentional philosophical mind-twister wherein there is no foundation for understanding. It is false wisdom posed in a riddle that has no solution beyond what I have shared, and even our most esteemed scholars have not interpreted what I share here in the correct manner.

Looking at the Zoroastrian concept of the Eternal Flame and the hive being associated with light and the Divine Spark within, when we look into some of these other Gnostic gospels, like *The Teachings of Silvanus*, we find the same elements of Zoroastrian 'light' referenced as Christ, as well as solar comparisons. We also see Wisdom portrayed in Ninhursag's feminine aspect. The following excerpts, when viewed with the knowledge about the hive make perfect sense:

*"Wisdom summons you in* ***her*** *goodness, saying, "Come to Me, all of you, O foolish ones, that you may receive a gift, the understanding which is good and excellent. I am giving to you a high-priestly garment which is woven from every (kind of) wisdom." What else is evil death except ignorance? What else is evil darkness except familiarity with forgetfulness? Cast your anxiety upon God alone. Do not become desirous of gold and silver, which are profitless, but clothe yourself with wisdom like a robe; put knowledge on yourself like a crown, and* ***be seated upon a throne of perception****. For these are yours, and* ***you will receive them again on high another time****."*

*"For* ***everything which is visible <u>is a copy</u> of that which is hidden****. For as a fire which burns in a place without being confined to it, so it is with the sun which is in the sky, all of whose rays extend to places on the earth. Similarly,* ***Christ has a single being, and he gives light to every place****. This is also the way in which he speaks of our mind,* ***as if it were a lamp which burns and lights up the place****. (Being) in a part of the soul, it gives light to all the parts."*

*"And **all is Christ**, he who has inherited all from the **Existent One**. For Christ is the idea of incorruptibility, **and he is the Light which is shining undefiled**. For the **sun** (shines) on every impure place, and yet it is not defiled. So it is with Christ: even if he is in the deficiency, yet he is without deficiency. And even if he has been begotten, he is (still) unbegotten. So it is with Christ: if, on the one hand, he is comprehensible, on the other, he is incomprehensible with respect to his actual being. Christ is all. He who does not possess all is unable to know Christ."*

*"**Cease being a tomb, and become (again) a temple, so that uprightness and divinity may remain in you.***

***Light the light within you**. Do not extinguish it! Certainly, no one lights a lamp for wild beasts or their young. Raise your dead who have died, for they lived and have died for you. **Give them life. They shall live again**!*

***For the Tree of Life is Christ**. He is Wisdom. For he is Wisdom; he is also the Word. he is the Life, the Power, and the Door. **He is the Light, the Angel, and the Good Shepherd. Entrust yourself to this one who became all for your sake.***

*Knock on yourself as upon a door, and walk upon yourself as on a straight road. For if you walk on the road, it is impossible for you to go astray. And if you knock with this one (Wisdom), you knock on hidden treasures.*

*For* ***since he (Christ) is Wisdom, he makes the foolish man wise. He (Wisdom) is a holy kingdom and a shining robe. For it (Wisdom) is much gold, which gives you great honor****. The Wisdom of God became a type of fool for you, so that it might take you up, O foolish one, and make you a wise man. And the Life died for you when he was powerless, so that through his death, he might give life to you who have died."*

[Bold emphasis mine]

Within these passages we find Christ associated with Wisdom, the Zoroastrian concept of Light and the associations with the sun, and the very telling admission that everything that is seen, meaning our human forms, are a *duplicate of what is hidden*, meaning the infectious hive cell within. When we have the valid keys of understanding to translate all this correctly, then the picture painted is not the glorified mystical land of enchantment it presents itself to be. Humanity has been sold a mystical bill of goods and humanity throughout the ages keeps chasing this tyrannical rainbow thinking it is something it's not.

The *Second Stele of Seth* within the Nag Hammadi corpus has this to share in the opening paragraphs:

> *"Great is the first aeon, male virginal Barbelo, the first glory of the invisible Father, she who is called "perfect".*
>
> *Thou (fem.) hast seen first the one who truly pre-exists because he is non-being. And from him and through him thou hast pre-existed eternally, the non-being from one indivisible,* ***triple power, thou a triple power, thou a great monad from a pure monad, thou an elect monad, the first shadow of the holy Father, light from light****.*
>
> *We bless thee, producer (fem.) of perfection, aeon-giver (fem.). Thou hast seen the eternal ones because they are from a shadow. And thou hast become numerable. And thou didst find, thou didst continue being one (fem.); yet becoming numerable in division,* ***thou art three-fold****. Thou art truly* ***thrice****, thou one (fem.) of the one (masc.). And thou art from a shadow of him, thou a Hidden One, thou a world of understanding, knowing those of the one, that they are from a shadow. And these are thine in the heart."*
>
> [Bold emphasis mine]

Within these short passages we see the Pythagorean and Platonic Monad and the tripartite feminine representing Ninhursag illustrated yet again. It is impossible to argue away the connection between Greek mystical hive philosophy and the Gnostic renderings in many places. The Greek Hecate is the

Gnostic Sophia in her tripartite representations. The Father, Mother, Son imagery harkens back to the Egyptian Osiris, Isis and Horus trinity and it is all the same presentation of Ninhursag in her triune hermaphroditic form presented through allegorical philosophical renderings. In many respects this could be analogous to the Veil of Isis, which I attest it is. As a side note in this chapter, I would like to call attention to part of what is found at Wikipedia under *Veil of Isis*:

> *"The veil of Isis is a metaphor and allegorical artistic motif in which nature is personified as the goddess Isis covered by a veil or mantle, representing the inaccessibility of nature's secrets. It is often combined with a related motif, in which nature is portrayed as a goddess with multiple breasts who represents Isis, Artemis, or a combination of both.*
>
> *The motif was based on a statue of Isis in the Egyptian city of Sais mentioned by the Greco-Roman authors Plutarch and Proclus. They claimed the statue bore an inscription saying* ***"I am all that has been and is and shall be; and no mortal has ever lifted my mantle."*** *Illustrations of Isis with her veil being lifted were popular from the late 17th to the early 19th century, often as allegorical representations of Enlightenment*

*science and philosophy uncovering nature's secrets."*

[Bold emphasis mine]

The inscription on this statue is little different than Jesus claiming to be the Alpha and Omega, the beginning and the end of all things, and this correlation cannot be overlooked when it purportedly comes from the lips of Ninhursag playing the role of Isis. The claim that no man hath ever lifted her veil is a direct brag about how the ignorance of humanity has not been able to see through the veil of illusion presented in this book. At last, Isis' veil is finally being lifted for the world to see the corruption that the goddess represents.

In many of the Gnostic writings we find our very existence referred to as being 'dead' if we cannot find that hive cell within ourselves and activate it. It is only when we give up our humanity and our waking consciousness that we are deemed worthy enough to exist in this tyrannical hive mystical framework. Only the hapiym hive cell holds value in all these traditions – the false concept of 'soul' or 'spirit', and your being human counts for nothing. You are considered dead in comparison to the hive cell that laid hidden within us. The human body was considered a prison or tomb in the Gnostic teachings, and the sooner the imprisoned hive cell could exit the tomb of the human form, the more joyous this false virus soul was expected to be, gaining freedom from the tomb of matter.

The same principles apply in modern Christianity, with the exception of the perception that one will be bodily resurrected to join their God in the afterlife. No such circumstance was ever going to happen, but it sells to the ignorant believers who yearn for that alleged Divine communion with their God, which in the end was only going to be their stolen human personalities joining the hive cluster. It has all been a gigantic hoax of monumental proportions, and the sad testimony of our species is that it has been kept secret by those who are fully aware of the cosmic hive and its tyrannical agenda who have worked in knowing collusion with the hive throughout the ages.

It is not my place to recap every text written by the Gnostics or any of the other sources throughout this volume. My purpose is to show the consistent thread that runs through all these traditions which have only appeared to change, through superficial doctrines making them appear to be different, when the fact is that the core elements all arise from the same source. Over the last 6,000 years we can observe a slow consolidation from the many gods to the few, from the physical gods to the metaphysical hive. This gradualist consolidation of power was designed to work toward a pinnacle that was to lead to total global tyranny, what people refer to as the New World Order, but who only have a superficial understanding of this tyranny at best. They can observe some of the outer permutations of this Aryan consolidation of power, but they are blissfully unaware of the overall hive agenda which lies behind the march toward global homogeneity.

The elite insiders to this game plan are as arrogant as the hive itself in referring to humanity as cattle, and the hive agenda has been driven and controlled by the global elite since the arrival of the Aryans on this planet over 5,000 years ago. The Gnostic texts, as with the Greek philosophical texts, were written *by* intellectuals *for* intellectuals. They have been written in a form of hidden code, which this book is now revealing. I am peeling away the blinders to show humanity the hidden con game taking place beyond its perception, so we can rid our species of this malignant hapiym hive poison once and for all. Despite all the smarmy rhetoric to convince people that their Globalist agenda is humanitarian in nature, they only consider themselves human and the rest of humanity as animals, merely beasts to be herded and controlled.

# 12. Pre-Renaissance Mysticism

I am not going to cover the era of the Neoplatonists in depth from the 3rd to 6th centuries AD as it is mostly a rehash of the Greek philosophers and their Platonic hive doctrines already presented appearing in a later era, although it passed through a process of refinement and syncretism with Egyptian religions. Neoplatonism never died, as much of the tradition was preserved in Islam after the Roman Church did its utmost to stamp it out along with Gnosticism, considering it heretical to the church doctrines. Islam carried forward Neoplatonism in the 9th century, as Wikipedia explains under *Platonism in Islamic Philosophy*:

> *"Medieval Islamic philosophy was steeped in both Aristotelianism and Neoplatonism from its 9th-century beginnings with Al-Kindi, but the influence of Neoplatonism becomes more clearly visible in the 10th and 11th centuries with Al-Farabi and Avicenna. Al-Farabi expanded on Plato's concept of an ideal city ruled by philosopher-kings to develop a political philosophy that could accommodate the religious and cultural diversity central to Islamic nations.*

*On the other hand, both al-Ghazali and Ibn Rushd vigorously opposed Neoplatonic views.*

*The characteristic of Neoplatonic thought in Islamic theology is that of emanation, linking God's transcendence with the corporeal reality of his creation. Islamic Neoplatonism was introduced by Al-Farabi, although Avicenna proved to have the greater influence. Both authors present a complex scheme of emanation.*

*Islamic Neoplatonism was allowed to flourish in the 10th to early 11th century, but there was a strong reaction against it in the later 11th century, especially from Al-Ghazali, who represents Islamic theology's "most biting attack on philosophy" at the time, and the severest reaction to Neoplatonism in particular (Netton 1998). Al-Ghazali's criticism evoked a counter-reaction by Ibn Rushd, who wrote a "systematic rebuttal of al-Ghazali's critique of Greco-Arab philosophy". While Ibn Rushd is trying to defend the possibility of philosophical thought as non-heretical, he does at the same time himself reject the theses of the Neoplatonist philosophers.*

*After the death of Ibn Rushd in 1198, the debate on Neoplatonism in Islam mostly comes to an end, and survival of Neoplatonic thought within Islam was mostly limited to Ismailism."*

Between the 6th and 9th century AD, we also find Neoplatonist ideas being shared by Christian mystics such as Pseudo-Dionysius the Areopagite from the late 5th to the early 6th centuries and whose work was apparently influenced by the Neoplatonist philosopher Proclus, both of which later influenced the 13th century Christian mystic, Meister Eckhart. For more information on these Christian mystics, refer to *List of Christian Mystics* on Wikipedia and research them independently on your own. You are only going to find the same hapiym hive perfidy with all of these mystics' visionary teachings when you look into them.

Within this list of Christian mystics, we find Hildegard von Bingen, who I covered in part in my book, *Revamping Psychology*, as one visionary who the hapiym hive manipulated through illness to do its bidding by insisting that she write down and catalogue all the messages the presumed hive 'angels' transmitted down through her. As Wikipedia related under *Hildegard of Bingen*, explaining her visions:

*"Hildegard said that she first saw* ***"The Shade of the Living Light"*** *at the age of three, and by the age of five she began to understand that she was experiencing visions. She used the term 'visio' to this feature of her experience, and recognized that it was a gift that she could not explain to*

*others. Hildegard explained that she saw all things in* ***the light of God*** *through the five senses: sight, hearing, taste, smell, and touch. Hildegard was hesitant to share her visions, confiding only to Jutta, who in turn told Volmar, Hildegard's tutor and, later, secretary. Throughout her life, she continued to have many visions, and in 1141, at the age of 42, Hildegard received a vision she believed to be an instruction from God, to "write down that which you see and hear."* ***Still hesitant to record her visions, Hildegard became physically ill****. The illustrations recorded in the book of Scivias were visions that Hildegard experienced, causing her great suffering and tribulations. In her first theological text, Scivias ("Know the Ways"), Hildegard describes her struggle within:*

*"But I, though I saw and heard these things,* ***refused to write*** *for a long time through doubt and bad opinion and the diversity of human words, not with stubbornness but in the exercise of humility,* ***until, laid low by the scourge of God, I fell upon a bed of sickness****; then, compelled at last by many illnesses, and by the witness of a certain noble maiden of good conduct [the nun Richardis von Stade] and of that man whom I had secretly sought and found, as mentioned above, I set my hand to the writing. While I was doing it, I sensed,*

*as I mentioned before, the deep profundity of scriptural exposition; and, raising myself from illness by the strength I received, I brought this work to a close – though just barely – in ten years. (...) And I spoke and wrote these things not by the invention of my heart or that of any other person,* ***but as by the secret mysteries of God I heard and received them in the heavenly places. And again I heard a voice from Heaven saying to me, 'Cry out therefore, and write thus!'***

Particular attention should be paid to Hildegard's plight in refusing to write down what 'God', or shall we say the hive virus, demanded that she write. Her refusal resulted in physical illness indicating beyond doubt that the hapiym hive virus did in fact control human physiology; in Hildegard's case bringing on debilitating physical illness that left her bedridden until she complied with the demands of the hive and wrote down what she was instructed, at which point she was 'magically' healed from the illness brought on by the virus itself.

Although mainstream materialists would rather deny all this as some form of psychosomatically induced illness, they overlook other factors that were also highly active and observable in the ancient world. When an adept in the 'science of God' was given the capability to manipulate the virus cell in others, they could cast 'spells' or generate curses which, through the activation of the hive cell living within their human host, could cause similar maladies. This is one reason our ancient ancestors feared magic spells and curses, for in the hands of a hive-trained adept, this type of 'magic' could bring on many varied symptoms. Contrary to modern rigid materialist scientific beliefs, these ancient fears were not predicated strictly on the superstitions of the ignorant masses, although superstition did play a part in many of these beliefs. Many people experienced the symptoms of these 'curses', never realizing that it was the infectious hapiym hive virus that could produce these physical symptoms within them.

St. Francis of Assisi started his quest to spread the word of the church and created the Franciscan Order based on a visionary experience. We also find Joan of Arc in the 15th century relying on her visions near the end of the 100 Years war with England and France, which have become legendary. Joan had been subject to visions since she was about 13 years old. These are only two further examples of many who are lesser known than these Christian mystics.

The visions provided by the hive were present throughout time. My original intent when I started this book was to catalogue a litany of quotes as provided in the previous chapters to illustrate the consistency of the doctrines that progress from Zoroastrianism into modern spiritual traditions. In doing my research I decided that there was no valid point in providing one repetitive example after another to prove my case. The consistency of the core hive doctrine of alleged Divine Oneness threads itself throughout human history, and the only variant is the interpretive nature of how the humans who sought to describe this Oneness of God translated it in their own style. It doesn't matter if the interpreter is the mystic Meister Eckhart, St. Augustine, Aleister Crowley in his occult traditions of Thelema handed down allegedly by the god Horus, or Emmanuel Swedenborg. The hapiym hive did its utmost, in collusion with the 'spirit' of the Anunnaki hermaphrodite Ninhursag, to shape the destiny of all humanity through a controlling intellectual elite, Ninhursag's Aryan tribes.

In all too many instances these artificially induced visionary states provided by the hive through activating the hive cell within its human host, usually under pressure of mental duress or deprivation, produced the wealth of varying religions we see today. The Muslim prophet Muhammed was no exception when he put himself in a cave and fasted and meditated, eventually producing his visions of the alleged angel Gabriel, the same angel who purportedly told Mary that she would give birth to the Christian Messiah, Jesus. As the story goes, when the angel Gabriel appeared before Muhammed, he held up a cloth with words on it and ordered Muhammed to read. Muhammed was illiterate and told the angelic apparition that he couldn't read, at which point this angel grabbed him by the throat and instructed him to "Recite!" Muhammed asked, "Recite what?", at which point, as the religious mythology of Islam goes, the angel responded, "Recite in the name of your Lord who has created, created man from a drop of blood. Recite, for your Lord is most generous...Who taught man what he did not know."

Needless to say, this experience scared the snot out of Muhammed and he bolted from the cave, but he was greeted about half-way down the mountain by the angel again at which point Gabriel told him that he was a "messenger of God". Over the next 21 years Muhammed was subjected to infrequent but intense visions that always left him debilitated after the fact, not unlike the circumstances of Hildegard von Bingen, and he is reported to have said that with each of these visions he felt that, "my soul has been torn away from me". These visionary trance states took a heavy physical toll, and after these trance-state visions, Muhammed was reported to have spoken in an 'ecstatic manner', and his actions and voice were out of character from his normal self. I share this story of Muhammed in order to build on information that will be presented in later chapters in regard to how the hapiym mind virus manipulated our bodies without our knowledge or consent, and how this presumably 'benevolent One God' who controls all was never above invoking states of physical discomfort or psychological fear to insure that its Will and desires were performed without question.

I realize what a large pill this is for anyone to swallow, particularly those who are approaching this book cold without any research into my previous work, but this volume is the culmination of all that came before it in what I have written. The pieces of fragmented human history are finally being sown together to present a tyranny on a cosmic scale that our materialist world simply refuses to believe existed. The adepts within the secret societies over the ages, like the Rosicrucians, the Freemasons, and those who created religions using the guidelines of these secret societies like Charles Taze Russel (Jehovah's Witnesses – Freemason), Joseph Smith (Mormonism – Freemason) and a litany of other members of the Freemasonic fraternity over the past few centuries since the Protestant Revolution, have carried within all these religions the hidden and secret doctrines of the hapiym hive agenda for control of the human mind, and ultimately this planet.

St. Ignatius Loyola, the creator of the Jesuit Order, also started his quest in creating that order after visions of the Divine Mary, thereby strengthening the worship of Mary within the Roman Catholic Church. Loyola himself was a devotee of the Black Madonna who, on his pilgrimage to Rome seeking to have his new Order sanctified by the Pope, stopped at virtually every chapel on the road from Spain to Rome that housed a statue of the Black Madonna, so he could pray and offer his continual devotion. The Black Madonna is recognized by many scholars as symbolizing the Egyptian goddess Isis and her son Horus. Wherever we track this mystical and supernatural God psychosis that plagues humanity, we will find the Mother Goddess and her Son in communion with the mystical hive traditions in one form or another.

I have provided the major keys to solving these mysteries of the hidden and invisible God of Oneness as nothing more than an intelligent and predatory hive virus that has infected the mind of humanity. All of our cultures worldwide have been shaped by this virus in every religious and mystical tradition we look into, from ancient shamanism into the modern New Age spiritual movements. It's all the same old song and dance being repackaged from one generation to the next. The outer doctrinal clothing may change, but the inner core tyranny of subjugation to the 'Divine Will' threads through all these traditions. Humans are viewed as nothing more that slave bodies to this hive virus while it lived. Our value in its eyes was only as that of a servant to its voracious desire to control everything as itself. Its spiritual doctrines were set as a lure to our species to draw us to its alleged supernatural power, and it did not hesitate to lie and fabricate false promises to humanity through artificially induced visions, dreams and beliefs along the way. Sadly, humanity is still so enchanted by these promises of their perception of immortality that this con game continues without the existence of the hive mind to perpetuate it. The lure to the supernatural is so deeply ingrained in the human psyche by the virus, that it is uncertain whether humanity will ever outgrow the lures the virus hive used to seduce our species. One thing is a certainty, materialism and Transhumanism are not the cure for this problem as it is the quest for immortality that drives science in this framework. The desire to live forever, which was a direct symptom of the virus itself, is so drilled into our minds that some are willing to give up our very humanity to preserve our virus-infected human ego personalities forever by seeking to merge us with machines to achieve this travesty.

Modern humanity is unwilling to face death in the general sense. It has been the concept of living forever in some happy afterlife that has stolen our humanity from us. We have become so focused on the promised eternal afterlife for so many thousands of generations that we have forgotten that death is part of the cycle of living. We do everything we can to avoid death or even think about death. We are obsessed with how to defeat death, so we can live forever. It was the seemingly immortal hapiym mind virus that infected our minds this way. Humanity is running away from death. The over-inflated ego personality produced by the hive virus with its instinctual necessity to cluster in herds and live eternally in the hive cluster in the sky has poisoned our minds. We are barely human any more, but mere puppets of these purportedly divine machinations. As much as the virus sought to steal from humanity, in the wake of its infection, humanity's consciousness is more hapiym virus than human. The hapiym mind virus has turned our entire species into mere caricatures of a human being. We have been infected with the virus for so long, we have never known what it is to be truly human without the virus symptomatology ruling our bodies and minds.

Although the hapiym hive clusters have been eliminated everywhere, we all live in its shadow, infected with the residual emotional and psychological habits the virus brought to our species. We took on the habits the virus used to manipulate our bodies and minds as nothing more than a food supply to drive its perfidious agenda. Mysticism and supernaturalism sit at ground zero where perpetuating the hive myth about the eternal existence of the human personality is concerned. Books have been written on this very subject.

In deciding to not present quotation after quotation in this book and altering direction mid-stream, so to speak, as an alternative I am offering a comprehensive list of books, articles and references from Wikipedia and other sources at the end of this volume. There is a wealth of information out there to verify what I have shared to date. The purpose of this volume was to supply the foundational information, the *key* for understanding, to decode all this mystical hornswoggle so humanity can finally give up on these false supernatural promises and choose a new destiny for itself – to take the road to discovering what it is to be truly human without the supernatural and mystical fabrications of the hive virus luring us down the road to cognitive destruction as a species. Sadly, even with the eradication of the virus, with the hands of the elite Aryan controllers on this planet who worked in active collusion of the hive still working toward that hive agenda, humanity is faced with a juggernaut for global control and homogenization that may be unstoppable. The outcome remains to be seen.

# 13. The Great Architect?

The lie that has been foisted on humanity at the instigation of the hive mind was that it was the creator of the universe, the Great Architect of all that is. Just as with all mystical traditions, this was merely another prevarication to seduce ignorant human beings into becoming doctrinaires for its agenda for total domination of the mind of the cosmos, particularly human species everywhere. One thing the hive mind was not short on was ego. But this should come as no surprise as the hive itself was only a replica of the first human mind it infected, and which died, becoming an immortal Xerox copy of that first human personality. There was nothing original about the virus other than how it was manufactured or came into being. As for the virus' primal origin, it is probably as close in age as the beginning of the cosmos. It goes so far back in time that it is incalculable to determine when and where it began, or by whom or what agency it came into being. One thing is certain, it did not create the universe, it was merely another type of predator *within* that creation. It was a near-immortal cancer of the mind in human hosts everywhere, a *predator*, just as don Juan described it, feeding on the human energy field and using us as little more than chickens in a coop, also as don Juan reported about this predatory virus from the stars.

The alleged Great Architect concept must be addressed within these pages for it is only another means through which the hapiym hive bragged about its supremacy over us lowly humans. In part, under *Great Architect of the Universe*, Wikipedia reports:

> *"The Great Architect of the Universe (also Grand Architect of the Universe or Supreme Architect of the Universe) is a conception of God discussed by many Christian theologians and apologists. As a designation* ***it is used within Freemasonry to represent the deity neutrally*** *(in whatever form, and by whatever name each member may individually believe in). It is also a* ***Rosicrucian conception of God****, as expressed by Max Heindel. The concept of* ***the demiurge*** *as a grand architect or a great architect also occurs in* ***gnosticism and other religious and philosophical systems****."*

> *"The Great Architect may also be a metaphor alluding to the godhead potentiality of every individual.* ***"(God)... That invisible power which all know does exist, but understood by many different names, such as God, Spirit, Supreme Being, Intelligence, Mind, Energy, Nature and so forth."*** *In the* ***Hermetic Tradition****, each and every person has the potential to become God,* ***this idea or concept of God is perceived as***

> ***internal rather than external.*** *The Great Architect is also an allusion to the observer created universe. We create our own reality; hence we are the architect. Another way would be to say that the mind is the builder."*
>
> [Bold emphasis mine]

The Gnostic concept of the demiurge is drawn directly from Plato's *Timaeus,* so with the concept of the Great or Grand Architect we come full circle to that hive Oneness consciousness. As these passages illustrate, the hive central command didn't care what it was called in what religion or tradition, even within materialist scientism and its concept of a designed clockwork universe along the line of Newtonian physics seeking to find a Unified Field Theory to explain everything is only a quest for the oneness of all things. It is the theology of the hive wrapped in scientific clothing.

Sir Isaac Newton is considered the primary father of modern science, yet it goes little reported that Newton's interest in alchemy and mysticism greatly outweighed the importance of his theory of gravity, committing almost a million words of text to alchemy and mystical research, substantially more than he devoted to his own scientific discoveries and innovations. Wikipedia confirms this when you look up *Isaac Newton's occult studies*:

> *"English physicist and mathematician Isaac Newton produced many works that would*

*now be classified as occult studies. These works explored chronology, alchemy, and Biblical interpretation (especially of the* ***Apocalypse****). Newton's scientific work may have been of lesser personal importance to him, as he placed emphasis on rediscovering the occult wisdom of the ancients. In this sense, some believe that any reference to a "Newtonian Worldview" as being purely mechanical in nature is somewhat inaccurate.*

*After purchasing and studying Newton's alchemical works, economist John Maynard Keynes, for example, opined in 1942 at the tercentenary of his birth that* ***"Newton was not the first of the age of reason, he was the last of the magicians."*** *In the Early Modern Period of Newton's lifetime, the educated embraced a world view different from that of later centuries. Distinctions between science, superstition, and pseudoscience were still being formulated, and a devoutly Christian biblical perspective permeated Western culture."*

[Bold emphasis mine]

In the present passages, one must be aware that the word Apocalypse does not only connote the end of the world, similar to the biblical context in the book of Revelation, but should be interpreted in the Greek context of seeking visions and/or revelations by having the direct experience of communion with the Divine. Newton worked ceaselessly combing through ancient texts trying to find the 'true religion' which he felt had been corrupted through the ages (*Alchemy and Eschatology: Exploring the Connections between John Dee and Isaac Newton*, Deborah E. Harkness). As a side note, John Maynard Keynes was a member of the British Fabian Society which works to this day in collusion with the Theosophical Society.

Newton was influenced by certain writings of John Dee, one-time astrologer to Queen Elizabeth I, and who himself, working through his associate Edward Kelley, who was a scryer (medium), had communications with who they thought were angels. These channeled communications served as the foundation to create the occult tradition known as Enochian magic, which has been one of the mainstays for occultists for the past few centuries. Dee was thoroughly convinced that these communications were with angels, although he kept most of these channeling sessions private rather than broadcast them too publicly out of fear of being accused of witchery in Elizabethan England.

Communications of this nature have occurred throughout the ages by the hive intelligence and have served to carve the direction for the advancement of humanity in a very specific yet dastardly direction. When we hear the word Creator, most people automatically default to the notion that Creation has already occurred. They view creation in the past tense. They do not perceive that however the universe came into being, that it is not meant to be a static creation, but the biblical story of the creation of everything by the singular God in six days, leaves everyone with the idea that Creation is static. God created it (past tense) so you can't mess with it.

To understand the mindset of the Aryan adepts throughout the ages, one must alter this perspective, particularly where the alleged Great Architect is concerned. The 'creation' is not complete, but is an ongoing enterprise perpetrated by the secret societies, the Fabian Society, the Theosophical Society and occult adepts and priests worldwide. The infectious hapiym hive virus was seeking to subdue the consciousness of all humanity, and its religious and spiritual doctrines about submitting to the Will of God are all testimony to this fact. When we throw communicating with the dead or the presumed angels of the Heavenly Hierarchy into this equation through *gnosis*, or the direct knowing of God through communicating with the Greek *daemons* and *geniuses*; the visions and communications to mystics, mediums and channelers throughout the ages, then the mystery over the ongoing agenda of the hive Grand Architect takes on its more sinister and realistic aspects. It is a work in progress, and that is why it is called The Great Work to these adepts and their globalist agenda.

One of the primary provisions of Renaissance and Hermetic tradition states their agenda clearly, to wit, "*Universal and General Reformation of the whole world*". In light of what has been illustrated thus far in this volume, you have to wonder just exactly what the 'reformation of the whole world' means, and who appointed these reformers to their task?

It has been the intellectual elite throughout the centuries who have spearheaded this ongoing Great Work, as it is referred to in Rosicrucianism, Freemasonry and modern Theosophy. This active interpretation of the hive as the 'Creator', the Great Architect of this designed destruction of human consciousness, is one of the greatest secrets the Aryan adepts and their acolytes have hidden in plain sight for thousands of years. They can refer to the Great Architect of the whole universe knowing full well that the general 'profane' population is going to automatically default to thinking that the Creation is finished, and the Creator stands outside the Creation watching his finished product. The Aryan adepts are fully aware of this default in human thinking and they rely on your misperceptions when they tell you the truth of their agenda with the Great Work and their Great Architect, knowing full well that you do not think in the correct manner to see through their cognitive charade. It is a tyranny hidden in plain view but which the vast majority of people overlook because of their thinking of Creator and Creation in the past tense. Your very ignorance is their greatest ally, and they don't bother explaining the truth of this because they know that humanity would pull them out of their positions of presumed authority and probably lynch the lot of them for their ongoing crimes against humanity in continuing with this agenda.

Spirituality and mystical traditions have been the mask of 'divine love' the hive hid this agenda behind, and the worship of the goddess Ninhursag in all her varied roles is re-emerging in today's culture. The Fabian-created Feminist movement is one of the strongest arenas for promoting this goddess over patriarchal God agenda. We see Temples to the Hindu Goddess Kali being erected in the west with all the same mystical trappings of old about Kali being the goddess of transformation, using the lure of mysticism to draw people into these revived ancient religions of hive filth. The growth of the Neo-Isis cult is part and parcel of this mystical revival, as is the spread of magical occultism. It doesn't matter which agenda people fall for in their pursuits of the supernatural, it is all planned by the hive Grand Architect and the Great Work continues unabated by its proponents worldwide, even in the absence of the hapiym virus and the hive. The psychological mindset that craves the supernatural and the mystical is so deeply ingrained in the human psyche that the planetary intellectual elite are fully aware that they can continue the Great Work to achieve global domination. For in their arrogance, they feel they can achieve it without the virus continually giving them the mystical inside track by using psychological programming instead to compete the Great Work. The only thing that will stop this juggernaut of cognitive tyranny is to shed every belief in the supernatural and assert your humanity over this inhuman virus agenda. If not, you will only remain a slave to these magical and mystical illusions.

To provide substantiation to what I am sharing with all of this, the Wikipedia reference under *Great Work* says this:

In regard to Hermeticism:

*"Eliphas Levi (1810–1875), one of the first modern ceremonial magicians and inspiration for the Hermetic Order of the Golden Dawn, discussed*

*the Great Work at length, expanding it from the purely alchemical towards the more spiritual:*

*Furthermore, there exists in nature a force which is immeasurably more powerful than steam,* ***and by means of which a single man, who knows how to adapt and direct it, might upset and alter the face of the world****. This force was known to the ancients; it consists in a* ***universal agent*** *having equilibrium for its supreme law, while its direction is concerned immediately with the great arcanum of transcendental magic*... **This agent...is precisely that which the adepts of the middle ages denominated the first matter of the Great Work***. The Gnostics represented it as* ***the fiery body of the Holy Spirit****; it was the object of adoration in the* ***secret rites of the Sabbath and the Temple, under the hieroglyphic figure of Baphomet or the Androgyne of Mendes****.*

*He further defined it as such:*

*"****The Great Work*** *is, before all things, the creation of man by himself, that is to say,* ***the full and entire conquest of his faculties*** *and his future; it is especially the perfect* ***emancipation of his will.****""*

In regard to Aliester Crowley's magical school of Thelema:

*"Within Thelema, the Great Work is generally defined as those spiritual practices leading to* ***the mystical union of the Self and the All****. Its founder, author and occultist Aleister Crowley, said of it in his book Magick Without Tears:*

*'The Great Work* ***is the uniting of opposites****. It may mean the* ***uniting of the soul with God****, of the microcosm with the macrocosm,* ***of the female with the male, of the ego with the non-ego****.'*

*For each individual* ***this Great Work may take different forms.*** *Crowley described his own personal Great Work in the introduction to Magick (Book 4):*

*'In my third year at Cambridge, I devoted myself consciously to the Great Work, understanding thereby* ***the Work of becoming a Spiritual Being,*** *free from the constraints, accidents, and deceptions of material existence.'*

*Within the system of the A∴A∴ magical Order the Great Work of the Probationer Grade is considered to be the pursuit of self-knowledge to, as Crowley said in The Confessions of Aleister Crowley, "obtain the knowledge of the nature and powers of my own being." However, Crowley continues, the Great Work should also be something that is integrated into the daily life of all:*

*I insist that in private life men should not admit their passions to be an end, indulging them and so degrading themselves to the level of the other animals, or suppressing them and creating neuroses. I insist that* ***every thought, word and deed should be consciously devoted to the service of the Great Work. 'Whatsoever ye do, whether ye eat or drink, do all to the glory of God'****."*

With the keys to understanding you now have in hand, you know what the concept of God means, what submitting the Will of your human self means, and what this alleged Great Work is seeking to do with humanity, i.e. give up being human, destroy your conscious self, and get in touch with the virus cell within and let it rule your life. This is the allegorical quest for the Holy Grail in romantic literature and the intellectual quest for the Philosopher Stone alluded to in all these hive-oriented mystical traditions.

As I have illustrated, the concept of the Holy Trinity represents the triune nature of Ninhursag's hermaphroditic nature which elevated with her hive virus cell when her form died. Jesus, as her fabricated Son, the Christ, is only a concept that fed the hive collective when it was alive. The quest for the Holy Grail, to find the 'Cup of Christ', was an invitation to turn within oneself and find the living virus cell inside. Once this connection could be made and maintained, then your humanity was gone, you become nothing but an active hive operative working to enslave all of humanity on this planet with concocted hive agendas.

The doctrines appear different because of the filtering systems of the humans who received these visions. If they were indoctrinated with Christianity, the visions were tailored to trick their sensibilities into believing they were angels, as in the case of John Dee, Emmanuel Swedenborg and countless others. If you were an adherent of other religions, your personal human filters were played upon, so the hive would feed your consciousness exactly what it wanted you to know to convince you of its holiness, as with Zarathustra and hosts of others throughout the ages. If you believed in the goddess, it was the goddess who appeared in these visionary states or through channeled communications. If you were a philosopher, then you were presented with the information the hive wanted you to know in terms of mathematics, astronomy or science and these entities were *daemons* or *geniuses* to your awareness. One's own internal waking consciousness set the stage for how these 'miraculous visions' and presumed 'divine communications' were interpreted, and this is why there is no homogenized doctrine presented by the hive beyond the hidden perennial philosophy. Beliefs set the stage for how all these intrusive hive visions and communications were interpreted by each individual. The hive virus knew us better than we knew ourselves. It knew our beliefs and our desires, and it played upon our humanity mercilessly to push forth its agenda of Oneness and cosmic Unity.

Insofar as automatic writing goes, the hive cell within could dictate through the medium of writing if the inner hive cell could gain enough control to transmit data through one in that manner. By controlling the human body, the hive cell within could have us write its mystical nonsense through the receiver. There is no mystery to this and nothing mystical, especially considering that the invasive hapiym virus could also control many aspects of our physiology as well as our subconscious awareness. There is a pragmatic explanation for all these mystical happenings if we can but remove the blinders from our own perception to see the deception taking place to control our species. With the virus hive dead and gone, then these mystical experiences should disappear from the stage of human advancement. That being so, it will not dissuade people from wasting their lives seeking mystical or occult powers or embracing the deceitful beliefs left in the wake of the virus infection. Our species is not yet a human species but is only a reflection of the mentality of the hive itself, until such time as individuals decide to set aside this fascination with the magical and mystical and remove these symptoms from their psyche. These beliefs *are* symptoms of that infection, and that is why this process is not one of 'spiritual growth', but one of psychological deprogramming and transcendence above ages of mystical psychological conditioning and knowing deceit.

The Great Architect is dead, its Great Work will never be finished as it had prefigured. All that is left is for humanity is to transcend this reliance, this *dependency* on the concept of God and Goddess as our metaphysical mommy and daddy, for it is all a contrived psychological dependency syndrome of a victimized human consciousness at the hands of the hapiym virus. It started with the presence of the offworld physical gods and their use of humans as their two-legged cattle, their *man-kine*. From there it progressed more into the metaphysical realm for direct experience and manipulation by the hive, and it really gained impetus when Ninhursag, with all her known abilities and neuroses gladly joined that hive in the sky. The next chapter is going to cover what the motivation is for those Aryan adepts who have been in the know since this shift to the metaphysical started.

# 14. The Making of Prophets

To start this chapter, I must digress into the psychological research of Boris Sidis from his book *The Source and Aim of Human Progress* and discuss some of his revelations on what he discovered and observed about the subconscious mind. What I will assert that Sidis in fact discovered was the nature of the hapiym virus intelligence operating within humanity as its subconscious mind. I am only going to share a few relevant observations to lay the foundation for what follows in regard to the visionary states induced by the hapiym hive collective on the consciousness of certain human hosts infected by the virus.

At first, Sidis speaks about our waking conscious state, which sorts through all the multitudes of stimuli in the world around us to organize and categorize this chaotic influx of perceptions into some order which helps us navigate the world around us. Sidis explains:

> *"The guardian-consciousness wards off, as far as it is possible, the harmful blows given by the stimuli of the external environment. In man, this same guardian consciousness keeps on constructing, by a series of elimination and selection, a new environment, individual and*

*social, which leads to an ever higher and more perfect development and realization of the inner powers of individuality and personality.*"

In contradistinction to this waking state, Sidis then goes on to describe the mind of the subconscious as a separate and distinct, yet indecipherable element from his level of perception. The following explanations provide us with guidance in this understanding:

> "*The upper and lower consciousness form one organic unity,—one conscious, active personality. Under certain abnormal conditions, however, the two systems of nerve-centres with their corresponding mental activities may become dissociated. The superior nerve-centers with their critical, controlling consciousness may become inhibited, split off from the rest of the nervous system. The reflex, automatic, instinctive, subconscious centres with their mental functions are laid bare, thus becoming directly accessible to the stimuli of the outside world; they fall a prey to the influences of external surroundings, influences termed suggestions. The critical, controlling, guardian-consciousness,* ***being cut off and absent, the reduced individuality lacks the rational guidance and orientation, given by the upper choice and will-centres, becomes the helpless***

***plaything of all sorts of suggestions, sinking into the trance states of the subconscious. It is this subconscious that forms the highway of suggestions, suggestibility being its essential characteristic. The subconscious rises to the surface of consciousness, so to say, whenever there is a weakening, paralysis, or inhibition of the upper, controlling will and choice-centres, or in other words, whenever there is a disaggregation of the superior from the inferior nerve-centers, followed by an increase of ideo-sensory, ideo-motor, sensori-secretory, reflex excitability; and ideationally, or rationally by an abnormal intensity and extensity of suggestibility.***"

"***The nature of abnormal suggestibility***, *the result of my investigations given in the same volume*, ***is a disaggregation of consciousness, a cleavage of the mind, a cleft that may become ever deeper and wider, ending in a total disjunction of the waking, guiding, controlling guardian-consciousness from the automatic, reflex, subconscious consciousness***. . . . *Normal suggestibility is of like nature,—it is a cleft in the mind; only here the cleft is not so deep, not so lasting as in hypnosis or in the other subconscious trance states ; the split is here but momentary; the* *mental cleavage, or the psycho-physiological disaggregation of the superior from the inferior centres with their concomitant psychic activities is evanescent, fleeting, often disappearing at the moment of its appearance."*

*"Suggestibility is a function of disaggregation of consciousness, a disaggregation* ***in which the subwaking, reflex consciousness enters into direct communication with the external world."***

*""The problem that interested me most was to come into close contact with the subwaking self. What is its fundamental nature? What are the main traits of its character? Since in hypnosis the subwaking self is freed from its chains, is untrammeled by the shackles of the upper, controlling self, since in hypnosis the underground self is more or less exposed to our view, it is plain that experimentation on the hypnotic self will introduce us into the secret life of the subwaking self; for as we pointed out the two are identical. I have made all kinds of experiments,* ***bringing subjects into catalepsy, somnambulism, giving illusions, hallucinations, post-hypnotic suggestions, etc****. As a result of my work one central*

*truth stands out clear, and that is the extraordinary plasticity of the subwaking self.*

***"If you can only in some way or other succeed in separating the primary controlling consciousness from the lower one, the waking from the subwaking self, so that they should no longer keep company, you can do anything you please with the subwaking self.*** *You can make its legs, its hands, any limb you like, perfectly rigid; you can make it eat pepper for sugar ; you can make it drink water for wine; feel cold or warm ; hear delightful stories in the absence of all sound* ***feel pain or pleasure; see oranges where there is nothing; you can make it eat them and enjoy their taste. In short, you can do with the subwaking self anything you like****. The subwaking consciousness is in your power, like clay in the hands of the potter. The nature of its plasticity is revealed by its extreme suggestibility."*

[Bold emphasis mine]

What needs to be understood from this diversion into psychology is that the hive cell that lived within our species until just a short time ago, was a malleable and separate form of intelligence. It was highly suggestible in weakened states of consciousness, either through hypnosis, artificially induced trance states through psychoactive substances, repeated mantras, drumming and dancing, meditative states and every other tool ever peddled by mystics throughout the ages to shut down their waking awareness, their 'guardian-consciousness', and allow the hive cell to come forth. I will assert that through direct and intentional intervention by the hive collective network that these visionary states could even be produced in certain humans, without warning and without their intentionally seeking these alleged 'divine experiences' in moments of emotional stress or duress. All the hive collective needed to do was choose their target, access the hidden hapiym hive cell within the subject, then produce these visionary states without warning. History is rife with reports of such visionary intrusions 'out of the blue' with some people.

In most cases, however, the human subject of such manipulation often actively sought these experiences, through praying, meditation, drug use or the other practices mentioned above. As Sidis noted in his own research:

> *""I wanted to get an insight into the very nature of the subwaking self; I wished to make a personal acquaintance with it. 'What is its personal character?' I asked. How surprised I was when, after a close interrogation, the answer came to me that there can possibly be no personal acquaintance with it,—**for the subwaking self lacks personality**."*
>
> *Under certain conditions a cleavage may occur between the two selves, and then the subwaking self may rapidly grow, develop, and attain (apparently) the plane of self-consciousness,*

*get crystallized into a person, and give itself a name, imaginary, or borrowed from history. (This accounts for the spiritualistic phenomena of personality, guides, controls, and communications by dead personalities, or spirits coming from another world, such as have been observed in the case of Mrs. Piper and other mediums of like type; it accounts for all the phenomena of multiple personality, simulating the dead or the living, or formed anew out of the matrix of the subconsciousness. All such personality metamorphoses can be easily developed, under favorable conditions, in any psycho-pathological laboratory)."*

[Emphasis in original]

Where Sidis' interpretive failure occurred was in approaching his explanation for these phenomena as simply a product of the human mind, mere illusions of suggestion and suggestibility. Lacking the knowledge of the hapiym hive virus, and the fact that *no* virus cell had any personality whatsoever beyond that of its human host, which it could only mimic, his conclusions could offer no other solution. The failure of the mind sciences in the face of such research was in the assumption that the hapiym virus was a natural part of the human biology. It never was, and that one fatal assumption has led to the mistreatment of multitudes of people at the hands of psychologists and psychiatrists since the profession was started.

Other factors that contributed to such hive collective invasions of human consciousness occurred when an individual was in stress due to illness or through Near Death Experiences (NDEs). Carl Jung himself suffered visions during a bout of serious illness in 1944, and actively sought such visions, even taking a trip to the desert like the Desert Fathers, seeking and beseeching to talk to his 'soul' for 25 days before the hive collective finally answered his yearning, like the Gnostic mystics of old and the Greek philosophers written about previously. Jung was also subject to at least two traumatic visions in 1913 and again in 1914, which he explains in his volume *The Red Book*, which he wrote and kept unpublished and secret until after this death. These visions and his years of study into mystical traditions are what laid the foundation for his metaphysical version of psychology, and which also led to his *Theory of the Collective Unconscious*.

Jung's book *Aion* is a compilation of his own years of study into mythology and mysticism seeking to understand what was, in essence, the metaphysical doctrine of the hive collective and the goddess Ninhursag in her discarnate hive association I have elucidated in this volume. *Aion* has left students of Jung baffled over the decades since it was written because none of them had the code key to deciphering what Jung was writing about in that volume. To be perfectly honest, I was hesitant to read the volume at all because I had seen at least one professor of Psychology say that it was one of the hardest works of Jung to understand, and downright frightening if it were true. Despite my personal hesitancy to pick up the book, I can say with complete honesty that I was startled to find the volume filled with mystical information that I am clarifying in this book. However, Jung could not see through what it all meant. I had very little difficulty understanding what he wrote in that volume in reference to the same subject matter presented in this book, and neither will any other scholar who reads *Aion* in light of the keys to understanding provided in this volume.

Given what I have revealed in this volume thus far about the nature of the hapiym hive collective, the nature of the hierarchal structure within the cosmic planetary hive, and how the hive cells on this planet were instinctually geared to establish that communion with the overall hive collective, I am going to share some passages from the extensive writings of one of the most noteworthy of Christian mystics from the Age of Reason, Emmanuel Swedenborg from his *Spiritual Diary* published in 1758. Within these passages you are going to see the verifying truth that I have shared in this volume about the nature of the hive cell that existed within humans, and the hive collective's agenda to 'bring Heaven down on Earth'. With the keys to understanding that I have provided in hand, as well as focusing on the highlighted passages below, this picture should become infinitely clearer.

> *"CONCERNING THE INHABITANTS OF THE EARTH MARS Spirits appeared in front to the left, who were said to be from the earth Mars, and who declared themselves to be holy; not that they were holy [in themselves], but the Lord, who is the Only Good, is their holiness.*

*As to the life of the inhabitants of that earth, I heard that they live in societies, but not under governments, the societies being such that they perceive immediately from the face, eyes, and speech, thus externally, whether they are among true associates,* ***whom they thus recognize, and to whom they adjoin themselves, <u>so as out of many to make one</u>. In this manner they know how to choose such companions for themselves as are congenial in temper and thought****, in which they are very rarely deceived; they become friends forthwith; yet they feel no aversion to others, as no such feeling as aversion or hatred exists among them,* ***but conjunction*** *according to states of mind, and by means of external things."*

*"Being in vision I spoke with spirits, of whom some said they wished to have me in their company. Accordingly, after some little delay* ***I was in consort with genii or celestial spirits****, and I then disappeared from the spiritual with whom I had previously been. These, not knowing whither I had withdrawn, sought me, saying that they knew not where I was. I was in fact in company with the* ***genii****, and while in that state they [the spiritual] seemed to disappear, although I was near by, and*

*heard them speaking, and seeking me."* *(March 19, 1748)*

*"THAT FALSITIES HYPOTHETICALLY ASSUMED ARE SOMETIMES CONFIRMED TO SUCH A DEGREE THAT THOSE WHO DO IT DO NOT KNOW WHAT THE TRUTH IS, AND THUS* ***ARE UNWILLING TO KNOW****. Let one fact be taken for an example. Spirits partly erring and partly malignant assumed a hypothetical position, viz.* ***the falsity that a spirit could enter into the body of a man, and thus live corporeally. This they were prompted to affirm solely from the fact that <u>a spirit with man thinks that he is the man.</u> But when I asserted that such was not the case they were unwilling to pay any attention to the reasons [which I adduced], for having once assumed in theory the falsity, they were intent upon confirming it; when the fact is, that as the spirit then thinks, apprehends, and wills in like manner with the man, and the appropriate acts follow, <u>the spirit therefore supposes that he is the man</u>****. But this does not last long; it only holds in those states [of the parties] which are analogous.*

*Moreover,* ***that a spirit should be able to pass into the body of another, and live in that body****, is at once absurd and impossible, for the* *consequence would be that the form of one would be changed into that of another,* ***the interior substances of the man would be entirely emptied out, and the substances of another applied, in their stead, to the fibers and vessels, while at the same time all that which had contracted a nature in the [life of] the body and been wrought into obedience to its proper form, would be assumed.*** *" March 20, 1748)*

*THAT THE PRIVILEGE OF CONVERSING WITH SPIRITS AND ANGELS MIGHT BE COMMON AND APPROPRIATE TO MAN.* ***Man was so created that he might hold interaction with spirits and angels, and thus heaven and earth be conjoined. Such was the case in the Most Ancient Church, such in the Ancient, and in the Primitive also there was a perception of the Holy Spirit. Such was the case with the inhabitants of other earths,*** *concerning which I have spoken before; for man is man because he is a spirit, with this only difference, that the spirit of man on the earth is encompassed with a body on account of its functions in the world. That heaven and earth are now separated, as respects our planet, arises from the fact that the human race has here, in the process of time, passed from internals to externals. - 1748, March 20.*

***THAT CERTAIN ONES IN HEAVEN CALL THIS EARTH A PUTRID WELL***. *When discoursing concerning a plurality of worlds, and [suggesting] that the inhabitants of this earth were too few to constitute the universal kingdom of the Lord, I perceived that this earth was called a well of stagnant water.-1748, March 20.*

***HE THAT IS LED BY THE LORD IS BLAMELESS. (A man although foul and polluted with defilements, yet while led by the Lord is exempt from blame; for whatever of truth and good he thinks, speaks, and acts is of the Lord, and whatever of false and evil of the devil, for man then knows that he does nothing of himself***. *- 1745, March 20.*

*"I said to them when they would fain have* ***induced their genius [upon me]***, *that it was sufficient to know what the Lord taught, to wit, that* ***He was One; that he who sees the Son sees the Father; that the Son alone is the door; that He is the way; that He is the mediation or Mediator; that He alone is the intercession or intercessor between the human race and the Father Himself; and again, that He is our Father***, *and that no other is to be thought of than He, because He alone*

*is the Mediation; that these things are sufficient, and that it is useless to go deeper into mysteries. - 1748 March 21.*

In the last passages, the 'Son' referred to is a double entendre. On one hand it is an allusion to Jesus (Ninhursag) the Son, and the subtler allusion refers to the hive cell within as the 'doorway' that serves as the mediator or intercessor to the 'God' of the hive collective, the Divine Oneness. I also ask the reader to take note of the passage where the hive considers Earth (and humanity) as putrid vessels for its alleged divine nature. In every mystical tradition our very humanity is disparaged, and we are only considered filth to the parasitic hive cell that lived within us.

Pay further attention to the passage that if one is working for the hive 'Lord', that their evil deeds are sanctified, and the individual is 'blameless' in serving this Lord, regardless of their personal perfidy in serving the hive collectivist agenda. This aspect will have keener relevance as we continue to expose the overall plan the hive had for our species through its Aryan agents over the ages, had it succeeded.

The underlined passage about the hive being present on other planets should be taken literally, for the hive collective was cosmic in scope. It was not just a local Earth plague, the hapiym virus has spread throughout the cosmos.

The most telling passage, also underlined, is the truth being told about how the 'spirit' moves in and thinks is the man. The hive cell in and of itself had no personality. For all intents and purposes, it was a blank Memorex tape that recorded everything about its human host, up to and including knowing how to manipulate our physiology so long as we were alive with the hive cell living within us. Through these communications with Swedenborg, we are being told the straight up truth about the hive cells, but Swedenborg challenged the truth he was told because it didn't fit his personal belief paradigm. He filtered out the truth being told in favor of his own human perceptions, thereby denying what he was told, however accurate it may be. As to its similarity to reincarnation, that will be covered in a later chapter.

Although Swedenborg didn't create any new religion, and his work was marginalized by many of his contemporaries, the influence of his writings in mystical and Hermetic circles since he had his visions has been very profound. I can't say with surety how his writings may have influenced the religion makers, the modern day 'prophets', but the hive ideology plays the same tune from Hinduism into modern New Ageism, from the Protestant Revolution to more modern offshoot religions like Mormonism, 7th Day Adventism, Unitarianism and others. Many of these religions were spawned by visions produced by the hive no different than those received by Mohammed, Ignatius Loyola, William Miller, Joseph Smith and loads of Christian mystics in the West as alluded to previously. The hive collective has been very busy seeking to manage the affairs of our species through lies, misdirection, false promises of an afterlife that no human was ever going to attain, and continual attempts of homogenized collectivist experiments on this planet including every religion through and including Marxism.

Another aspect of this virus in connection to Swedenborg's visionary communication stating that those who work for the 'Lord' are blameless, regardless of their actions, one should take note of Boris Sidis' observations in reference to the mind of the subwaking self, presented in his book *The Source and Aim of Human Progress*, because it is highly relevant to this discussion. Sidis explains:

> *“"The subwaking self dresses to fashion, gossips in company, runs riot in business-panics, revels in the crowd, storms in the mob, parades on the streets, drills in the camp, and prays in revival meetings. Its senses are acute, but its sense is nil.* ***Association by contiguity****, the automatic, reflex mental mechanism of the brute, is the only one it possesses.*
>
> ***"The subwaking self lacks all personality and individuality****; it is absolutely servile.* ***It has no moral law, no law at all****. To be a law unto one-self, the chief and essential characteristic of personality, is the very trait the subwaking self so glaringly lacks.*
>
> ***"The subwaking self has no will****; it is blown hither and thither by all sorts of incoming suggestions.* ***It is essentially a brutal self****. "The primary self alone possesses true personality, will, and self-control. The primary self alone is a law unto itself,—a personality having the power of*

*investigating its own nature, of discovering faults, creating ideals, striving after them, struggling for them, and by continuous efforts of will attaining to higher and higher stages of personality."*"

[Emphasis in original]

As I have explained in detail in my previous works, the hapiym virus infected its human hosts as a *tabula rasa*, a blank slate, upon which the personality of its human host imprinted the hive cell as a form of data recorder, thereby producing a personality *doppelganger*. This virus cell was not you, but its actions made you believe it was you through the beliefs you embraced and which it amplified through a form of cognitive chicanery. The virus hid itself from the awareness of its human host, and don Juan stated that this 'predator' had to stay hidden because of its own constant fear of being discovered. Be that as it may, the tyranny exhibited by the virus collective itself to deceive and delude humanity into buying into its myth of the afterlife has misdirected humanity for untold generations. Throughout this entire process of seeking the afterlife or our alleged perceptions about communion with God, or receiving supernatural occult powers, our species has forsaken its humanity to chase the pipe dream promises of the seemingly immortal hive believing it to be the maker of the universe, the One Cosmic Source, or God.

The thing that must be emphasized above all in reference to the hive collective is that its intelligence was nothing more than the stolen recorded knowledge of every human that ever lived. The alleged 'ancient wisdom' was stolen knowledge at best, and it must also be strongly emphasized that there is no Heaven and Hell as people perceive these concepts. Every human that ever lived had their consciousness elevate to the offworld hive collective upon the death of its human host. These recorded hive personalities include Attila the Hun, Genghis Khan, Adolph Hitler, Lenin, Stalin and Mao Tse Tung, along with every Saint or Holy Man. When we can accept this true nature of the hapiym virus cells, as difficult as this realization is to face, then we can finally start to grasp the tyranny represented by the hive and why the hive's claim that anyone working for the 'Lord' is blameless. This realization reveals one of the most shocking secrets hidden behind all these mystical traditions that leaves one's mind reeling at the massive level of deception perpetrated against our species.

This tradition of the alleged 'divine spark' in Greek religion can be traced back to the mythical Orpheus and the religion of Orphism, which celebrated the resurrection of the god Dionysus, one of the 'Son' personalities fabricated by Ninhursag. Within the Orphic tradition, the human soul was believed to be divine and immortal. Orphism, like many of the Greek Philosophical schools, was another mystery religion. The Orphic cult revered the goddess Persephone, and I will leave it to you to figure out who Persephone represented. It shouldn't be that hard to put together at this juncture.

Within the Orphic tradition, from fragmentary evidence found on gold plates, directions for how to pass through the underworld unharmed have been pieced together and translated into English by Claude Calame of Harvard University. The funerary poem is a set of instructions provided to the initiates of the mystery cult of Orpheus, who the poem refers to as the "*mystai* and *bacchoi*". The dead initiate is given directions to find a white (or shining) cypress and to drink from the "lake of Mnemosyne", the goddess of memory. "Guardians" protect this lake from the uninitiated and only through answering questions correctly is one given safe passage to the afterlife. Much of this Orphic tradition has been transmitted into modern Mormonism through the visions of Joseph Smith, the religion's founder, who also received his religious ideology from an alleged 'angel' named Moroni.

The Orphic initiate's ritual journey through the underworld very closely mirrors a similar set of tests presented in the *Tibetan Book of the Dead*, the *Bardo Thodol*. I suggested in my previous works that the Tibetan land of the Bardo is in fact representative of the hive collective cluster, and the ritual of the dead in the *Bardo Thodol* was to ensure that the hive cell exiting its human host retained its memory in the hive afterlife. The focus on the 'Lake of Mnemosyne' in the Orphic text illustrates a thread of consistency between these initiates and their death rites in comparison with the *Tibetan Book of the Dead*. This need of memory will be covered in depth in a later chapter.

In the Orphic ritual, the initiate was supposed to answer as to why he was wandering around in the underworld by the 'Guardians', to reply that he was "a son of Earth and the starry Heavens", and once their thirst was quenched from the drinking from the Lake of Mnemosyne, then they would be safely guided to the realm of the "*mystai* and *bacchoi*". If we remove all the mystical connotations from these death rituals and view these 'tests' as a manner for discriminating between the initiates into the varied mysteries, whether Tibetan, Orphic, Greek philosophical, Zoroaster's version of Hell as a testing ground, or any other mystical tradition that mirrors them, then we are confronted with the fact that the hive collective was very prejudicial in its suitability selection process for the afterlife. Given the hierarchal nature of the hapiym collective, this should really come as no surprise, particularly since it curried the minds of the intellectuals to form its own elite 'angelic' cadre of manipulators of humanity.

Just so the reader knows that such death rituals to help transition the hive cells into the afterlife did not escape the Christian practices of the Roman Church, Wikipedia provides us this information on the *Viaticum*:

> *"Viaticum is a term used especially in the Catholic Church for the Eucharist (also called* ***Holy Communion****) administered, with or without Anointing of the Sick (also called Extreme Unction),* ***to a person who is dying****, and is thus a part of the Last Rites. According to Cardinal Javier Lozano Barragán, "The Catholic tradition of giving the Eucharist to the dying* ***ensures that instead of dying alone they die with Christ who promises them eternal life****."*

> *"The word viaticum is a Latin word meaning "***provision for a journey***," from via, or "way". For Communion as Viaticum, the Eucharist is given in the usual form, with the added words*

***"May the Lord Jesus Christ protect you and lead you to eternal life"****. The Eucharist is seen as the ideal spiritual food to strengthen a dying person for the journey from this world to life after death."*

[Bold emphasis mine].

When we can shed ourselves of the illusion of Christ the man and see the Christ concept as the trinitarian hermaphrodite Ninhursag, the triune goddess, the transmitter of the Three to the 'One' of the hive, then the Catholic ritual of Viaticum is no different than the Orphic journey to the Underworld to transition the hive cell to the afterlife, or the Tibetan Buddhist ritual journey in the *Bardo Thodol*. It is just another hidden aspect to send the internal hapiym virus cell on its journey to join the eternal cosmic hive. In keeping with the Great Work agenda of the hive to Reform the Whole World, Wikipedia reports:

*"N.T. Wright argues that "God's plan is not to abandon this world... Rather,* ***he intends to remake it. And when he does, he will raise all people to new bodily life to live in it.*** *That is the promise of the Christian gospel"*

[Bold emphasis mine]

This promise by the God in the Bible to 'remake the world' is no different than the Hermetic belief in their One God to Reform the Whole World and the Great Work, or as it is known in esoteric circles, the *Magnum Opus*. The superficial trappings of the doctrine may appear different in exoteric traditional interpretation, but the esoteric meaning to the initiates in the know is no different, and this includes religious priests throughout the ages.

The greatest mystics over the ages have been the intellectuals, and philosophy has been their mainstay for promoting these ideas. In more ancient eras these intellectuals were the priests of the gods. The hive sought out and preyed on human intelligence, for the only way it could increase its own collective knowledge was through what the individual infectious hive cells could steal and record from their human hosts. For an avaricious mind virus with a serious hankering for conquering the universe, intelligence is what attracted it most. It is this stolen human intelligence, built into a cosmic hierarchy of replicated human intelligence, that constitute the alleged 'Ancient Wisdom' that all the hive doctrines profess to possess in one form or another.

Because of a form of, let's call it sympathetic resonance, the overall hive collective intelligence could tap into any human consciousness through the agent of the infectious hive cell within that person to produce these visionary states and thereby pipe down their doctrines through the hive cell to the human recipient of this fraud, believing that they were talking with God, angels or their 'soul'. This is exactly the case with Carl Jung and his catalogued experiences in *The Red Book*. In Jung's case, in his 1913 and 1914 visions, they were terrifying allegorical visions that Jung later translated to mean the forecast of WW I. These terrifying visions had a very profound effect on Jung's psyche and set the framework for his later theories in Psychology.

For the reader's greater understanding, I am going to share a personal experience with this kind of intrusion of consciousness. I have stated categorically that in most cases, certain conditions have to be met to lower the cognitive threshold of the affected individual, and I will discuss this now. In my younger days I did a lot of LSD in recreational drug use. I never used the substance for anything other than getting stoned. In all honesty, LSD never delivered the grand hallucinations to me that it did with others, and any hallucinatory aspects I did experience were extremely minimal. To be brutally honest, I felt cheated that LSD never delivered these 'trip' experiences that my friends all seemed to experience while doing the drug. I also did STP a couple of times, which was allegedly 10 time stronger than LSD, with the same lack of results. The same can be said of my experiences with psilocybin mushrooms. All I ever got out of these multiple experiences was the head-stone feeling that comes with the drugs.

Although I was raised in the Christian tradition, I don't count myself as ever having been very religious, and I didn't darken a church door from the age of 17 onward for the sake of worship. I didn't have any 'hunger' to know God. One night in the early 1970's I was doing an acid trip when out of the blue I got this heart-swelling emotion of love hit me, and a voice that wasn't a voice telling me that God loved me. You must understand that I was simply minding my own business and enjoying being stoned when this cognitive invasion occurred unbidden. What resulted as a matter of this intrusion into my psyche could be called the classic ecstatic experience, resulting in tears and being highly emotional to me at the time. Fortunately, after the fact, I chalked it up to just being a really weird acid trip, but I never forgot the overall experience, although the details of every instant of it are lacking in my memory. So, when I write about these invasive experiences, I am classifying them from the standpoint of having been subjected to one of them personally. I am not an outsider looking in trying to explain something I have not experienced myself.

I tell this story to illustrate the fact that one does not have to be actively pursuing God or the Divine for the hive to have intruded unbidden into one's consciousness. All it took was my waking state to be compromised by the LSD to open the door to this kind of cognitive chicanery.

Any kind of cognitive stress can lay the platform for this type of invasion. I have an acquaintance who had a similar experience after beseeching and fervently praying, seeking to know God. The stress of his yearning set the stage for the invasive hive collective to deliver him what he thought he was seeking. What the reader must understand about this process, particularly any psychologist seeking to understand these experiences, is that it is not just the desire that sets the stage for these types of cognitive invasion.

Millions of people over the ages have sought such experiences with nothing to show for their efforts. In the modern New Age arena, millions desire the mystical experience and are paying high fees for ayahuasca retreats and taking DMT seeking this alleged communion with the Divine and getting nothing in return for their time and energy, no matter how much they may desire the experience. For these hive-induced 'epiphanies' to occur requires a certain psychological mindset to set the stage for the invasion of consciousness. One must be in a self-induced state of mental distress or exhibiting a willingness to be subservient to the will of God to the point that they are willing to do anything to 'know God' before the hive collective could override the waking state of awareness. Without this psychological stress element, regardless of the simple desire to experience 'something cool' like a mystical occurrence, the stage isn't set for the intrusion to take place. One must be cognitively willing to 'give themselves up to God' or the Goddess in a fervent and stressful state before these things could take place. Once again this illustrates the compromise of the waking state required for these visions or encounters to take place. The hive capitalized on preying on us when we were at our weakest and our waking state was compromised or under psychological duress in some manner so the virus cell within could activate and create the experience with the overall hive collective.

This explains why these experiences are always related to occurrences after serious and almost fanatic religious devotion during revivals, when our waking state is compromised with certain psychoactive substances, serious illness, trance states induced by whatever means, and NDEs. It is a rare occasion indeed where one who is in control of their mental faculties could be preyed upon in this manner, and make no mistake, the hapiym hive collective was a predator *par excellence*. Any kind of psychological stress could produce the atmosphere for the hive collective to intrude into one's mind, and this is the factor that the field of Psychology has never figured out because it refused to investigate it except in the most materialist close-mindedness.

In the case of these mystical experiences throughout the ages, they leave a lasting impression on the one receiving these hive intrusions. You *never* forget the experience. In the case of religious zealots, the visionary experience where one firmly believes that they are talking with angels, and can establish a running relationship with the hive, as in the case with Swedenborg, then multiple volumes of hive mystical swill can be published to lure the public down the road to false mysticism. The Greek philosophers and their *daemons* and *geniuses* are indicative, at least to this author, of ongoing relationships with the hive to shape their doctrines and teachings, and this includes their genius in mathematics, rhetoric, grammar, geometry, astronomy and the other elements of Greek Classical education. All of these pursuits that transitioned into materialist science had their origins in seeking to figure out and define the Divine essence of Plato's Monad. Daemons, geniuses, angels, one's 'soul', the Gods and Goddesses, its all the same hive deception and the only thing that makes them seem different is the interpretive filters of the individual human mind being screwed with relating the experiences.

If one believes in God or angels, then the hive presented itself in that acceptable format. If one believed in occultism and dark magic, then the hive would present its doctrines in that manner, as it did with Aleister Crowley and his creation of the magical religion of Thelema. The hive didn't care what shape its doctrines took in the human psyche or how the cognitive filtering system of the individual human interpreted the data, the consistent tenets of the hive doctrine threaded through all these traditions, from Greek philosophy, Egyptian religion, Zoroastrianism, Hinduism, Christianity, Hermeticism and finally into Theosophy which is a blend of Fabian Marxism and all these foregoing mystical traditions passed down through Neoplatonism. In the modern arena of channeling, you can include in the foregoig list alleged Ascended Masters of the Theosophical variety as well as Aliens from whatever star system they want to lie about and claim to originate from. The ultimate aim of the game was to consolidate all these disparate seeming traditions into a homogenous whole of perception, blending Marxist collectivism with fake hive collectivist spirituality and mysticism to bring about the hive's design for a human new world order, over which would sit the angels and Ascended Masters of the hive to direct and control all of humanity forever. As crazy and science fiction as this may sound, all the evidence collected together creates this picture where the Hermeticists called for the "Reformation of the Whole World". I challenge the reader to give me any other logical explanation to refute where the evidence points in this regard without simple denial because the idea makes one very cognitively uncomfortable.

Once one experienced this profound Love jolt to the heart, (as I did during my own personal experience with the hive collective masquerading as God), artificially manipulated by the virus cell that lived inside us, they were sold American on whatever doctrinal bullshit the hive collective wanted to spew out to push forth its agenda if they remained convinced that the experience was what it presented itself to be. The emotional stimulation could not be denied, and if one was more susceptible than I was, these devotees very often turned into hive doctrinaires and religion makers, spreading the mystical hive poison as far as it could reach. Carl Jung's brand of mystical psychology is the hive's intrusion into the mostly materialist-oriented field of Psychology. His own writings betray his fascination with the mystical and any psychologist that relies on Jungian translations needs to see and understand what is at the root of his psychological theories. Jung's psychology was the hive's attempt to move its mysticism onto the therapist's couch to spread its poison that much farther. The recent development of Transpersonal Psychology and 'Spiritual Psychology' is only a continuation of the same hidden hive mystical agenda.

What I have elucidated is how prophets for the hive doctrines throughout the ages became the converts they were and why they pushed the religions they created at the direction of the hive collective itself. They were stone cold believers based on these experiences and the internal hive virus cell was intimately aware of what lie would sell to their particular human host. Humanity has merely been the tool of this subversive, collectivist tyranny by a space-borne mind virus, and it is past time that we rid ourselves of this cognitive poison and our fascination with the mystical false promises of the hive collective. It's time we claim our humanity and stop chasing mystical supernatural rainbows and promises that will never and have never applied to us as human beings. All that was being indoctrinated was the hive cell predator that lived within us. These hive cells, in all these mystery school and religious doctrines, were the 'living', and any human who did not give way to the internal hive infection was considered the 'dead'.

All the so-called prophets throughout the ages have been hive collective Pied Pipers, enticing and luring humanity down the road to its own destruction at the hands of this predatory virus. As uncomfortable as this makes us feel on a psychological level to admit these facts, choosing to ignore them is even more fatal to one's consciousness, for the habits left behind by the virus still control our minds and our cultures. To continue onward in the face of this only leaves the virus ruling our consciousness from its grave and will continue to deprive us of our very humanity. We will remain as changeless as the hive virus itself, simply repeating the same errors from the ingrained habits of the virus that still lie resident in our psyche and our body. The only way forward to find our humanity is to rid ourselves of this virus symptomatology and finally advance ourselves as a species and discover what we may truly become.

# 15. The Philosopher's Stone

To launch this chapter, we need to look at the word Alchemy and get a little information under our belt in regard to its meaning for those readers who may be unfamiliar with the term. Wikipedia informs us in part as follows:

> *"Alchemy is a philosophical and protoscientific tradition practiced throughout Europe, Africa and Asia. It aimed to* ***purify, mature, and perfect certain objects****. Common aims were chrysopoeia, the transmutation of "base metals" (e.g., lead) into "noble metals" (particularly gold); the creation of* ***an elixir of immortality;*** *the creation of panaceas able to cure any disease; and the development of an alkahest, a universal solvent.* ***The perfection of the human body and soul was thought to permit or result from the alchemical magnum opus*** *and, in the Hellenistic and western tradition, the achievement of* ***gnosis.*** *In Europe, the creation of a* ***philosopher's stone*** *was variously connected with all of these projects.*

*In English, the term is often limited to descriptions of European alchemy, but similar practices existed in the Far East, the Indian subcontinent, and the Muslim world. In Europe, following the 12th-century Renaissance produced by the translation of Islamic works on science and the Recovery of Aristotle, alchemists played a significant role in early modern science (particularly chemistry and medicine). Islamic and European alchemists developed a structure of basic laboratory techniques, theory, terminology, and experimental method, some of which are still in use today. However, they continued antiquity's belief in four elements and* ***guarded their work in secrecy including cyphers and cryptic symbolism. Their work was guided by Hermetic principles related to magic, mythology, and religion****"*

[Bold emphasis mine]

Just as the practice of modern Psychology finds its roots in mystical studies, as I reported in my book, *The Psychology of Becoming Human: Evolving Beyond Psychological Conditioning*, the birth of modern materialist science equally has its origins in mysticism and magic. Naturally, science would rather overlook these ignominious origins of its profession, but the truth is what it is, and it goes all the way back to ancient priesthoods studying the stars, reading omens in sheep's livers, prophesying by Oracles like Pythia at Delphi, or the seven classical subjects from Greek philosophical studies. No matter how much our materialist-oriented scholars want to whitewash the origins of modern sciences, they all have their foundation firmly laid in mysticism, magic and ancient religions.

I have not yet figured out exactly what the hive objective was in setting our species on the trail of scientific investigation through alchemy, what we know as chemistry today, but the lure of a formula that can turn lead into gold was enough to spark a greed factor in human beings to find this secret formula to make themselves rich. Kings throughout Europe sought out alchemists who they thought possessed the secret of the Philosopher's Stone with an eye to enrich their kingly larders with easy gold. The British Alchemist and mathematician and astrologer to Queen Elizabeth I once sold his services to the King of Prague in a quest to produce the Philosopher's Stone and create gold out of lead – unsuccessfully, of course.

I will suggest that the greed factor chasing this mysterious chemical solution was simply a ruse by the hive to spark humanity's advancement into the sciences. Despite the initial lure of wealth and the experimentation with chemistry and medicine, however, the real meaning of the Philosopher's Stone lay hidden in esoteric traditions and it had everything to do with hive manipulation, which I will prove and clarify in this chapter.

The mysterious Philosopher's Stone is an allegorical reference to the hive virus cell that resided inside is human hosts. The alchemical process of allegedly turning lead into gold was a hidden reference to overcoming one's human waking consciousness and learning how to find and connect with the hive cell within, thus the seeking of turning human 'lead' into the gold of the hive cell buried within. In modern occult and spiritual traditions this allegory is widely known and pursued in the belief that this spiritual alchemical process will make one more 'spiritual' or enlightened. This is the hidden meaning behind the superficial spiritual quest for the alleged Philosopher's Stone. No one was ever going to find their infinite soul as they perceive a soul to be but would only be connecting to the fraudulent virus cell living within them believing it to be their 'soul'. Thousands of generations of humanity have been deceived by this process of turning their human lead into virus gold, and it is far past the time that our species stops being deceived by these false teachings about striking spiritual gold and gaining supernatural powers or communing with the cosmic Oneness, Source or God.

In Carl Jung's book, *Aion*, he presents a tireless amount of research trying to solve the mysteries for which I am providing the key to understand in this volume. In his research he laid out all the connections with the fish in these allegorical stories, and how the fish, and or serpent or dragon, are associated with what is referred to as the *anima mundi*, or world soul. This world soul is referred to as a tripartite Father, Mother, Son representation of the Christian Trinity, above which sits the overarching consciousness of the hive soul, or eternal fire. Christ (not the man) is the *anima mundi*, and it bears every indicator of it being Ninhursag in her role as Hermaphroditus, the combined male and female that permeates all these doctrines telling people that they must unite the divine masculine with the divine feminine. With this key to unravel the code, then we are in a better position to understand the

Theosophical Society's dogma about the alleged Christ Consciousness, which has also permeated the New Age arena. It is not about the man Immanuel or what he tried to teach humanity, it is about the hive collective consciousness and the doorway through Ninhursag's triune personality that one must pass to find their own inner Philosopher's Stone and find communion with the hapiym virus hive. Without this key to understanding and deciphering these 'mysteries', when people read the Hermetic texts they can only come away confused and scratching their heads over what it all means. As an example, what follows was written by Johann Rosinus, most likely from his one volume of work, *Antiquitatum romanarum corpus absolutissimum* published in 1585:

> *"**This stone** is something which is **fixed more in thee [than elsewhere], created of God, and thou art its ore, and it is extracted from thee**, and wheresoever thou art it remains inseparably with thee. . . . And as man is made up of four elements, **so also is the stone**, and **so it is [dug] out of man, and thou art its ore, namely by working; and from thee it is extracted, that is by division; and in thee it remains inseparably**, namely by knowledge. [To express it] otherwise, **fixed in thee**: namely in **the Mercurius** of the wise; **thou art its ore: that is, it is enclosed in thee and thou holdest it secretly;** and from thee it is extracted when it is reduced [to its essence] by thee and*

*dissolved; for without thee it cannot be fulfilled, and without it canst thou not live, and so the end looks to the beginning, and contrariwise."*

[Bold emphasis mine]

With this passage we see all the elements present that I have deciphered on the reader's behalf. The statement that this Stone lies within us removes any possibility that it is some type of external stone, even though too many people have sought the Philosopher's Stone as a physical substance or a literal stone. As the passage states, this Stone was created by God (interpret that to mean the cosmic virus vector), and that 'thou art its ore', which is another cheapening allusion to you only being the ore to the alleged perfected stone of the virus cell within you. "The Mercurius of the wise" is a direct reference to Venus, another aspect of Ninhursag worshipped in Rome s the goddess of Love. So here again we find a veiled reference to the goddess in association with the hive hiding behind the mask of God. This passage states tacitly that this stone lies hidden within you, and once more we are confronted with the hidden hapiym virus cell lying internally beyond our waking awareness.

For a secondary perspective from another Hermeticist, Gerhard Dorn, we get some of the following information from his work, *Speculativae philosophiae*:

"***Learn from within thyself to know all that is in heaven and on earth, that thou mayest be wise in all things.*** *Knowest thou not that heaven* *and the elements were formerly one, and were separated by a divine act of creation from one another, that they might bring forth thee and all things?"*

[Bold emphasis mine]

Carl Jung relied upon and studied Dorn very heavily and even carried Dorn's works with him on a trip to India in 1928. Much of Jung's research in *Aion* is based on Dorn's writings and other esoteric writers and Christian mystics and provides a wealth of information in matters that are being discussed in this volume. After reading this volume and my revelations in the *We Are Not Alone - Parts 1-3* books, then a goodly portion of what Jung was seeking to understand in composing *Aion* will become clear by an order of magnitude.

What should be patently obvious at this point is that the Philosopher's Stone is a veiled reference to the hapiym virus cell that lived inside us until very recently, and that the process of changing lead into gold was an allegory of giving up one's own humanity in favor of a communion with the hive collective intelligence. The latter part of Dorn's claim in the passage above, to me, is merely misunderstanding or misdirection provided by the hive singularity as being the creator of the universe. You will see this specious claim in other similar religious and mystical doctrines around the planet. The hive intelligence did not create all that is where the universe its concerned, it is a bald face lie that the hive told foolish humans who were not informed enough to challenge the lie. We have been so wrapped up in seeking the beginning of everything and the fascination with some mystical higher power or force in the universe to question such claims and challenge them. This is the major reason humanity keeps falling for this spiritual braggadocio and its high time we shake this addiction from our minds.

The claim in the passage by Dorn that it was "formerly One but has been separated" is a direct allusion to the splitting of the hive virus into the individual cells that infected humanity. Through this willful act of the hive collective, then the virus cells that lived within individuals had an instinctual crave to reconnect with its 'maker'. There is no mystery here when we can see the virus as the driving element in all these mystical traditions.

To support my assertions in the last chapter about how one who is prone to devotion after a hive cell intrusion or inner cell activation when we are under states of mental stress, the 7th-8th century author Morienus Romanus wrote:

> *"This thing is extracted from thee, for thou art its ore; in thee they find it, and, to speak more plainly, from thee they take it; and* ***when thou hast experienced this, the love and desire for it will be increased in thee****."*
>
> [Bold emphasis mine]

The spark that ignites this desire was the artificial stimulation of the emotional center of the heart with a powerful feeling of Love. This is why we find Love at the center of all these doctrines, and I will discuss this Love aspect in greater detail in a later chapter as it is integral to the spreading of the virus when the hive was alive. There is nary a writer in religion or mystical esoteric traditions that didn't fall back on this Love card, to wit, the Love of Jesus, the Love of God, the Love of the Goddess, etc. Love permeates all these doctrines and when you couple the Love fascination with the Eternal Flame of Zoroastrianism, then you arrive at the modern spiritual mantras about Love and Light.

There are those who try to refute the association with ancient Egyptian religion with these Hermetic traditions, but the Pharaoh Akhenaten offers us *prima facie* evidence that the belief in the One True God of the Light was present in his religion of Aten. From the *Great Hymn to Aten* look-up on Wikipedia, we find some of the last passages to Ahkenaten's *Great Hymn* to the solar disc:

> *You are in my heart,*
> *There is no other who knows you,*
> *Only your son, Neferkheprure, Sole-one-of-Re [Akhenaten],*
> *Whom you have taught your ways and your might.*
> *[Those on] earth come from your hand as you made them.*
> *When you have dawned they live.*
> *When you set they die;*
> *You yourself are lifetime, one lives by you.*
> *All eyes are on [your] beauty until you set.*
> *All labor ceases when you rest in the west;*
> *When you rise you stir [everyone] for the King,*

*Every leg is on the move since you founded the earth.*
*You rouse them for your son who came from your body.*
*The King who lives by Maat, the Lord of the Two Lands,*
*Neferkheprure, Sole-one-of-Re,*
*The Son of Re who lives by Maat. the Lord of crowns,*
*Akhenaten, great in his lifetime;*
*(And) the great Queen whom he loves, the Lady of the Two Lands,*
*Nefer-nefru-Aten Nefertiti, living forever.*

There is no point in highlighting this passage with the information you now have in hand. All of the elements are apparent of the hive manipulation, the reference to the Love of the solar fire in Akhenaten's heart, the firm belief that it is solely his responsibility to bring this new religion about the One god to the world, the association with Re (Ninhursag), and the solar affiliation with the Eternal Flame of Zoroastrianism.

The carvings that survive of Akhenaten worshipping the one God as the solar disc has the sun's rays coming down, the end of which each have hands on them. Scholars are confused about the significance of the hands at the end of the rays, but I will suggest that the hands allegorically represent the manipulation of the hive into human affairs through the medium of the virus. Given the manipulative nature of the hive, such a suggestion should not be dismissed out of hand (no pun intended) as a telling of the truth through allegorical means. The hive intelligence loved rubbing our faces in our ignorance, even the ignorance of many of its mystical acolytes who didn't know the full hidden picture.

Now that we know what the Philosopher's Stone truly represents, then we need to look at the alleged Great Work and see through the hive agenda in pushing for this Reformation of the Whole World. What was the Great Work hiding from the masses that was such a deadly secret only whispered between Hermetic adepts over the ages? What is the dreadful secret hidden behind the superficial illusion of the Great Work? Before this work is finished the reader will see this secret in all its dastardly glory.

In the context of Hermeticism, the Philosophers Stone is 'in us' yet not 'of us', and is called the *veritas*, and "is to be sought not in us, but in the image of God which is in us." When we remove all the mystical elements from the Hermetic teachings and see the hapiym hive virus as the 'image of God which is in us', then once again the mystery disappears, and we find a rational pragmatic explanation for all this mystical innuendo. Because humanity has been so blinded by this God quest over the ages, only those who have achieved active communion with the hive and have worked knowingly within its precincts have been the adepts doing the Great Work. These adepts have been in the know for generations. As the Freemason Albert Pike freely admitted in his work, *Morals and Dogma*, "The adepts are the princes of Freemasonry." The initiatory rites of these secret societies and occult mystery traditions are what gave these adepts knowing access to the hive and who worked to fulfill its agenda to subdue the consciousness of all humanity to its 'Divine Will'.

Freemasonry is a religion, despite what many uninformed Masons at the lower levels may believe. To join the organization, one must profess a belief in God, although the name of that God doesn't matter within the ranks of Freemasonry for it is known at the highest degrees of the Craft that all representations of God lead to the same place, the inorganic hapiym hive collective.

The Philosopher's Stone is touted as the Holy Grail of Hermeticism. I covered in *We Are Not Alone – Part 3: The Luciferian Agenda of the Mother Goddess*, how the Holy Grail was a symbol of the womb, and that it directly correlated to Ninhursag in her goddess incarnations. With Ninhursag's hermaphroditism allegorically representing the Holy Trinity, then the Grail legends tie to Christianity has a more subtle and hidden meaning, particularly where the female 'three', or as Jung called it, the *anima* (female) aspect of the Trinity, runs rife through Hermetic and Christian mystical traditions. Hermaphroditism plays a central role in Hermetic literature, and with the understanding of Ninhursag the hermaphrodite playing both male and female roles in the Holy Trinity, we can now understand the mystery of one God in Three persons.

Just as the ancient Greek mystery philosophical doctrines reveal, no one reaches the Monad except through the triune aspect of Hecate. The later Christian rendition of Jesus, the Son of God and the female Holy Spirit would be rendered in a similar manner that, "No one comes to the Father except through me." There is no confusion in these correlations beyond the desire to deny what is patently evident when the mystery of the Trinity is revealed. The Christian Holy Trinity is nothing but the Greek Hecate acting as intercessor, or the one who vets the individual to test their worthiness to commune with the hive 'Father'. It matters not that the Christian interpretation covers both male and female aspects of the Trinity, for Ninhursag in her hermaphroditic state could play both roles quite easily, and she did throughout her existence.

Her desire was that all humans should become as she was, where the Divine Masculine merged and joined with the Divine Feminine, thereby replicating herself in human hosts. This mergence doctrine to strive for the hermaphrodite that allegedly is the price to pay to access God is found rampant in New Age doctrines as well and in Hinduism, Greek Hermetic traditions as well and in certain Gnostic gospels as in *The Gospel of Thomas* where is was written:

> *Jesus said to them, "**When you make the two one**, and when you make the inside like the outside and the outside like the inside, and the above like the below, **and when you make the male and the female one and the same, so that the male not be male nor the female female;** and when you fashion eyes in the place of an eye, and a hand in place of a hand, and a foot in place of a foot, and a likeness in place of a likeness; then will you enter [the Kingdom]."*
>
> [Bold emphasis mine]

When we read this passage, we see that the Greek Duad is at play where the two are to become one, the inner with the outer, and this represents merging the hive cell with the human body by allowing the hive cell to come forth to remove the duality and rule one's psyche. The reference to the male becoming female and vice versa ought to speak for itself in its meaning regarding the hermaphroditic nature of the doctrines of Ninhursag.

I want to share a couple other verses from the same Gospel as they highlight this hive manipulation through references to the Light, and the first verse also illustrates the vindictive nature of Ninhursag that I have explained in my other works.

> *"Jesus said, "Whoever blasphemes against the Father will be forgiven, and whoever blasphemes against the Son will be forgiven, but* ***whoever blasphemes against the Holy Spirit will not be forgiven either on earth or in heaven****."*"

> *Jesus said, "****It is I who am the light which is above them all. It is I who am the All. From Me did the All come forth, and unto Me did the All extend.*** *Split a piece of wood, and I am there. Lift up the stone, and you will find Me there."*
>
> [Bold emphasis mine]

I hope these brief passages illustrate how this hive doctrine pervades all these religious traditions, and also its insistence to continually brag about its magnificence. It was nothing but an ego on steroids, but given the fact that it was only a conglomeration of replicated human ego personalities to begin with, should we really be surprised? There was nothing holy about this virus masquerading as God. It was lying, deceitful, and it had its own agenda, with the twisted and vindictive personality of a lifelong persecuted hermaphroditic hybrid controlling the spiritual show on this planet in multitudinous guises.

I realize that I have drifted somewhat from the chapter title on the Philosopher's Stone, but all these seemingly dissimilar pieces weave together to create a tapestry of deception that defies human imagination. There are those that refuse to believe in any kind of conspiracy theories at all, but what I have illustrated so far provides a millennia's long agenda to deceive humanity through these alleged spiritual traditions. Once exposed, the evidence roars to be heard and acknowledged. We can continue to bend our brains trying to figure out all this mystical sleight of hand, or we can finally unmask the magician and its tricks. To continue to demand that the mystical promises of this cosmic deceiver virus are true and that we should dedicate our lives bending our knees to this fraud only shows a massive species psychosis for deceit and escapism. We are fortunate that the virus infection is eradicated, however our psyches are still plagued by its habits and our beliefs in its lies. Humanity must transcend all this mystical chicanery if they expect to advance as a species.

# 16. The Seven Rays

Although this chapter is titled the Seven Rays, we will be uncovering other aspects of this fascination with the number seven in other avenues of these mystical and religious traditions. For a bit of foundational knowledge, I will turn to Wikipedia under *Seven Rays*:

> *"The seven rays is an occult concept that has appeared in several religions and esoteric philosophies, since at least the 6th century BCE,* ***of the Aryan peoples*** *in both Western culture and in India. In the west, it can be seen in early western mystery traditions such as Gnosticism and the Roman Mithraic Mysteries; and in texts and iconic art of the Catholic Church as early as the Byzantine era. In India, the concept has been part of Hindu religious philosophy and scripture since at least the Vishnu Purana, dating from the post-Vedic era."*
>
> [Bold emphasis mine]

Take note of the fact that we are once again confronted with those enigmatic Aryan peoples where these traditions are concerned. I am going to present some of the information from Wikipedia in a different sequence than it appears on the page in order to provide a more linear historical context to all this seven rays ideology.

> *"In ancient Greek mythology, Zeus takes the bull-form known as Taurus in order to win Europa. Taurus is also associated with Aphrodite and other goddesses, as well as with Pan and Dionysus. The face of Taurus "gleams with* ***seven rays of fire****."*
>
> *The Chaldean Oracles of the 2nd century CE feature the* ***seven rays as purifying agents of Helios****, symbolism featured in Mithraic liturgy as well. Later, in the 4th century, Emperor Julian Saturnalia composed* ***a Hymn to the Solemn Sun, and in his Hymn to the Mother of the Gods spoke of "unspeakable mysteries hidden from the crowd such as Julian the Chaldean prophesied concerning the god of the seven rays****." In Greek Gnostic magic of the same era, colored gemstones were often used as talismans for medicine or healing; they were often engraved with a symbol borrowed from the Egyptian deity Chnuphis: a hooded serpent or great snake. The snake was shown with a lion's head, from which emanated either twelve or* ***seven rays****. The twelve rays*

*represented the zodiac, and the* ***seven rays*** *represented the planets, usually with the* ***seven Greek vowels engraved at the tips of the seven rays. The reverse sides of the talismans were engraved with a snake twisting around a vertical rod.*** *These were known as "Gnostic amulets" and were sometimes also engraved with the names Iao Sabao (the Archon Iao). Gnostic gems with Abraxas also featured the seven rays."*

[Bold emphasis mine]

Herein we find the connection with the Seven Rays of fire and the sun (Helios), following the Mazdaean traditions of Zoroaster and his seven Angels. Once again, we have that Mother Goddess sewn into this seven rays tapestry along with the sun, and we find the caduceus symbol associated with Hermes and the Babylonian god Ningizhidda, so it takes no imagination at all to figure out who this fascination with seven is associated with. So, let's take a look at this seven rays iconography in Christianity:

*"In early Christian iconography,* ***the dove of the Holy Ghost is often shown with an emanation of seven rays, as is the image of the Madonna,*** *often in conjunction with a dove or doves. The Monastery of St. Catherine on Mount Sinai, circa 565 CE, shows the Transfiguration of Christ in the apse mosaic,* ***with "seven rays of light shining from the luminous body of Christ***

*over the apostles Peter, James and John." In the present day Byzantine-style St. Louis Cathedral in Missouri, the center of the sanctuary has an engraved circle with many symbols of the Holy Trinity. The inscription reads:* ***"Radiating from this symbol are seven rays of light representing the seven gifts of the Holy Ghost.*** *""*

[Bold emphasis mine]

Now, let's take a look at Hinduism:

*"Agni is a Hindu and Vedic deity* ***depicted in three forms: fire, lightning and the sun****. In Hindu art, Agni is depicted with two or* ***seven hands****, two heads, and three legs. In each head, he has* ***seven fiery tongues*** *with which he licks sacrificial butter. He rides a ram or a chariot harnessed by fiery horses. His attributes are an axe,* ***a torch****, prayer beads and a flaming spear. Agni is represented as red and two-faced, suggesting both his destructive and his beneficent qualities, and with black eyes and hair.* ***Seven rays of light emanate from his body.***

*The Vishnu Purana, a post-vedic scripture, describes how* ***Vishnu "enters into the seven solar rays which dilate into seven suns." These are the "seven principal solar rays,"*** *the source of heat* *even to the planet Jupiter, and the* ***"seven suns into which the seven solar rays dilate at the consummation of all things.""***

[Bold emphasis mine]

Now, let's bring this all forward into our modern era and see what we can learn:

*"Beginning in the late 19th century,* ***the seven rays appeared in a modified and elaborated form in the teachings of Theosophy,*** *first presented by H. P. Blavatsky. The Theosophical concept of* ***the seven rays*** *was further developed in the late 19th and early 20th centuries in the writings of the Theosophists C. W. Leadbeater, and by other authors such as* ***Alice Bailey, Manly P. Hall****, and others, including notably the teachings of Benjamin Creme and his group Share International; and in the philosophies of organizations such as Temple of the People, The "I AM" Activity, The Bridge to Freedom, The Summit Lighthouse, The Temple of The Presence (1995) and various other such organizations promulgating what are called the* ***Ascended Master Teachings****, a group of religious teachings based on Theosophy.*

*As the New Age movement of the mid-to-late 20th century developed, the* ***seven rays concept appeared as an element of metaphysical healing methods such as Reiki*** *and other modalities, and in esoteric astrology."*

[Bold emphasis mine]

Are you starting to get a bit uncomfortable over all this seven rays information yet? If not, let's continue and look at the syncretic aspects of this doctrine:

*"Egyptologist Gerald Massey wrote in 1881 of what he described as connections between Vedic scripture, ancient Egyptian mythology and the Gospel stories. He theorized that the Archon Iao,* ***the "Seven-rayed Sun-God of the Gnostic-stones"*** *was also the "Serpent Chnubis," and "the Second Beast in the Book of Revelation." In 1900, he elaborated further, describing the unity of "the seven souls of the Pharaoh," "the seven arms of the Hindu god Agni," "the seven stars in the hand of the Christ in Revelation," and "the seven rays of the Chaldean god Heptaktis, or Iao, on the Gnostic stones."*

*Samuel Fales Dunlap, wrote in 1894:*

*"Moses was of the race of the Chaldeans. The Chaldean* ***Mithra had his Seven Rays****, and Moses his* ***Seven Days****. The other planets which circling around the sun lead the dance as round the King of heaven receive from him with the light also their powers; while as the light comes to them from the sun so from him they receive their powers that he pours out into the* ***Seven Spheres of the Seven Planets*** *of which the sun is the centre."*

*Dunlap wrote that* ***the idea of spirit as the ultimate cause is present in all of the great religions of the East*** *(which in the terminology of his time included the area now known as the Near East or Middle East), and that this idea can be found in "****the Seven Rays of the Chaldaean Mithra and the Seven Days of Genesis. From the Sun came fire and spirit****." According to Dunlap,* ***"this was the astronomical religion of the Chaldeans, Jews, Persians, Syrians, Phoenicians and Egyptians****."*

*Dunlap compared the* ***nimbus of Apollo to the seven rays of Dionysus,*** *presiding over the orbits of the* ***seven planets****. The seven rays are found also in the Chaldean mystery* ***of "the God of the Seven Rays, who held the Seven Stars in his hand, through whom (as Chaldaeans supposed)***

***the souls were raised."** Prior to the Christian era, this deity was known as Iao (the first birth) or Sabaoth (the Sun), and later described as **"Christos of the Resurrection of Souls."**"*

[Bold emphasis mine]

This section wouldn't be complete without taking the theosophical spin on all this:

*"**Syncretism is one of the core principles of Theosophy**, a religious philosophy originating with Helena Petrovna Blavatsky from the 1870s, and the seven rays appear repeatedly in the related writings. **Theosophy holds that all religions are attempts by the "Spiritual Hierarchy" to help humanity in evolving to greater perfection, and that each religion therefore has a portion of the truth.***

*Blavatsky wrote in the first book of The Secret Doctrine of an "**analogy between the Aryan or Brahmanical** and the Egyptian esotericism" and that the "seven rays of the Chaldean Heptakis or Iao, on the Gnostic stones" represent the seven large stars of the Egyptian "Great Bear" constellation, the seven elemental powers, and the Hindu "seven Rishis." She stated that **the seven rays of the Vedic sun deity Vishnu represent the***

***same concept as the "astral fluid or 'Light' of the Kabalists,"*** *and that the seven emanations of the lower seven sephiroth are the* ***"primeval seven rays,"*** *and* ***"will be found and recognized in every religion."***

[Bold emphasis mine]

What this little journey of investigation into the seven rays should prove beyond the shadow of a doubt is that there has been an ongoing agenda taking place beyond the awareness of all but the scholars and intellectuals throughout the ages. The average man in the street has no idea about this thousands of years old agenda to drive humanity in a specific direction with all these religious and spiritual doctrines.

So, let's take a look at Jewish traditions and our calendar. Saturday (Saturn's Day) is the $7^{th}$ day of the week, the day that God rested after his feat of creating everything in six days. In the Old Testament, we hear continual stories of Jews who *backslid* from the patriarchal worship of Yahweh and took to worshipping Canaanite gods, particularly Baal and Ashtoreth or Astarte/Ishtar. I have already illustrated the basis to establish the worship on Mt. Zion as a center for goddess worship. So, we have to ask just exactly what the seven-pronged menorah really represents with its candles and flames, and who is really being worshipped in this tradition? There is, naturally, contention about any correlation with Saturn and the seventh day of creation, but let's take a look at some information in regard to *Saturnalia* on Wikipedia and see if we can find any correlations:

*"The Saturnalia was the dramatic setting of the multivolume work of that name by Macrobius, a Latin writer from late antiquity who is the major source for information about the holiday. In one of the interpretations in Macrobius's work,* ***Saturnalia is a festival of light*** *leading to the winter solstice,* ***with the abundant presence of candles symbolizing the quest for knowledge and truth****.* ***The renewal of light*** *and the coming of the new year was celebrated in the later Roman Empire at the Dies Natalis Solis Invicti, the* ***"Birthday of the Unconquerable Sun"****, on 23 December."*

*"The first inhabitants of Italy were the Aborigines, whose king, Saturnus, is said to have been a man of such extraordinary justice,* ***that no one was a slave in his reign, <u>or had any private property</u>, but all things were common to all, and undivided, as one estate for the use of every one****; in memory of which way of life, it has been ordered that at the Saturnalia slaves should everywhere sit down with their masters at the entertainments,* ***the rank of all being made equal****."*

*—Justinus, Epitome of Pompeius Trogus 43.3*

[Bold emphasis mine]

Curiously enough, the Jewish holiday Hanukah is also known as a Festival of Light that entails lighting candles, usually nine in contradistinction to the usual seven-candle menorah. There is naturally contention as to who started the tradition first, but all I want to point out is the similarities in the rituals and the association with the flame and solar seven rays cultism.

What I ask the reader to pay attention to in particular in the last segment is the aspect of community property where no one owns anything. This is no different than the Marxist ideology, as is the modern battle cry of equality by Social Justice Warriors. None of this is by accident, and all of it is linked to Saturn, or shall we say Ninhursag in this instance. All of the seven rays' doctrines fold into her role as the alleged Christ, the solar cultism, festivals of Light and the Light being associated with wisdom or knowledge. If you think for one minute that all these things are not connected and being played out in the modern global political arena you have another thing coming.

Returning to the subject of Saturn, aside from Saturn's beneficent side, there was a darker aspect of Saturn that is represented in an alter ego that thrived on chaos. This concept of chaos and liberty followed Ninhursag and her doctrines throughout the ages. A glaring example of this association is found with Ninhursag's hidden identity posing as the lady Liberty in the French Revolution, which ultimately resulted in the Reign of Terror. So, let me digress and share a few facts about the French Revolution from Wikipedia under the *Cult of the Supreme Being* title:

*"The Cult of the Supreme Being (French: Culte de l'Être suprême) was a form of deism established in France by Maximilien Robespierre during the French Revolution. It was intended to become the state religion of the new French Republic and a replacement for Roman Catholicism and its rival, the Cult of Reason."*

*"Robespierre believed that reason is only a means to an end, and the singular end is virtue. He sought to move beyond simple deism (often described as Voltairean by its adherents) to a new and, in his view, more rational devotion to the godhead.* ***The primary principles of the Cult of the Supreme Being were a belief in the existence of a god and the immortality of the human soul****. Though not inconsistent with Christian doctrine, these beliefs were put to the service of Robespierre's fuller meaning,* ***which was of a type of civic-minded, public virtue he attributed to the Greeks and Romans. This type of virtue could only be attained through active fidelity to liberty and democracy.*** *Belief in a living god and a higher moral code, he said, were "constant reminders of justice" and thus essential to a republican society."*

[Bold emphasis mine]

There are those that claim that Robespierre was a Freemason, but there is not a lot of evidentiary documentation to support this contention. It shows without question, however, that his new State sanctioned religion and its bloody consequences have the hive single God fingerprints all over it. Robespierre's ideology was notoriously left-wing in its political orientation, which is why I bring this into the discussion at this time. I also ask the reader to remember the information handed down to Emmanuel Swedenborg where it was stated that anyone doing the work of God, regardless of their actions, was blameless.

Taking into consideration the aspects of Saturn named above, then we need to take a look at lady liberty in a painting produced by Eugène Delacroix in 1830. Wikipedia, under the look-up *Liberty Leading the People*:

> *"Liberty Leading the People (French: La Liberté guidant le peuple [la libɛʁte gidɑ̃ lə pœpl]) is a painting by Eugène Delacroix commemorating the July Revolution of 1830, which toppled King Charles X of France. A woman personifying the concept and the* ***Goddess of Liberty*** *leads the people forward* ***over a barricade and the bodies*** *of the fallen, holding the flag of the French Revolution –* ***the tricolour flag****, which remains France's national flag – in one hand and brandishing a bayonetted musket with the other. The figure of Liberty is also viewed as a symbol of*

*France and the French Republic known as* ***Marianne.****"*

*"Delacroix depicted Liberty as both an allegorical goddess-figure and a robust woman of the people.* ***The mound of corpses acts as a kind of pedestal from which Liberty strides, barefoot and bare-breasted****, out of the canvas and into the space of the viewer. The* ***Phrygian cap*** *she wears had come to symbolize liberty during the first French Revolution, of 1789–94. The painting has been seen as a marker to the end of the Age of Enlightenment, as many scholars see the end of the French Revolution as the start of the romantic era.*

***The fighters are from a mixture of social classes, ranging from the bourgeoisie represented by the young man in a top hat, a student from the prestigious École Polytechnique wearing the traditional bicorne, to the revolutionary urban worker****, as exemplified by the boy holding pistols. What they have in common is the fierceness and determination in their eyes. Aside from the flag held by Liberty, a second, minute tricolore can be discerned in the distance flying from the towers of Notre Dame."*

[Bold emphasis mine]

What we find in the elements highlighted is the Phrygian cap associated with the god Attis, the consort of the Mother Goddess Cybele. Also pay attention to the fact that within Delacroix's painting that the goddess liberty is attended and followed by the working class and college students, no different than today's SJW agenda playing out around the world. The mound of corpses she uses as her 'pedestal' are equally representative of every Marxist revolution since Marxism was written as a political theory. None of this is accidental, and the rise in neo-goddess cultism goes hand in glove with all of this political activism and revolution-mindedness today. For some greater understanding of our goddess friend, let's take a look at the goddess *Eris* in Wikipedia and see what we find:

> *"In Hesiod's Works and Days 11–24, two different goddesses named Eris are distinguished:*
>
> *So, after all,* ***there was not one kind of Strife alone, but all over the earth there are two****. As for the one, a man would praise her when he came to understand her; but the other is blameworthy: and they are wholly different in nature. For one fosters evil war and battle, being cruel: her no man loves; but perforce, through the will of the deathless gods, men pay harsh Strife her honour due.*

*But the other is the elder daughter of dark Night (Nyx), and the son of Cronus* ***who sits above and <u>dwells in the aether</u>, set her in the roots of the earth****: and she is far kinder to men. She stirs up even the shiftless to toil; for a man grows eager to work when he considers his neighbour, a rich man who hastens to plough and plant and put his house in good order****; and neighbour vies with his neighbour as he hurries after wealth****. This Strife is wholesome for men. And potter is angry with potter, and craftsman with craftsman and beggar is jealous of beggar, and minstrel of minstrel."*

[Bold emphasis mine]

I realize that some readers may feel that I am stretching things too far with all this goddess stuff, but I have studied the varying roles of Ninhursag in depth over the years, and what the reader should pay attention to in all these diverse-seeming roles are the threads of commonality and consistency. One cannot look at the goddess Liberty astride her pedestal of corpses and not see the goddess Eris as equally responsible for sowing discord between neighbor and neighbor, particularly when one is rich, and one is not. This is all exemplified in our modern leftist political spectrum with Social Justice Warriors screaming for equality against the rich. The doctrines of Eris are running the Fabian Marxist agenda in global culture today. It is all part of the Hermetic "Reformation of the Whole World". The Freemasonic saying of *Ordo ab Chao* (Order out of Chaos) illustrates the hive's overall agenda for the homogenization of humanity through artificially-induced chaos and revolution.

I will now get back on track with the seven rays topic and show how this fascination with the number seven threads into Christianity. We have to look no further than the Seven Seals in the book of Revelation. Looking up *Seven Seals* in Wikipedia informs us:

> *"The Seven Seals is a phrase in the Book of Revelation that refers to seven symbolic seals (Greek: σφραγῖδα, sphragida) that secure the book/scroll, that John of Patmos saw in his Revelation of Jesus Christ. The opening of the seals of the Apocalyptic document occurs in Revelation Chapters 5-8 and marks the Second Coming. In John's vision, the only one worthy to open the book/scroll is referred to as both the "Lion of Judah" and the "Lamb having seven horns and seven eyes"."*

In the present context of Revelations, the Lion of Judah is equated with Christ. The reference to the lamb with seven horns could be an allusion to Hermes the Shepherd, who is often portrayed in art and statuary carrying a ram. To see this correlation between Hermes and Jesus we need to look up *Kriophoros* in Wikipedia:

*"Free-standing fourth-century CE Roman sculptures, and even third-century ones, are sometimes identified as "Christ, the Good Shepherd", illustrating the pericope in the Gospel of John, and also the second-century Christian literary work The Shepherd of Hermas. In two-dimensional art, Hermes Kriophoros transformed into the Christ carrying a lamb and walking among his sheep: "Thus we find philosophers holding scrolls or a Hermes Kriophoros which can be turned into Christ giving the Law (Traditio Legis) and the Good Shepherd respectively" (Peter and Linda Murray, The Oxford Companion to Classical Art and Architecture, p. 475.)."*

It seems no matter where we turn we find these goddess/Hermes connections with the Christ concept of Christianity. They become inseparable because, I assert, they all rise from the same tradition and from the same formulators, Ninhursag and the hapiym hive collective. The concept of sheep representing humanity under the 'guidance' of the Hermetic shepherd only fits the pattern of what has been shown in this book so far. Again, the reader is free to deny it, but I don't think the correlations can be effectively refuted.

Now, let's take a look at this number seven thing and a few others in the book of Revelation. The first thing I ask you to notice is that the Revelation of John is no different than any other visionary 'visit' by some disembodied hive personality passing itself off as an angel as revealed in the first 2 verses. Take this into consideration when giving credence to these alleged 'prophecies'.

***Rev.1***

*"[1] The Revelation of Jesus Christ, which God gave unto him, to shew unto his servants things which must shortly come to pass; and he sent and signified it by his angel unto his servant John:*

*[2] Who bare record of the word of God, and of the testimony of Jesus Christ, and of all things that he saw.*

*[4] John to the* **seven** *churches which are in Asia: Grace be unto you, and peace, from him which is, and which was, and which is to come; and from the seven Spirits which are before his throne;*

*[5] And from Jesus Christ, who is the faithful witness, and* ***the first begotten of the dead, and the prince of the kings of the earth****. Unto him that loved us, and washed us from our sins in his own blood,*

*[8] I am* ***Alpha and Omega, the beginning and the ending, saith the Lord****, which is, and which was, and which is to come, the Almighty.*

*[10] I was in the Spirit on the Lord's day, and heard behind me a great voice, as of a trumpet,*

*[11] Saying,* ***I am Alpha and Omega, the first and the last:*** *and, What thou seest, write in a*

*book, and send it unto the* ***seven*** *churches which are in Asia; unto Ephesus, and unto Smyrna, and unto Pergamos, and unto Thyatira, and unto Sardis, and unto Philadelphia, and unto Laodicea.*

*[12] And I turned to see the voice that spake with me. And being turned, I saw* ***seven golden candlesticks****;*

*13] And in the midst of the* ***seven candlesticks*** *one like unto the Son of man, clothed with a garment down to the foot, and girt about the paps with a golden girdle.*

*[14] His head and his hairs were white like wool, as white as snow; and his eyes were as* ***a flame of fire****;*

*[16] And he had in his right hand* ***seven stars****: and out of his mouth went a sharp twoedged sword: and his countenance was* ***as the sun shineth*** *in his strength.*

*[18] I am he that liveth,* ***and was dead; and, behold, I am alive for evermore,*** *Amen; and have the keys of hell and of death.*

*[20] The mystery of the* ***seven stars*** *which thou sawest in my right hand, and the* ***seven golden candlesticks****.* ***The seven stars are the angels of the seven churches: and the seven candlesticks which thou sawest are the seven churches****.*

***Rev.3***

*[1] And unto the angel of the church in Sardis write; These things saith he that hath the* ***seven Spirits of God, and the seven stars****; I know thy works, that thou hast a name that thou livest, and art dead.*

***Rev.4***

*[1] After this I looked, and, behold,* ***a door was opened in heaven****: and the first voice which I heard was as it were of a trumpet talking with me; which said, Come up hither, and I will shew thee things which must be hereafter.*

*[2] And immediately* ***<u>I was in the spirit</u>****: and, behold,* ***a throne was set in heaven, and <u>one</u> sat on the throne****.*

*[3] And he that sat was to look upon like a jasper and a sardine stone: and there was* ***a rainbow round about the throne****, in sight like unto an emerald.*

*[4] And round about the throne were four and twenty seats: and upon the seats I saw four and twenty elders sitting, clothed in* ***white raiment****; and they had on their heads crowns of gold.*

*[5] And out of the throne proceeded lightnings and thunderings and voices: and there were* ***seven lamps of fire burning before the throne, which are the seven Spirits of God."***

[Bold emphasis mine]

I think I have offered enough of this hive swill to make my case to show that the prophetic prognostications in the book of Revelation are just more of the same old garbage as illustrated in these other traditions. You have seen the One on the throne in heaven, the seven angels, the seven candlesticks, the eyes like fire, and Ninhursag's claim to be the Alpha and the Omega so that there should be no doubt as to just who the 'visionary' Jesus Christ in John's Apocalypse represents. To provide some additional zing to this over-zealous fascination with the number seven, the number of colors in a rainbow is seven, and the number of spikes on Lady Liberty's crown in New York harbor is also seven. This is also present in the seven subjects of classical Greek education promoted by the universities. We are having our faces rubbed in this hive and Ninhursag-created mysticism and symbolism, yet we are unaware of the brazen agenda taking place before our very eyes.

The rainbow symbol is associated with the LGBT agenda, and Ninhursag as Aphroditus promoted homosexuality and transsexuality and the lowering of sexual boundaries in that cult. Looking up *Aphroditus* in Wikipedia informs us of the following:

> *"Aphroditus (Greek: Ἀφρόδιτος Aphroditos) was a male Aphrodite originating from Amathus on the island of Cyprus and celebrated in Athens in a* ***transvestite rite****.*

*Aphroditus was portrayed as having a **female shape and clothing like Aphrodite's but also a phallus, and hence, a male name**. This deity would have arrived in Athens from Cyprus in the 4th century BC. In the 5th century BC, however, there existed **hermae of Aphroditus, or phallic statues with a female head**.*

*According to Macrobius, who mentions the goddess in his Saturnalia, Philochorus, in his Atthis (referred to by Macrobius), **identifies this male-female god with the Moon** and says that at its sacrifices men and women exchanged clothing. Philostratus, in describing the rituals involved in the festivals, said that the image or the impersonator of the god was accompanied by a large train of followers in which girls mingled with men because the festivals allowed **"women to act the part of men, and men put on woman's clothing and play the woman"**.*

*Aphroditus is the same as the later god **Hermaphroditus**, whose name means "**Aphroditus in the form of a herm"**—a statue shaped as a quadrangular pillar surmounted by a head or bust, and first occurs in the Characters of Theophrastus. Photius also explained that Aphroditus was Hermaphroditus, and cited fragments from Attic* *comedies mentioning the divinity. In later mythology* ***Hermaphroditus came to be regarded as the son of Hermes and Aphrodite****."*

[Bold emphasis mine]

It is not accidental that the rainbow has become the symbol of the current LGBT movement given the nature of Ninhursag's goddess teachings of the past that surrounded her own hermaphroditic nature and her promotion of sexuality of all kinds. People do not generally realize that all this symbolism has meaning for those who are in the know, and their usage goes beyond the superficial notice of the masses. There is presently a Christian counter-movement using a motto of, "God wants his Rainbow back", that serves as a point of conflict over using the rainbow as a symbol for the LGBT movement. The rainbow has also become a banner for modern spiritual teachings in the New Age and you will find no shortage of books promoting New Age spirituality with rainbows adorning the covers of their books and posters for their spiritual seminars. The reader needs to realize that there is a more sinister agenda taking place hiding behind the beauty of the rainbow.

If you think for one minute, after all the evidence presented thus far in this book, that this is remotely accidental, then you need to check your head. I will ask the reader this; if I am so in error on what I propose, then why do all these pieces fit seamlessly together? If I was in error in these assessments, then there would be glaring holes on all this, yet the more I dig, the more I find correlations that only bolster my assertions. Only the willfully blind can ignore the mountain of building evidence here. Denial won't make the evidence disappear, and without the keys to solving this code that I provide, it is all just a grand mystery, and those who have sought to solve these mysteries to this day remain baffled. It all either comprises an incomprehensible mystery known by a select few mystics and esotericists over the ages, or there is a solution to the mystery. Our greatest minds, like Carl Jung, couldn't figure this stuff out and you can tell by his writings that it near drove him crazy trying to make sense of it and apply empirical psychological explanations for all of it.

The rabid revolutionary tone of the modern leftist political spectrum encapsulating the Feminist agenda, the LGBT agenda, the SJW social revolutionaries tied in with the other two, and the revival of modern goddess cultism puts the explanation for all these things in one neat little package with a *big*, Marxist revolutionary red ribbon on the box. As with the goddess Eris, the cult of Dionysus was also about chaos. The hive collectivism is mirrored in Fabian Marxist collectivism, as has been the regimentation of herd mentality and tribalism over the ages of human history. Collectivism and homogenization has always been the agenda of the hapiym hive. Although the virus is eliminated, its habits still rule our consciousness and we are but shadows of that virus, continually playing out its agenda in our total blind ignorance. If we do not utilize the cure to rid ourselves of this symptomatology by first facing up to the truth of our circumstances and its origin, then we are likely doomed as a species.

# 17. Rosicrucians and the Chemical Wedding

Within Rosicrucianism, which is a continuation of the mystical Hermetic underground stream of knowledge that wove its way through the Renaissance period with the likes of Giordano Bruno and others who the Roman Church branded as heretics, (Bruno himself being burned at the stake in 1600), we find the 17$^{th}$ century continuation of the doctrines of Ninhursag and the hidden hive wisdom progressing into the Age of Reason. The primary symbol of the Rosicrucians is the Rose and the Cross, in which the cross represents man and the Rose represents the soul. A curious fact that must be noted in reference to the Greek story about the creation of the rose is that the goddess of flowers, Chloris, came upon a dead nymph and turned her into a flower. She asked for the assistance of the goddess Aphrodite and the god Dionysus. Aphrodite gave the rose its beautiful color and Dionysus provided it nectar. I have already established that Aphrodite and Dionysus were different aspects of Ninhursag. With the creation of the rose by these two gods, we thereby associate Ninhursag with the Rosicrucian Rose in an allegorical form, or hidden doctrine.

The Golden Cross of the Rosicrucian Order allegedly represents man, and the symbol of the Rose sits on the cross where the human heart would rest. The Rosicrucian ideology is another of those, similar to Gnosticism, that promotes the 'perfecting of the soul' and the elevation of the human with the Divine. We have modern apologists like Lynn Picknett and Clive Prince in their book *The Forbidden Universe*, who make the erroneous assertion that the Renaissance Hermeticists were persecuted by the Roman Catholic Church because they promoted the ideas of Copernicus's theory of heliocentricity and that the Earth orbited the sun, in opposition to the Church doctrine of the universe revolving around the Earth. Picknett and Prince's take is that the Roman Church was averse to science based on Copernicus' theory. There may be some truth to this on one level, but as with all apologists of their favored doctrines, Picknett and Prince omit a lot of facts, the most important being that it wasn't just the science in which the Roman Church found heresy, but in the re-emergence of Hermetic solar cultism pushed by the Neoplatonist philosophies. Within the circles of those surrounding the De Medici family, as I covered in *WANA- Part 3*, we find the more public re-emergence of the Neoplatonic Hermetic doctrines displayed allegorically in much Renaissance artwork. If one looks at these Renaissance paintings, we often find the subjects in the painting with one finger pointed skyward. This single finger pointing to the sky, particularly in many of the religious paintings of the Renaissance era, signifies the Platonic concept of the Monad, or One God. The artist Raphael's painting, *The School of Athens,* is filled with dedicatory representations of Zoroaster, Plato, Pythagoras and other Greek philosophers. In this painting, you see Plato with his index finger pointing skyward denoting the belief in the Monad or the One God.

As Wikipedia informs us in reference to *The School of Athens* painting:

> *"In the center of the fresco, at its architecture's central vanishing point, are the two undisputed main subjects: Plato on the left and Aristotle, his student, on the right. Both figures hold modern (of the time), bound copies of their books in their left hands, while gesturing with their right. Plato holds* ***Timaeus****, Aristotle his* ***Nicomachean Ethics****.*
>
> *It is popularly thought that their gestures indicate central aspects of their philosophies, for Plato, his Theory of Forms, and for Aristotle, his empiricist views, with an emphasis on concrete particulars. Many interpret the painting to show a divergence of the two philosophical schools. Plato argues a sense of timelessness whilst Aristotle looks into the physicality of life and the present realm."*

The Catholic Church always leaned toward Aristotelian philosophy in its universities over the esoteric ideas of Plato. Where Plato contemplated his philosophy on translating the esoteric meaning of the Monad into the human sciences, Aristotle was more materialist oriented, seeking to separate the science of man from the esoteric concept of Plato's 'ideas' that science should be the translation from the Monad to man. Aristotle's more materialistic view would naturally be more acceptable to a Church that wanted the bailiwick of translating God for the masses kept separate from Aristotle's materialist view of logic and science, maintaining the Church's religious dominion. In Aristotle's philosophy the soul and the body comprised different aspects of the form, in contradistinction to Plato's idea that the soul was separate and a part of God. To show this more materialistic viewpoint, Aristotle said that the soul is the "first actuality of a natural organic body" *(De Anima ii 1, 412b5–6)*. This places the soul as part of the natural material world and would leave the metaphysical supernatural aspect of saving souls in the hands of the Church, thereby being less threatening than the Platonist and Neoplatonist ideology that man could find God on his own without priestly intercessors.

A bit of information on Plato's philosophy should be addressed here in part so one can see the doctrine synopsized for broader understanding. I am not interested in wider discussions with philosophers over how they might conjecture the overall meaning of Plato's dialogue in *Timaeus*, but only want to present a bit of information from Wikipedia on *Timaeus* for the reader's understanding:

> *Timaeus begins with a distinction between the physical world, and* ***the eternal world****. The physical one is the world which changes and perishes: therefore it is the object of opinion and*

*unreasoned sensation.* ***The eternal one never changes****: therefore it is apprehended by reason.*

*The speeches about the two worlds are conditioned by the different nature of their objects. Indeed, "a description of what is* ***changeless, fixed and clearly intelligible will be changeless and fixed,****" while a description of what changes and is likely, will also change and be just likely. "As being is to becoming, so is truth to belief". Therefore, in a description of the physical world, one "should not look for anything more than a likely story".*

*Timaeus suggests that since nothing "becomes or changes" without cause, then the cause of the universe must be* ***a demiurge or a god****, a figure Timaeus refers to as* ***the father and maker of the universe****. And since the universe is fair,* ***the demiurge must have looked to the eternal model to make it,*** *and not to the perishable one. Hence, using the eternal and perfect world of "forms" or ideals as a template, he set about creating our world, which formerly only existed in a state of disorder."*

[Bold emphasis mine]

We can but wonder what type of 'reason' Plato applied when interpreting the divine and changeless intentions of the hapiym hive. Plato's philosophy, put forth here, is the same as the virus ideology no matter which form it masked itself from human consciousness. Being a virus that could only mimic the intelligence of its human host, it was as unchangeable as any other pathogen known to modern medical science. Its only concern was to spread itself and grow its colony of infection larger. Citing Wikipedia further along regarding how Plato saw the purpose of the universe:

> *"Timaeus continues with an explanation of the creation of the universe, which he ascribes to the handiwork of a* ***divine craftsman.****,* ***The demiurge, being good, wanted there to be as much good as was the world. The demiurge is said to bring order out of substance by imitating an unchanging and eternal model*** *(paradigm). The ananke, often translated as 'necessity', was the only other co-existent element or presence in Plato's cosmogony. Later Platonists clarified that* ***the eternal model existed in the mind of the Demiurge.***
>
> [Bold emphasis mine]

Within this short passage we find the reference to the Great Architect as the 'divine craftsman', as well as how the hive Demiurge is seeking to bring its collectivist 'order' to humanity out of the chaos of being human, serving as the harbinger to the Freemasonic term, *Ordo ab Chao*. The alleged 'eternal model' existing in the 'mind' of the Demiurge is naught but the spread of the collectivist mind virus into each and every human on a knowing basis – in other words, the forsaking of our human consciousness in favor of the hive collectivist intelligence where one replaces the other. This was the grand design, or Great Work, of the hive in bringing order out of chaos, the subsummation of human consciousness into the hive collective.

To understand how these things have been hidden and wrapped in Christian symbolism, where only the initiates into the Hermetic doctrines of the hive could understand their symbolic meaning and still be displayed in plain sight, masquerading in Christian garb, we now need to take a look at the meaning of the Cross in Rosicrucian symbolism. I will once again turn to Wikipedia for a synopsis of the symbolism under the reference *Christian Cross*:

> *"The cross-shaped sign, represented in its simplest form by a crossing of two lines at right angles,* ***greatly predates*** *the introduction of Christianity, in both East and West. It goes back to a very remote period of human civilization. It is supposed to have been used not just for its ornamental value, but also with* ***religious significance.*** *It may have represented* ***the apparatus used in kindling fire, and thus as the symbol of sacred fire or as a symbol of the sun,*** *denoting its daily rotation. It has also been interpreted as* ***the mystic representation of***

***lightning*** *or of the god of the tempest, or* ***the emblem of the Aryan pantheon and the primitive Aryan civilization.***

*Another associated symbol is the ansated cross* ***(ankh or crux ansata)*** *used in ancient Egypt. It was often depicted in the hands of the* ***goddess Sekhmet****, and as a hieroglyphic* ***sign of life*** *or of the living. Egyptian Christians (Copts) adopted it as the emblem of the cross. In his book, The Worship of the Dead, Colonel J. Garnier wrote: "The cross in the form of the 'Crux Ansata' ... was carried in the hands of the Egyptian priests and Pontiff kings as* ***the symbol of their authority as priests of the Sun god and was called 'the Sign of Life'.****"*

[Bold emphasis mine]

There are a few points that need to be made in reference to these passages and some necessary expansion. I'm sure you have already seen the correlations with the solar cultism that mirrors that of the Aten worship in Egypt and Zoroastrianism, the association with fire and lightning in the previous passage, and our dear friends the Aryans holding center stage once again.

The symbol of the ankh has seen a revival in recent decades as a jewelry adornment. The ankh is the cross with the loop at the top, and as I revealed in the *WANA* series of books, represents the womb of the Mother Goddess, the giver of life. This same womb symbolism is found in the Omega sign, which Ninhursag in her varied roles wore as a hairstyle and is also found in representations in Hindu temples as the yoni.

Although the Egyptian goddess Sekhmet is mentioned in this passage, the goddess was represented in many Near Eastern traditions sitting atop a lion throne, one of whom was Ashtoreth, or Astarte. For more information on this lion affiliation, look up *Lion-throned Goddesses of Western Asia* (link in references section). In many of these ancient carvings you are also going to find other symbols like the winged solar disc, the Tree of Life, the serpent uraeus, the lotus, the planet Venus and other symbolic representations that all point to Ninhursag in her many guises.

So, to get back on track and not wander too far afield of the subject at hand, the Rosicrucian Cross, although having the appearance and leaving the impression of Christianity to the ignorant masses, holds a more ancient meaning of the sun disc and the eternal flame associated with the hive collective going all the way back to Zoroastrianism, as well as the Rose being associated with Aphrodite and Dionysus. Despite the superficial appearances of mainstream Christianity to Christian eyes, the symbolism is wholly pagan by Christian definitions. It is through such symbolic devices of hidden meaning that the adepts and acolytes of the 'Sacred Science' hide their messages in plain sight and go totally unperceived by the masses.

Since I have broached the subject of the yoni in this chapter, I feel it is appropriate to provide some information in regard to that so the reader can see how all these 'spiritual' traditions fold into one another. Under *Yoni* on Wikipedia we find:

*Yoni (IAST: yoni; Sanskrit: "womb", "uterus", "vagina", "vulva", "abode", or "source") is a stylised representation of* ***female genitalia representing the goddess Shakti*** *in Hinduism. Within Shaivism, the sect dedicated to the god Shiva,* ***the yoni symbolises his consort****. The male counterpart of the yoni is the lingam.* ***The union of the yoni and lingam represents the eternal process of creation and regeneration, the union of male and female principles, and all existence****. In art and sculpture, this union is represented by a cylinder (lingam, often interpreted as a stylised phallus) resting within a spouted dish (yoni)."*

[Bold emphasis mine]

Here again we find that hermaphroditic mergence of the male and the female allegorically presented through the lingam (phallus) joined within the yoni (vagina) where the two represent one, once joined in this holy communion merging the feminine and masculine. With this information now in hand, let's take a look a closer look at Rosicrucianism, allegedly the launching organization of later Freemasonry. In Wikipedia, under the lookup, *Chymical Wedding of Christian Rosenkreutz,* we find:

*The Chymical Wedding of Christian Rosenkreutz (German: Chymische Hochzeit Christiani Rosencreutz anno 1459) is a German book edited in 1616 in Strasbourg. Its anonymous authorship is attributed to Johann Valentin Andreae. The Chymical Wedding is often described as the third of the original manifestos of the mysterious "Fraternity of the Rose Cross" (Rosicrucians), although it is markedly different from the Fama Fraternitatis and Confessio Fraternitatis in style and in subject matter.*

*It is an allegoric romance (story) divided into* ***Seven Days, or Seven Journeys****, like* ***Genesis****, and recounts how Christian Rosenkreuz was invited to go to a wonderful castle full of miracles, in order to assist the* ***Chymical Wedding of the king and the queen,*** *that is, the husband and the bride.*

*This manifesto has been a source of inspiration for poets, alchemists (the word "chymical" is an old form of "chemical" and refers to* ***alchemy****—for which the* ***'Sacred Marriage' was the goal)*** *and dreamers, through the force of its initiation ritual with processions of tests,* ***purifications, death, resurrection, and ascension*** *and also by its symbolism found since the beginning with the invitation to Rosenkreutz to assist this Royal Wedding.*

*The invitation to the royal wedding includes the **Monas Hieroglyphica** associated with **John Dee**.*

*There is some resemblance between this alchemical romance and **passages in the Bible** such as:*

*The **kingdom of heaven is like unto a certain king, which made a marriage for his son**, and And when the king came in to see the guests, he saw there a man which had not on a wedding garment: (Matthew 22:2,11 KJV)*

*And I John saw the holy city, **new Jerusalem, coming down from God out of heaven**, **prepared as a bride** adorned for her husband. (Revelation 21:2)*

The highlighted portions should illustrate the repeating pattern of the Seven symbolism in this tale that I covered in the last chapter. The biblical passages are an allusion to this divine wedding and there has been no shortage of Hermetic indoctrination and propaganda in the modern spiritual arena and within Christian churches referencing the 'Bride of Christ'. There is, however, not one single reference in the Bible that use the term Bride of Christ.

As with many things in these allegorical references, there is often a double entendre and a reversal of content. In the Chemical Wedding, Christ is presumed to be the groom, and the hive, or hosts of Heaven take on the role of the Bride, theoretically the Holy Spirit. The Rosicrucians are relying on Christian perception of Jesus the man to be accepted as the groom in this mystical wedding ceremony, and the bride to represent the female Holy Spirit. It is an intentional inversion to confound and confuse in the exoteric arena of the masses hiding the true esoteric meaning to their adepts.

The chemical wedding brings in more than one concept and blends them all together, for within the Hermetic doctrines we find the concept of the mergence with the male and female, based on Ninhursag's hermaphroditism, symbolized by the chemical wedding of the bride and groom, and merging the two into one (a presumed family unit). The other aspect is the merging of the hive mind with the human mind in a form of chemical wedding using esoteric 'alchemy', where the Demiurge brings the New Jerusalem (the hive collective) from Heaven down to Earth and asserts its will and creates its kingdom on Earth.

The way our species has been indoctrinated to categorize most things as either one way or another, most do not think with the minds of allegory and hidden agendas like these esoteric Hermetic philosophers. Most people interpret things in a straightforward and superficial manner, categorizing things in a strictly dualistic, black or white sense of perception. We have been indoctrinated to think this way, and this is one reason that the majority of people can't see through the hidden subversive agenda in all these esoteric traditions through their masked symbolism.

Now, insofar as additional information, the *Chymical Wedding* stated that John Dee's *Monas Hieroglyphica* was engraved on the wedding invitation or appears in the text of the book next to the wedding invitation. Dee's symbol, in his own words, represents "*the moon; the sun; the elements; and fire*". The symbol is a stylized ankh, with a moon crescent atop the circle, once again displaying all the elements of the hive solar ideology mixed with those of Ninhursag. Within the circle of the ankh, we find a single dot, which is referred to as the *circumpunct,* and represents both the sun and the Monad in Pythagorean philosophy and represents the alchemical 'gold' to Hermeticists and Kabbalists. You can see this symbol on every Target retail store as its logo. It is also an allegorical representation of the All-seeing eye in a simplistic form and is found in the Arab world as the *nazar boncoğu* which is supposed to protect one from the 'evil eye'. It must be remembered that John Dee had a many-years long relationship working with alleged 'angels' with his scryer associate Edward Kelley, and there is little doubt to this author about the origin of the symbol arising from these communications. Wikipedia reports under *Monas Hieroglyphica*:

> *"The Hieroglyphic embodies Dee's vision of* ***the unity of the Cosmos*** *and is a composite of various esoteric and astrological symbols. Dee wrote a commentary on it which serves as a primer of its mysteries. However, the obscurity of the commentary is such that it is believed that Dee used it as a sort of textbook for a more detailed explanation of the Hieroglyph which he would give in person. In the absence of any remaining detail*

*of this explanation the full significance of the glyph may never be known."*

*"The existence of the Hieroglyph* ***links Dee to Rosicrucianism****, but in what way remains obscure. The Hieroglyph appears on a page of the Rosicrucian Manifesto Chymical Wedding of Christian Rosenkreutz, beside the text of the invitation to the Royal Wedding given to Rosenkreutz who narrates the work."*

[Bold emphasis mine]

In contradistinction to the last sentence of the first paragraph above, I think I have capably provided the full significance of the glyph and what it represents in esoteric circles of interpretation. In Dee's symbol we find the merging of Ninhursag's hermaphrodite symbolism represented with the ankh, the moon and the solar logos, and also the Monad of the hive, the sun and fire, effectively merging the two into one, all in one single symbolic representation.

I want to digress somewhat and focus a bit on the local conflict and competition between Enki (Yahweh) and Ninhursag. In earlier traditions, which have mostly been expunged from the Bible, Asherah was the consort of Yahweh, and there have been many inscriptions unearthed that reference Yahweh and his Asherah to show this once ancient partnership. As I noted in the *WANA* books, Enki and Ninhursag carried on a serious love/hate relationship for millennia, working together when they could both profit from it, and going after each other hammer and tong when they didn't. In most cases it was the latter circumstance that guided both their hands in this conflict to rule humanity, and the next chapter is going to explain some of the seeming dichotomy in the Bible and why, to this day, there are many unanswered mysteries and contradictions present in that body of work.

# 18. Explaining Contradictions in the Bible

As previously noted, Enki and Ninhursag worked together in the early eras of the ancient Near Easter religions. While Ninhursag subsumed many different goddess identities and created equally as many fictitious other identities, Enki was also doing the same thing with some of his competing adversaries. I realize how confusing this may all sound to the reader, but one should not assume that Enki and Ninhursag were the only two Anunnaki gods carving out territory for themselves in the ancient past. They had many competitors, and just as monopolistic organizations subsume smaller businesses to secure their monopolies and remove the competition, the ancient wars between kingdoms and their tutelary gods was a process of a similar enterprise, although more politically motivated. Over thousands of years of warfare, Enki and Ninhursag were finally able to either eliminate or subjugate their competition to the point that they became the two primary adversaries on the world stage where both were seeking to force their brand of devotion on the human population of this planet. This is why through ancient historical accounts we see a constant thread of continuing religious syncretism taking place.

As much as scholars and their materialistic perspectives want to protest what I am presenting, the historical records leave a lot of evidence where this consolidation of power is concerned. They would rather attribute this syncretizing all the gods to human priesthoods, and by maintaining that idea, they fail to grasp the true historical nature of what was taking place. By relegating the ancient gods to the realm of the mystical, fanciful or mere superstitious statuary representations, they completely miss what took place in our ancient past. They are blissfully unaware of the genuine power struggle that took place in our past with physical entities who called themselves gods and how humans and their armies were only pawns in this larger game for power and control of this planet. To entertain such ideas psychologically challenges the arrogant view of our species and thinking that we have always been in charge of our own destiny. Such ideas totally undermine our cultural perception of ourselves because it illustrates that we have *never* been in charge of our own destiny as a planetary species. Psychologically speaking, this is a huge and bitter pill to swallow, but such strong denial is what drives our intellectual academics. There have been volumes written where these scholars are seeking to solve the meaning of these mysteries, but they all approach their research with the false foundational premise that these stories and traditions are simply myth, and walk away puzzled regardless of the amount of research time they spend ro compose their academic papers trying to impress others.

In light of what I am proposing about the ongoing conflict between Enki and Ninhursag, we only need turn to the Bible itself to see this illustrated. To modern Christians this is a simplistic war between Christianity and Paganism, but there is a deeper tale to be gleaned from the biblical writings that goes beyond these superficial dualistic interpretations which cuts right to the heart of the conflict between God and Satan. I am not going to do an exhaustive examination of the entire Bible, but I am only going to offer certain verses necessary to substantiate my assertions and clear the muddy waters of misunderstanding in regard to the story being told between the alleged morality tales contained in the book.

If we can accept the premise I assert, then the first place we want to undo a major point of confusion in Christian scholarship to this day is the apparent dichotomy between Isaiah 14:12-14 and Revelation 2:26-29, where in Isaiah the Morning Star refers to Satan or Lucifer, and in the Revelation passages refers to Christ as the Morning Star. Let's look at the NIV translation of Isaiah 14:12-14 to get the first glimpse at this Biblical conundrum:

> *12. How you have fallen from heaven, morning star, son of the dawn! You have been cast down to the earth, you who once laid low the nations!*
>
> *13. You said in your heart, "I will ascend to the heavens; I will raise my throne above the stars of God; I will sit enthroned on the mount of assembly, on the utmost heights of Mount Zaphon.*
>
> *14. I will ascend above the tops of the clouds; I will make myself like the Most High."*

Here is the King James Version to remove all confusion about who is being referred to in these passages:

> *12. How art thou fallen from heaven, O Lucifer, son of the morning! how art thou cut down to the ground, which didst weaken the nations!*
>
> *13. For thou hast said in thine heart, I will ascend into heaven, I will exalt my throne above the stars of God: I will sit also upon the mount of the congregation, in the sides of the north:*
>
> *14. I will ascend above the heights of the clouds; I will be like the most High.*

In the context of this presentation, Lucifer should be interpreted to represent Ninhursag as Lucifer. Lucifer as the Morning Star is a direct reference to the planet Venus and there is no doubt whatsoever as to what these verses indicate; that Ninhursag (Lucifer) said that she will Ascend to heaven and exalt herself above the stars of God (Enki/Yahweh), and will sit on the mount of congregation (the hive) in the sides of the north. In Hermetic traditions the North represents the hive in allegorical form. Lucifer (Ninhursag) further states that she will "ascend above the heights and will be like the "most High". This latter part is another of those double entendre statements. The polemic, delivered as a criticism of Lucifer, is being leveled by Yahweh/Enki in regard to Ninhursag's ambition to elevate herself above Yahweh's control as the self-proclaimed "most High". But the "most High" from Lucifer's claim is to 'ascend' and become part of the hapiym hive collective as "like the most High" as the center of the hapiym collective. Until one can understand this double entendre, the verses make only superficial sense in the dualistic realm of perception.

Now, let's take a look at where the Christian confusion comes in with the reference to Christ as the Morning Star in the second book of Revelation:

> *[1] Unto the angel of the church of Ephesus write;* ***These things saith he that holdeth the seven stars in his right hand, who walketh in the midst of the seven golden candlesticks;***
>
> *[2] I know thy works, and thy labour, and thy patience, and how thou canst not bear them which are evil: and thou hast tried them which say they are apostles, and are not, and hast found them liars:*
>
> *[3] And hast borne, and hast patience, and for my name's sake hast laboured, and hast not fainted.*
>
> *[4] Nevertheless I have somewhat against thee, because thou hast left thy first love.*
>
> *[5] Remember therefore* ***from whence thou art fallen****, and repent, and do the first works; or else I will come unto thee quickly, and will remove thy* ***candlestick*** *out of his place, except thou repent.*
>
> *[6] But this thou hast, that thou hatest the deeds of the Nicolaitans, which I also hate.*

*[7] He that hath an ear, let him hear what the Spirit saith unto the churches; To him that overcometh will **I give to eat of the tree of life**, which is in the midst of the paradise of God.*

*[8] And unto the angel of the church in Smyrna write; **These things saith the first and the last, which was dead, and is alive;***

*[26] And he that overcometh, and keepeth my works unto the end, to him will I give power over the nations:*

*[27] And he shall rule them with a rod of iron; as the vessels of a potter shall they be broken to shivers: even as I received of my Father.*

*[28] **And I will give him the morning star.***

*[29] He that hath an ear, let him hear what **the Spirit** saith unto the churches.*

[Bold emphasis mine]

In these passages we are once again confronted with an inversion of perception. These allusions are about Christ, which most Christians think of as Christ the man, Son of God, but taken in the context of the code keys I have provided in this volume, a different picture emerges and we see that Christ is Ninhursag, "the first and the last" (Alpha and Omega), and also the one to be "given the morning star". Ninhursag had died and risen, just like the story of Jesus' Resurrection (albeit not bodily) as I have asserted in earlier chapters in this book. When one can see the inversion and the allegory in these passages in relationship to the passages in Isaiah condemning Lucifer as the morning star, then the seeming contradiction and dichotomy in Revelation disappears. The polemic in Isaiah is from Enki's perspective as God almighty, and the Revelation passages are put forth from Ninhursag's perspective as the living Christ of the hive transformation through a vision provided to John of Patmos. There is no dichotomy except that of perception and lack of information. Lucifer, the morning star (Venus/Ninhursag) *is* Christ the morning star in the New Testament format. The only difference is whose viewpoint is being expressed, Ninhursag's or Enki's, and how we interpret the texts.

Asherah, as with most goddesses, was associated with trees and groves, also represented in the Hermetic and Kabbalistic traditions as the Tree of Life. The hive promoted Intellect, and Ninhursag always promoted herself as the goddess of Wisdom and Intellect. The competition between Yahweh and the goddess appears as early as the Garden of Eden story in Genesis with the serpent of wisdom and knowledge (Ninhursag) enticing Eve to eat from the Tree of Knowledge, thereby corrupting Yahweh's plan to keep humanity ignorant and subservient to his will. The Garden of Eden story illustrates the difference between Enki and Ninhursag and how they each chose to rule the mind of humanity, i.e. one through perpetual ignorance and subservience to himself, the other through limited provided knowledge or wisdom and gaining devotion from this sharing of wisdom. The goddess in all these mystery traditions was the provider, the womb of knowledge, the nurturing and caring Mother, and represented fertility which was reflected in her sexual rites. This stands in stark contradiction to the patriarchal ways of Enki/Yahweh demanding groveling subservience to his will. Make no mistake in thinking that either one of these options did not lead to tyranny over human consciousness, for both of these power-hungry monsters only had human subjugation as their goal. The only variance was in how they each chose to implement it. Once the hive element was introduced through mystical doctrines, the hidden tyranny only became more subversive – more 'mysterious'.

With this information in hand, then we need to do a further analysis of some selected biblical verses. Although many of these are leveled at the backsliding of Israel into their old Canaanite religious practices, they are as much a polemic against Ninhursag as they are aimed at Israel.

***Jeremiah 2:13***

*"For My people have committed two evils:* ***They have forsaken Me, the fountain of living waters****, to hew for themselves cisterns, broken cisterns that can hold no water.*

[Bold emphasis mine]

For those who wish to contest my assertion that the Yahweh of the Old Testament is in fact the Sumerian Enki, the highlighted portion above brings this into sharp focus, as the illustrations and carvings of Ea (Yah), or Enki always portray him with waters flowing from him. Enki is the epitome of the 'living water' in Sumerian lore and iconography, and the biblical God's assertion that he is the 'fountain of the living water' is pretty inarguable by comparison when we look at these ancient renderings of Ea/Enki throughout the Fertile Crescent. This may be contested but I don't think it can be effectively refuted.

The following verses could be viewed as a double entendre set of sayings as well where, on one hand they are referring to Israel, and on the other can be seen as direct polemic against Ninhursag and her brand of goddess cultism.

***Jeremiah 2:20***

*"For long ago I broke your yoke and tore off your bonds;* ***But you said, 'I will not serve!' For on every high hill and under every green tree you have lain down as a harlot.***

***Jeremiah 3:6***

*Then the LORD said to me in the days of Josiah the king, "Have you seen what faithless Israel did?* ***She went up on every high hill and under every green tree, and she was a harlot there.***

***Jeremiah 7:18***

*"The children gather wood, and the fathers* ***kindle the fire,*** *and the women knead dough to* ***make cakes for the queen of heaven****; and they pour out drink offerings to other gods in order to spite Me.*

***Hosea 2:1-16***

*Say to your brothers, "Ammi," and to your sisters, "Ruhamah."*

*"Contend with your mother, contend, For* ***she is not my wife, and I am not her husband; And let her put away her harlotry from her face and her adultery from between her breasts.***

*Or I will strip her naked and expose her as on the day when she was born. I will also make her like a wilderness, make her like desert land and slay her with thirst.*

*"Also,* ***I will have no compassion on her children, because they are children of harlotry****.*

*"For* ***<u>their mother</u> has played the harlot; she who conceived them has acted shamefully.*** *For she said,* ***'I will go after my lovers, Who give me my bread and my water, my wool and my flax, my oil and my drink.'***

*"Therefore, behold,* ***I will hedge up her way with thorns, and I will build a wall against her so that she cannot find her paths****.*

*"She will pursue her lovers, but she will not overtake them; and she will seek them, but will not find them. Then she will say, 'I will go back to my first husband, for it was better for me then than now!'*

*"For she does not know that it was I who gave her the grain, the new wine and the oil, and lavished on her silver and gold, which they used for Baal.*

*"Therefore, I will take back My grain at harvest time and My new wine in its season. I will also take away My wool and My flax given to cover her nakedness.*

*"And then* ***I will uncover her lewdness in the sight of her lovers, and no one will rescue her out of My hand.***

*"I will also put an end to all her gaiety, her feasts,* ***her new moons, her sabbaths and all her festal assemblies.***

*"I will destroy her vines and fig trees, of which she said, 'These are my wages which my lovers have given me.' And I will make them a forest, And the beasts of the field will devour them.*

*"I will punish her for the days of the Baals when she used to offer sacrifices to them and adorn herself with her earrings and jewelry, and follow her lovers, so that she forgot Me," declares the LORD.*

*"Therefore, behold, I will allure her, bring her into the wilderness and speak kindly to her.*

*'Then I will give her her vineyards from there, And the valley of Achor as a door of hope. And she will sing there as in the days of her youth,*

***as in the day when she came up from the land of Egypt***.

*"It will come about in that day," declares the LORD, "That you will call My Husband and will no longer call My Lord.*

[Bold emphasis mine]

We can continue to read this as Yahweh complaining about Israel's wayward religious devotion, but I think it is safer to translate that these verses are highly illustrative of Enki's scorn for Ninhursag and her religious practices as the Mother Goddess, Yahweh's Asherah. The tribes of Israel never received the tribute in worship as alluded to in these passages, so his polemic is aimed at 'the mother' for receiving them. The vindictive tone in these verses can't be overlooked, and I think it is equally as fair a representation of Enki's resentment toward Ninhursag personally as they are a reflection of those Israelites who went back to her religious cults in their alleged backsliding. It should also be noted that 'she' "came up from the land of Egypt", so any protest that Ninhursag was any kind of strictly Hebrew goddess should be immediately dismissed. These verses, in this author's opinion, accurately frame the conflict between these two ancient Anunnaki gods and their demands on their human worshippers. For some additional insight into this war I offer the following verses.

***Hosea 4:12-14***

*"My people consult their wooden idol, and their diviner's wand informs them; For* ***a spirit of***

***harlotry** has led them astray, and they have played the harlot, departing from their God.*

*They offer sacrifices on the tops of the mountains and burn incense on the hills, under oak, poplar and terebinth, because their shade is pleasant. Therefore your daughters play the harlot And your brides commit adultery.*

*I will not punish your daughters when they play the harlot or your brides when they commit adultery, for the men themselves go apart with harlots and offer sacrifices with temple prostitutes; so the people without understanding are ruined."*

**Jeremiah 44: 14-17**

*None of the remnant of Judah who have gone to live in Egypt will escape or survive to return to the land of Judah, to which they long to return and live; none will return except a few fugitives."*

*Then all the men who knew that their wives were burning incense to other gods, along with all the women who were present—a large assembly—and all the people living in Lower and Upper Egypt, said to Jeremiah,*

*"We will not listen to the message you have spoken to us in the name of the LORD!*

*We will certainly do everything we said we would: **We will burn incense to the Queen of***

***Heaven and will pour out drink offerings to her just as we and our ancestors, our kings and our officials did in the towns of Judah and in the streets of Jerusalem. At that time we had plenty of food and were well off and suffered no harm.***

[Bold emphasis mine]

I could go on and on with Enki's vitriolic condemnation over the competing worship of Ninhursag, but I think there is little point to add repetitive fuel to this fire. If the reader wants more, the Bible is replete with more information in this regard. Of all the other gods present at that time in many places, we do not see the same level of vitriol aimed at any others like that leveled at Ninhursag and her rituals, her mountaintop places of worship, her sacred groves, and her rites and festivals of sexual and drunken revelry. This is indicative of a personal war between these two 'gods' that transcends any of the other 'Baals' present all across the ancient Near East.

To add to this information on the relationship between Yahweh and Ninhursag as his consort Asherah, we only need to look at Wikipedia under *Asherah* for more information:

*Asherah (/ˈæʃərə/) in ancient Semitic religion, is a mother goddess who appears in a number of ancient sources. She appears in Akkadian writings by the name of Ašratu(m), and in Hittite as Aserdu(s) or Asertu(s). Asherah is generally considered identical with the Ugaritic goddess 'A̲tirat.*

*Asherah is identified* ***as the queen consort*** *of the Sumerian god Anu, and Ugaritic El, the oldest deities of their respective pantheons,* ***as well as Yahweh, the god of Israel and Judah****. This role gave her a similarly high rank in the Ugaritic pantheon. Despite her association with Yahweh in extra-biblical sources,* ***Yahweh in the Bible commands the destruction of her shrines so as to maintain purity of worship to Yahweh Himself.*** *The name Dione, which like 'Elat means "Goddess", is clearly associated with Asherah in the Phoenician History of Sanchuniathon, because the same common epithet ('Elat) of "the Goddess par excellence" was used to describe her at Ugarit. The Book of Jeremiah, written circa 628 BC, possibly refers to Asherah when it uses the title "Queen of Heaven"[b] in Jeremiah 7:16-18[7] and Jeremiah 44:17-19, 25."*

*"Between the 10th century BC and the beginning of their exile in 586 BC, polytheism was normal throughout Israel;* ***it was only after the exile that worship of Yahweh alone became established, and possibly only as late as the time of the Maccabees (2nd century BC) that***

***monotheism became universal among the Jews.*** *Some biblical scholars believe that* ***Asherah at one time was worshipped as the consort of Yahweh****, the national God of Israel. There are references to the worship of numerous gods throughout Kings: Solomon builds temples to many gods and Josiah is reported as cutting down the statues of Asherah in the temple Solomon built for Yahweh (2 Kings 23:14). Josiah's grandfather Manasseh had erected one such statue (2 Kings 21:7)"*

*"William Dever's book Did God Have a Wife? adduces further archaeological evidence—for instance, the many female figurines unearthed in ancient Israel, (known as Pillar-Base Figurines)—as supporting the view that in Israelite folk religion of the monarchal period, Asherah functioned as a goddess and consort of Yahweh and was worshiped as the Queen of Heaven, for whose festival the Hebrews baked small cakes.*

*The word Asherah is translated in Greek as alsos, grove, or alse, groves, or occasionally by dendra, trees; Vulgate in Latin provided lucus or nemus, a grove or a wood (thus KJV Bible uses grove or groves with the consequent loss of Asherah's name and knowledge of her existence to*

*English language readers of the Bible over some 400 years). The association of Asherah with trees in the Hebrew Bible is very strong. For example, she is found under trees (1K 14:23; 2K 17:10) and is made of wood by human beings (1K 14:15, 2K 16:3-4). Trees described as being an asherah or part of an asherah include grapevines, pomegranates, walnuts, myrtles, and willows (Danby:1933:90,176)."*

As mentioned previously, Raphael Patai offered very powerful and convincing evidence of Asherah as the consort Goddess of the Jews in his book, *The Hebrew Goddess.* Another extensive presentation is, *History's Vanquished Goddess ASHERAH: God's Wife* by Darlene Kosnik. This particular volume is filled with images from all around the ancient Near East for those interested in archaeological pictorial evidence of the reach of Ninhursag's goddess cults. The archaeological evidence of a conjoined worship in temples of Yahweh and Asherah is very powerful, as is the evidence of a falling out between Enki and Ninhursag in those roles as the previous biblical verses highlight. This further bolsters my contention about their on again-off again relationship, the last parting which resulted in the major thrust of this presentation. Once those two parted ways for the last time, their competing doctrines became murderous to one another and humanity has been the casualty in the game ever since.

To put the capstone on this chapter, we will look at one more inversion in the book of Revelation and that is from chapter

17 in reference to the Great Whore of Babylon. When you read these passages, you have to reverse their meaning from the standard Old Testament admonishments against the Goddess and her cult. Citing the passages from Wikipedia under *Whore of Babylon* we find:

> *"The "great whore", of the biblical Book of Revelation is featured in chapters 17 and 18:*
>
> *17:1 And there came one of the seven angels which had the seven vials, and talked with me, saying unto me, Come hither; I will shew unto thee the judgment of the great whore that sitteth upon many waters:*
>
> *17:2 With whom the kings of the earth have committed fornication, and the inhabitants of the earth have been made drunk with the wine of her fornication.*
>
> *["Fornication" is interpreted/translated as "idolatry" in the Amplified Bible (AMP), the New American Bible mentions "harlotry"]*
>
> *17:3 So he carried me away in the spirit into the wilderness: and I saw a woman sit upon a scarlet coloured beast, full of names of blasphemy, having seven heads and ten horns.*
>
> *17:4 And the woman was arrayed in purple and scarlet colour, and decked with gold and precious stones and pearls, having a golden cup in*

*her hand full of abominations and filthiness of her fornication:*

*17:5 And upon her forehead was a name written, MYSTERY, BABYLON THE GREAT, THE MOTHER OF HARLOTS AND ABOMINATIONS OF THE EARTH. [King James Version; the New International Version uses "prostitutes" instead of "harlots"].*

*17:6 And I saw the woman drunken with the blood of the saints, and with the blood of the martyrs of Jesus: and when I saw her, I wondered with great admiration.*

*17:9 And here is the mind which hath wisdom. The seven heads are seven mountains, on which the woman sitteth. [King James Version; the New International Version Bible and the New American Bible use "hills" instead of "mountains"].*

*17:10 And there are seven kings: five are fallen, and one is, and the other is not yet come; and when he comes, he must continue a short space.*

*17:11 And the beast that was, and is not, even he is the eighth, and is of the seven, and goes into perdition.*

*17:12 And the ten horns which thou saw are ten kings, which have received no kingdom as yet; but receive power as kings one hour with the beast.*

*17:15 And he said unto me, The waters which thou sawest, where the whore sitteth, are peoples, and multitudes, and nations, and tongues.*

*17:18 And the woman which thou sawest is that great city, which reigns over the kings of the earth.*

*— Revelation 17:4–18 (various)"*

In this context, and many Protestant researchers have figured this out, the Great Whore of Babylon represents Rome and the Roman Church, which is a city built upon seven hills. The Saints in this context refer to those hapiym 'souls' who were persecuted and martyred by the heretical zealots of the Roman Church, i.e the Gnostics and mystics throughout the ages, not the assumed Christian saints fed to the lions in the Roman Coliseum. The reference to Babylon is a direct allusion to the monotheism of Enki/Yahweh which was brought out of Babylon by the Yahwists after the Jewish exile and noted previously, not the goddess Ninhursag in this context.

The fact that the woman was arrayed in purple and red signifies the garments of the Roman Church clergy. To Ninhursag and the hive's divine mystical traditions, Rome is the unequivocal Great Whore who has corrupted the teachings and persecuted the divine 'Christ' consciousness represented by Ninhursag and reflected in the hapiym hive collective. It has nothing to do with evangelical Christian superficial thinking and everything to do with Ninhursag as Christ casting her own polemic against Enki's Church in Rome, which has controlled kings and states throughout the ages since its establishment.

If one doesn't have the key to understanding these things as I have provided in this book, then only dichotomy and confusion appears between the Old and New Testament renderings of the great harlot. In the Old Testament, the harlot was the Goddess Ashera/Ashtoreth. In the New Testament, in the framework for interpretation I have provided, the great harlot is Enki's church in Rome, which has persecuted the hive mystics from its inception.

The majority of people can't perceive things beyond their beliefs to interpret these texts in any manner other than their standard rigid belief structure. They do not perceive innuendo, nor do they perceive the inversions presented in these doctrines. They have one picture and all the contradictions are expected to fit into simplistic dualistic perceptions and interpretations of this picture. They have not developed the discernment to perceive anything beyond what they have been told to believe where their beliefs are concerned. People simply think too small to perceive this larger picture, and to perceive anything beyond accepted beliefs creates fear and cognitive dissonance to anyone who can't accept an alternative perspective than the belief they have adopted and made part of their very personality.

We have to read the New Testament in the light of visionary experiences that mirror the Zoroastrian and hive doctrines of Light. Paul was blinded by the Light and saw visions of the resurrected Jesus on the road to Damascus. Regardless of his own interpretations of this hive induced vision, all the elements are present to substantiate this argument. I ask the reader to remain open-minded enough to ponder my assertions when you read the following passages about the *Conversion of Paul the Apostle* from Wikipedia:

> *"Acts of the Apostles discusses Paul's conversion experience at three different points in the text, in far more detail than in the accounts in Paul's letters. The Book of Acts says that Paul was on his way from Jerusalem to Syrian Damascus with a mandate issued by the High Priest to seek out and arrest followers of Jesus, with the intention of returning them to Jerusalem as prisoners for questioning and possible execution. The journey is interrupted when* ***Paul sees a blinding light****, **and communicates directly with a divine voice.***
>
> *Acts 9 tells the story as a third-person narrative:*
>
> *As he neared Damascus on his journey, suddenly* ***a light from heaven flashed around him****. He fell to the ground* ***and heard a voice say to him****, "Saul, Saul, why do you persecute me?"*
>
> *"Who are you, Lord?" Saul asked.*

*"I am Jesus, whom you are persecuting," he replied.* ***"Now get up and go into the city, and you will be told what you must do."***

*The men traveling with Saul stood there speechless; they heard the sound but did not see anyone. Saul got up from the ground, but when he opened his eyes he could see nothing. So they led him by the hand into Damascus. For three days he was blind, and did not eat or drink anything.*

*—Acts 9:3–9, NIV*

*The account continues with a description of Ananias of Damascus* ***receiving a divine revelation*** *instructing him to visit Saul at the house of Judas on the Street Called Straight and there* ***lay hands on him to restore his sight*** *(the house of Judas is traditionally believed to have been near the west end of the street). Ananias is initially reluctant, having heard about Saul's persecution, but obeys the divine command:*

*"Lord," Ananias answered, "I have heard many reports about this man and all the harm he has done to your holy people in Jerusalem. And he has come here with authority from the chief priests to arrest all who call on your name."*

*But the Lord said to Ananias, "Go!* ***This man is my chosen instrument to proclaim my name to the Gentiles*** *and their kings and to the people of Israel. I will show him how much he must suffer for my name."*

*Then Ananias went to the house and entered it. Placing his hands on Saul, he said, "Brother Saul, the Lord—Jesus, who appeared to you on the road as you were coming here—has sent me so that you may see again and be filled with the* ***Holy Spirit."*** *Immediately, something like scales fell from Saul's eyes, and he could see again. He got up and was baptized, and after taking some food, he regained his strength.*

*—Acts 9:13–19, NIV*

Through this conversion and Paul's subsequent healing of his temporary blindness, we see all the elements of typical ecstatic conversion when induced by the hapiym virus. I will assert that the hapiym virus cell inside Paul caused his temporary blindness, and that the intercession of another human whose own internal hive cell (Ananias) was active, was able to remove this physiological impairment that was also instigated by Paul's internal hive virus cell. I realize how much this may stretch the reader's imagination to accept the fact that the hapiym virus could impact us not only on the mental, but also the physiological level, but there have been too many similar reported cases in many cultures around the world to dismiss this out of hand.

Just as Paul was induced to change completely from a persecutor of Christians as a direct result of his 'divine' intervention, it has happened innumerable times throughout the ages, and only materialist scientists are so readily willing to discount these occurrences and refuse to investigate them. I explained my own experiences at the hands of this pernicious hive collective masquerading as God, and I will fully assert that Paul's conversion was based on the same kind of cognitive intrusion that I personally experienced, as have others throughout time.

We also have to look at the impact of Pauline Christianity and the collectivist herding impact it has had on the world for almost 2,000 years. We can ignore all this and chalk it up to some guy who had a psychotic episode and self-induced temporary blindness, or we can face the facts and see the episode for what it was and admit the massive detrimental psychological impact it has played on the human psyche for generations. Paul's conversion, based on this intrusive, artificially induced hive visionary state, was equally as powerful as the vision of the angel Gabriel with Mohammed that led to the creation of the religion of Islam, or the visions provided to Emmanuel Swedenborg, William Miller, Joseph Smith and countless others around the world. We can no longer afford to look at these things as disparate and isolated 'subjective' incidents but must finally mature our consciousness enough to see the repeating pattern in all these invasions of human consciousness and accept what they represent. We ignore this evidence at our own peril, for until we can clear our psyche of the residual effects of this virus and how it controls our perceptions to this day, we are still a slave to its designs.

# 19. The Tao Te Ching, Fuxi and Nuwa

At this point of this presentation the reader must now be aware that nothing is as it seems and that there is also no simple way to reveal this information. The vastness of this interwoven tapestry of mysticism can't be explained in a linear fashion but must ever be approached in an almost spherical way of thinking to concatenate all the disjointed pieces together to create the whole picture. There is no single aspect of this that can be explained or described as a singular element that will provide the comprehensive understanding required to truly perceive the greater whole. Compartmentalized thinking that 'this is this' and 'that is that' will always leave one lacking when trying to comprehend the larger picture. In the realm of mystical teachings, this has been done intentionally to ensure that the information is kept out of the hands of the 'profane,' and has been reserved for the intellectual classes of mystics and philosophers to serve as humanity's 'guides' to understand this deception. This wide distribution of fragmented pieces has kept this alleged spiritual mysticism ever a mystery to the masses. The mystery attracts, for if people knew what is presented in this book beforehand, they would be wise enough to stay away from all these mystical contrivances knowing full well that they are not what they present themselves to be.

Before we can start to unravel these traditions, we often need to search for the root of certain doctrines to see their origin. It is from these roots, provided we have enough information in hand to see through the stories, that we can see the evolution of mystical ideas. In addressing and exposing the *Tao Te Ching* as just another mystical spinoff of the Anunnaki goddess Ninhursag, we will start this part of the exposé at the root. To lay this foundation we are going to refer again to Wikipedia with the lookup of *Queen Mother of the West* where we find:

> *"The Queen Mother of the West, known by various local names, is a goddess in Chinese religion and mythology, also worshipped in neighbouring Asian countries, and attested from ancient times. The first historical information on her can be traced back to oracle bone inscriptions of the fifteenth century BC that record sacrifices to a "Western Mother". Even though these inscriptions illustrate that she predates organized Taoism, she is most often associated with Taoism. From her name alone some of her most important characteristics are revealed: she is royal, female, and is associated with the west. The growing popularity of the Queen Mother of the West, as well as the beliefs that she was the dispenser of prosperity, longevity, and eternal bliss took place during the second century BC when the northern*

*and western parts of China were able to be better known because of the opening of the Silk Road"*

*"She is also known in contemporary sources as the Lady Queen Mother. In the Maternist current of Chinese salvationist religions she is the main deity and is called upon as the Eternal Venerable Mother.*

*Tang writers called her "Golden Mother the First Ruler", the "Golden Mother of Tortoise Mountain", "She of the Nine Numina and the Grand Marvel", and the "Perfected Marvel of the Western Florescence and Ultimate Worthy of the Cavernous Darkness". Commoners and poets of the era referred to her more simply as the "Queen Mother", the "Divine Mother", or simply "Nanny" (Amah)."*

*"The first mentions of the Queen Mother date back to the oracle bone inscriptions of the Shang dynasty (1766 – 1122 BC)."*

*"Western Mother refers to an archaic divinity residing in the west. The exact nature of the Mother divinities in the Shang dynasty is unclear, but they were seen as powerful forces*

*deserving of ritual by the people of the Shang dynasty.*

*Originally, from the earliest known depictions of her in the "Guideways of Mountains and Seas" during the Zhou dynasty, she was a ferocious goddess with the teeth of a tiger, who sent pestilence down upon the world. After she was adopted into the Taoist pantheon, she was transformed into the goddess of life and immortality."*

*"One of the earliest written references to the Queen Mother comes from the writings of the Taoist writer Zhuangzi (c. fourth century BC):*

*The Queen Mother of the West obtained it* ***[the Dao]****[...] [...]and took up her seat at Shao kuang. No one knows her beginning; no one knows her end.*

*Zhuangzi describes the Queen Mother as one of the highest of the deities, meaning* ***she had gained immortality and celestial powers.*** *Zhuangzi also states that Xiwangmu is seated upon a spiritual western mountain range, suggesting she is connected to not only the heavens, but also to the west."*

I apologize for the length of the quotations, but within these passages we are finding all of the elements of what has come in the previous chapters in this book. It is indisputable from the information just offered that the goddess (Ninhursag) is the presenter of the Dao, or Tao. The Wikipedia citation just shared has substantially more information to provide on the *Queen Mother of the West* for those interested in a deeper study of the matter.

Within these passages we see the dualistic nature of this goddess as both a force for positive as well as having an aggressive nature who is associated with delivering pestilence. In this respect, the Queen Mother of the West brings forth images of the Hindu goddess Kali where her personal characteristics are concerned. Given the foundation just established, then we realize that the 'she' referred to in the Tao is Ninhursag in her elevated 'celestial' capacity as a representative of the hapiym cosmic hive.

Under the Wikipedia reference for *Chinese salvationist religions* we find:

> *"Chinese salvationist religions or Chinese folk religious sects are a Chinese religious tradition characterised by a concern for salvation (moral fulfillment) of the person and the society. They are distinguished by* ***egalitarianism****,* ***a founding charismatic person*** *often informed by a* ***divine revelation, a specific theology written in holy texts****, a millenarian eschatology and* ***a***

***voluntary path of salvation****, an embodied experience of the* ***numinous*** *through healing and* ***self-cultivation****, and* ***an expansive orientation through evangelism and philanthropy****."*

[Bold emphasis mine]

I ask the reader's forbearance as I finish painting this picture based on the evidence at hand. For those who are unfamiliar with what egalitarianism means, Wikipedia defines *Egalitarianism* as:

*"Egalitarianism (from French égal, meaning 'equal') – or equalitarianism – is a school of thought that prioritizes equality for all people. According to the Stanford Encyclopedia of Philosophy, Egalitarian doctrines maintain that* ***all humans are equal in fundamental worth or social status.*** *According to the Merriam-Webster Dictionary, the term has two distinct definitions in modern English: either as* ***a political doctrine that all people should be treated as equals and have the same political, economic, social and civil rights****; or* ***as a social philosophy advocating the removal of economic inequalities among people, economic egalitarianism, or the decentralization of power****. Some sources define egalitarianism as the point of view that equality reflects the natural state of humanity."*

[Bold emphasis mine]

With this definition we find that within the Taoist theory of egalitarianism as a salvation ideology, where one seeks communion with the divine, we also have the correlative roots of Marxist egalitarian ideology, *"from each according to his ability, to each according to his needs."* Given this context, the spiritual side washes the hand of the materialist Marxist side, and it has followed through the western mystical traditions under the banner of *Liberty, Equality, Fraternity* which I covered previously. It doesn't matter which mask it hides behind, the overall hapiym hive agenda was the homogenization of humanity into a consolidated herd. The virus drew no distinction between the sacred and the profane where delivering its ideologies of herd consolidation were concerned, as will be discussed in depth in a later chapter. But we can no longer afford to see these things as separate and distinct from each other, for in truth, these ideologies are woven so tightly together into this tapestry that they are truly inseparable.

Before I get too far afield of this chapter topic, I only want to add that the word numinous is a derivative of the Latin word *Numen*, which Wikipedia informs us in part:

> *"Numen, pl. numina, is a Latin term for* ***"divinity"****, or a* ***"divine presence", "divine will."*** *The Latin authors defined it as follows. Cicero writes of a* ***"divine mind"*** *(divina mens), a god* ***"whose numen everything obeys,"*** *and a* ***"divine***

***power"*** *(vim divinam)* ***"which pervades the lives of men.""***

[Bold emphasis mine]

With this explanation now in hand, then we can see that all these references to the numinous mean a source of presumed divine inspiration, whether that is receiving visions or hearing the voice of God or the Goddess represented by the intrusive hive cell within one's form when the virus was alive. Whenever we are confronted with the term 'divinely inspired' we should cringe at its implications in light of the information presented in this book. Also pay attention to how the numen 'pervades the lives of men'.

I am not going to do an exhaustive analysis of the *Tao Te Ching* but am only going to provide some relevant passages to illustrate my point that the writings of Lao Tzu are just another facet of hive spiritual ideology with the goddess Yao (Ninhursag) as the primary driving agent to deliver the teachings. I am going to use the translation of the Tao by James Legge from 1891 found in *The Sacred Books of the East No, 39.*

*"(Conceived of as) having no name, it is the Originator of heaven and earth; (conceived of as) having a name,* ***it is the Mother of all things****."*

*"Under these two aspects, it is really the same; but as development takes place, it receives the different names. Together we call them the*

***Mystery****. Where the Mystery is the deepest is the gate of all that is subtle and wonderful."*

*"****Heaven and earth do not act from (the impulse of) any wish to be benevolent****; they deal with all things as the dogs of grass are dealt with.* ***The sages do not act from (any wish to be) benevolent****; they deal with the people as the dogs of grass are dealt with."*

*"Heaven is long-enduring and earth continues long. The reason why heaven and earth are able to endure and continue thus long is because they do not live of, or for, themselves. This is how they are able to continue and endure.*

*Therefore* ***the sage puts his own person last,*** *and yet it is found in the foremost place;* ***he treats his person as if it were foreign to him****, and yet that person is preserved. Is it not because he has no personal and private ends, that therefore such ends are realised?"*

*"We look at it, and we do not see it, and we name it* ***'the Equable.'*** *We listen to it, and we do not hear it, and we name it 'the Inaudible.' We try to grasp it, and do not get hold of it, and we name it 'the Subtle.' With these three qualities, it cannot*

*be made the subject of description; and hence we blend them together and obtain* ***The One****."*

*"**The (state of) vacancy should be brought to the utmost degree**, and that of stillness guarded with unwearying vigour. All things alike go through their processes of activity, and (then) we see them return (to their original state). When things (in the vegetable world) have displayed their luxuriant growth, we see each of them return to its root.* ***This returning to their root is what we call the state of stillness****; and that stillness may be called a reporting that they have fulfilled their appointed end."*

*"Tao is* ***one****. It was in the beginning. It will remain for ever. It is impersonal, eternal,* ***immutable, omnipresent, bodiless, immaterial. It cannot be perceived by the senses. It is nameless. It is indescribable."***

From another translation of the Tao Te Ching we find:

*"The mystery of the valley is immortal;*
***It is known as the Subtle Female.***
***The gateway of the Subtle Female***
*Is the source of the Heaven and Earth."*
*(Chapter 6)*

*"The beginning of the world*

*May be regarded as the* ***Mother of the world.***

***To apprehend the Mother,***

***Know the offspring.***

***To know the offspring***

***Is to remain close to the mother,***

*And free from harm throughout life."*

*(Chapter 52)*

[Bold emphasis mine]

Starting with the last stanza, the offspring refers to the hapiym virus cell. Find the virus cell within and you would connect to Ninhursag, the triple goddess "Mother" of the hive. Know the offspring (hive cell) and you will know the Mother. Mystery resolved.

In the prior passage, the state of vacancy referred to is the setting aside of one's waking state of consciousness so the internal hive virus 'subconscious' could come to the forefront and rule our psyches. This state of stillness was achieved by slaying the waking state of one's awareness, that part of us that the mystics refer to as ego. In my teachings explaining attaining the second cognition state of awareness, it is the slaying of the false ego, the mimic virus habits still present in our species, that must be overcome. One must understand these two separate and distinct definitions of what is called the ego before we can read through teachings like the Tao and other mystical traditions and grasp their true 'mystical' meaning.

This Taoist seeking of the One is only the striving to kill our waking consciousness to form that same communion with the hive collective of intelligence that every other mystical tradition teaches. We have to disenchant ourselves from the idea that this overarching concept of God, Source, the One or the cosmic Creator of all that is was a wholesome ideology. It all led to a form of spiritual egalitarianism and homogenization of one's mind and folded it into the hive collective consciousness. Just as modern Fabian Marxist ideologies and Social Justice Warriors pound their political pulpits about equality, we must see all these ideologies as homogenization, usually at the lowest rung of the ladder. It matters not whether the homogenization was achieved through religious and spiritual ideologies or through materialist ventures like Marxist ideologies, the outcome was destined to be the same had the hive been able to fulfill its agenda for our species. Just as Lao Tzu revealed, the job of the sage was not to see benevolence. If one had to lie down with dogs to achieve the agenda of the Tao, it was wholly permissible.

In the context of Taoist thinking as well as that of the Gnostics and Neoplatonists, it is the world of man that is dirty and corrupted, and only through allegedly merging with the divine could humanity find its value. I can think of a no more hateful doctrine to profess than 'my way or the highway, thus sayeth the Lord', yet this hive ideology permeates every religious and political ideology on the planet. Be a part of our herd or you will suffer for disagreeing with our ideology. Our cultures worldwide are evidence of this hive collectivist thinking. The core doctrine is the same, only the outer clothing changes to mask the same ill intent against humanity. In this book I am declaring with a megaphone, once and for all, this mystical collectivist King has no clothes!

So, let me change course and address the other aspect of this chapter title and take a look at Fuxi and Nuwas. Looking up *Fuxi* on Wikipedia we find:

> *"Fuxi (Mandarin: [fǔ ɕí]; Chinese: **伏羲**), also romanized as Fu-hsi, is a culture hero in Chinese legend and mythology, credited **(along with his sister Nüwa女娲)** with creating humanity and the invention of hunting, fishing and cooking as well as the Cangjie **system of writing** Chinese characters c. 2,000 BCE. He was also known as Paoxi (t **庖犧**, s **庖牺**), also romanized as Pao-hsi. Fuxi was counted as the first of the **Three Sovereigns** at the beginning of the Chinese dynastic period. Fuxi was an ancient Chinese god who was said to show the ancient Chinese people how to domesticate animals."*
>
> [Bold emphasis mine]

Now let's look up *Nuwa* in Wikipedia and see what we can discover to add to this story:

> *"Nüwa or Nügua is the **mother goddess** of Chinese mythology, **the sister and wife of Fuxi**,*

*the emperor-god. She is credited with creating mankind and* ***repairing the Pillar of Heaven****. Her reverential name is Wahuang (Chinese: 媧皇; literally: "Empress Wa").”*

[Bold emphasis mine]

Are we starting to see a repeating pattern here? If not, I ask the reader to look up Fuxi and find the illustration that represents Fuxi and Nuwa. You will find an alleged brother and sister whose torsos below the waist are entwined serpents, just like the twin serpents on the staff of Hermes and also in the Sumerian god Ningishzida, who I asserted previously was a representation of Ninhursag in the role of a god rather than goddess. What is of particular interest in the ancient paintings representing Fuxi and Nuwa is that Fuxi holds a carpenter’s square and Nuwa is holding compass. These paintings of the blended male and female Fuxi and Nuwa holding the compass and the square predate the origin of Freemasonry and their use of the symbols by more than a thousand years. The intertwined aspect of the male with the female, coupled with the compass and the square represent the merging of the divine (the circle, compass) with the material (the square), When the two are merged, then we get the triangle, allegedly representing body, mind and spirit, but the triangle also represents the triune nature of the hermaphrodite Ninhursag. The painting also represents that blending of the alleged divine masculine and feminine that is ever present in Ninhursag’s doctrines.

Within the mystical traditions, body, mind and spirit could be accurately interpreted as the form, the intellect and the hive collective. It is through subduing our waking state of consciousness that the form is conquered at the hands of the intellect, so the collective divine mind can rule by creating this mystical triangle through 'squaring the circle' in esoteric terminology. Intellect in and of itself is not consciousness. The circle represents the presumed Oneness of the hive collective that is seeking to move its intelligence into material form. Since the virus itself had no true mind of its own, all it could ever be was the mimicked intelligence of its human hosts. This is why there is so much emphasis on the mind/intellect within these mystical traditions dating back beyond the creation of Greek philosophy.

As noted by what is offered in this chapter, the way of the Tao was already ancient when Lao Tzu wrote the Tao Te Ching in the $6^{th}$ century BC. In China, Confucianism was the materialist response to the mystical Tao and institutionalized Buddhism, just as Theosophy and Marxism are linked together in the West. Once again, we see repeating patterns in all this if we can remove the blinders of compartmentalized thought believing that there is really a difference in the collectivist mentality provided through both avenues of intellect.

As Taoist tradition states, it was the Queen Mother of the West who introduced these alleged spiritual traditions to the East. We find the same celestial connection with the Chinese Queen Mother that we find in the assertions I have made about Ninhursag giving up her form and elevating her hive cell to the hive cosmic collective. The evidence just keeps mounting, in my opinion, and the picture it paints all points the same direction.

This chapter would not be complete if we did not discuss, at least briefly, the symbol of the Tao, the yin-yang symbol. In the primary sense, people see this symbol as representing a balance between positive and negative, or light and dark. The fact that they are combined as seemingly dualistic principles in a single whole, actually represents a *trinity*, once again. In Chinese traditions, the light and dark are often equated with the sun (light) and the moon (dark), two aspects of Ninhursag's symbol usage in other traditions. The triune aspect of the yin-yang symbol that goes unnoticed by most is comprised in the circle which signifies that, under unity (the hive), light and dark are equal and there is no distinction where the whole is concerned. It takes the light and dark, or the positive and negative combined to comprise the whole of the trinity represented in the symbol. This dualistic nature of positive and negative is also presented in other aspects of Ninhursag's personality where she is the mother goddess on one hand and the goddess of chaos and destruction on the other, as with the Queen Mother of the West in Chinese Taoist traditions, as well as with the goddess Kali in Hindu traditions.

Given that the Tao was the invention of the Queen Mother of the West, we must look at this triune aspect of the symbol to understand its hidden meaning. Regardless of the dualistic first impression, the symbol must be viewed as a symbol of trinity, to wit – positive, negative and balance – at least as far as the Taoist ideology is interpreted. No matter where we find these alleged divine ideologies with a goddess association, we find this repeating triune nature, with Hecate; Osiris, Isis and Horus; Father, Son and Holy Spirit in Christian traditions; or through the triune representation of the Tao symbol. Only our compartmentalized dualized blindness prevents us from seeing all these correlations, and it cannot, in contradiction to certain scholarly schools of thought, all be attributed to cultural borrowing. The traditions are too ancient and too homogenous in what they seek to present through these mystical ideologies. Naturally, there is always room for protest and disagreement, but the reader is challenged to provide better explanations for all these things than what is presented in this book that ties them together in such a cohesive manner. Scholars throughout the centuries have not been able to piece this puzzle together, at least in the mainstream arena of academia. The intellectual adepts, however, have always had an inside track, and that is why one must study their material as well as mainstream academics to piece this all together. Ignoring one branch of research in favor of the other leaves the picture incomplete, despite the hidden knowledge of the intellectual adepts. As the reader is discovering, the researcher must cast a wide net to put this all together. Solving these mysteries will not be achieved with compartmentalized thinking and the tunnel vision begotten through one's selected beliefs and filters. Unfortunately, it is exactly this kind of tunnel vision that has prevented this information from being revealed over the centuries, and it explains why our mainstream scholars, locked within their academic specialties, have not figured it out.

# 20. Magic and Other Occult 'Sciences'

The word occult generally means hidden from view, but I am going to provide what Wikipedia has to offer in defining *occult* to bring the picture into clarity:

> *"The occult (from the Latin word occultus* ***"clandestine, hidden, secret"****) is* ***"knowledge of the hidden"****. In common English usage, occult refers to* ***"knowledge of the paranormal"****, as opposed to "knowledge of the measurable", usually referred to as science. The term is sometimes taken to mean* ***knowledge that "is meant only for certain people"*** *or that* ***"must be kept hidden"****, but for most practicing occultists it is simply the study of a deeper spiritual reality that extends beyond pure reason and the physical sciences. The terms esoteric and arcane can also be used to describe the occult, in addition to their meanings unrelated to the supernatural.*
>
> *It also describes a number of magical organizations or orders, the teachings and practices taught by them, and to a large body of*

*current and historical literature and spiritual philosophy related to this subject.*

*Occultism is the study of occult practices, including (but not limited to) magic, alchemy, extra-sensory perception, astrology, spiritualism, religion, and divination. Interpretation of occultism and its concepts can be found in the belief structures of philosophies and religions such as Gnosticism, Hermeticism, Kabbalah, Theosophy, Ancient Egyptian religion, Obeah, modern paganism, Eastern philosophy (including Indian philosophy), Western esotericism and Christian mysticism."*

[Bold emphasis mine]

As we can tell by reading these definitions, everything in this book is considered to be occultism. It should be evident that the occult covers a wide and varied range of subjects, including magic. I have asserted in my other works that what people consider magic is nothing more than one using certain energies programmed to do certain things. Energy itself is neutral, and its usage, whether for good or bad, is reliant on the person who programs that energy to do specific tasks. I realize that materialist mainstream thinkers are automatically going to discount this notion because it doesn't fit into their tunnel-vision perception of material reality. Such things simply don't exist in a 5-sense realistic sense where scientific investigation is concerned. It is purely balderdash. But then, this whole presentation is balderdash by that same limited cognitive standard of measurement.

There is not really any sound argument that can be put forth that refutes the evidence that there is a serious global increase for the interest in magic, as illustrated by the huge popularity of the Harry Potter series of books and movies, citing only one example. There has been a rise of occult and magic oriented websites where members share their spellcasting recipes and where the website sages promote themselves and their self-proclaimed knowledge of occult practices. Other so-called spiritual websites also cater to the occultists within their membership ranks and these spiritual websites have become a hodgepodge gathering point attracting membership from anyone seeking some form of mystical 'enlightenment'. Occultism is big business in today's world. The homogenization of all these mystical occult and spiritual traditions is a major thrust of the Theosophical Society and its umbrella organizations worldwide. This much can't be effectively refuted by anyone who has done just a little bit of investigative research.

With more Fabian Marxist influence and control in the mass media and the constant assault on Christianity, particularly the more rigid ideologies of the evangelical wing of Christianity, the psychological manipulation focused against Christianity doesn't provide similar condemnation of the Islamic faith. Such persistent assaults have steered many people away from traditional Western religion and into the arms of New Age mystical beliefs and occultism. The Theosophical Society's worldwide network of religious homogenization operating under the banner of its Lucis Trust organization, blending the mystical doctrines of the East and West, has provided fruitful ground to attract many people into the realm of mystical spirituality which, despite the selective blindness of the ignorant seeker into the divine, is still occultism.

Lucis Trust and the Fabian Society have very deep pockets, and the Lucis Trust organization has 30,746 (or more) charitable organizations worldwide safely nestled under its umbrella, including the United Nations, which is itself considered a charitable trust. The establishment for this worldwide organization goes back to the beginning of the Theosophical Society when the Fabian Annie Besant joined the organization and set up housekeeping for the Theosophical Society in India. In time, Alice Bailey, another member of the Fabian Society, worked through the ranks and eventually started a breakaway group called the Arcane School while still promoting the general doctrines of Theosophy.

Bailey established 'telepathic' contact with her alleged Ascended Master guide from the Spiritual Hierarchy, Djwal Khul, in 1919, the same year she met her second husband, a judge and 33rd Degree Freemason named Foster Bailey. For some biographical information on *Alice Bailey* provided by Wikipedia we find:

> *"Alice Ann Bailey (June 16, 1880 – December 15, 1949) was a writer of more than twenty-four books on theosophical subjects, and* ***was one of the first writers to use the term New***

***Age**. Bailey was born as Alice La Trobe-Bateman, in Manchester, England. She moved to the United States in 1907, where she spent most of her life as a writer and teacher.*

*Bailey's works, written between 1919 and 1949, describe a wide-ranging system of esoteric thought covering such topics as **how spirituality relates to the Solar System,** meditation, healing, **spiritual psychology**, **the destiny of nations, and prescriptions for society in general**. She described the majority of her work as having been **telepathically dictated to her by a Master of Wisdom, initially referred to only as "the Tibetan" or by the initials "D.K.",** later identified as Djwal Khul. Her writings bore some similarity to those of Madame Blavatsky and are among the teachings often referred to as the **"Ageless Wisdom".** Though Bailey's writings differ in some respects to the Theosophy of Madame Blavatsky, they have much in common with it. She wrote on **religious themes**, including Christianity, though **her writings are fundamentally different from many aspects of Christianity** or other orthodox religions. Her vision of **a unified society** included **a global "spirit of religion" different from traditional religious forms and including the concept of the Age of Aquarius**."*

[Bold emphasis mine]

I want to pause for a moment before continuing and bring attention to a number of revelations offered in this section. Pay attention to the fact that Bailey is one of the first writers to use the term New Age and also heavily promoted the idea of the Age of Aquarius, both ideas which were launched in earnest in the 1960s. The song by the band the 5th Dimension, *Aquarius/Let the Sunshine In*, served as a public anthem to launch the New Age in the minds of the 60s era drug revolution. It was a piece of psychological spiritual propaganda and won the Grammy Award for the best song and best album in 1969.

Also note that Bailey, like so many mystics of the past, including Greek philosophers, religious 'seers' and Hermetic mystics throughout the ages, got her information through 'telepathic' means provided by an alleged Spiritual Hierarchy. The concept of an Angelic Hierarchy can be traced back directly to Pseudo-Dionysus the Areopagite in the 5th century AD. Bailey was only continuing in those mystical footsteps. Similar forms of angelology exist in Christianity, Islam and Jewish traditions where in the more mainstream references they are referred to as Cherubim and Seraphim, or those who sit close to the Throne of God.

Within these passages we also find reference to the Solar System which is only the old Zoroastrian Solar Flame ideology rearing its ugly head in the 20th century under Bailey's guidance, as well as the agenda to address 'the destiny of nations' through 'prescriptions for society in general'. In simplistic terms, Bailey's

Theosophical ideology promoted through the hands of her hive manipulator, Master D.K., was a form of spiritual social engineering. Continuing with Wikipedia:

> *"Bailey was born to a wealthy middle class British family and, as a member of the Anglican Church, received a thorough Christian education*
>
> *Her autobiography states that* ***at the age 15,*** *on June 30, 1895, Bailey was visited by a stranger,* ***"... a tall man, dressed in European clothes and wearing a turban" who told her she needed to develop self-control to prepare for certain work he planned for her to do****. This turned out to be the creation and publication of 19 books together with educational and meditation work* ***that reached into "practically all the countries of the world"****. (p. 63-64)."*
>
> *"Alice and Foster Bailey founded the Lucis Trust in 1922. Its activities include the Arcane School, World Goodwill, Triangles, a quarterly magazine called The Beacon, and a publishing company primarily intended to publish Bailey's many books. The Arcane School gives instruction and guidance in meditation, via correspondence, based on the ideas in Bailey's books. World Goodwill is intended to promote better human*

*relations through goodwill which they define as "love in action". That "action" included support of the* ***United Nations****. The* ***"Triangles"*** *are* ***groups of three people*** *who agree to link up in thought each day and to meditate on right human relations, visualising* ***light and love pouring into human minds and hearts****, followed by the use of the Great Invocation. It is not necessary for each person to link in thought at the same time each day and need only take a few moments of time.*

*"Alice and Foster Bailey founded,* ***"Lucifer Publishing Company". ("'Lucifer' and 'Lucis' come from the same word root, lucis being the Latin genitive case meaning of light.")*** *After the first two or three years, the name was changed to* ***"Lucis Publishing Co."*** *(The Theosophical Society also used the name "Lucifer" for its early magazine.) In 1923, with the help of Foster Bailey,* ***Alice Bailey founded the Arcane School****, which is* ***part of Lucis Trust****. This school provides educational correspondence, meditation instruction, and guided study based on her writings."*

*"Bailey's writings includes a detailed exposition of the* ***"seven rays"*** *which are presented as the fundamental energies that are behind and*

*exist throughout all manifestation. They are seen as the basic creative forces of the universe and* ***emanations of Divinity*** *that underlie the evolution of all things. The rays are described as* ***related to human psychology, the destiny of nations****, as well as the planets and stars of the heavens. The concept of the seven rays can be found in Theosophical works. Campbell writes that* ***Bailey, "... was the first to develop the idea of the seven rays,*** *although it can be found in germ in earlier Theosophical writings."* ***The seven rays also appear in Hindu religious philosophy."***

[Bold emphasis mine]

The reader should see that Alice Bailey and the Theosophical Society sit at ground zero where launching the modern spiritual movements in the West are concerned. What the biographical information on Bailey conveniently overlooks was her membership in the Marxist-oriented British Fabian Society before moving into Theosophy. The Wikipedia post on Alice Bailey is very extensive, but I am only going to offer one more passage and then move forward.

*"Bailey taught a form of* ***universal spirituality*** *that transcended denominational identification, believing that, "Every class of human beings is a group of brothers. Catholics, Jews, Gentiles, occidentals and orientals* ***are all***

***the sons of God." She stated that* all religions originate from the same spiritual source*, and that humanity will eventually come to realize this, and as they do so, the result will be the emergence of* a universal world religion and a "new world order"*."*

[Bold emphasis mine]

From the standpoint of the hive hierarchy and its infection within humanity, we are being told the truth by Bailey about all religions originating from the same spiritual source, except there was nothing truly 'spiritual' about any of it. It was all hive virus manipulation deceiving humans who had a keen desire to experience the supernatural in one form or another. The present Leftist agenda to create a New World Order is part and parcel of the teachings of Theosophy, and the untold truth about this agenda is the linkage between Fabian Marxism and Theosophy.

Annie Besant, who managed the Indian wing of the Theosophical Society was a co-founder of the Fabian Society and established Co-Freemasonic Lodges under her organization International Order of Co-Freemasonry in many places throughout the British Empire. Besant herself was a leading Speaker for the Fabian Society as well as the Marxist Social Democratic Federation (SDF). Besant was a strong proponent of women's rights (Feminism) and birth control in an era where such ideas were wholly unthinkable, and was involved in Marxist union activities, including the Bloody Sunday demonstration in 1887, which was organized by the Marxist SDF. Her writings show that she was a devout Atheist, so we have to wonder just what kind of 'spirituality' she was promoting by moving from the Marxist Fabian Society to the Theosophical Society, eventually taking over its operations in India after an apparent split between her and the America branch. At least that is how the cover story goes.

Despite being President of the Theosophical Society in India, Besant did not give up her activist ideologies, and she played a key role in the Indian Independence Movement pushed forth by another Theosophist, Mahatma Ghandi. For further information on Besant, see the extensive Wikipedia references under *Annie Besant.*

The point of this exposition thus far is to illustrate the association between these alleged spiritual teachings and the Marxist Globalist agenda being shoved down the throat of the world through ideologies like multiculturalism and the apparent push to harmonize the world's religions and create a secular cum spiritual New World Order. This has all been delivered, by the way, at the hands of the same mystical hive manipulators that it has throughout recorded human history. Where, in the past, these efforts were more regional and fragmented, with the age of electronic communication and mass media control, the race to homogenizing the human race is taking place in earnest to ideally fulfill the hapiym hive agenda of total world domination. It isn't going to happen insofar as the realization ached for by the hive collective, but its human Aryan proponents are not going to give up just because their hive masters are suddenly missing in action. They have come too far to give up their game now.

Through all of this we find the elements of revolution at every turn instigated by religious zealots over the ages. The destruction of the past has been an element in all these movements where they are wont to replace and rewrite the past to conform to their own ideologies, illustrated in Christianity tearing down old pagan monuments and places of worship, including one of the destructions of the Library of Alexandria, which Islam finally completed centuries later, and which we are observing on the American landscape at the hands of the Leftist movement today with the destruction of Civil War statues. The tactics are always the same and the ultimate result is the reshaping of society, "Reforming the Whole World", in accordance with the Hermetic hive agenda. Occultism lies at the center of all these movements, and at the center of occultism lies the hive ideologies and Ninhursag in one goddess representation or another, no matter which form they take.

I am not here to preach and endorse this type of occultism, but to expose it for the lie it presents itself to be. The first challenge is to acknowledge that these 'mysteries' have perpetuated themselves throughout the ages, and despite mainstream materialist scientific and academic denial, the metaphysical aspect exists where these hive doctrines are concerned. The mystical enchantment and lure still fascinates and draws the majority of people on this planet into its web. It has always been a lure to the waking ego to possess supernatural powers or, in their sense of insufficiency, be acknowledged in some manner by their God, which perpetuates this dependency on the divine lie – and make no mistake, it is a psychological dependency syndrome of the worst kind.

After untold generations of being told by gods, priests and authorities of all kinds that we are lesser beings, we have become a race of psychologically insecure people who can only seek to reach that supernatural something outside ourselves to give us some sense of value as a human being. It is a species-wide insecurity complex, a psychosis that keeps us ever looking outward to find some external force or power to make us feel strong through acknowledgement of supernatural means to give us personal worth, or even better, to elevate our presumed status above other men when we can attain magical or spiritual powers. Even these hive doctrines that tell us to look within to find our 'souls' were only there so we could find our inner hive cell and thereby connect to the external metaphysical world of the Divine hive collective.

The planetary hapiym virus collective didn't care what it peddled to ignorant humans so long as it could lure people into its mystical and collectivist clutches. The unimprinted hive cell had no sense of good or evil and only sought to expand the hive infection itself. The collective possessed *no* morality, and as illustrated in the last chapter about the Tao, the hive sage was not seeking benevolence, but would lie down with dogs to fulfill its agenda for conquering the human mind. The collective did not possess any inherent sense of right or wrong, good or evil, and it drew no distinction in creating whatever lures it could fabricate to entice humans into giving up their consciousness and replace it with the hive collective mentality. In its simplest sense, the hapiym hive collective could be compared to a multinational corporate conglomerate that ate up all its competition and offered every product it could produce to create its overall monopoly. The hapiym hive collective didn't care what brand of its beliefs it could get you believed so long as you believed some of it.

No two people think the same or are lured by the same concepts, and as such, the hive had to remain ever diverse in the mystical product lines it offered to continue its monopoly. At its core, the hive doctrines are predicated on the same tyranny and the same agenda for control, but the packaging and merchandising has continually changed over the millennia to suit the mystical needs of any particular cultural milieu. When we can understand this agenda as nothing more than a continual sales campaign with an unscrupulous hive collective CEO, then we can come to terms with the fact that it favored tyranny as much as it favored benevolence in order to fulfill its ultimate agenda. With this knowledge in hand, then we must accept that the hive virus drew no delineation between good and evil except in the most superficial sense.

In occultism the argument still rages over the goodness of white magic over the evil of black magic, but the creator of the Church of Satan, Anton LaVey had it right when he said:

> "*White magic is supposedly utilized only for good or unselfish purposes, and black magic, we are told, is used only for selfish or "evil" reasons. Satanism draws no such dividing line. Magic is magic, be it used to help or hinder. The*

*Satanist, being the magician, should have the ability to decide what is just, and then apply the powers of magic to attain his goals."*

*"Satanism is not a white light religion; it is a religion of the flesh, the mundane, the carnal - all of which are ruled by Satan, the personification of the Left Hand Path."*

[Source Wikipedia, *Black Magic*]

When we can accept that the personality of Ninhursag was truly that of a conscienceless psychopath, and that her psychotic personality elevated to a high position of authority in the hive hierarchy (which all the evidence in this book substantiates), then we arrive at the discomfiting fact that within the hive doctrines, there is only the superficial appearance of allowable good versus evil. Each doctrine fabricated by Ninhursag and the hive was tailored to lure as many people as it could into its collectivist ideologies, and I don't care how much one wants to argue the point, religions are as much a collectivist herd endeavor as are political ideologies like Marxism. We see this duality of personality in the Chinese Queen Mother of the West, and we see an even more pronounced version of it in the bloodthirsty Hindu goddess Kali, who is illustrated as wearing a necklace of skulls, a belt of cut off human hands, and four arms. In one hand she holds a bloody sword and in the other a severed human head which bleeds into a bowl held by the hand below it, with her $4^{th}$ hand covered in blood, standing on the corpse of Shiva. This imagery,

I assert, is the most accurate description of the dark and bloody nature of Ninhursag and I don't care what any goddess aficionado or Hindu apologists try to peddle me to dissuade me from seeing Ninhursag in her Kali impersonation as she actually was. The bodies beneath the feet of the French goddess Liberty stand as a testimony to the bloody trail of Ninhursag's 'goodness' as a goddess.

I am not going into an in-depth analysis of Kali found in her many guises in the Hindu tradition in this volume as it is more confusing than the number of god/goddess roles Ninhursag played in the Near East and the West. What should be noted of Kali is that she is one of the three goddesses who sprang from the mind of the Mother Goddess Durga, nailing down another triune aspect of Ninhursag in the Hindu goddess pantheon. Another different trinity aspect in Hinduism is that of Kali, Vishnu and Shiva. Wikipedia informs us in part about *Kali* this way:

> *"Kali's earliest appearance is that of a destroyer of evil forces. She is the goddess of one of the four subcategories of the Kulamārga, a category of* ***tantric Saivism****. Over time, she has been worshipped by devotional movements and tantric sects variously as the* ***Divine Mother, Mother of the Universe****, Adi Shakti, or Adi Parashakti.* ***Shakta Hindu and Tantric sects additionally worship her as the ultimate reality or Brahman.*** *She is also seen as divine protector and the one who bestows moksha, or* ***liberation.*** *Kali is*

*often portrayed standing or dancing on her consort, the Hindu god Shiva, who lies calm and prostrate beneath her. Kali is worshipped by Hindus throughout India."*

*"Hugh Urban notes that although the word Kālī appears as early as the* ***Atharva Veda****, the first use of it as a proper name is in the Kathaka Grhya Sutra (19.7). Kali appears in the Mundaka Upanishad (section 1, chapter 2, verse 4) not explicitly as a goddess, but as the* ***black tongue*** *of the* ***seven flickering tongues of Agni, the Hindu god of fire.****"*

[Bold emphasis mine]

Of the four Vedas, the *Atharva Veda* is a book of magical charms, so it should be no surprise that Kali's first appearance in India and the Hindu religious structure occurs in a book of magic spells. This mirrors Ninhursag as Hecate in Greek traditions as the goddess of witches and sorcerers. In reference to tantra, that word has a broad and diverse philosophical meaning within Hinduism, with three primary schools of tantric thought, all of which feature the goddess Kali at their center. The word tantra itself translates to mean, *loom, weave, system*. Given the nature of how this hive web of deceit has been woven and Ninhursag's role with the hive, as illustrated in this volume, then the meaning of tantra takes on a more expanded and realistic meaning than the philosophical religious meanings in Hindu religious practices. With

Ninhursag/Kali sitting in the middle of tantric religious philosophy and ritual practices, there is much to be gleaned in understanding just what is being *woven* with the facts presented this book in hand.

For those unfamiliar with the Hindu religion and its holy books, Wikipedia offers these brief explanations under *Vedas*. (As an FYI, you can translate Indo-European in these passages to mean Aryan).

> *"The Sanskrit word véda* ***"knowledge, wisdom"*** *is derived from the root vid-* ***"to know".*** *This is reconstructed as being derived from the Proto-Indo-European root *u̯eid-, meaning* ***"see" or "know"."***

> *"The Vedas (/ˈveɪdəz ˈviː-/; Sanskrit:* वेद *veda, "knowledge") are a large body of knowledge texts originating in the ancient Indian subcontinent. Composed in Vedic Sanskrit, the texts constitute the oldest layer of Sanskrit literature and the oldest scriptures of Hinduism. Hindus consider the Vedas to be apauruṣeya, which means "****not of a man, superhuman****" and "****impersonal, authorless****"."*

> *"The Veda, for orthodox Indian theologians, are considered* ***revelations seen by ancient sages after intense meditation****, and texts*

*that have been more carefully preserved since ancient times. In the Hindu Epic the Mahabharata, the creation of Vedas is credited to* ***Brahma****. The Vedic hymns themselves assert that they were skillfully created by Rishis (sages), after* ***inspired creativity****, just as a carpenter builds a chariot."*

*"Transmission of texts in the Vedic period was by oral tradition, preserved with precision with the help of elaborate* ***mnemonic techniques****."*

[Bold emphasis mine]

What these passages reveal is the same pattern of visionary interdiction to formulate the Hindu holy books as with other religions like Zoroastrianism, Christianity and Islam. Brahma in this context should be seen as the overall hive collective consciousness. In some traditions, as shown above, Kali is equated with Brahma, which should come as no surprise with the information you now possess in reading this book thus far. Brahma is the cosmic hive overmind, of which each human is only a divine fragment, or Atman. I trust you can see the similarities in all this with the concept of cosmic Oneness that permeates modern New Age spiritual traditions and Plato's Monad, and all the spiritual nonsense of humans all possessing a *divine spark* within them.

The representation of Kali in the previous passages equates her with the black tongue of Agni's seven tongues of fire. I assert that this has a direct correlation with the Black Flame of the Left Hand path of black magic. The Black Flame is the dark divine spark allegedly present in the aspiring black magician with which he or she must get in touch to become an adept. Regardless of whether one pursues the path of white magic or black, we will find elements of the hive doctrines embedded within them. So, we will take a glimpse at some information that Wikipedia can supply us about *Black Magic*:

> *"Black magic has traditionally referred to* ***the use of supernatural powers or magic*** *for evil and selfish purposes. With respect to the left-hand path and right-hand path dichotomy, black magic is the malicious, left-hand counterpart of the* ***benevolent white magic****. In modern times, some find that the definition of "black magic" has been convoluted by people who define magic or ritualistic practices that they disapprove of as "black magic"."*

> *"Like its counterpart* ***white magic****, the origins of* ***black magic*** *can be traced to the primitive, ritualistic* ***worship of spirits*** *as outlined in Robert M. Place's 2009 book, Magic and Alchemy. Unlike white magic, in which Place sees parallels with primitive* ***shamanistic efforts to achieve closeness with spiritual beings****, the rituals that developed into modern "black magic" were*

*designed* ***to invoke those same spirits*** *to produce beneficial outcomes for the practitioner."*

[Bold emphasis mine]

Robert Place is correct in his assessment above. Whether one is performing black or white magic, *the same spirits*, meaning the hapiym hive collective, are being invoked to work whatever magic is being formulated, or whatever energy is being programmed. Contrary to dualistic thinking and perceptions of the religious or the spiritual, every alleged encounter with otherworldly 'spirits' has resulted from direct interface with the hapiym hive collective. It doesn't matter if one is using white magic to create a religion, (although religionists do not recognize creating religions as a form of magic), or whether one is using black magic to push forth an agenda of personal greed and seeking power, whenever one relied on these assumed otherworldly 'spirits', they were being manipulated and played by the hapiym hive collective. This includes all the books that Alice Bailey wrote through the guidance of her Ascended Master Djwal Khul and every other person that channels or presents channeled messages in the New Age arena. It doesn't matter whether it's prophecies delivered by alleged Christian mystics carrying messages from 'Angels of the Lord', or teachings in philosophy by the daemons and geniuses of the Greek philosophers, *it's all the same thing!* There is absolutely no distinction beyond that of the individual human's perception and how their own cognitive filtering system chooses to interpret and believe these things. One man's miracle is another man's magic spell.

Whether one sees this manipulation through communing with these alleged spirits as magic or a miracle of God, when one is deceived into believing they are talking to spirits, the deception is all the same. Granted, until now humanity has had no real source of information in regard to the virus hive and its wiles to be aware of this perfidy, but even then, the lack of questioning by those who not only experienced these things, but by those who trust in them, is illustrative of far too much trust when more critical questions should be asked when unseen entities appear in our minds to screw with our psyche. Trusting alleged holy men throughout the ages has been a major human failing, and it is all because we *want* to believe in something greater than ourselves. Our materialist science has failed us miserably by discounting such things exist and its utter refusal to investigate what may be behind it all. The earliest framers of the field of Psychology like William James and Pierre Janet were delving into solving the issue of mediums and mystics, but their efforts were soon overshadowed by materialist scientism which quashed further investigation into such subject matter. I covered this aspect in creating the field of Psychology in my book, *The Psychology of Becoming Human: Evolving Beyond Psychological Conditioning*. Selective blindness on both sides of the equation has allowed humanity to be deceived by this agenda for far too long. This type of cognitive tyranny must come to an end for humanity to advance and realize its true potential as a species.

The Latin interpretation of the word occult as 'secret and clandestine' must be paid attention to within these occult traditions of every nature. Their traditions have always been hidden from lower level initiates into the occult bailiwick, whether it was the mysteries of the Greek philosophers, or held in the hands of the high priests. There has always been a hidden hierarchy present in every occult tradition and this can be traced back throughout human history. Religious bodies are just as occulted as were pagan practices.

Within religious bodies we find secret inner doctrines of the esoteric preserved exclusively for the priestly elect while the masses are fed exoteric doctrines of feel-good swill to get them to conform to the religious collective ideology. There has always been a secret inner circle of the elite, made up of the intelligentsia who so arrogantly hold themselves in higher esteem than the human herds or initiates they seek to direct. This elite class of intellectuals, as has been shown time and again with the evidence presented in the book, has been spearheaded by Ninhursag's Aryans. This doesn't mean that they haven't drafted other intellectuals into their ranks over the ages, but these Aryans have held the highest positions of the most secretive leadership positions in all these mystical organizations, and by mystical organizations I include secret societies like the Rosicrucians, the Freemasons and the Jesuit priesthood within the Catholic Church, just to name three of the most well-known organizations. These secret societies are by no means restricted to the West as they are found around the world in every culture.

Within this cadre of black magicians, we can also include the Theosophical Society and the Fabian Society who collude to create their globalist spiritual cum Marxist New World Order, teaching the perennial philosophy of hive collectivist ideologies.

One of the most damning pieces of evidence of this perfidy to seek global hive hegemony over humanity is Alice Bailey's book, *The Externalization of the Hierarchy*. On its face, this book looks like your typical Love and Light spiritual doctrine, but to understand what is really being revealed by the so-called Ascended Masters who channeled this hive swill down to Bailey, it must be totally inverted to see the true picture of the hapiym hive collective's agenda. When the picture painted in that book is turned upright and not viewed upside down as it is presented, it is a very contrived and planned agenda for the total domination of our planet and our species. As much as your mind rebels screaming that this is not reality as you know it and see it, it *is* the reality of the global elite, and humanity better be wising up very soon to stop this globalist juggernaut from placing all of humanity under a faux spiritual Marxist ideology.

I am not running on fantasy and fear by telling this story. I have provided an overwhelming amount of evidence in all my books to convince even the staunchest skeptic with the information to see through this agenda for tyranny, provided they don't insist on living in the land of denial. Only the willfully blind can deny the mountain of evidence available to see through this agenda. Denial of the agenda will not make it go away any more than sticking your fingers in your ears going la la la.

Whether we view it as black magic or white magic, spirituality or demonology, speaking with the dead or channeling angels, saints or aliens, it's all cut from the same cloth of deception, and its high time that humanity wakes itself from the dream. Even though the virus hive has been eliminated, we all still rent its psychological residual symptoms space in our psyches. The only way to cognitive salvation and true cognitive healing is to rid ourselves of these false beliefs and our dependency on things outside ourselves, particularly what we think is supernatural.

I am not going to do an in-depth analysis of all the aspects of black versus white magic but leave it up to the reader to investigate such things for themselves if they are interested. You now have the keys to unravel the puzzle if you have a mind to. You also have the personal responsibility to free your own mind from this tyranny of beliefs. No one can do it for you but yourself.

It is no accident that certain occultists were burned at the stake for heresy during the Renaissance era and afterwards. I do not justify what the Roman Church did at the hands of the Inquisition, as I see most of it as an illicit means to steal people's property and push forth its own collectivist religious ideologies through fear. But I also see where those occultists presented a real and present danger to the Church's hegemony had their mystical doctrines proceeded unchecked and expanded. In our present era, with the advancement in electronic communication and mass media, through the contrived and concerted efforts of the Fabian and Theosophical Societies, we see mysticism unbound and running unchallenged on the planet except by the most rigid believers in their religious ideologies.

We live in a world driven by the spiritual deception that the Roman Church feared and which we witness every day. The conflict between the alleged right and left is a religious war, with Christians lined up on one side and the Socialist Marxist mystical religionists on the other, with both sides poised to eliminate each other once the tinder box of powder gets ignited. This conflict is ages old, it has only taken on a different guise in our present generation. The question remains as to whether humanity is going to outgrow the hive's mental herd indoctrination or possibly destroy half the world's population trying to settle ages old scores; or whether we can, as a species, as a single human race, develop the wisdom to throw these herd ideologies in the trash bin where they belong and choose to advance ourselves as a species.

This homogenization of allegedly opposing doctrines can even be seen in what is called *Theistic Satanism*, which Wikipedia informs us:

> *"Theistic Satanism or spiritual Satanism is an umbrella term for religious beliefs that consider Satan as an objectively existing supernatural being or force worthy of supplication, with whom individuals may contact, convene and even praise, rather than him being just an archetype, symbol or idea as in LaVeyan Satanism. The individual belief systems under this umbrella are practiced by loosely affiliated or independent groups and cabals. Another characteristic of Theistic Satanism is the use of ceremonial magic.*
>
> *The history of theistic Satanism, as an existing spiritual path practiced by people, is obscured by a number of groups accused of being*

*devil-worshippers who asserted that they were not, such as in the witch trials in Early Modern Europe. Most actual theistic Satanist religions exist in relatively new models and ideologies, many of which claim to be independent of the Abrahamic religions."*

*"The internet has increased awareness of different beliefs among Satanists, and has led to more diverse groups, but* ***Satanism has always been a pluralistic and decentralised religion****. Scholars outside Satanism have sought to study it by categorizing forms of it according to whether they are theistic or atheistic, and referred to the practice of* ***working with a literal Satan as theistic or "traditional" Satanism****. It is generally a prerequisite to being considered a theistic Satanist that the Satanist accept a theological and metaphysical canon involving one or more god(s) who are either Satan in the strictest, Abrahamic sense, or* ***a concept of Satan that incorporates gods from other religions (usually pre-Christian), such as Ahriman or Enki.*** *A small, now-defunct Satanist group called Children of the Black Rose* ***equated Satan with the pantheistic the All****."*

[Bold emphasis mine]

Given that Satan represents Ninhursag, as I elucidated previously, then this homogenization of Satanism should be of little surprise to the reader at this juncture in this presentation. It is nothing more than another avenue of expanding the market to lure more people into the mystical web of deceit. As I stated previously, the monopoly of ideologies simply keeps expanding, bringing new generations into the same old hive mystical song and dance. With the vast funding and diversification of the Lucis Trust organizations and think tanks worldwide, Theosophy has shown its colors where adapting and creating new mystical ideologies is concerned. The overall agenda, as stated previously, is to create a homogenous humanity under the New World Order agenda of Theosophy and Marxism. As much as people would like to attribute this all to a war between a metaphysical God and Satan, it has common elements on both sides of the occult equation. Humanity would be well advised to take note of this deceptive agenda and outgrow the dependency on the supernatural and create our own destiny as a species, rather than have it dictated by the duplicated and stolen personalities of dead humans that gravitated to the hive collective posing as gods, goddesses, angels, devils, daemons or Ascended Masters. To do otherwise only leaves our species slaves to that hidden and pernicious agenda.

# 21. The Aryans and the Dual Creation

We are now going to step into difficult territory where proving my assertions about the Aryans is concerned, and we are going to have to rely upon a lot of inferred textual evidence from different places in order to weave this tapestry together. What must be stated categorically from the outset is that we cannot fully rely on the veracity of ancient texts. As should be patently obvious, there has been a persistent agenda to hide the facts from our species, and when it comes to textual evidence left by the Anunnaki gods Enki and Ninhursag, there has been an intentional propaganda campaign to paint them in the best light and to exclude anything that challenges these formulated images of their greatness. The ancient texts from many lands are guilty of this intentional obfuscation of facts, and we have to assemble many disparate pieces to try and winnow out what truth may be buried within them. One thing is certain, we can take nothing at face value and must resort to allegory and innuendo to read through much of this godly propaganda and find the real story hidden within these tales. In this chapter, I can only provide the evidence and my insights predicated on the evidence available and leave it to the reader's discretion as to whether they agree with the interpretations or not.

As has already been illustrated, everything has been kept as an intentional mystery where our presumed history and perception of history is concerned. There is substantial evidence of an elite group of individuals who has chosen to keep their secrets hidden from the masses throughout the ages of recorded history as this hive collectivist agenda has taken shape over the last 4,000 years. This secrecy is not questionable based on the wealth of available evidence. Whether one can accept this conspiratorial version of our history is based totally upon the willingness of the individual to face the facts.

None of us wants to believe that our species has been manipulated at the hands of ancient so-called gods or their acolytes over the ages. In materialist scientism, Darwin's theory of evolution is more palatable to those who insist on humans holding center stage and who seek an acceptable explanation in competition to the supernatural Creationist beliefs. Proponents on both sides of this argument are living in a state of cognitive denial for the simple reason that their beliefs make them psychologically comfortable. We have a wealth of information, even with a corrupted and propagandized history, that tells us where our species came from, but willful blindness and denial keeps most people from admitting this fact. Such facts cheapen our over-inflated species self-image. I realize the abyss that must be crossed to accept these ideas as it was not something that I just bought into out of hand myself. It has taken me decades of painstaking research to formulate these conclusions, and no shortage of cognitive dissonance to come to term with these facts along the way. The reader is invited to do their own forensic investigation into these matters and reach their own conclusions.

It has been noted by numerous biblical scholars that within the pages of the book of Genesis we find two separate creation stories. The first is found in Genesis 1 and the second story of the creation of humans is found in Genesis 2. In Genesis 1 we find that god created man and woman on the 6th day of creation, and also that it was not a singular effort for as the biblical verses note, God says let 'us' make man in our image, which defies the concept of a singular ever-present God (NIV translation):

> *26 Then God said, "**Let us make mankind in our image, in our likeness**, so that they may rule over the fish in the sea and the birds in the sky, over the livestock and all the wild animals, and over all the creatures that move along the ground."*
>
> *27 So God created mankind in his own image, in the image of God he created them; male and female he created them.*
>
> *28 God blessed them and said to them, "Be fruitful and increase in number; fill the earth and subdue it. Rule over the fish in the sea and the birds in the sky and over every living creature that moves on the ground."*
>
> *29 Then God said, "I give you every seed-bearing plant on the face of the whole earth and every tree that has fruit with seed in it. They will be yours for food.*

*30 And to all the beasts of the earth and all the birds in the sky and all the creatures that move along the ground—everything that has the breath of life in it—I give every green plant for food." And it was so.*

*31 God saw all that he had made, and it was very good. And there was evening, and there was morning—**the sixth day."***

[Bold emphasis mine]

Within these passages we find that the Old Testament God was not alone in this creation, and I asserted in my *We Are Not Alone* book that the God of the OT actually had nothing to do with creating humans on this planet, but only claimed credit for the deed after the fact when there were no longer any voices of opposition left to challenge his claim. The fact that it says 'let us' is indicative of more than one hand at play in the creation mythology, represented in the term Elohim, which is plural.

Now, let's move on to the second creation found in Genesis 2 (NIV translation):

*"4 This is the account of the heavens and the earth when they were created, when the Lord God made the earth and the heavens.*

*5 Now **no shrub had yet appeared on the earth and no plant had yet sprung up**, for the Lord God had not sent rain on the earth and there was no one to work the ground,*

*6 but streams came up from the earth and watered the whole surface of the ground.*

***7 Then the Lord God formed a man from the dust of the ground and breathed into his nostrils the breath of life, and the man became a living being."***

[Bold emphasis mine]

Comparing the two sets of verses from these chapters in Genesis should illustrate that they are two separate stories as the sequence of events do not match, and many scholars over the ages see this as two separate and distinctive creation stories. Although some apologists try to assert that it is only the story told from two different points of view, it does not address the contradiction of two separate creations of humans taking place.

In order to unravel this mystery, we have to turn to some of the source legends from more ancient cultures that shaped the Genesis stories to arrive at the solution of this conundrum, and they are found in Sumerian and Babylonian mythological literature about the creation of humans by the Anunnaki god Enki and the goddess Ninhursag. The first creation story, outside the Genesis story, was brought to public awareness outside the realm of academic scholarship, sensationalized and connected to the Anunnaki through the populist works of Zechariah Sitchin in his *Earth Chronicles* series of books. What Sitchin promoted was the creation story presented in the Sumerian tablets whereby earth human slaves, or *lullu*s, were created by the Anunnaki god Enki, after many trial and error failures. This list of presumed failures in creating humans can be found in the Sumerian text entitled *Enki and Ninmah.* These early human creations are referred to as *lullû amēlu*, basically translating to mean 'primitive workers', and these first humans were created by the god Enlil after the lower class Anunnaki workers (*igigu*) rebelled and demanded that a new creature be created to take the workload off themselves. Enki later took credit for the creation of humans to glorify himself and ultimately write Enlil's role as the genetic creator of earth humans out of the story. Enki and Ninhursag were both notorious for claiming the attributes and accomplishments of others and stating that they were ultimately the performers of those deeds, when in fact they were simply lying to elevate their status in the eyes of their human worshippers. What should also be noted in this more ancient telling of the creation of humans was that the god Enlil was a living, breathing being who had the capability to genetically create a new class of worker beings. Enlil was not some invisible supernatural god living the far reaches of the cosmos as people perceive God to be in their religious illusions.

The second creation story is where our focus needs to be in this chapter as it is the one where Ninhursag actually did play a seminal role in creating the Aryan breed of humans, and this second creation is found in both the *Epic of Gilgamesh*, but particularly in the *Atrahasis Epic*. In the book *Primeval History – Babylonian, Biblical and Enochian* by Helge S. Kvanvig, we find this second creation focused upon in the chapter 1.3.3 where the two creations are noted; the first creation of the *lullû amēlu* by the god Enlil, and a secondary creation of a different type of human by Ninhursag, who is referred to in these passages as *Bēlit-ili.* As

Kvanvig notes, in the creation of the first *lullû amēlu*, it was a pretty cut and dry creation of the new human being. What this later passage reveals, however, is a second creation allegedly formed by mixing the original human creation with that of a god, creating a different race of human beings:

> *"On the first, seventh, and fifteenth days of the month*
> *I will institute a cleansing rite, a bath.*
> *Let one god be slaughtered!*
> *And the gods be thereby cleansed!*
> *In his flesh and blood,*
> *Let Nintu mix clay (tittu)!*
> *Both god and man (ilumma u awilum),*
> *may they mix together in clay!*
> *Forever after let us hear the drum (uppu)!*
> *In the god's flesh, let there be a spirit (etemmu)!*
> *Let it make known the living being (balta), its sign!*
> *So that it will not be allowed to be forgotten, let there be a spirit (etemmu)!*
> *(I iv, 206–217)"*

> *"Belet-ili, you are the mistress of all gods,*
> *you have created lullû amelu,*
> ***now shape the king (lugal), ma-li-ku a-me-lu.***
> *Surround his stature with good,*
> *form his appearance harmonical, make his body beautiful!*

***Then Belet-ili shaped the king, the ma-li-ku lú.***

*(Creation of Humankind and the King rev. 31–36)"*

[Bold emphasis mine]

What Kvanvig and other scholars take note of is that in the original creation of humans, there is no death of a god whose blood or spirit is mixed with this second human creation called a *maliku amelu,* or king (*lugal*). This is indicative of the creation of a ruling or 'royal' race of humans created from the blood of the dead god who was the organizer of the *igugu* rebellion against Enlil who demanded the creation of a worker race to take the burden of labor off their shoulders. (Kvanvig pp. 55-57).

As Kvanvig observes, this second race of humans is instilled with the 'spirit' of the slain leader of the *igugu* rebellion, who it is presumed from the legend to have a flair for 'planning and rebellion', and whose blood is allegedly used to create a secondary type of 'royal' human *maliku amēlu* to rule over the original *lullû amēlu* created by the 'Great God' Enlil. This, I assert, is the Aryan race that has served as the intercessory masters over humanity working for their creator, Ninhursag, and also serving Enki in the roles of priests and kings since their arrival on this planet c. 3760 BC, using the start date of the Jewish calendar as a hallmark, which coincides closely with the mysterious appearance of the enigmatic Aryans into Earth history determined through archaeological excavations and other areas of research.

As to whether the secondarily-created Aryan race actually arose from the blood of a sacrificed god as the foregoing passages relate is a matter of conjecture, for we must take all of these self-glorification stories composed by Enki and Ninhursag with a certain grain of salt. The importance of these passages is that a second race of human beings *was* created as kings and overlords over the original humans created on this planet. This new breed was skilled in planning and rebellion, and were designed to serve as overlords above the first humans created on this planet.

For further evidence of this rulership of the second race over the firstborn humans, we only need to look at the stories in the Bible where the second son bilks the firstborn son out of their birthright through deception as with the story of Jacob and Esau, and how Jacob deceived his blind father to claim that birthright. We see a similar second son analogy with that of Abraham's firstborn Ishmael and the second son Isaac. These stories are allegorical representations of the wile and deceptive genius on the part of Jacob, and allegedly of bloodline between Ishmael and Isaac, which places the second son, or shall we just say the Aryans, as superiors over the firstborn humans on this planet. We have to read between the lines of the allegory in these stories to see their true meaning and what humanity has had rubbed in its face about these alleged Aryan second sons deceiving and ruling humanity since their arrival on this planet.

As much as such a concept shocks our conscious, the doctrines of Adolph Hitler and his ideology of the Aryan Master Race bear this out, although his claim that the Aryans were all blond-haired and blue-eyed, I assert, was a deliberate ploy to misdirect from the truth that the Aryans are represented across the racial spectrum, and not just as Hitler idealized them. Too many scholars have noted that with the Aryan migrations since their mysterious appearance out of nowhere, we find a small number of elite individuals eventually setting themselves up as overlords over more pliable populations who cave into their tyranny and their deceptions, as well as their generally terroristic tactics throughout the ages.

We only need to look at the most well-known tyrant conquerors throughout recorded history to see the Aryans at play in many racial varieties, from the Persian conquerors, to the Egyptian Pharaohs, from the Hyksos to Alexander the Great to Atilla the Hun and Genghis Khan. Each and every world conqueror throughout human history brought the same thing with their ideas of conquest, and that is a collectivist kingdom of tyranny intended to spread worldwide, no matter the mask of benevolence they tried to hide behind. The Aztec empire in the West was no different in its demand for collectivist cultural worship and bloodshed than the Mayans and Incas. We can translate these Aryan ideologies of tyranny and apply them to Adolph Hitler, Lenin, Stalin and Mao Tse Tung. We find their fingerprints in Marxist collectivism and the murderous policies of the Jewish operatives of Communism like Lazar Kaganovich and others whose trail of terrorism and bloodshed have been responsible for over 100 million deaths in the last century alone. We find the same agenda with the tyrannical expansion in the Roman Church with their bloodthirsty missionaries killing millions while trying to convert them to the faith, as well as the expansion of the British Empire with its own sense of racial self-righteousness seeking to tame the savage wherever their ships set anchor. While humanity is taught to separate and compartmentalize all these issues as somehow different, when we can remove these factors of compartmentalization and see the common consistency that threads throughout our known history, we find a drastically different picture than the illusion of history we have been indoctrinated to believe.

The rise and fall of the mythical phoenix is the symbol of the agenda of the Aryans and the hapiym hive collective. Wikipedia reports in regard to the *Phoenix (mythology):*

> *"**Associated with the Sun**, a phoenix obtains new life by **arising from the ashes of its predecessor**. According to some sources, the phoenix dies in a show of flames and combustion, although there are other sources that claim that the legendary bird dies and simply decomposes before being born again. There are different traditions concerning the lifespan of the phoenix, but by most accounts the phoenix lived for 500 years before rebirth. Herodotus, Lucan, Pliny the Elder, Pope Clement I, Lactantius, Ovid, and Isidore of Seville are among those who have contributed to the retelling and transmission of the phoenix motif.*
>
> *In the historical record, **the phoenix "could symbolize renewal in general as well as the sun, time, the Empire, metempsychosis,***

***consecration, resurrection, life in the heavenly Paradise, Christ, Mary, virginity, the exceptional man, and certain aspects of Christian life*". "

[Bold emphasis mine]

If we look at human history and the incessant march of the Aryans across that stage of our past, the phoenix represents the rise and fall of civilizations, the constant reshaping of the psyche of humanity, with the death of the phoenix illustrated by the destruction and conflagration of war, murder, population elimination, and the failure of old religions. With the Aryan phoenix ever-rising, new models can be born on the same old repetitive designs, with the inexorable march toward an ultimate collectivist syncretism designed to homogenize humanity and make its consciousness ripe for the harvesting of the hapiym hive collective. Virtually every person of renown we have held up as the shapers of history will, in the end, be shown as part of this hive agenda working toward a form of tyrannical climax with the Aryan second sons ever using the rest of humanity as their worker drones and cannon fodder in their incessant wars, who from ancient times were designed to take on the labor of the lazy Anunnaki gods.

It doesn't matter which collectivist ideology is utilized to create this state of world domination, for the doctrinal packaging made no difference to the hive collective, its agenda was total domination of our species. Mysticism and religion were equally acceptable forms of tyranny to perform this task as was Nazism, Communism or the rule of single tyrants throughout our recorded history. There is no facet of this tapestry that is disconnected from the other, for it all arises from the same whole – the collective mind of the hapiym virus. Until humanity as a species can finally accept this horrible truth and stop the tyranny, these agendas, pushed forth by Aryan elitists and their collaborators, will continue to rule the uninformed and ignorant masses who feel powerless to stop it. The first place to stop this tyranny lies within yourself and cleaning up the residual habits of the hapiym virus in your own mind that leave you fearful and believing that you are a lesser being and have no control over your personal destiny as a fully functional human being.

As much as we are repelled by admitting what I have shared in this chapter, an honest analysis of the tyrants throughout history and their terroristic tactics, regardless of their apparent differing racial visage or location on the planet, exposes the common Aryan tactics throughout time. It's time we take off the blinders of our ignorance and face these truths, for if we don't, the future looks grim indeed. The evidence for this abounds in research by a wealth of scholars from many field specialties, but each is blinded by how they *want* to view the world rather than taking the world and our history for what it actually presents to us when the evidence is weighed without one demanding to protect their perceptual comfort zones.

When we run the comparison between these more ancient texts and what became the Bible stories, we can see that the Bible is more of a *Reader's Digest* version and compilation of a litany of other stories from Babylon, Sumeria, Assyria, Egypt and other lands around the Fertile Crescent. The Bible is a condensed version of all these prior stories, regardless of what Judaists, Christians and Muslims want to believe about the sanctity of the book. It is one of the biggest frauds every perpetrated in human history and, when viewed in the correct interpretive light, it can all be reduced to a war between two competing offworld gods and one's intimate and incestuous relationship with the hapiym hive collective.[ii] The religious ideological wars of today are only an extension of this millennia's old war between Enki and Ninhursag, masked behind different religious and political ideologies, all working to serve the agenda of one or the other. Presently, the doctrines of Ninhursag and the hive have the upper hand in this conflict as Enki's believers seem to have taken on the defensive position on the modern political stage. 99% percent of humanity is, as it always has been, putty in the hands of the Aryan psychological controllers who have always been in the know about this secret agenda while the rest of humanity has been nothing more than the moldable clay the varied Aryan tribes use as cannon fodder to fulfill their separate agendas. The ultimate goal will always be the same, total global domination. The only thing that differs is how the different Aryan tribes compete to see which one of their ideologies wins the game of king of the mountain. In the end, only Ninhursag and the hive was going to be the ultimate victor.

The one saving grace for humanity in all this is that the competing Aryan tribes each seem to want to rule the world in a different fashion. The only thing they can all agree on is that one Aryan tribe or another will become the ultimate rulers of this planet and humanity. The infighting amongst the Aryan ranks is no different than the infighting illustrated in their maker Ninhursag, and her fellow-traveler brother Enki. Enki picked his favorite tribe, the Jews, as his primary Aryan representatives, but they are no less Aryan than any of the rest. Most Christians do not recognize the bait and switch that occurs in the Bible where the stories start out talking about Hebrews and then are replaced with Jews, eventually making the terms synonymous, but the switch is there, and it is very obvious when one can see through the charade. The levels of intentional deception in the Bible are both profound and shocking, and with the polarities present in the world either believing and defending it by religionists, and the opposing atheistic side wanting to discredit it entirely by ignoring it, the real story being told in the book is utterly overlooked.

Not content to just be kings and priests, many of these Aryan rulers proclaimed themselves gods, as with the Caesars, Pharaohs, Japanese and Chinese emperors, Natchez rulers, the Saliendras, Majapahit kings, the Dalai Lamas, Inca Emperors and Nepalese Kings. Through giant statuary iconography others are elevated to near godhead like Lenin, Mao, Saddam Hussein, and multitudes of others. Here again, we must look at the commonalities of the Aryan tyrants to see the continuing historical pattern of our self-proclaimed ruling elite. The evidence is all around us and psychologists are still trying to figure out the mind of the tyrant. Given what is shared in this book, the psychopathy of the Aryan breed, creations of Ninhursag and colluders with the hapiym hive collective, then I think we can finally identify the root of the problem. There is always room for contention to what I present, but it is going to take something more powerful than simple denial and disagreement to effectively refute it all. Denial will no longer suffice as an edifice for cognitive comfort.

The reason this has all been overlooked as part of a comprehensive whole is because people view things as isolated incidents. We have no sense of history, particularly when our history is whitewashed generation after generation to present a superficial image of our past that the ruling elite want us to see. Most people do not look for common threads, but instead focus on what they think are the differences between such events, particularly when they take place in disparate regions of the planet. But if we look at the agenda of these world conquerors, we find the same single collectivist element in all their actions, no matter where they lived on the planet or during which era of history they reared their tyrannical heads. There is no difference in them other than the generational doctrines that try to paint them as different to the ignorant masses. The core elements of their actions are *always* the same.

The majority of people on this planet are unwilling to even entertain the idea of a conspiratorial view of history, and even those who do can scarcely imagine an agenda that spans thousands of years because they can't perceive what the ultimate aim of such a long-term agenda can possibly mean. Before this book is complete, this agenda is going to become frighteningly clear in its scope and deviousness.

# 22. The Goddess and the Hive in Islam

Although Islam is another offshoot of the patriarchal religion perpetuated by Enki as the God of the Old Testament, and apologists for Islam claim that Allah is just a different name for the same God, have no doubt that Ninhursag's goddess traditions, in collusion with the hapiym hive collective, appear in the religion of Islam as well, particularly in Sufism, which is the mystical branch of Islam. As is being illustrated in this volume, every religion has certain elements of the mystery of the hive embedded within them when one has the eye to read through the scriptures to see both Enki and Ninhursag present in all these varied scriptures, and Islam is no exception. As with all these traditions we must turn to the esoteric writers to see through the superficial exoteric doctrines and find the hidden mystical mysteries hidden within them.

The difficulty with an undertaking in the scope of this book is that it amounts to a form of synopsizing high points of topics that require substantially more in-depth research to glean full understanding of the topics presented herein. Deeper research only serves to validate these synopsized high points, not refute them, but establishing the trail of evidence to present my case is a laborsome undertaking at best. Although what is presented in this volume may seem like cherry-picking to some readers, further investigation into these topics will reveal a deeper and more substantiating amount of information that supports rather than undermines my assertions.

The first place we are going to make a stop in discovering the hive ideology within Islamic Sufi tradition is the word *Akhir* – found in the Quran at Sūrah al Hadid 57.1-3 which read:

> *57.1 Whatever* ***is in the heavens and earth exalts Allah, and He is the Exalted in Might, the Wise****.*
>
> *57.2 His is* ***the dominion of the heavens and earth.*** *He gives life and causes death, and He is over all things competent.*
>
> *57.3* ***He is <u>the First and the Last</u>, the Ascendant and the Intimate, and He is, of all things, Knowing.***
>
> [Bold emphasis mine]

We find the claim by Ninhursag as being the Alpha and Omega in these passages and how all things on Heaven and Earth represent the Wise Allah. If Allah is the First and the Last, then Allah is Ninhursag. Allah's dominion is also referenced in passages 57.4-6 where we are informed:

> *"57.4 It is He who created the heavens and earth in six days and then established Himself above the Throne.* ***He knows what penetrates into the earth and what emerges from it and what***

***descends from the heaven and what ascends therein; and He is with you wherever you are.*** *And Allah, of what you do, is Seeing.*

*57.5* ***His is the dominion of the heavens and earth.*** *And to Allah are returned [all] matters.*

*57.6 He causes the night to enter the day and causes the day to enter the night, and* ***he is Knowing of that within the breasts****."*

[Bold emphasis mine]

Given the nature of the hive virus infection then all of these statements about Allah wholly represent the hive cells that resided within humans and how the overlord of the hive collective could see into the 'human breast' through the advent of the hive virus infection. Since Islam is an offshoot of the Jewish Bible, Enki gets a little nod as the God who created the world in 6 days, but what all these verses collectively reveal is Ninhursag as the First and the Last, as well as the permeating nature of the hapiym virus represented by Allah. The reference to the "Ascendant and the Initiate" from verse 57.3 can be read to mean knowing the 'Inner and the Outer', which is also found in the Hermetic traditional slogan of "As above, so below, As within, so without." Again, understanding the nature of the hapiym virus as being both a transcendent space-borne hive collective (the outer, the above) corresponding with the hive cell that dwelled in humans (the inner, the below), then the mystery provided by these sayings evaporates and the truth reveals itself for its true, yet hidden meaning.

Another passage in the Quran, 112.1-4 reveals the hive nature of Allah when it states:

> *"112.1 Say,* ***"He is Allah, [who is] One****,*
> *112.2 Allah, the* ***Eternal Refuge****.*
> *112.3* ***He neither begets nor is born****,*
> *112.4 Nor is there to Him any equivalent."*
>
> [Bold emphasis mine]

In these passages we find the same doctrine of Oneness or the Monad as we find in the Platonic traditions and the monotheism of Akhenaten. When we look at *Allah as a Lunar deity* on Wikipedia we find the following excerpts:

> *"The word Allah predates Islam. As Arthur Jeffrey states:*
>
> *The name Allah, as the Quran itself is witness, was well known in pre-Islamic Arabia. Indeed, both it and* ***its feminine form, Allat,*** *are found not infrequently among the theophorous names in inscriptions from North Arabia."*
>
> *"The* ***crescent moon symbol*** *used as a form of blazon is not a feature of early Islam, as would be expected if it were linked to Pre-Islamic pagan roots. The use of the crescent symbol on Muslim flags originates during the later Middle Ages.*

*14th-century Muslim flags* ***with an upward-pointing crescent*** *in a monocolor field included the flags of Gabes, Tlemcen (Tilimsi), Damas and Lucania, Cairo, Mahdia, Tunis and Buda."*

[Bold emphasis mine]

Although religious apologists argue that the crescent moon symbol on Islamic flags has no pagan predecessor, I must argue in the alternative where the moon crescent is associated with Ninhursag in her many roles played in many lands. The five-pointed star is associated with the goddess Isis and is associated with the star Sirius in Egyptian religious lore, as well as the five-pointed star being associated with Eliphas Levi's illustration of the hermaphroditic representation of the Baphomet. The pentacle is also a central symbol in occultism, as is the moon crescent, so any arguments that there is no predicate for the crescent moon and pentacle star having no pagan predecessors falls flat in lieu of substantial data to the contrary.

To find more about the hive doctrines within the Quran we can look at the word *Qalb*, or *ayn al-qalb* which translates to mean 'eye of the heart'. Under *Qalb* on Wikipedia we find:

*"In Islamic philosophy, the qalb, or heart, is the origin of intentional activities,* ***the cause behind all of humans intuitive deeds****. While the brain handles the physical impressions,* ***qalb (the heart) is responsible for apprehending****. Heart and*

*brain work together,* ***but it is the heart where true knowledge can be received.***

*In Islamic thought, the heart is not the seat of feelings and emotions, but of rūḥ:* ***the immortal cognition****, the* ***rational soul.***

*In the Quran, the word qalb is used more than 130 times.*

[Bold emphasis mine]

When we look at the concept of *qalb* where the heart and certain sensory perceptions associated it with represent 'reason', then we must also remember the Greek philosophers and their high endorsement of 'reason' in their traditions. *Qalb* states categorically that this type of 'reason' is not a process of the brain but is a form of intellect or cognition interpreted through the heart and associated with the concept of the presumed soul. Through this understanding, then we must approach the concept of reason as something completely different than the Age of Reason type of purely intellectual materialist Reason associated with the mind.

Now, let us look into Sufism a bit and see what we can discover in reference to that mystical branch of Islam. The first stop is Wikipedia under *History of Sufism*:

*"Sufism is the mystical branch of Islam. A Sufi is a Muslim,* ***who seeks for annihilation of the ego in God****."*

*"The exact origin of Sufism is uncertain. Some sources state, Sufism emerged during the Islamic Golden Age from about the 9th to 10th centuries. However Islamic scholars predating the Islamic Golden Age were referred to as Sufis, like Hasan of Basra. According to Ibn Khaldun Sufism was already practiced by the Sahaba, but with the spread of material tendencies, the term Sufi was just applied to those who emphasize the spiritual practice of Islam."*

[Bold emphasis mine]

With this brief history established, let's look up *Sufism* on Wikipedia for more information into the mystical belief system:

*"Sufism, or Taṣawwuf, which is often defined as "Islamic mysticism",* ***"the inward dimension of Islam"*** *or "the phenomenon of mysticism within Islam", is a mystical trend in Islam "characterized ... [by particular] values, ritual practices, doctrines and institutions" which began very early in Islamic history and represented "the main manifestation and the most important and central crystallization of" mystical practice in Islam.*

*Practitioners of Sufism have been referred to as "Sufis", an Arabic word which is believed by historians to have originally indicated the* ***"woollen clothes*** *(ṣūf) or rough garb" worn by the early Islamic mystics. Historically, they have often belonged to different ṭuruq, or* ***"orders"*** *– congregations formed around a* ***grand master*** *referred to as a mawla who traces a direct chain of teachers back to the Islamic prophet, Muhammad."*

*"The original meaning of sufi seems to have been "one who wears wool (ṣūf)", and Encyclopaedia of Islam calls other etymological hypotheses "untenable". Woollen clothes were traditionally associated with* ***ascetics and mystics****. Al-Qushayri and Ibn Khaldun both rejected all possibilities other than ṣūf on linguistic grounds.*

*Another explanation traces the lexical root of the word to ṣafā, which in Arabic means* ***"purity".*** *These two explanations were combined by the Sufi al-Rudhabari (d. 322 AH), who said, "The Sufi is the one who wears wool* ***on top of purity"****.*

[Bold emphasis mine]

Within these passages we finally start to find some correlations with the later Rosicrucianism and Freemasonic fraternal orders, which were also overseen by a Grand Master. The

Sufi's wore the rough woolen garments to represent their asceticism, and a key part of a Freemason's regalia is a sheepskin apron. It is also reported that the mysterious Essenes also were issued a lamb skin apron after their three years of initiation into the Essene hierarchy. The Greek god Dionysus (Ninhursag in one of her son roles) was also associated either with the Ram or the Lamb, as the mystical Jesus is the Lamb of God. These associations readily explain sheepskin aprons and woolen garments worn by these mystical acolytes and their hidden importance to these occult traditions.

Part of tracking these mystery traditions through history comes with the affiliation of symbols used by the mystery schools and the secret societies. Just as the paintings of Plato illustrate him with a single index finger pointed skyward indicated his divine Monad, within Muslim tradition we find the same gesture called the *tawhid*, which represents the affirmation of the unity of a singular God. As Wikipedia explains it under the reference *Tawhid*:

> *"Tawhid (Arabic: tawḥīd, meaning* ***"oneness [of God]"*** *also romanized as tawheed, touheed or tevhid) is the* ***indivisible oneness concept of monotheism*** *in Islam. Tawhid is the religion's central and single-most important concept, upon which a Muslim's entire faith rests. It unequivocally holds that* ***God is One*** *(Al-ʾAḥad) and Single (Al-Wāḥid), therefore the Islamic belief in God is considered* ***Unitarian****."*

> *"There is an **uncompromising monotheism** at the heart of the Islamic beliefs (aqidah) which is seen, from an Islamic standpoint, as distinguishing Islam from other major religions. However, Tawhid is analogous to the monotheistic concept of God in Judaism as declared in the Shema Yisrael, the Jewish declaration of faith. Tawhid is also analogous to **Christian Unitarianism** adhered to by a minority of Christian denominations which reject a **trinitarian position of God in Christianity**, which is in contrast to most Christian faiths that ascribe to the Trinity (God as three persons in one being; the Father, Son, and Holy Spirit). Further Tawhid requires Muslims not only to avoid worshiping multiple **gods but also to relinquish to strive for money, social status or egoism**.*
>
> [Bold emphasis mine]

Within these passages we find that blending of doctrines that we also find present in the Bible between Enki on one hand, and Ninhursag and the hive collective on the other. Although the *tawhid* symbolism represents the Platonic idea of the Monad, of which all beings are only small parts, Islam has also adopted the notion of Enki as a supreme and singular God from the Old Testament and equates him with Allah in the more exoteric aspects of the religion. The relinquishment of the ego in the Sufi

Islamic religious context once again refers to allaying the waking state of being human and subverting that aspect of ego to find the will of Allah within, which is the basis of Islam meaning 'submission' to the will of god. As a side note before I continue, the symbol of the Unitarian Church is the flame, harkening back to Zoroastrianism and the Eternal Flame. The best way to track these hive ideologies is to observe the symbols used in them, whether corporate, political or religious. The symbols tell more than people realize.

Within the Sufi esoteric teachings, we find the same aspect of annihilating or the extermination of the waking self to attain communion with the eternal, expressed in the Arabic concept of 'subsistence'. This Sufi concept of universal Oneness is no different than is found in all the hapiym hive teachings. The misconception that the inner infectious hive virus cell was the soul is no different in Sufism than in these other hive belief systems. The outer dressing may be changed to appeal to a Muslim audience, but at the end of the day its all the same old hive deception at its core. While the followers of the superficial exoteric teachings of Islam keep their eyes focused on rewards in the afterlife, the Sufis, like all other mystical traditions, want to reap the benefits of the hive connection to the Divine in this life.

Because humanity has been incessantly indoctrinated with afterlife promises and the desire for their human personality to extend into the eternal, these doctrines sell to a human population that is so insecure in its own existence as human beings that the psychosis presented with mystical religions is overwhelming. The mystery schools are more appealing to the avaricious individual who doesn't want to collect on the afterlife promises but wants their spiritual cake in this life as well as the in afterlife. Mystical Islam in this respect is no different than any other mystical doctrine, regardless of whether it is wrapped in Muslim ideology or not. It's just more of the same hive collective ideology wearing a different doctrinal garb.

Although in our modern world with revolutionary Muslim organizations like Isis performing terroristic acts and its adherents believing they will reach the afterlife as martyrs for their god, or other suicide bombers harboring the same beliefs, the concept of religious martyrdom predates the creation of Islam as a religion. Early Christianity was not much different with its adherents seeking their own form of martyrdom, although they did not perform acts of terrorism to attain their martyrdom. As Wikipedia informs us about martyrdom under *Christian views on suicide*:

> *"Suicide was a common problem among early Christians. The most notable pro-suicide group was the Donatists, who believed that by killing themselves they could attain martyrdom and go to Heaven. They were eventually declared heretics. Most early theologians of the Catholic Church considered suicide as murder and thus a mortal sin in the absence of circumstances that could mitigate the sinfulness of the act.*
>
> *In the fifth century, St. Augustine wrote the book The City of God, in it making Christianity's*

*first overall condemnation of suicide. His biblical justification for this was the interpretation of the commandment, "thou shalt not kill", as he sees the omission of "thy neighbor", which is included in "thou shalt not bear false witness against thy neighbor", to mean that the killing of oneself is not allowed either. The rest of his reasons were from Plato's Phaedo.*

*In the sixth century AD, suicide became a secular crime and began to be viewed as sinful. In 1533, those who committed suicide while accused of a crime were denied a Christian Burial. In 1562, all suicides were punished in this way. In 1693, even attempted suicide became an ecclesiastical crime, which could be punished by excommunication, with civil consequences following. In the 13th century, Thomas Aquinas denounced suicide as an act against God and as a sin for which one could not repent. Civil and criminal laws were enacted to discourage suicide, and as well as degrading the body rather than permitting a normal burial, property and possessions of the suicides and their families were confiscated."*

The fact that suicide had to be declared a secular crime only illustrates how many early Christians felt that suicide and dying for their God was a free pass to heaven. Other Christians under later Muslim rule would publicly proclaim their Christian beliefs knowing that they would most likely be put to death under Muslim law (see *Martyrs of Córdoba* on Wikipedia), thereby believing their martyrdom would give them passage to the afterlife. One can only view these obsessions with the afterlife and the willingness to give up one's life as a psychosis, and humanity must outgrow this psychosis if it is every going to evolve past all these self-destructive belief systems.

# 23. Reincarnation?

We are now going to delve into one of those touchy areas where Buddhism, Hinduism and many facets of Eastern religions have been fed into Western spiritual beliefs, and that is the topic of reincarnation. Given the nature of the hive virus, we must now reanalyze the concept of reincarnation in light of the virus' existence. What follows in this chapter is going to be highly uncomfortable for many people to face, in fact probably everyone who reads this chapter is going to come away very disconcerted because their perception of reality is going to be challenged more than it has been so far. The information to follow is where this whole hive agenda turns into a true horror story where our species advancement is concerned.

In Chapter 14 I brought up the *Tibetan Book of the Dead* and what is called the *Bardo Thodol*. In Wikipedia under *Bardo Thodol* we find:

> *"The Bardo Thodol (Tibetan: བར་དོ་ཐོས་གྲོལ, Wylie: bar do thos grol, "Liberation Through Hearing During the Intermediate State") is a text from a larger corpus of teachings, the Profound Dharma of Self-Liberation through the Intention of the Peaceful and Wrathful Ones, revealed by*

*Karma Lingpa (1326–1386). It is the best-known work of Nyingma literature, and is known in the West as the Tibetan Book of the Dead.*

*The Tibetan text describes, and is intended to guide one through, the experiences that the consciousness has after death, in the bardo, the interval between death and the next rebirth. The text also includes chapters on the signs of death and rituals to undertake when death is closing in or has taken place."*

*"According to Tibetan tradition, the Liberation Through Hearing During the Intermediate State was composed in the 8th century by Padmasambhava, written down by his primary student, Yeshe Tsogyal, buried in the Gampo hills in central Tibet and subsequently discovered by a Tibetan terton, Karma Lingpa, in the 14th century."*

The *Tibetan Book of the Dead* is a compilation of spells and chants that, when possible, one receives near their death in preparation for the afterlife. It is designed to strengthen their memory, no different than the Greek belief in maintaining the memory after death on the journey through the underworld presented in Chapter 14. The memory of the human host is very important in the transition of the hive cell to the celestial hive collective, and the spells and chants contained in the *Bardo Thodol* are designed to insure the memories of the human host as the hive cell moves into the afterlife. In Tibetan tradition, these memories bear import where reincarnation is concerned as well. I will offer more elaborate discussion on reincarnation at the end of the chapter, but for now, I ask the reader to focus on the perception of reincarnation strictly in reference to the recycling of hive cells into human form.

The importance of *Tibetan Book of the Dead* is when it was discovered, not when it was allegedly written. The book's discovery predates the birth of the first Dalai Lama. In Wikipedia under *1st Dalai Lama* we are informed:

> *"Gedun Drupa was born in a cowshed in Gyurmey Rupa near Sakya in the Tsang region of central Tibet, the son of Gonpo Dorje and Jomo Namkha Kyi, nomadic tribespeople. He was raised as a shepherd until the age of seven. His birth name (according to the Tibetan Buddhist Resource Center, his personal name) was Péma Dorje (Tibetan: པདྨ་རྡོ་རྗེ་, "Vajra Lotus"). Later he was placed in Narthang Monastery. In 1405, he took his śrāmaṇera (novitiate) vows from the abbot of Narthang, Khenchen Drupa Sherap.*
>
> *When he was 20 years old, in about 1411, he received the name Gedun Drupa upon taking the vows of a bhikṣu (monk) from the abbot of*

*Narthang Monastery. Also at this age he became a student of the scholar and reformer Je Tsongkhapa (1357–1419), who some say was his uncle. Around this time he also became the first abbot of Ganden Monastery, founded by Tsongkhapa himself in 1409. By the middle of his life, Gedun Drupa had become one of the most esteemed scholar-saints in the country.*

*Tradition states that* ***Palden Lhamo, the female guardian spirit of the sacred lake****, Lhamo La-tso,* ***promised the First Dalai Lama in one of his visions "...that she would protect the reincarnation lineage of the Dalai Lamas." Since the time of Gedun Gyatso, who formalized the system, monks have gone to the lake to meditate when seeking visions with guidance on finding the next reincarnation."***

[Bold emphasis mine]

In the highlighted passage above we are once again confronted with the female deity associated with water promising the first Dalai Lama that she would protect the reincarnation lineage of the Dalai Lamas. This devotion to the goddess was recorded in one of the books written by Gedun Drupa entitled, *Praise of the Venerable Lady Khadiravani Tara*. If we look up Tara (Buddhism) on Wikipedia we find:

*"Tara (Sanskrit: तारा, tārā; Tib. སྒྲོལ་མ, Dölma) or Ārya Tārā, also known as Jetsun Dölma (Tibetan language: rje btsun sgrol ma) in Tibetan Buddhism, is a* ***female Bodhisattva in Mahayana Buddhism*** *who appears as* ***a female Buddha*** *in Vajrayana Buddhism. She is known as the* ***"mother of liberation"****, and represents the virtues of success in work and achievements. She is known as Tara Bosatsu in Japan, and occasionally as Duōluó Púsà in Chinese Buddhism.*

*Tara is a meditation deity whose practice is used by practitioners of the Tibetan branch of Vajrayana Buddhism to* ***develop certain inner qualities and understand outer, inner and secret teachings*** *about compassion and emptiness."*

[Bold emphasis mine]

I think at this point we can figure out who Tara represents without much commentary. Along with the Vedanta form of Hinduism, Mahayana Buddhism is greatly emphasized in Theosophical teachings. Given the Mother Goddess associations and the goddess connection with Lucifer as the Morning Star in Theosophical teachings, one can start to better grasp the homogenization process taking place with all these goddess hive traditions.

So, let's return to the Dalai Lama and its promise from the goddess of the lake to insure the line of the Dalai Lamas and see what we can glean from this promise, especially considering that the *Tibetan Book of the Dead* was discovered shortly before the birth of the first Dalai Lama. We now know that Ninhursag was the intermediator between the human hive cells and the hive collective. For her to promise continuity of the line of the Dalai Lamas would not have been a hard promise to fulfill once we understand the nature of the virus and how it could be manipulated in human hosts.

The first myth that must be shattered where the 'line' of the Dalai Lamas is concerned in the fact that the current Dalai Lama is the same hive personality of the first Dalai Lama. Reincarnation is believed to be an act whereby a soul is born into a new human form to continue the cycle of karma. Where the fear of Hell and eternal damnation serve as the whip to coerce other religionists into adhering to their religious beliefs, karma is used as the whip in Eastern ideologies to discipline their religious believers and keep them in line. If you do good things in this life, like honoring the gods and goddesses, you get a better shake in the next life. If you do bad in this life, you can regress your position in the next life. Regardless of which tactic is used to enforce these religious ideologies, control through fear lies at the heart of the doctrines.

Now, let's look at the alleged reincarnation and selection of the Dalai Lama and see what we can find. Under *Succession of the 14$^{th}$ Dalai Lama* at Wikipedia we find:

*"Following the Buddhist belief in the principle of reincarnation, the current Dalai Lama is believed* ***to be able to choose the body*** *into which he is reincarnated. That person, when found, will then become the next Dalai Lama. According to Buddhist scholars it is the responsibility of the High Lamas of the Gelgupa tradition and the Tibetan government to seek out and find the next Dalai Lama following the death of the incumbent. The process can take a long time. It took four years to find the 14th (current) Dalai Lama, Tenzin Gyatso. The search is generally limited to Tibet, although* ***the current Dalai Lama has said that there is a chance that he will not be reborn****, and that if he is, it would not be in a country under Chinese rule. To help them in their search, the High Lamas may have visions or dreams, and try to find signs. For example, if the previous Dalai Lama was cremated, they can watch the direction of the smoke to suggest where the rebirth will take place. When these signs have been interpreted and a successor found,* ***there are a series of tests to ensure that they are the genuine reincarnation of the previous Dalai Lama. They assess the candidate against a set of criteria, and will present the child with various objects to see if they can identify those which belonged to the previous Dalai Lama.*** *If a single candidate has been*

*identified, the High Lamas will report their findings to eminent individuals and then to the Government. If more than one candidate is identified, the true successor is found by officials and monks drawing lots in a public ceremony. Once identified, the successful candidate and his family are taken to Lhasa (or Dharamsala) where the child will study the Buddhist scriptures in order to prepare for spiritual leadership."*

[Bold emphasis mine]

So, let's analyze what this passage tells us in light of everything you now know. We know that the hive cells could move in and out of human bodies when they found a human host whose own hive cell was weak and undeveloped, for instance that of a child. Given the information and spellcasting involved in the *Bardo Thodol* insuring the memory of the hive cell within the Dalai Lama, then the hive cell that infected the current Dalai Lama is the same hive cell that has been 'reincarnating' into human children for the last 544 years. There has been no process of rebirth of this alleged soul, but it has in fact been a reinsertion of the first Dalai Lama's hive cell into successive human children for all these centuries. This is why the identification of objects of the prior Dalai Lama is part of the testing criteria for the candidates, and also why the memory preservation spells in the *Bardo Thodol* are so important when each Dalai Lama is preparing to die.

With the promise of Ninhursag, highest functionary of the hive to insure the lineage of the Dalai Lamas, and the ability of hive cells to migrate into other human forms, then the lie of this type of reincarnation should become evident. There is no genuine reincarnation from the standpoint of the hive deception, it was a process of usurpation of the Dalai Lama's hive cell over a weaker hive cell in a human child that allowed the hive cell of the original Dalai Lama to keep *reinserting* itself onto the world stage generation after generation for over five centuries. It has been a deceptive game of body snatching, and this hive cell has never once gone through a process of 'rebirth' in the strictest sense of the word as people perceive reincarnation. When the old human vehicle wore out, the hive cell elevated to the collective just long enough to find a suitable human host into which it could reinsert itself and continue its own form of religious tyranny as the leader of the Buddhist world.

I realize how shocking such an idea is to one's consciousness, but the story actually gets worse, because the hive cell of the Dalai Lama is not the only powerful hive cell that has reinserted itself into human form after the original human host died, although the spirit (and I use that term loosely here) of the Dalai Lama is the easiest to prove it happens. We have other instances of alleged hive walk-ins through NDEs where one's personality completely changes after a near death experience, usually turning them into some kind of spiritual zealot, preaching the love and light doctrine of the hive, or developing skills in art and music that the original hive owner of the form didn't possess. The Maharishi Mahesh Yogi, guru to the Beatles and other celebrities and the creator of Transcendental Meditation, pointedly admitted that he was a walk-in. But everyone falsely assumed he was a soul and not a hive cell impostor who walked in.

In one of Rudolph Stenier's books, he received channeled information that Alexander the Great was very close to the philosopher Aristotle who was one of his tutors. As Steiner reports from his 'heavenly' sources, the spirits of Alexander and Aristotle 'reincarnated' into two Age of Reason personalities centuries later, the names which escape me at the moment. But the point is that we have a number of sources that talk about souls walking in or reincarnating in this manner, and we must now view all of these cases of reinserting hive cells as probably taking place much more often than we can imagine. We have to wonder how many mystics, Greek Philosophers, Gnostics, priests and Aryan Warlords have been hive cells reinserting themselves repeatedly throughout recorded history driving humanity closer and closer to that collective corral, at which time the hive decided to usurp all human consciousness and replace it with hive cells. A prospective date for this full onslaught invasion was slated for Dec. 21, 2012 in line with the prophetic Mayan Calendar where the world's consciousness was supposed to 'shift'. Fortunately for humanity, this hive invasion didn't take place, and with the subsequent elimination of the hive collective everywhere, it will never happen.

This is uncomfortable information if my assessment is correct, for it means that even at the hands of the Aryan invaders, the hive has been controlling human affairs for a very long time and we have not remotely been in charge of our destiny as a species. For those who still have doubts about these assertions I direct you to a book written by Charles W. Leadbetter in 1915 entitled *Invisible Helpers.* Leadbetter was a member of the Theosophical Society and, although mainstream materialist psychologists and scientists want to deny such things occur, Leadbetter recounts his own personal experience with these 'invisible helpers', which I assert was the hive virus collective. As stated previously, not everyone who experienced encounters and interface with the hive collective was of low intelligence but were in fact some of the most intellectual people throughout the ages. This tracks through from the interface in the ancient mystery schools of the Greek Philosophers and the priesthoods in Egypt, India and elsewhere into modern times. In fact, it is reported in Alice Bailey's book, *The Externalization of the Hierarchy*, that the hierarchy would prefer that people don't believe in the hierarchy's existence for it gives them more latitude to fulfill their Divine agenda. Deception always works best in secrecy.

The refusal of humanity to acknowledge these things only leaves us as unwitting slaves to this agenda for total planetary control over our species. Even with the elimination of the hive collective and the living hive cells within our species, we are still programmed to do its will through our cognitive and emotional habits. We are still slaves to the agenda through our programming at the hands of psychological manipulators worldwide, whether they be religious authorities or political authorities. Our species fascination with the supernatural, our desire to be something more than human because we are dissatisfied with our lot in life of being 'lowly' humans, allows this chicanery to continue. Even with the lack of fulfillment of these mystical desires being removed with the elimination of the virus, the mental fascination to become supernatural, to connect with the Divine, to become Gods, drives the agenda of slavery ever forward. Transhumanism is just the next piece of this desire to be something more than what we are. With Transhumanism, some are totally willing to give up their very humanity and merge with machines if it will give them eternal life or enhanced computer-like cognitive processing abilities. It's all the same thing wrapped in different packages, and at the root we find a species that is so dissatisfied with itself that it is unwilling to discover what it can be without the effects of the hapiym mind virus controlling our very destiny as a species.

Through thousands of years of religious and spiritual indoctrination, our humanity and our acceptance of being human has been so cheapened that none of us want to be human. We want to turn into some mystical creature that makes us more than human, so we can escape being what we are, when we have yet to discover what being fully human actually entails. The doctrines of the hive virus and its egotistical authority that continually cheapened our very existence lies at the root of this dissatisfaction. We have taken the doctrines of a liar to establish our sense of self-worth, an external authority whose only goal was to eliminate human consciousness and replace it with its own collectivist sameness. It is no different than the character Agent Smith in the second episode of *The Matrix* franchise remaking the world in his image. If you want to perceive the overall hive agenda with Ninhursag running the show, then that *Matrix* film should show it to you in all its allegorical glory. This is the Great Work touted by the Hermeticists, Theosophists and Freemasons. This is the real hidden agenda behind all this.

Given the research into the subconscious, we must now face the reality that practices like past-life regression hypnotherapy are dodgy practices at best. As reported in Chapter 14, the work of Boris Sidis into the subconscious revealed that there is nothing wholesome about the hive cell that dwelled within us. It had no sense of right or wrong and it was an inveterate liar, which can only be expected from a mind parasite whose only agenda could be achieved through deceit and misdirection. When one subjected themselves to past-life regression hypnotherapy and reached the hive cell within the client, they were in touch with their own inner virus cell liar. This being the case, then any information delivered about alleged past lives must come into question insofar as their reliability of reporting is concerned.

'Most people seek out therapists for this type of therapy because they are curious who they may have been in a past life. They are enchanted with the idea of being something special in a past life like a King, Prince or Princess, and that will somehow give them a sense of value and purpose in this life. They are already staged to accept whatever lie the inner hive cell told them about themselves to bolster their own ego beliefs.' The hive cell knew us more intimately than we think we know ourselves. It knew exactly how to manipulate us into believing what *it* wanted us to believe, so lying to us from the subconscious state to glorify its host personality falls right in line with the continual hive deception. This being the case, based on what Sidis and other researchers into the subconscious unearthed, then the practice of regression hypnotherapy should come under great scrutiny. At one time I gave credence to such practices. I can no longer provide that credence I once did in light of what I know now.

Given the nature of the hive infection, we have all been herd animals, seeking collectivist thinking and external herd endorsement to our ideas and our beliefs. There is a distinct difference in wanting to associate with other people and being *compelled* to do so as a result of the collective hive mind infection. The presumed concept of humans being social animals must now come under equal scrutiny as much as everything else we believe. The herding collectivist instinct was not necessarily a human instinct as much as it was the instinct of the virus itself. Until humanity rids itself of all these collectivist virus habits, we have no idea what we are nor what we can become as a virus free species taking control of our own minds and our own destiny. We have not yet discovered what it means to be human. We have been wind-up toys to a pernicious and controlling mind virus, subject to the whims of the hive and those who collaborated with the hive to herd us in the direction it wanted to fulfill its own power-hungry agenda for control of our species.

With the virus' capability to exchange one hive cell with another in a human body within its cosmic herd framework, then we can't help but wonder about our alleged history as a species. If these higher-level hive cells within the hierarchy of the Brotherhood of Light have been reinserting themselves into different human hosts over the ages and have remained in communion with the great goddess, the overseer of the hive agenda, is there really any human history at all, or has it all just been a massive experiment in hive social engineering seeking to find the right workable solution to finally overcome human consciousness and remake the world in its image? Everything we think we know must come into question. We have to exhibit the courage as a species to right this multigenerational wrong of tyranny and reverse it, but that will never happen so long as we refuse to face the problem and do not seek to rectify it in our own psyche first on an individual basis.

If we look up *Hermetic Brotherhood of Light* on Wikipedia we find:

> *"The Hermetic Brotherhood of Light was a Fraternity* ***that descended from the Frates Lucis*** *in the late 18th century (in turn, derived from the German Order of the Golden and Rosy Cross), and was the seed from which Ordo Templi Orientis was created."*
>
> [Bold emphasis mine]

I have provided more than enough information that the reader should be able to see what this alleged Brotherhood of Light (Frates Lucis) actually is. The fact that this Brotherhood 'descended' should have an equally obvious meaning. How many of these hive 'Brothers' were the hive cells of dead personalities who reinserted themselves into human forms to create these fraternities and push forth the hive agenda? Are we expected to believe that this was all nothing more than human invention? And if so where did they 'descend' from? We have been told the truth for generations and it has been right in front of our faces, yet we either perceive it as a mystery or seek it out to satisfy our own ego's desires to experience the supernatural. In either case, we have been blinded to the true agenda taking place on this planet and the manipulation of our species by the hive collective infection that rules our minds.

Since I have broached the subject of this cosmic Brotherhood, let's take a look at what is known as the *Great White Brotherhood* on Wikipedia and see what we can decipher about it:

> *"The Great White Brotherhood, in belief systems akin to Theosophy and New Age, are said to be* ***supernatural beings of great power who spread spiritual teachings through selected humans****. The members of the Brotherhood may be known as the* ***Masters of the Ancient Wisdom or the Ascended Masters****. The first person to talk about them in the West was Helena Petrovna Blavatsky (Theosophy), after she and other people* ***claimed to have received messages from them****. These included Aleister Crowley, Alice A. Bailey, Guy Ballard, Geraldine Innocente (The Bridge to Freedom), Elizabeth Clare Prophet and Benjamin Crème."*

> *"The idea of a* ***secret organization of enlightened mystics, guiding the spiritual development of the human race****, was pioneered in*

*the late eighteenth century by Karl von Eckartshausen (1752-1803) in his book The Cloud upon the Sanctuary;* ***Eckartshausen called this body of mystics, who remained active after their physical deaths on earth, the Council of Light.*** *Eckartshausen's proposed* ***communion of living and dead mystics, in turn, drew partially on Christian ideas such as the Communion of the Saints, and partially on previously circulating European ideas about secret societies of enlightened, mystical, or magic adepts*** *typified by the Rosicrucians and the Illuminati."*

[Bold emphasis mine]

With the information provided in this book, taken with a heavy dose of pragmatism, it takes no imagination whatsoever to see through the mystical aspect of the Great White Brotherhood. Eckharthausen's assessment about his alleged Council of Light being comprised of dead human souls, given all the foregoing information in this book, illuminates us to the hive's continual intervention into the affairs of humanity, particularly where spiritual endeavors are concerned. Our species has been herded mercilessly into these presumably spiritual corrals to ensnare and enslave our consciousness with these alleged mystical beliefs for thousands of years of our existence. While the adepts and collaborators with the hive slavishly used the term 'guiding humanity', a more realistic assessment would be *steering humanity* down the road of mystical enchantments that the hive wanted us to go. We have been herded like cattle into these mystical cesspools of disinformation at the discretion of the hive, Ninhursag and her schools of mystical adepts for at least 4,000 years. This is what comprises the 'invisible college', which Wikipedia informs us:

> *"The Invisible College has been described as a precursor group to the Royal Society of London, consisting of a number of natural philosophers around Robert Boyle. It has been suggested that other members included prominent figures later closely concerned with the Royal Society; but several groups preceded the formation of the Royal Society, and who the other members of this one were is still debated by scholars*
>
> *The concept of "invisible college" is mentioned in* ***German Rosicrucian pamphlets in the early 17th century****. Ben Jonson in England referenced the idea, related in meaning to Francis Bacon's House of Solomon, in a masque The Fortunate Isles and Their Union from 1624/5. The term accrued currency for the exchanges of correspondence within the Republic of Letters."*
>
> [Bold emphasis mine]

I will leave it to the reader to decide whether the Invisible College has strictly to do with the establishment of the Royal

Society, particularly considering that the concept originated in Rosicrucian circles. The Invisible College associated with the Royal Society is responsible, however, for establishing the peer review system that controls all academia as a form of intellectual censorship, which suited the hive agenda quite well by obfuscating mystical information and studies in favor of purely materialistic endeavors and scientific denial. It was the establishment of the Royal Society where the intellectuals in England set the tone for what was 'acceptable' scholarship was and what met the King's approval and could be presented to academics and the public. It became an academic censorship bureau and its influence still strangles academic inquiry to this day through the peer review system. I covered this in my book *The Psychology of Becoming Human.*

The association with white in this brotherhood is based on the concept of purity, which is why so many mystics from ancient times wore white robes or white garments. The white of this alleged purity is also associated with the white light seen by many of these earthly adepts who had their visionary encounters with the Divine, such as the Apostle Paul on the road to Damascus. There is hidden symbolism in all these things that people generally overlook, just as noted earlier about the Dionysus association with the ram or the lamb being symbolically translated into woolen garments or lambskin aprons worn by both the white-wearing Essenes and part of the Freemason's regalia.

I have provided substantial food for thought in this chapter about alleged reincarnation and how the hive cells could reinsert themselves into human forms if it was warranted that their presence was necessary in human form to drive the hive agenda forward. As difficult as this may be for us to accept, I think the evidence offered is enough to justify my assertions and make the reader quite uncomfortable facing the truth of this assessment. The world we perceive is not what we believe it to be. No one wants to admit betrayal in any case, but when that betrayal is revealed by facing the total lie of our most cherished beliefs, it is a terribly difficult pill to swallow, but swallow it we must if we ever expect to transcend this hidden tyranny. Humanity has been scammed in the most merciless fashion imaginable. Our entire species has been victimized by a con game whose vastness staggers our imagination, but it is not something the admission of which can't be transcended. We are stronger than we believe ourselves to be. We only need find that strength and courage to face this tyranny and refuse to allow it to rule our consciousness any longer. The situation may be difficult, but it is not hopeless.

# 24. Channeling as a Force for Change

In Chapter 8 I brought up Spiritism and the fascination with humans fretting over their chances of living in the afterlife and how it became a religious movement. Wikipedia informs us about *Spiritism* this way:

> *"Spiritism is a spiritualistic philosophy codified in the 19th century by the French educator Hippolyte Léon Denizard Rivail, under the codename Allan Kardec; it proposed the study of* ***"the nature, origin, and destiny of spirits, and their relation with the corporeal world"****. Spiritism soon spread to other countries, having today 35 countries represented in the International Spiritist Council.*
>
> *Spiritism postulates that humans are essentially immortal spirits that temporarily inhabit physical bodies for several necessary incarnations to attain moral and intellectual improvement. It also asserts that* ***spirits, through passive or active mediumship, may have***

***beneficent or malevolent influence on the physical world.***"

*"Emanuel Swedenborg (January 29, 1688 – March 29, 1772) was a Swedish scientist, philosopher, seer, and theologian. Swedenborg had a prolific career as an inventor and scientist. At 56,* ***he claimed to have experienced visions of the spiritual world and talked with angels, devils, and spirits by visiting heaven and hell. He claimed he was directed by the Lord Jesus Christ to reveal the doctrines of his second coming.***

*Swedenborg, however, warned against seeking contact with spirits. In his work Apocalypse Explained, #1182.4, he wrote, "Many persons believe that man can be taught by the Lord by means of spirits speaking with him. But those who believe this, and desire to do so, are not aware that it is associated with danger to their souls." See also Heaven and Hell #249*

*Nevertheless, Swedenborg is often cited by Spiritists as a major precursor for their beliefs."*

[Bold emphasis mine]

Some of the founders of psychology investigated Spiritist mediums in the late 1800s while working to shape the field of psychology. Both Pierre Janet and William James (the Father of American Psychology) cut their psychological teeth while investigating paranormal phenomena associated with spirit mediums. Naturally, with the advancement of materialist viewpoints in psychology, these founding investigations into the supernatural by these early psychologists is swept under the rug in modern academic classrooms. I covered these mystical studies extensively in my book *The Psychology of Becoming Human.*

Both Janet and James were members of the Society for Psychical Research (SPR), which was first organized in Great Britain as an associate organization of both the British Fabian Society and the Theosophical Society. These three cousin organizations almost had a revolving door leadership where members from one group would take leadership roles in one or both of the others over time. Pierre Janet eventually created the French branch of the SPR while William James went on to create the American branch of the SPR. The primary focus of the SPR in those early days was establishing contact with and investigating mediums.

The SPR gained its notoriety in exposing fraudulent mediums, and at one time actually exposed Madame Blavatsky as a fraudulent parlor medium (which she was). But I have asserted in my other works that while the SPR was exposing mediums on one hand to legitimize its existence and exposing fraudulent mediums, it was also in the business of scouting out genuine clairvoyants who could work as intermediaries with the hive hierarchy, as did Madame Blavatsky and Alice Bailey. Through these scouting endeavors, both the Theosophical Society as well as the Fabian Society were able to fill their ranks with adepts they could convert to their way of thinking, believing that they were fulfilling the Divine Will of the hive while performing their skills as magical adepts. The skills of generations of mystical adepts were handed down from ancient Egypt, India, Persia and Greece, through Hermeticism, people like Emmanuel Swedenborg and other 'visionaries' who created divergent religions, into the modern era channelers that really boomed in the 1980s onward. With the association between the Fabian Society, the Theosophical Society and the SPR, this process became refined and became global in scope. The hive finally had three powerful organizations through which it could work to push forth its agenda for conquest of the human psyche through psychological manipulation (SPR), spiritual manipulation (Theosophy) and the body politic (Fabian Society). These three organizations created an unholy trinity, and it takes little imagination to figure out who the triune being was manipulating the show from hive central.

What I have illustrated in the pages of this book is a gradualist progression of tyranny throughout human history, manipulated by the hapiym hive virus, and which has amplified and speeded up in the last 500-600 years once Ninhursag was able to better consolidate her power on this planet. The Lucis Trust organization created by Alice and Foster Bailey has been the primary vehicle through which the funding is funneled to its almost 31,000 worldwide organizations which comprise a global network of power controlling the political, spiritual and psychological arenas planetwide.

The Theosophical Society played an integral role in the formation of the United Nations, a charitable Trust operating under the banner of the Lucis Trust umbrella masquerading as a world governing body, and the Theosophical Society played a serious role in trying to create the League of Nations as the starting point of the later UN. This unholy trinity and all its subdivisions and organizations worldwide has been the driving force of the hidden hive agenda on this planet. Within this structure you have the mystical supporters of the agenda of the Great Work found in Vedanta Hinduism, Mahayana Buddhism, Freemasonry, Sufism, Rosicrucianism, Satanism, Occultism, the Ordo Templi Orientis, Aleister Crowley's religion of Thelema, Mormonism, Scientology and untold host of others. This has been a contrived and concerted effort to eventually bring in the supremacy of goddess worship in all Ninhursag's varied roles over the ages as the Mother Goddess.

For hundreds of years these efforts were hidden from the public eye, and only the adepts on Enki's side of the equation served to remotely slow the agenda through the Roman Church. This is not meant to justify the actions of the Church of Rome but is only an illustration of the ongoing conflict between the doctrines and control between Enki and Ninhursag's separate ideologies. Humanity in general has only been pawns in this global game for control of this planet.

With the push for spirituality present in the world today, where most people do not call themselves religious, but do classify themselves as spiritual, Ninhursag and the hive agents on this planet are no longer hiding in the dark when their agenda can be seen. Certain segments of Freemasonry are coming out of the shadows and professing their belief in the goddess, and how they have believed in her all along. No one is allowed to join a Freemasonic lodge if they do not profess a belief in a Divine Being. The religion of the member doesn't matter so long as they profess this belief in a higher power. Freemasonry, like any other church, is a religion. It pays homage to the Great Architect, and I have already shown who the Great Architect is.

The only major resistance to this expanding agenda being driven by Ninhursag and the hive is Enki's variants of Christianity, most particularly Protestant evangelicals. The stage is set for a war with the Leftist goddess worshippers lined up on one side and Christians lined up on the other in a defensive posture. When one understands the nature of this ancient war between Enki and Ninhursag, then the political tableau that is unfolding on the world stage between the Left and the Right can be seen for what it is, a final showdown between the beliefs of two ancient adversaries.

As much as you may not put credence in all this New Age spiritual swill, those who are in possession of the money and power on this planet do take it all very seriously. This becomes patently obvious when you have channelers like Lee Carroll, the man who allegedly channels some group entity named Kryon, invited with all seriousness to channel before a group at the United Nations. This was not a one-time occurrence. Carroll has channeled Kryon for the S.E.A.T. organizations within the UN body of organizations in 1995, 1996, 1998, 2005-07 and 2009. These were not speaking engagements by Carroll *about* Kryon, they were actual live channeling sessions where Carroll set his human consciousness aside and let this presumed Kryon entity 'Of Magnetic Service' address the gathered audience directly.

The Theosophical Society, the Fabian Society and the SPR have been doing this kind of work with the hive for well over a century, and you would be well advised to take the information in this book as seriously as the intellectual world-shapers over the centuries have done. If this were all just New Age frill and fancy, then you have to ask why invisible entities like Kryon are being given legitimacy anywhere in the alleged world governing body of the UN. This is as serious as it gets, and the fate of humanity has been in the hands of this collectivist viral predator since this species was created. With Ninhursag's hive cell joining the hive, the agenda only became more subversive and more dangerous to humanity. As I said previously, the hive cells are dead everywhere, but the infected human ego is still plagued with the symptoms of the virus. We cannot cure ourselves as a species so long as these residual symptoms control our consciousness, and presently, mysticism and the incessant desire for supernatural solutions to our problems are the poisons that keep us frozen like a deer caught in the headlights of an oncoming car.

Just as the Spiritists captured the imagination of those wanting assurances of their loved ones living happily in the afterlife, modern spiritual channelers provide the same kind of false salve to the egos of those seeking assurances of their place with the Divine hive. They have been sold a mystical lie of enchantment that few have the stamina or courage to throw away, and this has more to do with the humanity's fear of not having some cosmic overseer or God to guide our species in our psychotic insecurity as a species. The enchantment and lure of mystical solutions to our lives leaves everyone trapped in these beliefs prisoners in their own minds. Even when faced with the truth they would rather deny it and embrace the supernatural lies for the expedient reason that it simply makes them *feel good* to embrace the fallacious beliefs. It is a dependency syndrome unimaginable except for those who can see through the charade and accept reality rather than deny it and live in a cognitive illusion.

# 25. What is Zionism and the End Times?

We are now going to embark on a sensitive political and religious subject, and that is the question about what Zionism is. Over my years of research, I have paid attention to enigmas, particularly those where there seems to be no readily apparent answer. When it comes to classifying what Zionism is, we find one of those enigmas, because it means different things to different people. On one hand it is said to be a religious movement associated with the return of God's people to Israel. On another hand it is presented as political Leftist ideology associated with Marxism. The fact is that Zionism is one of those enigmatic subjects about which you just can't get a straightforward answer, and when I find something as unanswerable as what is Zionism, then I sense that there is something that is intentionally not being told. What I am going to attempt to do in this chapter is finally provide an explanation about what Zionism really is and what the secret it is hiding represents. My answers are not going to be pleasant to face, but it must be weighed against all the information provided in this book. I will leave it up to the reader's discretion to determine whether my assessment is correct or not.

I have already established that Ninhursag had her temple atop Mt. Zion in the kingdom of Judah located in modern day Jerusalem. Mt. Zion is presently where the Muslim Dome of the

Rock mosque is located. It is allegedly from this huge rock inside the temple that the prophet Mohammed was carried up to heaven and had his visionary communications with God, what the Muslims refer to as the Mi'raj in reference to Mohammed's Night Journey (see *Isra and Mi'raj* on Wikipedia for more). It is the giant rock inside this temple complex that holds particular significance for all three major Western religions based on the Bible. Under *Dome of the Rock* on Wikipedia we find, in part:

> *"The site's great significance for Muslims derives from traditions connecting it to the* ***creation of the world*** *and to the belief that the Prophet Muhammad's Night Journey to heaven started from the rock at the center of the structure.*
>
> *In Jewish tradition the rock bears great significance as the* ***Foundation Stone, the place from which the world expanded into its present form*** *and where God gathered the dust used to create the first human, Adam; as the site on Mount Moriah where Abraham attempted to sacrifice his son; and as* ***the place where God's divine presence is manifested more than in any other place****, towards which Jews turn during prayer."*
>
> [Bold emphasis mine]

Before continuing we also need to look up *Foundation Stone* on Wikipedia for a more definitive explanation of this rock:

*"The Foundation Stone . . .is the name of the rock at the centre of the Dome of the Rock in Jerusalem. It is also known as the Pierced Stone because it has a small hole on the southeastern corner that enters a cavern beneath the rock, known as* ***the Well of Souls****. There is a difference of opinion in classical Jewish sources as to whether this was the location of the Holy of Holies or of the Outer Altar. According to those that hold it was the site of the Holy of Holies, that would make this the holiest site in Judaism (Tanhuma, chapter 10).*

***Jewish tradition views the Holy of Holies as the spiritual <u>junction</u> of Heaven and Earth, the axis mundi****, and is therefore the direction that Jews face when praying the Amidah The other view, that this was the site of the Outer Altar, would explain the holes in the stone which served various sacrificial purposes in the Outer Altar. From a classical Jewish textual standpoint, there is no conclusive opinion on the matter."*

[Bold emphasis mine]

There has been some contention over the ages about the location of Mt. Zion, with presently 3 locations being potentially identified as Mt, Zion, one of them being the current Temple

Mount where the Dome of the Rock is situated. Its present location is identified as what is known as the Western Hill, but it remains undetermined as to whether this was the original Mt. Zion. The location of the Dome of the Rock is referred to as the Upper Eastern Hill and was the accepted location of Mt. Zion for many centuries. My personal feeling is that the present site of the Dome of the Rock was the original Mt. Zion and I will provide my reasoning for this as follows.

In many of Ninhursag's alter ego goddess roles, the worship of stones in correspondence with her other identities was not uncommon. For some preliminary background on stone worship, we will look at Wikipedia under *Baetylus*:

> *"Baetylus (also Bethel, or Betyl, from Semitic bet el "house of god") is a word denoting* ***sacred stones that were supposedly endowed with life****. According to ancient sources, these objects of worship were meteorites, which were dedicated to the gods or revered as symbols of the gods themselves. A baetyl is also mentioned in the Bible at Bethel in the Book of Genesis in the story of Jacob's Ladder.*
>
> *In the Phoenician mythology related by Sanchuniathon, one of the sons of Uranus was named Baetylus. The worship of baetyls was widespread in the Phoenician colonies, including*

*Carthage, even after the adoption of Christianity, and was denounced by Augustine of Hippo."*

*"In Rome, there was the stone effigy of* ***Cybele, called Mater Idaea Deum****, that had been ceremoniously brought from Pessinus in Asia Minor in 204 BC. Another conical meteorite was enshrined in the Elagabalium to personify the Syrian deity Elagabalus.*

*In some cases an attempt was made to give a more regular form to the original shapeless stone: thus Apollo Agyieus was represented by a conical pillar with a pointed end, Zeus Meilichius in the form of a pyramid. Other famous baetylic idols were those in the temples of Zeus Casius at Seleucia Pieria, and of Zeus Teleios at Tegea. Even in the declining years of paganism, these idols still retained their significance, as is shown by the attacks upon them by ecclesiastical writers.*

*A similar practice survives today with the* ***Kaaba's Black Stone*** *although there is no veneration or mention of it in the Quran."*

[Bold emphasis mine]

Although most of the baetylus stones may have been meteorites, I don't think we should arbitrarily assume that all of them were. The current black meteorite stone that sits at the center of the Kaaba in Mecca was once dedicated to the goddess Al'lat in part of a trinitary goddess cult that predated Islam. If you look up *Al-lat* on Wikipedia you will find that Al'lat was the regional variant of the Mother Goddess in Arabia and has the same associations as Ishtar, Cybele, Magna Mater, Athena and other goddess alter egos Ninhursag played in other places. In some traditions Al'lat was considered the consort wife or possibly the daughter of Allah. Cybele herself was associated with stone worship, particularly cubes, derived from her name variant *Matar Kubile*. Around the world today in major cities you will find massive black cube statues (Google Black Cube Statues to see these statues), which all represent the Mother Goddess based on Cybele.

Cybele was also known as Lady of the Mountain, so the association of the goddess Cybele with the mountain top is an indisputable reference to Ninhursag – *Nin* = (Lady) *Hursag* = (of the Mountain). With Cybele and Al'lat's association with stones, whether meteoric or not, the large stone that served as the Holy of Holies on the Temple Mount would be wholly in keeping with Mt. Zion as Ninhursag's ancient temple stronghold in Jerusalem.

One other aspect of stones being affiliated with Ninhursag in her guise of Hermes is found in the Greek word *herma*. As Wikipedia informs us about *herma*:

> *"In the earliest times Greek divinities were worshiped in the form of a heap of stones or a shapeless column of stone or wood. In many parts*

*of Greece there were piles of stones by the sides of roads,* ***especially at their crossings****, and on the boundaries of lands. The religious respect paid to such heaps of stones,* ***especially at the meeting of roads****, is shown by the custom of each passer-by throwing a stone on to the heap or anointing it with oil. Later there was the addition of* ***a head and phallus*** *to the column, which became quadrangular* ***(the number 4 was sacred to Hermes)****."*

*"In ancient Greece the statues were thought to ward off harm or evil, an apotropaic function, and were placed at* ***crossings, country borders and boundaries*** *as protection, in front of temples, near to tombs, outside houses, in the gymnasia, palaestrae, libraries, porticoes, and public places,* ***at the corners of streets****, on high roads as sign-posts, with distances inscribed upon them. Before his role as protector of merchants and travelers,* ***Hermes was a phallic god, associated with fertility, luck, roads and borders****. His name perhaps comes from the word herma referring to a square or rectangular* ***pillar of stone****, terracotta, or bronze; a bust of Hermes' head, usually with a beard, sat on the top of the pillar, and male genitals adorned the base."*

[Bold emphasis mine]

Through this Hermes association with the stone *herma*, coupled with their placement at crossroad, borders and porticos, we find another affiliation with stone reverence and Ninhursag in the role of Hermes and the *herma*.

Another indicator that Jerusalem was the center of Ninhursag's worship is found in the name *Shalim* which Wikipedia tells us:

> *"Shalim (Shalem, Salem, and Salim) is a god in the Canaanite religion pantheon, mentioned in inscriptions found in Ugarit (Ras Shamra) in Syria. William F. Albright identified Shalim as the god of dusk, and Shahar as god of the dawn. In the Dictionary of Deities and Demons in the Bible,* ***Shalim is also identified as the deity representing Venus or the "Evening Star", and Shahar, the "Morning Star"****. His name derives from the triconsonantal Semitic root S-L-M. The city of Jerusalem was named after him, and the biblical King Solomon may also have been."*

> *"A Ugaritic myth known as The Gracious and Most Beautiful Gods, describes Shalim and his brother Shahar as offspring of El through two women he meets at the seashore. They are both nursed by* ***"The Lady", likely Anat (Athirat or Asherah),*** *and have appetites as large as "(one) lip to the earth and (one) lip to the heaven." In other*

*Ugaritic texts, **the two are associated with the sun goddess.**"*

[Bold emphasis mine]

Given the fact that Shalim and Shahar are both associated with the morning and evening star, which is Venus, and that they are nursed by Asherah most likely, it would not be an incorrect surmise that these two 'brothers' were male roles played by Ninhursag, and that she was responsible for establishing Jerusalem from the start. Their association in Ugaritic texts with the sun goddess should also not be overlooked. If this is so, then Jerusalem would have been the place Ninhursag established her temple on Mt. Zion. Given the fact that in her other goddess roles elsewhere, her associations with stones would naturally draw her to the giant stone on top of Mt. Zion to serve as a natural pedestal from which she could rule the kingdom of Judah.

There was obviously a back and forth between Enki and Ninhursag during this period because at least two Kings of Judah rebuilt the temple against Yahweh's mandates, and both king Ahab, and later King Manasseh reinstalled the Asherah and reinitiated worship of the Hosts of Heaven within these temples. There is no shortage of biblical enmity against these kings for their alleged backsliding into the original worship practices of the kingdom of Judah. I have already pointed out that the Hosts of Heaven represented the discarnate hive personalities who, by the temple phase in Israel, Ninhursag had already joined in the Divine hive hereafter. 2 Kings 21:4-6 states about Manasseh:

*"4 He built altars in the house of the LORD, of which the LORD had said, "In Jerusalem I will put My name."*

*5 For he built altars for* ***all the host of heaven*** *in the two courts of the house of the LORD.*

*6* ***He made his son pass through the fire, practiced witchcraft and used divination, and dealt with mediums and spiritists****. He did much evil in the sight of the LORD provoking Him to anger...."*

[Bold emphasis mine]

Through these brief passages we find the temple being re-commemorated to Asherah and Baal, totally against Yahweh's wishes. To further prove Yahweh's distaste of the Heavenly Hierarchy I provide the following versus where Yahweh and his prophets condemn the heavenly hosts along with the whore Asherah:

*2 Kings 17:16 And they abandoned all the commandments of the Lord their God, and made for themselves metal images of two calves; and* ***they made an Asherah and worshiped all the host of heaven and served Baal****.*

*Jeremiah 19:13 The houses of Jerusalem and the houses of the kings of Judah—all the houses on whose roofs offerings have been offered* *__to all the host of heaven__, and drink offerings have been poured out to other gods—shall be defiled like the place of Topheth.*

*Jeremiah 8:2 And they shall be spread before **the sun and the moon and all the host of heaven, which they have loved and served, which they have gone after, and which they have sought and worshiped.** And they shall not be gathered or buried. They shall be as dung on the surface of the ground.*

*Isaiah 34:4 **All the host of heaven shall rot away,** and the skies roll up like a scroll. **All their host shall fall,** as leaves fall from the vine, like leaves falling from the fig tree.*

*Isaiah 24:21 On that day the Lord will punish **the host of heaven, in heaven**, and the kings of the earth, on the earth.*

[Bold emphasis mine]

These passages leave no question as to who is associated with the host of heaven, and it is not Yahweh – it is Asherah. There is no grey zone in this distinction based on these verses. With these clearly inarguable condemnations of the host of heaven and its association with Asherah, then one must reach the logical conclusion that if Jesus is to return with the Hosts of Heaven in the end times, there is no way he can be the Son of *this* Old Testament God. The only viable alternative explanation is the one I offer in this book, and that is the fact that Jesus is the Son of Asherah, or Ninhursag, although the use of Sonship is merely another one of her fictitious personality constructs.

Of all the tribes of Israel in the Old Testament, the tribe of Judah is the one that suffers the most scorn and persecution of Yahweh. As I pointed out it was the tribe of Judah, symbolized by the Lion, one of Ninhursag's long-standing symbolic icons, that was eventually taken away to Babylon in captivity. It should be noted that the national god of Babylon was Marduk, allegedly the son of Enki, but in actuality only a different role that Enki/Yahweh played in another land. Marduk was a fabricated alter ego for Enki just as Ninhursag used her many alter-egos in many other lands – Ishtar, Athena, Al-lat, Cybele, Anat, Asherah, etc. So, the invasion from Babylon and the casting of Ninhursag's Tribe of Judah into exile is but one more illustration of the war between Enki and Ninhursag, with Nebuchadnezzar II serving as Enki's client king to subjugate the 'sinful' (and non-tax paying) Tribe of Judah. This exile and captivity lasted until Babylon was conquered by the Persians, whose national god was Ninhursag as her alter ego, Ahura Mazda, at which time the Judah captives were set free.

With these facts and this perspective in hand, much of the Old Testament storytelling takes on a different texture and we can finally get to the root of what was actually taking place without all the mystical religious malarkey to blur the picture. Most Christians don't bother to question the story being told here, but simply take it as religious fact. They ignore the apparent contradictions because in all their Bible study courses they focus on the prophetic appearance of Jesus and the end times more than the foundational actions of the stories being told. Had more Christians truly engaged in Bible study rather than working with their religious confirmation bias, they may have raised the questions I did and come to different conclusions about their faith in light of these contradictions over the heavenly host. Despite what has been expunged in the biblical fabricated stories, there Is enough evidence for the wise scholar to see through the charade once they know what to look for.

As with everything biblical, we are often looking at two or three meanings to certain terms, and host of heaven is one of those terms. To some, the host of heaven means the stars in the sky, particularly when considering the use of astrology in the ancient world, and Hebrew mythology and later Kabbalah are not lacking in astrological forecasting. Another format for the host of heaven is found in the Book of Enoch, where the host of heaven is often associated with the Angels and those who rebelled and ultimately bred with the daughters of men to create the Nephilim, or giants in the Old Testament. In neither of these contexts does the term host of heaven bear the same weight and significance that I have placed on the meaning for host of heaven as the hapiym hive collective who lined up behind Ninhursag in her personal war against Enki for control of this planet. In the context of the verses provided above, this is the only explanation that makes any sense, and it is the one that is not explained within the Old Testament, it is only alluded to as a term and the reading audience is left to figure out what it means on their own, which no theological scholar has done since the Bible was compiled.

Another aspect that should be weighed in this equation is that if the host of heaven refers to the Angels, then why does Enki/Yahweh spurn his own alleged Angels in these passages? This doesn't make any sense in the interpretive context of wanting to tear down and destroy the host of heaven *in* heaven as related in Isaiah 34: 4 in the verses cited. Given the content of the polemic against Asherah and her association with the host in heaven, along with all the other hallmarks of condemnation against Ninhursag/Asherah offered here and in Chapter 7, only my explanation for the host of heaven as the hapiym hive collective fits the story line.

Before continuing further into discussing Zionism, it must be noted that the Oneness professed in all the modern spiritual doctrines, or the monotheism expressed in the solar worship of the Aten disc in Akhenaten's sun religion, are not the same as the monotheistic worship of Enki as the sole God of the Old Testament. Enki was a narcissistic sociopathic personality who loved the praise of others and had no problem mandating the murder of others who did not give him the homage and worship he felt he was due as God Almighty, and this part of his personal character is seen throughout the Old Testament. For a direct correlation of this assertion that Yahweh/Enki was a narcissist in his sociopathy, I direct the reader to an ancient Sumerian text entitled *Enki and the World Order* (pdf link in References section). When you read this particular text and compare it to the personality of Yahweh in the Old Testament, you are going to see many direct correlations with the psychological composition of a narcissistic sociopath.

Establishing that Ninhursag/Asherah was the point of worship for the Tribe of Judah, who were the alleged 'backsliders' to the ancient religion of the goddess, can now be defined as Zionism with her worship center being situated on Mt. Zion in Jerusalem. It was a city that she herself established as the Canaanite god Shalim (Venus), and we have zeroed in on a major hidden part of the Bible storytelling. Because Mt. Zion was primarily a cult center of goddess worship in ancient Canaan and for the Tribe of Judah, we now have the information to follow Zionism through the centuries.

Zionism is much like Judaism or Jewishness. Asked about whether a Jew is a designation of a race or a religion, either answer may be provided depending on who the question is asked of and answered by. I have attested in my other works that the Jews are only one faction of the Aryan invader tribes who arrived on this planet ca. 3760 BC, which is the starting date of the Jewish calendar, and through which the Jews still track their historicity.

One thing that must be explained is that one does not have to be Jewish or embrace the Jewish religion to become a Zionist. There are a few million Christian Zionists who have been deceived into believing alleged biblical prophecy and who harbor the ideological belief that the return of the Jews to the Holy Land is a prophetic harbinger to the Second Coming of Christ. Unbeknownst to most Protestant Christians, there was a concerted propaganda effort to plant this idea in their churches before the push for the Zionist State of Israel was established. This blind support for the establishment of Israel was used as a public pressure mechanism to sway governmental decisions to continually support Israel, which the United States still heavily funds to this day on an annual basis, and this doesn't take into consideration supplying the Israeli armed forces with top of the line American made weapons.

What most Protestant Christian Zionists do not understand, and which most refuse to accept when presented with the facts, is that the State of Israel was a contrived Marxist agenda manipulated by the Marxist Fabian Society, working through Lord Alfred Balfour, who was a close associate with high ranking members of the Fabian Society. The so-called Balfour Declaration was a private letter sent by Lord Balfour to the Zionist Rothschild banking family member Baron Lionel Walter Rothschild, expressing the British government's support for a Jewish homeland in Palestine. This letter was composed on Nov. 2, 1917, so the plan was launched to establish the State of Israel through machinations of the Marxist Fabian Society and the Zionist Rothschild banking consortium using the British government as the vehicle to attain that goal. After WW I, Palestine fell under the control of Great Britain as a protectorate.

As early as 1900 the 6 million number was already being floated in the American Press. I will provide but a few examples to support this contention from a short piece entitled *Two hundred "Six million Jews" allegations from 1900-1945*:

*1900 - Stephen S. Wise, New York Times, June 11, 1900: "There are 6,000,000 living, bleeding, suffering arguments* ***in favor of Zionism.***"

*1902 - Encyclopaedia Britannica, 10th Edition, Vol. 25, 1902, page 482: "While there are in Russia and Rumania six millions of Jews who are being systematically degraded ..."*

*1902 - Samuel W. Goldstein, New York Times, November 27, 1902:* ***"PLEA FOR ZIONISM*** *... In answer I would say: Does Dr. Silverman represent the 6,000,000 Jews in Russia, 300,000 in Roumania and the 1,000,000 in Galicia?"*

*1904 - Israel Zangwill, New York Times, October 20, 1904: "The problem does not relate to the American Jews, but to the 6,000,000 in Russia. The Russian Government has consented to allow the Jews to leave,"*

*1905 - New York Times, January 29th, 1905: "He declared that* ***a free and a happy Russia, with its 6,000,000 Jews, would possibly mean the end of Zionism, since the abolition of the autocracy would practically eliminate the causes that brought Zionism into existence.***"

*1911 - Max Nordeau speaking at The 1911 Zionist Congress. Hecht, Ben. Perfidy. NY; Julian Messner. 1961. page 254: "But the same righteous Governments, who are so nobly, industriously active to establish the eternal peace, are preparing, by their own confession, complete annihilation for six million people,"*

*1914 - New York Times, December 2nd, 1914, page 12: "APPEAL FOR AID FOR JEWS. ... the plight of more than 6,000,000 Jews ... upon the Jewish people, more than nine millions of whom live in the countries at war and over six million of these in the actual war zone in Poland, Galicia and the whole of Russian frontier."*

*1915 - The Sun (NY), June 6, 1915, section 5, page 1: "Six million Jews, one-half of the Jewish people throughout the world, are being persecuted, hounded, humiliated, tortured, starved. ... six million Jews in Russia ... are being tortured so mercilessly."*

[Bold emphasis mine]

These should be enough of the two hundred instances of the propaganda designed to get the 6 million persecuted Jews number into the mind of the public before the 6 million of the Holocaust ever happened. What should be noted by most Western readers is that there was another revolution in Russia against the Tzar in 1905. Looking at *1905 Russian Revolution* on Wikipedia we find:

> *"According to Sidney Harcave, author of The Russian Revolution of 1905 (1970) four problems in Russian society contributed to the revolution. Newly emancipated peasants earned too little and were not allowed to sell or mortgage their allotted land. Ethnic minorities resented the government because of its "Russification", discrimination and repression, such as banning them from voting and serving in the Imperial Guard or Navy and limited attendance in schools. A nascent industrial working class resented the government for doing too little to protect them, banning strikes and labor unions. Finally,* ***radical ideas fomented and spread after a relaxing of discipline in universities allowed a new consciousness to grow among students****."*
>
> [Bold emphasis mine]

What should be taken note of in this brief passage is that it was the banning of labor unions and the indoctrination on universities of students that allowed the revolutionary incentive to be built. Also, during and after this initial revolution, the minority Jewish population was able to insert itself into positions of governmental power. The ideology of this revolution is no different than any other Marxist revolution – incite the public into sentiments of riot and eventually undermine the government. Although the 1905 revolution brought about some political change, it was not enough for the radical Marxists, and the Bolshevik Revolution of 1917 was just around the corner to complete the destruction of Russia, and in time, murder close to 60 million people. Hitler's 6 million seems paltry in comparison to this murderous carnage.

It should be noted from the earlier highlighted passage that "a free and happy Jewish community would undermine the need for Zionism". This is indicative of the fact that Zionism only flourished under the banner of Jewish Communist malcontents. There really is no other way to interpret such a statement. Ergo, Zionism is hooked to revolutionary Marxism like a Siamese twin.

So, let's move forward to the Christian misconception about God's people returning to the Holy Land and expose that lie. The primary driving force of the establishment of Israel, despite the Balfour Declaration, was Marxist terrorism at the hands of such organizations as the Irgun and the Stern Gang. If we look up *Irgun* on Wikipedia we find in part:

> *"The Irgun ("The National Military Organization in the Land of Israel") was a Zionist paramilitary organization that operated in Mandate Palestine between 1931 and 1948. It was an offshoot of the older and larger Jewish paramilitary organization Haganah (Hebrew: Defence). When the group broke from the*

*Haganah it became known as the Haganah Bet (Hebrew: literally "Defense 'B' " or "Second Defense"), Irgun members were absorbed into the Israel Defense Forces at the start of the 1948 Arab–Israeli war. The Irgun is also referred to as Etzel, an acronym of the Hebrew initials, or by the abbreviation IZL.*

*The Irgun policy was based on what was then called* **Revisionist Zionism** *founded by Ze'ev Jabotinsky. According to Howard Sachar, "The policy of the new organization was based squarely on Jabotinsky's teachings: every Jew had the right to enter Palestine; only active retaliation would deter the Arabs; only Jewish armed force would ensure the Jewish state"*

***Two of the operations for which the Irgun is best known are the bombing of the King David Hotel in Jerusalem on 22 July 1946 and the Deir Yassin massacre, carried out together with Lehi on 9 April 1948.***

***The Irgun has been viewed as a terrorist organization or organization which carried out terrorist acts****. Specifically the organization* ***"committed acts of terrorism and assassination against the British, whom it regarded as illegal***

***occupiers, and it was also violently anti-Arab"*** *according to the Encyclopædia Britannica. In particular* ***the Irgun was described as a terrorist organization by the United Nations, British, and United States governments****; in media such as The New York Times newspaper; as well as by the Anglo-American Committee of Inquiry, the 1946 Zionist Congress and the Jewish Agency. Irgun's tactics appealed to many Jews who believed that any action taken in the cause of the creation of a Jewish state was justified,* ***including terrorism****."*

[Bold emphasis mine]

Now, let's take a look at the other side of this Jewish terrorist equation, that being the Stern Gang, alternatively known as Lehi. Under *Lehi*, Wikipedia informs us in part:

*"Lehi - (Lohamei Herut Israel – Lehi, "Fighters for the Freedom of Israel – Lehi"), often known pejoratively as the Stern Gang, was a Zionist paramilitary organization founded by Avraham ("Yair") Stern in Mandatory Palestine. Its avowed aim was to evict the British authorities from Palestine by resort to force, allowing unrestricted immigration of Jews and* ***the formation of a Jewish state, a "new <u>totalitarian</u> Hebrew republic"****. It was initially called the National Military Organization in Israel, upon*

*being founded in August 1940, but was renamed Lehi one month later. According to Jean E. Rosenfeld,* ***the group admitted to having used terrorist attacks****.*

*Lehi split from the Irgun militant group in 1940 in order to continue fighting the British during World War II.* ***Lehi initially sought an alliance with Fascist Italy and Nazi Germany, offering to fight alongside them against the British in return for the transfer of all Jews from Nazi-occupied Europe to Palestine****. Believing that Nazi Germany was a lesser enemy of the Jews than Britain,* ***Lehi twice attempted to form an alliance with the Nazis****. During World War II, it declared that* ***it would establish a Jewish state based upon "nationalist and totalitarian principles"****. After Stern's death in 1942, the new leadership of* ***Lehi began to move it towards support for Joseph Stalin's Soviet Union****. In 1944,* ***Lehi officially declared its support for National Bolshevism. It said that its National Bolshevism involved an amalgamation of left-wing and right-wing political elements – Stern said Lehi incorporated elements of both the left and the right*** *– however this change was unpopular and Lehi began to lose support as a result."*

[Bold emphasis mine]

So much for the Christian misperception about God's people returning to the Holy Land. Members of the Irgun and Stern Gang, mostly comprised of Eastern European Communist Jews who were never Semites, went on to hold high positions of power in Israeli government. Former Lehi leader Yitzhak Shamir became Prime Minister of Israel in 1983. Menachem Begin had also been a leader of the Irgun before he eventually became Prime Minister of Israel. This is the history of Israel that is kept hidden from the blind propagandized eyes of Western Protestant Christians with their eyes ever turned heavenward anticipating the return of Jesus with his heavenly host to purify all humanity and remove all the sinners who disagree with them and cast them into Hell.

Given the fact that Marxism is the foundation for Zionism in modern Israel, and that revolutionary tactics, just like those used following the Lady Liberty in the French Revolution, then we should have no problem linking Zionist Marxist world government to Ninhursag and the hive's agenda for the total domination for humanity on this planet. Zionism, like Christianity, is also a messianic movement, and Jewish messianism is present in the Dead Sea Scrolls and can be found in the Bar Kokhba revolt, the last of the three Jewish revolts against the Romans. As Wikipedia informs us about Bar Kokhba revolt:

> *"Simon Bar Kokhba took the title Nasi Israel and ruled over an entity that was virtually independent for two and a half years. The Jewish*

*sage Rabbi Akiva* ***identified Simon Bar Kosiba as the Jewish messiah****, and gave him the surname "Bar Kokhba" meaning "Son of a Star" in the Aramaic language, from the Star Prophecy verse from Numbers 24:17: "There shall come a star out of Jacob". The name Bar Kokhba does not appear in the Talmud but in ecclesiastical sources. The era of the redemption of Israel was announced, contracts were signed and a large quantity of Bar Kokhba Revolt coinage was struck over foreign coins."*

[Bold emphasis mine]

I bring in the Bar Kokhba story to elucidate the bent of Jewish messianism and its revolutionary tendencies over the ages. Christians have accepted Jesus as the only messiah, yet Jews throughout the ages keep looking for a Jewish messiah. Bar Kokhba was only one of them. In the 17th century there appeared another Jewish claimant to the title messiah, *Sabbatai Zevi*, which Wikipedia informs us about:

*"Sabbatai Zevi (other spellings include Shabbetai Ẓevi, Shabbeṯāy Ṣeḇī, Shabsai Tzvi, and Sabetay Sevi in Turkish) (August 1, 1626 – c. September 17, 1676[1]) was a Sephardic ordained Rabbi, though of Romaniote origin* ***and a kabbalist****, active throughout the Ottoman Empire,* ***who claimed to be the long-awaited Jewish***

***Messiah.** He was the founder of the **Sabbatean movement.***

*In February 1666, upon arriving in Constantinople, Sabbatai was imprisoned on the order of the grand vizier Ahmed Köprülü; in September of that same year, after being moved from different prisons around the capital to Adrianople (the imperial court's seat) for judgement on accusations of fomenting sedition, Sabbatai was given by Köprülü, in the name of the Sultan Mehmed IV, the choice of either facing death by some type of ordeal, **or of converting to Islam. Sabbatai seems to have chosen the latter by donning from then on a Turkish turban**. He was then also rewarded by the heads of the Ottoman state with a generous pension for his compliance with their political and religious plans. Some of his followers also converted to Islam—about 300 families who were known as the Dönmeh (converts). He was later banished twice by the Ottoman authorities who were tired of his schemes and discovered him singing psalms with the Jews. He later died in isolation."*

[Bold emphasis mine]

Sabbatai Zevi is just one example of the typical Zionist Jew who is willing to do anything to push the Zionist agenda forward. Just as Zevi converted to Islam and won the scorn of religious Jews who were not believers in the Kabbalah, other Zionists have chosen to don new clothing to push forth the hive collectivist agenda. After the Bolshevik Revolution it was reported by a Russian Communist defector, Bella Dodd, that during the 1930s, 1100 Communists allegedly converted to and inserted themselves as Catholic priests. The collectivist agenda of the hive means that the perpetrators of this ongoing Great Work to take over the minds of humanity will stop at nothing to fulfill its tyrannical agenda. Leftist Marxism promoted by the Fabian Society, coupled with the mystical spirituality of the Theosophical Society, which has spread into all modern spiritual beliefs, is the seductive poison through which these would-be world rulers control the psyche of humanity. Zionism is just another phrase for deception in this process, and all too many gullible Christians have fallen for the prophecy myth to question any of this. The motto of the Israeli Mossad is, By Deception Shall We Do War.

Another thing that should be noted that is of particular interest is that the word Zion has no predecessor etymology. This means there is no predicate history for this word before Ninhursag named the mountain in Jerusalem as her temple site. Despite the many varied interpretations of Zionism through the ages, there is no previous etymological history from which the word derived. It appears as suddenly as her temple cult as Asherah and Baal in the kingdom of Judah. Baal was symbolized by the golden calf. If we keep in mind that in Egypt one of Ninhursag's alter egos was the cow-headed goddess Hathor, then the golden calf would simply represent another Son connotation in her repeating pattern of

Mother and Son deceptive perfidy. So, it is highly likely that she played the role of Baal which was specifically associated with her Asherah cult in Judah, no different than the Mother-Son association with Isis and Horus. It must be clarified, however, that the word Baal simply meant Lord, and throughout the entire Middle East we see numerous gods designated with the predicate of Baal. For the most part, except in biblical context, Baal itself was not a proper name, but simply a designator of a god as Lord, not unlike the predicate *En* designating Lord in Sumerian.

Although Ninhursag established her mountain retreat in Judah while she was still in physical form, the name she chose for that mountain carried her personal energetic imprint, whether she physically occupied the location or not. Just as the name Ninhursag translates to mean Lady of the Mountain in Sumerian, she had long associations with mountains well before establishing Ur-Shalim (Jerusalem). Even the name Jerusalem is a derivative of a name she created, so the entire city is constructed upon a fictitious character she created as the god Shalim. We must also pay attention to the fact that this particular piece of real estate has probably been the most contested and bitterly fought over territory since its beginning, and that the *three* major Western religions all have a vested interest in controlling it. Doesn't it strike you as strange that once again we find the three associated with all this contention? Perhaps it is only accidental, but one thing I have learned in my years of research into these subjects is that there is nothing accidental about any of this.

If we look at the Muslim belief about that huge rock sheltered under the Dome of the Rock as being the place where

Heaven meets Earth, and we take into consideration that Ninhursag had given up the ghost of her physical form so she could join the hive, then this particular perception of Heaven meeting Earth through the aegis of that rock takes on a more sinister meaning. That giant stone is situated on top of a mountain at its pinnacle. Through one sense, it could be interpreted as lying between Heaven and Earth, although it rests firmly on the ground. At first gloss this may not have much meaning, or seem somewhat confusing, but I am going to expand your perceptual awareness by explaining this.

As the goddess Hecate, Ninhursag in her triune form found her energies in spaces that lied between places. She was the goddess of the crossroads, particularly where three crossroads met, for at a crossroad, there lies the junction which is not any of the three roads, so it is a space *in between* the roads where the crossroad is none of the roads that meet at the junction. Hecate was also the goddess of doorways, gates or portals, for a doorway is neither inside nor outside, but lies in a nether region in between them. To understand the importance of this, we must always keep in mind Ninhursag's hermaphrodite form, which was male, female and the androgyne. Through taking on the alter egos of gods she could use her magical energies to cast spells from the masculine aspect, and from the goddess side she could cast spells from the female aspect. The androgyne part of her, the blending of the male and female, where she was neither one nor the other, is the in between part of her through which she could program and harness energies from nether regions, or voids. That stone on top of Mt. Zion, from the standpoint of her energetic programming abilities, represented a void, caught between Heaven and Earth. In this regard, the Muslim interpretation about the stone is correct.

As shared previously, the Foundation Stone in Jewish beliefs, is also a junction between Heaven and Earth provided the stone lied at the center of the Holy of Holies, which I assert that it did. For more substantiating evidence of this we need to look at the word Shekinah, which was the Holy Spirit that inhabited the Holy of Holies in the Jewish temple. Wikipedia shares about the *Shekinah* in part this way:

> *"The Shekhinah represents the* ***feminine attributes of the presence of God.*** *(Shekhinah being a feminine word in Hebrew), based especially on readings of the Talmud."*
>
> *"The Shekhinah is associated with the* ***transformational spirit of God*** *regarded as the source of prophecy:*
>
> *After that thou shalt come to the hill of God, where is the garrison of the Philistines; and it shall come to pass, when thou art come thither to the city, that* ***thou shalt meet a band of prophets coming down from the high place with a psaltery, and a timbrel, and a pipe, and a harp, before them; and they will be prophesying****. And the spirit of the LORD will come mightily upon thee, and*

*thou shalt prophesy with them,* ***and shalt be turned into another man.*** *— 1 Samuel 10:5–6"*

*"Sabbath Bride*

*The theme of the Shekhinah as* ***the Sabbath Bride*** *recurs in the writings and songs of 16th century* ***Kabbalist****, Rabbi Isaac Luria. The Asader Bishvachin song, written in Aramaic by Luria (his name appears as an acrostic of each line) and sung at the evening meal of Shabbat is an example of this. The song appears in particular in many siddurs in the section following Friday night prayers and in some Shabbat song books:*

*Let us invite the Shechinah with a newly-laid table and with a* ***well-lit menorah*** *that casts light on all heads.*

***Three*** *preceding days to the right,* ***three*** *succeeding days to the left, and amid them the* ***Sabbath bride*** *with adornments she goes, vessels and robes ...*

*May the Shechinah become a crown through the six loaves on each side through the doubled-six may our table be bound with the profound Temple services.*

*A paragraph in the Zohar starts: "One must prepare a comfortable seat with several cushions and embroidered covers, from all that is found in the house, like one who prepares a canopy* ***for a bride****. For* ***the Shabbat is a queen and a bride****. This is why the masters of the Mishna used to go out on the eve of Shabbat* ***to receive her on the road,*** *and used to say:* ***'Come, O bride, come, O bride!'*** *And one must sing and rejoice at the table in her honor ...* ***one must receive the Lady with many lighted candles, many enjoyments, beautiful clothes, and a house embellished with many fine appointments ...****"*

[Bold emphasis mine]

With all the foregoing now in hand we find that the Shekinah is the feminine aspect of God, that it resided in the Holy of Holies within the temple precincts, and that the seven candles of the Menorah represent the Shekinah as a Bride in the Sabbath celebrations according to Kabbalistic traditions. We also find the echoes of the Hermetic traditions of the Chemical Wedding, the Bride of Christ, the emphasis on the candle flames with the Shekinah harkening back to Zoroastrian beliefs and the Eternal Flame of Ahura Mazda as well as the flame association with the Hindu Agni. And this is not overlooking the importance of that number seven in the candlesticks. Are we starting to see the noose tighten around defining what Zionism is?

As illustrated, the Zionist movement is both a messianic movement where Jews are looking specifically for a Jewish messiah. It is also and has always been a collectivist movement, which is why it can fold itself into Marxism without there being any conflict once the illusion and confusion can be seen through. One does not have to be a Jew to be a Zionist. Any Aryan or uninformed individual can support the Zionist agenda in its many permutations without having a clue what is going on with it.

For those Christians who have bought into Bible prophecy believing that Communist terrorist Jews returning to Israel constitutes the concept of a religious people returning to the Holy Land, they are gravely misinformed, but then, they were propagandized by Zionist agents preaching from their church pulpits for decades to buy into this belief as I have illustrated in this chapter.

Another aspect of this that I have not yet shared in this book is also found in Ninhursag's alter ego, Hecate. Hecate was the goddess who served as the guide to the underworld. Returning to the shared passages from Wikipedia where it stated that the stone on Mt. Zion covers a cavern referred to as 'the Well of Souls'. Once again, when we associate Ninhursag with the Shekinah and the Holy of Holies with Hecate's role as the guide to the underworld and the afterlife, then all the pieces fit seamlessly together. Some readers may feel that this is a stretch, but given all the information shared in this book, all things must be considered as a whole, not as separate pieces.

Mother Goddess cults were often associated with caves or caverns, as with the Cult of Mithras and others. A cave or cavern was considered to be a womb of the Earth Mother Gaia, so numerous religious cults and mystery schools held their ritual ceremonies underground or in caves. With the cavern under that rock on Mt. Zion being alluded to as the Well of Souls, we are looking at another mother goddess womb correlation, as well as an underworld connotation which would relate to Hecate as the guide into the underworld after death. This would correlate Shekinah with Hecate without any disruption in perception and that stone on the mountain being a boundary above the underworld and situated below Heaven.

Western religions have all done their damndest to distance themselves from their Pagan roots. Just because religionists deny these origins does not mean they are not still there at the root of their religions. It is because of intentional obfuscation and the mental compartmentalization based on denial that people have not made the correlations I have made in this book. It is the *refusal* to look at these things that keeps humanity blinded from them, and there is nothing worse in my estimation than willful ignorance.

There is one other piece I want to add to this puzzle, and that is another contentious topic surrounding a book called The *Protocols of the Learned Elders of Zion*, which was made public and translated into English in 1905 by the author Sergei Nilus. The original Russian addition was released in 1903. The reason I am bringing up this controversial work is not because I give it credence for what it was presented to be, a worldwide Jewish agenda, but due to the fact of what it has become.

It has been proven definitively that the *Protocols* are a plagiarism on a novel produced by Eugène Sue, a French author with socialist leanings who serialized his work in 90 segments from 1842-1843 called *The Mysteries of Paris* which, as Wikipedia states about that novel: "*Its realistic descriptions of the poor and disadvantaged became a critique of social institutions, echoing the socialist position leading up to the Revolutions of 1848.*" At that time, it was presented with an anti-Catholic, anti-Capitalist spin on the work, which is in keeping with Ninhursag's Zionist agenda since the creation of the Roman Church.

Another person whose work was plagiarized in order to create Nilus' version of the Russian Protocols was Maurice Joly from his polemic criticism of the political ambitions of Napoleon III in his book, *Dialogue in Hell*. Between these two authors we find the launching point of what eventually became the propaganda piece called *The Protocols*.

You may be wondering why I bring this up at all. The importance of the work is not that it is a forgery, but the agenda that is put forth in the volume that, if you look at the world around you, has come into being using the tenets in that book. There is nothing that says, forgery and plagiarism notwithstanding, that the British Fabian Society did not have access to this book and use it as a guide to shape their own globalist Marxist agenda. If you think about it, what better way to hide their agenda in plain sight than to discredit the book, leave the Jews holding the bag, then push forward Ninhursag and the hive's agenda for control using that book as the model through which to subvert everything that has taken place at the hands of the hive-colluding Fabian Marxists. It would only be another means of deceiving the public and leaving the Jews as the fall guys to the British Fabian wing of the

Aryan brotherhood. I have stated that these Aryan tribes have competed with each other since they parted ways after their arrival on this planet, and they have been involved in an incessant game of king of the mountain between themselves ever since. A deception of this nature would be right in keeping with their overall agenda of deception, so such a possibility should not be ruled out.

Having laid the groundwork for understanding Zionism and the globalist agenda, let's now look at so-called End Times prophecies. All three Western religions are based on messianic beliefs. The Jews are looking for their Jewish messiah, the Christians are waiting for the return of Jesus, and even Islam holds a belief that Jesus will return for Judgment day after their Mahdi arrives, and who will rule Islam for a period of time before Jesus returns for Judgment day. Just as there have been false Jewish messiahs like Bar Kokhba and Sabbatai Zevi, the Muslims have had numerous claimants who declared themselves to be the awaited reformer of Islam over the centuries.

In Hinduism, it is the return of Vishnu (another fictitious alter ego of Ninhursag) who will return on a white horse ending the present era, or Kali Yuga. Even Theosophy has promoted the idea of a world redeemer whom they call Maitreya, or World Teacher. In fact, a goodly portion of world religions believe in some kind of Last Days or End Times prophecy. What the reader must realize is a couple different aspects of prophecy before we can go further in explaining all this End Times prophetic nonsense.

In the first instance, humans are a tremendously insecure species, and I have provided enough information in this book that explains why this species has this type of psychological insecurity. Prophecies lie in the realm of the supernatural. All too many humans want their lives spelled out for them, and if it can come from some presumed supernatural source, like a mystic, medium, astrologer, oracle, psychic or prophet, so much the better. These days we do not have oracles like the Oracle at Delphi, so we have modern channelers to spread the presumed prophetic swill of the hive. For more basic personal life questions, people turn to the presumed supernatural powers of the Psychic Hotline or Tarot card readers. The reader needs to realize that it is this same reliance on supernatural explanations for our humdrum lives as mortals that keeps this supernatural circus alive and filling the bleachers, as well as filling the pockets of these supernatural promoters. There has always been a profit margin where prophets are concernd.

In the context of the hive agenda, what is presented as prophetic visions was in fact a long-term plan. There is a distinction between a presumed prophecy and broadcasting a plan masqueraded as prophecy. Because of the supernatural element involved in alleged prophecy, visions and divine communications received by mystics and prophets, people are misdirected into believing that these prophecies are a mandate that will all come to pass, without question. Through sowing the anxiety associated with these prophecies, it created one hell of a food supply for the hapiym virus on this planet and also served as an energetic food source for the cosmic hive collective. The continual anticipation, dread and disappointment over these fraudulent prophecies over the ages has caused wars, mass movements and paranoia throughout the generations.

We have had two instances of a form of millennial type fever to use as examples. The first occurred with the global trepidation over Y2K, and the most recent was the prophetic fiasco associated with the Mayan calendar and the Shift in Consciousness nonsense heavily promoted by the Theosophists and the New Age leading up to 2012. In both cases there was a lot of anxiety or excitement beforehand, depending on one's belief system, and in both cases, there was a serious emotional letdown for many when their beliefs, either in the Second Coming or the magical Shift in Consciousness didn't occur. Others breathed a sigh of relief when the world didn't come to an end in either case. Regardless of where you fell in this set of emotions, the hapiym virus fed like a Thanksgiving dinner over the emotions generated from both the lead up to, and the disappointment or relief after these two dated events. When you can understand the feeding nature of the hapiym virus being based on human emotions, then you can understand how prophecies manipulate our emotions and have throughout time. Prophecy is a weapon used to generate human emotional energies, so the virus could feed on our species while the hives were still alive. End of story.

When we look at the biblical prophecy brought forth in the Book of Revelation, we are looking at Ninhursag and the hive's ultimate game plan. This is true for every End Times prophecy embedded in any religion that professes such an ideology. The form of the prophecy may vary from religion to religion, but the ultimate result was intended to be the same thing – the completion of the Great Work. This was the point at which the stone would be placed on top of the pyramid as the capstone to bring in the full-fledged world government and tyranny worked toward by Ninhursag, the hive and the Aryans for the last 4,000 years. This is what all these End Times prophesy in all these varied religions portended. For an excellent brief, yet thorough overview of prophecy fever over the ages, I suggest reading a NY Times article by Peter Steinfels from 1999 called, *Beliefs; Millennial fears in the year 1000: apocalypse then, apocalypse now and apocalypse forever.*

With the information I have shared in this chapter, then the reader is now apprised of the full agenda for all these mystical traditions and what the planned-for outcome was to be had the hives not been removed to stop this millennia's old agenda on this planet. I have drawn the lines of interconnectedness to illustrate how all these mystical and supernatural traditions dovetail together through the perennial philosophy and the alleged Great Work into a monumental plan for tyranny and the subjugation of the entire human species on this planet. In all of these religious traditions, the 'sinners' were all to be eliminated and humanity was supposed to enjoy peace forever. Sinners in this case should be interpreted to mean any human who disagreed with the hive collectivist ideology to rule the world.

To close this chapter, I want to focus on one last verse from the Book of Revelation and explain its meaning and remove the final mystery from this prophetic puzzle; Revelation 1:7:

*"Behold, he cometh with clouds; and every eye shall see him, and they also which pierced him: and all kindreds of the earth shall wail because of him. Even so, Amen."*

I have heard any number of people ask the question over the years how, when Christ returns, every eye and every person will see him coming on the clouds. They can't comprehend what circumstance would allow people on a different side of the planet to see Jesus coming back on his clouds of glory with the heavenly host. There is a very simple and pragmatic explanation to all this when we understand the workings of the hive virus within us.

Almost every mystic throughout the ages, and virtually every prophet had visions. When one was infected by the hapiym virus, it had the capability to artificially induce visions, with or without the tools of meditation, drugs, trauma or NDE states to trigger these visions. When the time was right for the Great Work to come to completion, I assert that the invading hive, led by Ninhursag, intended to trigger this visionary state in as many humans as possible to create this worldwide vision through which every eye would 'see' his return. Such a wide scale artificially induced visionary experience would allegedly bring the world together, and the hive cell of Ninhursag and other members of the heavenly host hive could reinsert their hive consciousness into human beings and thereby become world rulers, thereby bringing Heaven onto Earth. Pretty sickening, isn't it. Fortunately, it will never to come to pass. With the destruction of the hapiym hive virus everywhere, humanity is now only left with its false beliefs and the psychological conditioning manipulated by its earthly allies. All of this can be overcome, and the virus habits will eventually die out by attrition if not by other means, which will be the topic of the closing chapter.

# 26. How Rank was Established in the Hierarchy

I would be remiss at this juncture if I did not take a bit of time to explain what established rank and power in the hive collective's heavenly host hierarchy. It is only through understanding this system of rank establishment that we can understand how a creature like Ninhursag could elevate herself to virtual second in command over all of the hive's 'heaven'.

Where modern scholarship fails us is when it views textual evidence from ancient civilizations through the lens of Christian religious thinking and accepting Western monotheism as the foundation for their scholarly assumptions. There is not a single scholar, to my knowledge, that is willing to acknowledge the presence of physical beings who came from the skies who lived on this planet and called themselves gods. The idea is too challenging for the invisible God supernaturalist believers as well as the believers in human superiority through the Darwinian evolutionary theory to accept. Yet we have thousands of pieces of textual evidence that support this contention, particularly the Ras Shamra texts from Ugarit in northern Syria, where the texts refer to a Council of the Gods. I can assure you that in the context of these literary recordings that it wasn't a bunch of pagan idol worshippers dragging the stone statues of their gods together for a meeting. They were real beings and they had council meetings and they also continually fought with each other for ultimate supremacy between themselves.

Before humanity as a whole can remove itself from such stunted denial-thinking we are going to have to shed our safe-zone cognitive illusions. In both examples just cited, supernaturalism and materialistic denial keep us from not only seeing the truth of our past as a species, but also keeps us from accepting these truths. These ideas challenge our species identity and the residual false persona of the hapiym virus infections keeps our denial deeply rooted in our psyche.

Such concepts become even more disturbing when we face the fact that our entire planetary species has been controlled through an invisible energetic mind virus whose only goal was to use our emotions as a food source. Such a horror story is simply too much for most to come to terms with on a psychological basis. Thus, we ignore the uncomfortable and the unknown and willingly embrace the world of lies we have intentionally been fed by those self-appointed elite whose only concern is to control us as their global labor force.

With the confusing elements of the existence of ancient physical gods on one hand, who lorded it over our species as their cattle, we are equally resistant to facing the information that adds a secondary form of mental tyranny presented by the virus infection on the other hand. Denying both of these circumstances of reality is a very easy thing to do when our esteemed academics are living as much in this world of denial as the dumbed-down cultures their intellectualism overshadows.

Humanity has been conditioned to submission, regardless of the false ego bravado of the breast-beaters who scream they are free. The level of self-enforced ignorance is truly staggering. The human psyche has never been free. We are enslaved within a cognitive illusion which *can* be shattered if we will but find the courage to see through the illusion and gain our own cognitive freedom. But freedom always comes with a price, and in this case, it is the price of acknowledging the truth of what's presented in this book and all my other works. One can't escape the mind trap of the illusion if they continually demand to embrace it because of their cultural and psychological conditioning.

So, let's turn to the main thrust of this chapter and discuss how rank was established in the hapiym hive hierarchy, and you are going to see it reflected in many of the practices used on this planet to keep its cosmic machine running, when it was still functional. The first place I want to point as a foundational reference is to Wikipedia under *Veneration for the dead*:

> *"The veneration of the dead, including one's ancestors, is based on love and respect for the deceased. In some cultures,* ***it is related to beliefs that the dead have a continued existence, and may possess the ability to influence the fortune of the living. Some groups venerate their direct, familial ancestors. Certain faith communities, in particular the Roman Catholic***

***Church, venerate saints as intercessors with God, as well as pray for departed souls in Purgatory.***

*In Europe, Asia, and Oceania, and in some African and Afro-Diasporic cultures, the goal of ancestor veneration* ***is to ensure the ancestors' continued well-being and positive disposition towards the living, and sometimes to ask for special favours or assistance****. The social or non-religious function of ancestor veneration is to cultivate kinship values, such as filial piety, family loyalty, and continuity of the family lineage. Ancestor veneration occurs in societies with every degree of social, political, and technological complexity, and it remains an important component of various religious practices in modern times."*

[Bold emphasis mine]

At first glance, the concept of ancestor veneration is connected with the belief in the afterlife and the continuation of the personality after death. But what I want to call attention to is the fact that the hapiym virus cells fed on human emotions. This also includes what the individual virus cell fed on in the hive afterlife hierarchy. The emotions presented by loved ones after death contributed to the virus cell's food supply in the afterlife so long as it was remembered. This is why we create gravestones and visit graves to place flowers on the graves of lost loved ones, because the dead are remembered and the emotions or dedication in remembering them fed the individual hive cell in the hive collective afterlife. The more a person is remembered or acknowledged after their death, the greater that particular hive cell's rank elevated in the collective's afterlife. Although the human host is dead, the name lived on through the infectious virus cell that stole its host's personality.

I have already illustrated how Ninhursag as Hecate was the guide for people's souls to the underworld and the afterlife. In one of her alter ego roles which I have already firmly established, *Hermes*, Wikipedia informs us:

> *Hermes was also* ***"the divine trickster"*** *and* ***"the god of boundaries and the transgression of boundaries****, ... the patron of* ***herdsmen, thieves, graves****, and heralds." He is described* ***as moving freely between the worlds of the mortal and divine, and was the conductor of souls into the afterlife****. He was also viewed as the protector and patron of roads and travelers.*
>
> [Bold emphasis mine]

With the character of Hermes and how people believed the stories in the ancient world that he would trick the gods, usually in favor of humans, people were being conditioned to accept deceit if it was for the right purpose. Despite modern hairsplitting over the term threshold and boundary, a boundary is also a void area like a threshold. A boundary is the line between two places just as a doorway or gate presents a line between the inside and the outside. Given the fact that Hermes was the patron of graves, we find another association right out of Ninhursag's playbook, particularly when it is Hermes who conducts souls into the afterlife. Bearing all these things in consideration, and given the premise that Ninhursag's hive cell could conduct souls into the afterlife, being the trickster and deceiver that the Hermes character denotes, what happened when a hive soul was *not* conducted to the collective afterlife? Would we not have a discarnate hive 'spirit' without a human host form left in the nether regions of Earth to play havoc on those sensitive enough to perceive them? How many ghost or poltergeist stories have you heard in your life? Or stories of demon possession, or maybe that should be *daemon* possession, for the former term is a Christian corruption of the latter? Why are there so many stories about ghosts being in graveyards?

For centuries people have tried to figure out where ghosts come from and how to get rid of these pesky and scary haunters. Paranormal investigators, or shall we call them ghost hunters, flocked to the membership of the Society for Psychical Research, along with those who believed in Spiritism to investigate such matters. These were not your everyday Joe's or Jane's in the street, but some of the most intellectual people of their era, like the father of American Psychology, William James. What did their investigations into the paranormal really yield in the form of their elitist understanding? What went unreported in their journals? Through what I have brought forth in this book about the hive's ability to alter our senses, to artificially induce visions or make us hear things that aren't there and go bump in the night, is it really that much a stretch of the imagination to see discontented hive cells who can't find their way to hive heaven screwing around with those humans who are psychically sensitive? Is this really superstition, or is there a strong basis in fact to frame an answer to these questions? How much emotional energy did these maverick hive cells feed on from the fear they begat in their target human subjects? How much fear does the idea of ghosts stir up in people to this day? I think I may have solved this big riddle of the paranormal, but I will leave it to the reader to decide for themselves whether these explanations lie on pragmatic, solid ground or not.

Now, let's look at all these people set up on pedestals as our idols, regardless of who or what they were in life. We have ancient bloody Aryan warlords like Genghis Khan and tyrants like Adolph Hitler, Mao Tse Tung, Lenin and Stalin whose names live on through historical accounting. We are not allowed to forget these people. We have the Sigmund Freud's of the world, the George Washington's, the Greek Philosophers, movie actors and actresses, and an innumerable number of other famous people whose name lives on after their deaths like dead Presidents. We may love them, or we may hate them, but their names generate emotional energies, even if they are emotions of admiration or awe, fear or the desire to emulate them. The higher one was placed on a pedestal as an authority and the more people who knew about them and contributed any kind of energy to their memory, the higher the rank their disincarnate hive cell possessed in the hive afterlife. Are we now starting to understand the importance of hero worship in all this duplicity?

When it comes to alleged holy men, as with the Ascended Masters in the Theosophical doctrines, Hindu Yogis, Buddhist monks, Christian Saints and martyrs – those who can *really* gather some acknowledgement on a very large scale as human beings, then the hive cell that infected those human hosts was highly elevated in that hierarchy of heavenly structure. What you see in all these elevations of rank is that there is very little room for the common man in the hierarchal hive structure, which is why most humans are reduced to ancestor veneration at best to provide emotional table scraps to our dead relatives in the afterlife while those whose names are constantly put in front of our face through history books and religious and academic veneration sat at the banquet tables in the hive afterlife, energetically speaking.

The individual human will pass away, but through the parasitic hive mind virus and personality mimic, the energy provided in the afterlife was to be found because their 'name lives on'. In ancient cultures the worst thing that could happen to a person was to have their name erased to never be spoken of again, even by family members after their death. There are a number of cultures that used this tactic to turn their backs on people when they were exiled or executed. In the Roman culture is was called *Damnatio memoriae,* and Wikipedia explains it this way:

> *"Damnatio memoriae is a modern Latin phrase literally meaning "condemnation of*

*memory", meaning that a person must not be remembered.*

*It was a form of dishonor that could be passed by the Roman Senate on traitors or others who brought discredit to the Roman State. The intent was to erase the malefactor from history.*

*Damnatio memoriae, or* ***oblivion, as a punishment was originally created by the peoples of Ephesus after Herostratus set fire to the Temple of Artemis,*** *one of the Seven Wonders of antiquity.* ***The Romans, who viewed it as a punishment worse than death, adopted this practice****. Felons would literally be erased from history for the crimes they had committed."*

*"In ancient Rome, the practice of damnatio memoriae was* ***the condemnation of Roman elites and emperors after their deaths****. If the senate or a later emperor did not like the acts of an individual, they could have his property seized****, his name erased*** *and his statues reworked. Because there is an economic incentive to seize property and rework statues, historians and archaeologists have had difficulty determining when official damnatio memoriae actually took place, although it seems to have been quite rare."*

> *"It is unknown whether any damnatio memoriae was totally successful* ***as it would not be noticeable to later historians, since, by definition, it would entail the complete and total erasure of the individual in question from the historical record****. It was difficult, however, to implement the practice completely. For instance, the senate wanted to condemn the memory of Caligula, but Claudius prevented this. Nero was declared an enemy of the state by the senate, but then given an enormous funeral honoring him after his death by Vitellius."*
>
> [Bold emphasis mine]

I find it highly amusing that our historians can claim that *damnatio memoriae* was ineffective based on a handful of incidents where it didn't work, and memory erasure was not complete, as in the case of the named emperors. If there were total erasure of one's name then, as stated, no one would be the wiser because they would have been removed from the annals of history, period! I ask the reader to also pay close attention to the fact that this practice didn't exist until someone burned one of Ninhursag's Temples to the ground. Artemis was allegedly the twin sister of Apollo, the sun god, and in some stories the daughter of Demeter, an unchallenged fertility goddess alter ego of Ninhursag. Demeter was also the goddess that controlled the cycle of life and death. Demeter and her daughter Persephone were the central figures in the Eleusian Mysteries celebrations that occurred every five years, and during which the participants drank *kykeon* as part of the mystery ritual as it was sacred to Demeter, but I digress.

We should also take note of the fact that *damnatio memoriae* seemed to be reserved for the elite class as the most severe form of punishment imaginable. Given all I have shared here and the insider knowledge of the Aryan elite, this practice takes on a more damning meaning, (excuse the pun). To remove the name of one of these elite was tantamount to eternal oblivion in the hive hierarchy.

Contrary to materialist thinking, name erasure had a devastating effect on a discarnate hive cell who had nothing upon which it could feed in the afterlife. Being relegated to an existence of non-remembrance would have amounted to a sentence to Hell for a hive cell. We even find this practice spelled out in the Old Testament in regard to the Book of Life where it says directly, "*Let them be blotted out of the book of the living, and not be written with the righteous.*" I ask the reader to ponder just what such a threat really meant in the context just revealed? And then let's take this Christian insistence to always want to pray for someone's soul if you don't believe like they do. Every facet of our lives is affected by these things on a subliminal energetic emotional level and we are blissfully ignorant about their true meaning, wandering around in our materialist illusion aching for the afterlife to hurry up and get here and whisk us away from being human.

As I have illustrated in this book, the Bible is an admixture of the God of the Old Testament, Yahweh/Enki, in the role as one of the physical Council of the Gods, which is referred to in a number of verses in the Bible, as well as participating in such a Council through the plural designation *Elohim*. This is one aspect of a heavenly host in certain biblical references. The other side of the equation is where we find the doctrines of Ninhursag as both the goddess Asherah/Astarte also cavorting and colluding with the hive heavenly host, which I have shown that Yahweh totally disparaged. We must view all these things in the context revealed in this book to glean true understanding of what is taking place within the pages of the Bible, as well as other mystical religions touting 'everlasting life' in heaven, regardless of what religious doctrine it is wrapped within. With this understanding, then we can perceive what a truly damnable experience it would have been for a hive cell that left its human host to lose its energetic food supply forever by having its host's name expunged from the hive's Book of Life. Such a thing would amount to a virtual death sentence, not dissimilar than a life lived by a vampire that could never feed. I feel no pity for these virus cells, I am only clarifying what all this religious threatening truly means.

In order to clarify this a bit more, lets look at what Wikipedia has to say about *Ancestor veneration in China*:

> *"Chinese ancestor worship, or Chinese ancestor veneration, also called the Chinese patriarchal religion, is an aspect of the Chinese traditional religion which revolves around the ritual celebration of the deified ancestors and tutelary deities of people with the same surname organised into lineage societies in ancestral*

*shrines. Ancestors,* ***their ghosts, or spirits****, and gods are considered part of "this world", that is, they are neither supernatural (in the sense of being outside nature) nor transcendent in the sense of being beyond nature.* ***The ancestors are humans who have become godly beings, beings who keep their individual identities.*** *For this reason, Chinese religion is founded on veneration of ancestors.* ***Ancestors are believed to be a means of connection to the supreme power of Tian as they are considered embodiments or reproducers of the creative order of Heaven.****"*

[Bold emphasis mine]

Within this short passage we can see how the Chinese concept of Tian is no different than the concept of the Oneness of the Divine hive found in any other religious or spiritual ideology. The fact that their beliefs recognize that the human personality lived on as a form of ghost or spirit in no way diminishes my assertion about the hive infection. The Chinese concept that the spirits of their ancestors were 'embodiments and reproducers of the creative order of Heaven' defines the hive virus for what it actually was and how it spread itself as infectious 'reproducers' of the cosmic collective. Greeks harbored similar beliefs that the spirits of the dead could pester or haunt the living, which is one reason they resorted the using curse tablets seeking justice or compelled performance from the dead in their graves. See *Curse Tablets* on Wikipedia for more understanding if you are interested.

With our over-busy modern thinking and reliance on materialist perspectives, it is easy to discount the psychic sensitivities of our ancestors, but we must consider that they did not have the same elements that assault our consciousness on a daily basis back then that we do in our modern cultures. They didn't have electrical noise, automobiles and all the other pollutions that serve to overload our senses to dampen our own psychic capabilities. They did not have the hustle and bustle to distract them as our modern towns and cities do, and outside the marketplaces, theaters or political arenas of their eras, they did not have the same noise distractions to contend with that our modern culture overwhelms our senses with on a daily basis. As a result of these modern distracting pollutants for our senses, we have become dulled beyond imagining compared to the cognitive sensitivities of our ancestors who lived substantially quieter and simpler lives.

It is very easy for us in our modern aeries of technological superiority to look back and consider that our ancestors were just stupid, superstitious, and gullible in the face of all our presumed knowledge, but given what I have shared in this chapter, they may have had every right to be jumpy, what with the presence of offworld gods on one hand and the invisible mind virus remnants (ghosts) moving around to haunt them in reality on the other. When we look to the past we all have the bad habit of wanting to project our modern perceptions into the ancient world and analyze our ancestors using *our* point of view. By doing so we cheapen the world they lived in by trying to overlay our perceptions onto their reality. We can't use our limited dumbed-down state of technological advancement and sensory overload as the measuring stick to decipher the world in which they lived.

We live in a world where, in the more advanced nations, entertainment options lie at our fingertips. In the ancient world, such escapist opportunities did not exist, particularly in colder climes when people were pretty much homebound during winter's harsher months. An excellent study that puts life in the ancient world into perspective is *The Chemical Muse: Drug Use and the Roots of Western Civilization* by D. C. A. Hillman, PhD. Hillman does an excellent job of elucidating the harsh conditions of everyday life in the ancient world without all our modern conveniences, like FDA approved drugs easily available at the local market or drug store whenever we get sniffles or a headache. He does a superb job of outlining the conditions of life without anesthetics for even the simplest of injures, let alone gaping war wounds from battles fought with swords, spears, axes and arrows. The simplest wound could lead to death in those times without antibiotics. Through his realistic reanalysis of our past and how our ancestors lived, then it is not that big a leap to perceive the impact of the gods and even the hapiym virus on the cultures of those ages.

Without wanting to sound like a book review, Hillman did his doctoral thesis on drug use in the ancient world. Where he ran into trouble with his thesis and where he almost failed to get his degree is when the examination board instructed him to remove the part of his thesis that dealt with recreational drug use in the ancient world with plants like opium and other psychotropic substances. He was forcefully coerced to edit out the truth from his research findings because it went against the moral constraints of academia and presented a picture of our esteemed ancient philosophers, in some cases, as psychedelic drug users communing with the Divine. The examination review board was more interested in protecting the public image of these ancient philosophers than they were interested in the truth the evidence provided in his thesis revealed. This is exactly the kind of close-minded monolith my own body of work is up against where meeting overly-strict academic standards is concerned. I will have more to add on this topic in a later chapter.

Be that as it may, when we can take the exhaustive research Hillman did into recreational drug use in the ancient world, and couple it with all the information provided in this book, we must face the fact that our ancestors were more in touch with the hive metaphysical world then than we are today. Regardless of some of the misinterpretations over their experiences with the gods and the hive, the same fascination still plagues our species today with the quest for the supernatural and the mystical experience. There is a tremendous evidentiary trail to substantiate all this if people will but remove the blinders of their own indoctrinated perceptions to see the reality beyond their perceived religious and cultural illusions.

Returning to the topic of the hive personality being fed by energies, the original race that created this species, the same race from which the supreme god Enlil written about in the ancient texts across many lands in the ancient Near East came from, those I refer to as the Orioners, were energy sensitives in a similar manner to the hive collective. The Orioners were particularly focused on harvesting and feeding on the energies produced by fear because, as anyone knows, fear emits a lot of energy. The Anunnaki race of hybrids also had this same ability to feed on energies. Whether that sensitivity came about as a direct result of their fish genetics being spliced with the genetics of the Orioners would only be a point of conjecture and I have no evidence either way as to how or why Enki and Ninhursag had these same energetic feeding capabilities.

Regardless of the source of this energetic sensitivity, the Anunnaki noticed that there were other subtler human emotional energies to be harvested than just fear. Humans emit a wide variety of emotions, everything from the ebullience of joy to the deepest of depression, and all ranges of subtler emotions in between. Since Enlil's species primarily focused on producing and harvesting fear energies, this left the door open for Anunnaki like Enki and Ninhursag to start their own brand of energy harvesting, collecting all the 'unused' human emotional table scraps that Enlil's breed paid no attention to. Both Enki and Ninhursag discovered that the energies of love and devotion could be equally as powerful as that of fear, although they did not hesitate to mix love with fear to keep their own human energetic food supply going to make themselves more powerful to gain supremacy over their Anunnaki rivals. The Bible is a testimony of how Enki/Yahweh used fear and demanded love and devotion to him alone, so this point is inarguable with nothing plausible to refute the practice. Through such methods of creating temples of worship and devotion, coupled with creating multitudes of alter egos in different regions, Enki and Ninhursag created for themselves a powerful source of energy to harvest to make themselves stronger and eventually defeat all their rivals until it came down to just the two of them in a locked-horn battle for the ultimate supremacy over this species and this planet. This is the basis of the conflict shown in the biblical passages shared in this book, and this is what was behind their incessant war. Humanity was only the energetic pawns in their game.

I have not been able to pinpoint when or how it was that Ninhursag stumbled upon her awareness of the hive collective, but one thing about her, regardless of her psychopathy, she was a genius at perfidy, deception and gathering power unto herself, as the description of Hermes elucidates, the consummate trickster. The ancient Sumerian texts relate how Enki was given magical powers called *mes* (pronounced mays) by Enlil. I discussed in *We Are Not Alone – Part 1*, how the energy from a *me* could be embedded into a ring, a crown, priestly robes or mitres, or any other symbol of authority or power. The Orioners were totally patriarchal and misogynistic. Once they discovered how to create life through advanced genetics, they had little need for their own women unless they chose to breed offspring, which did not happen often since they were technically immortal. Women were second class citizens in their culture and any other culture they ruled or conquered, and a hermaphrodite like Ninhursag, in their eyes, was an aberrant monstrosity beneath notice. To understand her psychopathy, we must envision this creature as an unacknowledged genius, with an unquenchable thirst for power and control, and her constant battle with the patriarchal mindset of Enlil who wouldn't give her the time of day. Enki, as the selected Anunnaki overlord for the region of the world allocated to the Anunnaki breed, ancient Mesopotamia, was given aspects of Enlil's magic to keep this patriarchy in place. This is one major reason Ninhursag could never unseat Enki on the physical plane, because no matter what she did, Enki could call on the *mes* given him by Enlil and shut her down at every turn. You can only imagine how mad this made Ninhursag, not only in the irate sense, but also in turning her into a raging bloodthirsty psychopath, as evidenced in her roles as the battle goddess Anat, or more acutely, as the Hindu Kali.

How or whenever Ninhursag discovered the hive and figured out the power structure of the hierarchy will probably forever be unknown, but what we must take away from this is that through the alliance with the hive, she finally found her way to circumvent and undermine Enki and the *mes* supplied to him by Enlil, where she could gain supremacy over this species and this planet. She saw this alliance with the hive collective as her ultimate shot at victory. However she gained her understanding of the hierarchal nature of the hive collective, she knew that to attain and maintain rank in that hierarchy she would need a constant supply of energy to sustain her own hive cell after death and ascend to the top of the hive hierarchy. It is at this point, after conquering all their physical adversaries, that the doctrines in the ancient world shift from dedication to the physical gods and the direction of human culture shifts to the metaphysical aspects of religion and spirituality. I have yet to identify the exact point of this shift, but it appears to have started by at least the 2nd millennium BC where we see the more mystical aspects start creeping into religious doctrines with Zoroastrianism and spread all across the known world at that time, as all the information in this book substantiates.

Ninhursag started establishing her afterlife power supply by creating all these varied mystical religions with her sitting dead center as the receiver of these energies, either as a god or goddess, creating the mind control systems of metaphysical devotion that have been transmitted down into the modern era. Where Ninhursag was concerned, the outer dressing of the religious ideologies she created made no difference so long as one of her alter ego personalities served as the conduit to funnel energy to her. By doing this she guaranteed herself the highest position attainable in the hive hierarchy after dying, so all these pieces had to be in place before she finally died, in whichever manner she chose to off herself and leave the physical plane.

I realize that this story all seems like some kind of science fiction flight of fancy, but one thing cannot be denied, and that is the impact all these mystical and supernatural traditions play on the human psyche to this day. The situation is having a very profound effect in our world today as I will explain as we move forward.

I have already explained the truth of Ninhursag hidden behind the Theosophical Society and Freemasonic reference to Lucifer as the Light Bringer and how their interpretation of Lucifer as the planet Venus implicates Ninhursag as Lucifer. I covered this aspect extensively and in depth in *We Are Not Alone-Part 3: The Luciferian Agenda of the Mother Goddess*. This book has exposed the link between the hive and the Mother Goddess at every turn and has exposed Ninhursag and the hive's hidden tyrannical mystical agenda. I didn't make this stuff up. I have provided what I consider an irrefutable trail of evidence throughout this book to prove these assertions. The only thing I bring to this equation is the correct manner with which to interpret what all this information means and remove the millennia's old mystery from the equation. As hard to swallow as all this is, the evidence supports it, even the story of Ninhursag and her agenda, no matter how 'crazy' it may sound to our present way of thinking nor how uncomfortable it makes us feel psychologically to entertain or accept these ideas.

Rudolph Steiner was one of those alleged refugees from the Theosophical Society. He may have broken away from the Theosophical Society, but he did not break away from working with the hive players when he created Anthroposophy as an alternative mystical belief system similar to Theosophy. In one of Steiner's books where he shared some of his channeled communications with his own hive deceivers, who called themselves the 'Michael Group', relying on the name of the biblical angel to foist their deception on him, they admitted that they had started avidly influencing human affairs about 500 years ago which, at the time Steiner wrote this book, would have been right around the Renaissance era. Although the hive prevaricators were inveterate liars where it came to pushing the hive agenda forward, they also loved telling their stupid human acolytes and adepts the truth, particularly when they felt the truth was too obscure to understand. They lied about being associated with the

Archangel Michael, they told the truth about how the hive's efforts on this planet escalated in the last 500 years or more.

The expansion of mystical traditions during these past few centuries stands as testimony to this increase in focus pushing hive mystical ideologies where we see the Hermeticists pushing for scientific advancement and the establishment of organizations like the Rosicrucian Society occurring closely together. We also find the hive intruding on the minds of people like Dr, John Dee and his magical angel transmissions developing the system of 'Enochian Magic' which is very big in modern occult circles, and other Christian visionaries like Emmanuel Swedenborg. The hive produced its visions of the Mother Mary for Ignatius Loyola who created the Jesuit Order, and Christianity was imported to the Western hemisphere where Catholicism and Mary worship still control the minds of most Latin Americans. Catholicism and Christianity spread round the world and was in direct competition, as it is today, with the mystical visionary religion of Islam. About 500 years ago, the hive was open for business and they spared no efforts to spread their mystical doctrines through every venue they could create with their vision-infected human stooges.

Since ancient times, Ninhursag was able to keep her agenda alive though such devices as the mystery schools, traditions of Kabbalah, Hermeticism, Gnosticism and virtually every other belief that challenged Enki and Enlil's patriarchal systems of control. By creating the identity of Jesus, she created a great field of energy harvesting, and she harvested energies of fear through the character of Satan or Lucifer. By the time Mohammed has his vision, Ninhursag was safely ensconced in the leadership role of the hive collective and probably had as much a hand in producing Mohammed's visions as she did the Apostle Paul on the road to Damascus or to Zoroaster as Ahura Mazda. In our modern Feminist-driven culture, you hear constant protests against the 'patriarchy' voiced at almost every turn. The term patriarchy has become a buzzword for Feminists, transgenders, gays and lesbians in the West for the past few decades now, and there is probably not one of them who spouts their protest against the invisible patriarchy who has a clue about what is actually taking place and what agenda they are actually serving. They are only stooges for the Theosophical, Fabian Marxist, hive goddess agenda, devoting their emotional energies to undermining Western culture in this blind ignorance and political parroting of emotional theater. The emotional energies created through artificially created wars, WWI and WW II for instance, had to be phenomenal feeding frenzies for the entire hive collective, and Ninhursag's Fabian Society and Marxist ideologies fed the conflicts by manipulating the creation of conflicts, fulfilling her role as the goddess of chaos and destruction.

As noted in earlier chapters, the spread of occultism and goddess worship, cults of witchcraft and sexuality are all escalating to create resistance to the primarily Christian elements of society who still adhere to the Old Testament doctrines of the vindictive and narcissistic god of the Jews. I have illustrated through the evidence provided in this book that we are looking at a 4,000-year old agenda leading to a presumed culmination at this point in human history. I have also stated that the hive virus has been eliminated, yet we all carry the psychological programming and indoctrination of these two ancient gods and the virus infection symptomatology in our psyches. Denying all this leaves is with a false sense of cognitive security, safely nestled in the arms of our individual perceptual illusions. The psychological programming through media manipulation of all kinds -- movies, the news, video games, TV and the internet, is irrefutable when one takes off the blinders to see the deliberate manipulation of our consciousness. Some people are starting to wake up from the illusion, but the lack of honest information keeps them lost in a never-never land of quasi-despair on one hand, and the hope that some Divine power will rescue them from the fire of chaos that burns around them on the other. We must remember the motto of the Freemasons, *Ordo ab Chao* – Order out of Chaos. Through the application of the Hegelian dialectic the chaos is artificially produced as the whip to drive humanity into the mystical religious corral of hive collectivist beliefs. Mysticism and supernaturalism is the carrot, contrived chaos is the stick driving all of humanity into that corral.

This sense of despair where some are partially removed from the illusion is by design, for when people are psychologically stressed in this manner, steering them into the quagmire of mystical or supernatural solutions is a simple task. Meditate! Pray! Ask for Divine guidance! Forsake the patriarchal God, embrace the Goddess! The world is falling apart and only the belief in the Divine and mystical is what gives people hope in a world artificially incited to chaos, and we do not even realize the method through which we are being psychologically herded. We are caught in the illusion at every turn and refuse to acknowledge the illusion to even seek the exit from the corral.

Through Ninhursag's personal machinations to create her power base over the past 4,000 years, she became second in command over the hive. The hierarchy became her pyramid and all these mystical traditions are nothing more than a cosmic Ponzi scheme to keep our species ever the losers in this contest over consciousness. Just as Steiner's hive manipulators told him about the pressure being amped up for the last 500 years, with the establishment of the Theosophical Society, the Fabian Society and the Society for Psychical Research in the late 1800s, the pressure to fulfill the hive agenda was amplified even more. Through control of the publishing houses, academia, the press, and a virtually unlimited supply of funding through the Lucis Trust organizations worldwide, humanity is being herded into a collectivist New World Order corral, which has been the designated endgame of Ninhursag ever since she gave up the ghost and joined the hive. The hive is dead, its ideologues are not. Ninhursag's Aryan spawn still control the financial, religious, educational, political and manufacturing capabilities of our species worldwide, and humanity is but the pawn in their game for power and control.

The noose of the supernatural hive agenda is tightening around humanity's neck, and our entire species is blissfully ignorant of the perfidy of what has been behind it all. We have been so psychologically programmed to embrace the illusions our captors have fed us that we are willing to die defending the false ideologies and beliefs rather than heal ourselves and give up the illusionary false reality for genuine sanity. We each make ourselves casualties in this war for human consciousness by defending these mystical and supernatural illusions, and if humanity doesn't choose to wake up and change itself, then it deserves the fate it receives while waiting on the fictitious Divine intervention to fix it all for them.

I have provided the reader all the information necessary to see through this mystical illusion and remove themselves from this web of mystical deceit and supernatural dependency, but it is still the responsibility of the reader to free their mind from this psychological reliance on supernatural beliefs. This is not an easy task and is only one part of the psychological healing process necessary to free oneself from the virus' residual symptomatology, but it can be done with hard work and consistent effort. I have provided the tools in all my books to help anyone who genuinely wants out of this morass to free themselves, but the decision has to be an individual one, and it has to be sincere if one intends to succeed. The process of freeing one's mind doesn't come as easily as professing a belief in the Divine, anyone can do that. In fact, humanity has been taking that easy road to destruction for 4,000 years. Don't you think it's time for a change?

For thousands of years we have placed people on pedestals. At first it was our gods who stood over us on their pedestals. That giant rock under the Dome of the Rock was just one of Ninhursag's pedestals, just as every mountaintop from which she ordained her mandates as Cybele, Anat, Hera and a host of other alter ego personalities. When the gods disappeared, then we started placing our Aryan overlords up on those abandoned pedestals, continually elevating them above ourselves and standing in their shadows as subservient lesser beings to their presumed authority and notoriety. As I have noted in my other work, it is not human history we have been taught, but the history of our Aryan overlords and masters, and those intellectualist sycophants who want a piece of their authoritarian pie whose history we have shoved down our throats in our educational institutes, or more accurately, our brainwashing and indoctrination classrooms. These are our academics, our politicians, our priests and preachers, and humanity can't seem to live without some pedestal shadow of greatness to stand beneath. The etymology of pedestal translates from the Latin to mean foot-stand. A more apt interpretation where humanity is concerned in our world where our authorities reside on pedestals we put them upon would be *footstool*. We place our politicians, movie stars, rock and country music idols, academic intellectuals, gurus, saints and mass murderers up on pedestals so we can stand in the awe of their shadows, all the while making ourselves nothing but their footstools as a species. This is a truly sad testimony for a species that has such potential for greatness. We are not even a footnote in our own history, we are barely extras on the planetary movie set. It is up to us to change this or become totally subjugated slaves more than we already are. If the Fabian Marxist ideologues have their way, billions will die to put their global tyranny in place. They don't care which rank and file religious zealots they use as tools to perform this mass execution of half or more of the population on this planet to finally pull the noose tight around humanity's neck. We have *always* been disposable goods to meet their ends. If you don't believe they are up for the task, just look up *Georgia Guidestones* on Wikipedia and have a cup of coffee in your world of illusion while the reality revealed about the Georgia Guidestones soaks in and takes a bite of your consciousness.

# 27. The Virus Vector

Having explained what I have about the hapiym hive collective and Ninhursag's role as what one might call the second in command of the overall hive collective, then I'm sure the reader has wondered exactly what the infectious vector of the virus is. How does it spread within our species? I have been aware of the destruction of the virus collective since shortly after it occurred, and I wrote my book, *The Energetic War Against Humanity: The 6,000 Year War Against Human Cognitive Advancement*, using that volume to explain the workings of the cosmic mind virus in detail.

Since I wrote that book I contemplated heavily trying to figure out how the virus spread itself. I sought to discover exactly what the infectious vector of the virus was, and I finally realized that the one thing all humans have in common is the desire to love and be loved. Psychologists have come down on the side of thinking that this one core *need*, and need is the operative word, is one of the major factors in developing humans. They have done extensive studies seeking to prove that the removal of love interface in infants can leave them scarred for life.

Through my own contemplation and analysis I reached the conclusion, without delving into this psychological research, that love had to be the virus infection vector. One only has to look at every religious or mystical tradition on the planet to find the Love of God at the center of virtually every religion on the planet. The Eastern philosophical doctrines that have been imported to the West through the concerted efforts of the Theosophical Society all have this Love concept at their core. We only have to look at our popular culture to see how we cannot escape the propaganda of love. We are saturated with songs about love, unrequited live, being victims of love, falling in love again, songs about heartbreak, seeking vengeance for spurned love, and the litany goes on and on. We are bombarded with TV shows and films about love, sappy romantic comedies that keep women ever yearning for finding Mr. Right and films about depression over lost loves, love loss from death and the same propaganda for love in all its aspects continually assaults our senses.

Through the Hermetic mystical systems, we ceaselessly hear about brotherly love, with Philadelphia, Pennsylvania touting itself as the City of Brotherly Love. We hear about Mother Love and we are all instructed to love our neighbors as we love ourselves. We are forced to love our siblings, when often times they are underserving of our love, particularly if they have been abusive towards us. The point of all this is that we can't escape this incessant love indoctrination. New Age religions, which have all spawned from Theosophy, have Love at the center of their teachings. Love is the answer, we are told, but who has bothered to ask that if love is the answer, what is the question it answers?

The human fascination with emotional love is paramount and it has been a mainstay of tortured and enamored poets throughout the ages. Humanity has gone to every extreme to understand love and catalogue its varied effects on our hearts and psyches, but in doing so, we have only been cataloguing symptomatology without ever understanding what the root of all this emotional anxiety is surrounding love, where it originates or why we are so fixated by this emotion above all others as a species. As the psychologists accurately note, love is a need, and being needy as it is, it denotes a dependency, no different than a drug addiction. Humans are addicted to love, and we are never allowed to forget this addiction with the constant saturation through Harlequin love novels, religious ideologies telling us God loves us and that we should love our gods. We are reminded in poetry throughout the ages, through tales that make us love our heroes and their tales of valor. Without being one bit facetious, love is everywhere, and we can't escape its clutches.

Love is humanity's greatest weakness, not is greatest strength. All it takes to destroy an individual is withdraw your love from them and you will level them. I don't care how much a part of you wants to try and rationalize this away, love is our weakness as a species. Everyone revels at falling in love, from experiencing that heart-swelling feeling of ebullience and joy over falling in love, this same heart-swelling feeling of love can be found in every ecstatic mystical or religious experience that has ever been recorded, whether it is attained through a religious revival meeting, or when one's cognitive guard is dropped through using psychotropic substances so the virus cell inside us could trigger that love elation within us. If you read the accounts of the mystical visionaries throughout the ages you are going to find this ecstatic feeling of love coupled with their visions. It is the hallmark of the hive collective's intrusion on our consciousness when the inner hive cell could assert itself to peddle us the love emotion. Any concerted effort into studying these mystical or religious experiences bears this out. There is not one single recorded instance of the visionaries that doesn't tout love as part of the visionary experience. This evidence is overwhelming and cannot be effectively refuted.

Love is the vector point through which a mother passes on the virus to her offspring. This is not to put any blame on women, for men are equally at fault where their children are concerned in most cases, but it is that burst of motherly love at birth that serves as the conduit for the hapiym virus to replicate itself like an amoeba and jump from one person to the next in a never-ending cycle of reproduction through replication.

To understand the spread of the virus, we must rely on one of the most ancient forms of life on this planet as our example, and that is the amoeba. The amoeba replicates itself through what is called binary fission. When it replicates, it creates a full-sized mirror cell of itself. Most readers have probably not considered the fact that every amoeba alive today is the same amoeba that started this replication process eons ago. Each amoeba is only a mirror reflection, a doppelganger of that first amoeba cell that replicated itself in this manner. In essence, every amoeba today is the same amoeba that started this process. It is *changeless*, and each amoeba cell is *exactly the same* as its predecessor without variance.

Although the hapiym hive virus was an invisible energetic virus, its manner of replication was no different than the process of binary fission utilized by the physical amoeba. Each virus cell was a duplicate of the one before it, and once it infected the human body, its tactics for control were the same in everyone, i.e. control through emotional manipulation. Love was the transmission vector that served as the fertile ground to transmit the virus from human to human in its never-ending quest to remake the universe in its image.

I realize that by making these assertions that many are going to want to call the idea hogwash for the simple fact of how they hold the emotion of love in a position of sanctity in their mind. But if you were a predatory virus that wanted to infect a target species, what method would you use to target that species? Would you not target its weakest point? And as psychological studies have shown, the desire to love or be loved is paramount in our psyches. We must now ask, why is the overwhelming *need* to love or be loved present in our being? Is it really a human need, or is it perhaps the need of the virus to be accepted in its herd milieu? One thing is certain, we are all suckers for love, and within mystical traditions, seeking that ecstatic experience of the presumed love of the cosmos, God, Source or Oneness is the carrot that has lured billions into the mystical clutches of the virus through the millennia, from the ancient primeval shamans into to modern New Age religions.

Chasing the ecstatic experience is the foundation of Transpersonal Psychology and is most likely the criteria driving the new offshoot branch of Psychology – Spiritual Psychology. The doctrines of finding the ecstatic love experience and joining with the One are everywhere, and they are exquisitely joined in the Feminist-oriented neo-goddess ideologies. Love, the Goddess and Oneness are so intertwined when one reads the literature on it, it's sickening. One prime example of this can be found in the book, *Dancing in the Flames: The Dark Goddess and the Transformation of Consciousness* by Marion Woodman and Elinor Dickson. These two authors are from the Jungian school of psychological thinking, relying on dream interpretations and other aspects of Carl Jung's metaphysical psychology to provide therapy to their clients. They are both proselytes for the goddess Kali as the Dark Goddess or the Mother Goddess of the Earth, and also promote the concept of cosmic oneness with the goddess as the intercessor to tapping into that Divine consciousness. They have used their practices to promote goddess worship on their therapist couches and have, in my estimation, turned their psychological profession into a form of ancient priestess proselytizing. This is no different than Transpersonal Psychology endorsing the use of psychotropic entheogens as a means to reach the Divine and find the communion with the One through drug use and seeking the ecstatic love experience.

Love is the vector, whether one wants to admit it or not, and it was not until I sat down to write this chapter of the book that I discovered an ancient text written 1800 years ago or thereabouts that validates everything I have presented in this book about Love, the Goddess and the Hive. Many may choose to not believe that I reached my own conclusions about the virus vector before stumbling over this ancient information, but when I found it, all I had committed to the page was the title of this chapter and nothing more. The validating information of all I have revealed thus far in this chapter can be found in the writings of the Neoplatonist philosopher Plotinus, in his body of work entitled *The Enneads* which was edited and compiled by his student Porphyry about 270 A.D.

Since this is a philosophical work, I am going to take on the task of translator to explain what it shows in modern English and remove the vague philosophical overtones and let the reader decide whether Plotinus' exposition *'On Love'* from his *Third Ennead* substantiates what I have shared thus far throughout this book and in this chapter. I am not going to share the entire treatise, but only as much as is required to substantiate my own assertions, although they will be somewhat lengthy. To start this investigation, I will pick up part way through Plotinus' dissertation where he seeks to lay out the distinction between the love of the good, and physical human love. In these philosophical writings of ages past, the Good is an allusion to the hive.

Plotinus writes:

> *"Now everyone recognizes that the emotional state for which we make this 'Love' responsible* ***rises in souls aspiring to be knit in the closest union with some beautiful object, and that this aspiration takes two forms, that of the good whose devotion is for beauty itself****, and that other which seeks its consummation in some vile act. But this generally admitted distinction opens a new question: we need a philosophical investigation into the origin of the two phases.*

*It is sound, I think, to find **the primal source of Love in a tendency of the Soul towards pure beauty, in a recognition, in a kinship, in an unreasoned consciousness of friendly relation**. The vile and ugly is in clash, at once, with Nature and with God: **Nature produces by looking to the Good, for it looks towards Order which has its being in the consistent total of the good,** while the unordered is ugly, a member of the system of evil and besides, **Nature itself, clearly, springs from the divine realm, from Good and Beauty; and when anything brings delight and the sense of kinship, its very image attracts.**"*

[Bold emphasis mine]

The reader should take note of the alteration in the lower case used of good and beauty in the opening phrases to being capitalized by the end of this passage. What Plotinus is telling us is that Nature, or what these philosophers allude to as Nature, is Divine and associated with Good and Beauty. Our impressions of nature are not what these philosophers referred to as Nature. Their interpretation of Nature is that of the celestial Divine exhibited as the Good and Beauty. Also pay attention to the emphasis on kinship and how Beauty and the Good attract. The 'beautiful object' is a veiled allusion to the hive collective, the Oneness, as further passages will reveal.

He continues:

*"Reject this explanation, and no one can tell how the mental state rises and what are its causes: it is the explanation of even copulative love, which is the will to beget in beauty;* ***Nature seeks to produce the beautiful and therefore by all reason cannot desire to procreate in the ugly.***

*Those that desire earthly procreation are satisfied with the beauty found on earth, the beauty of image and of body;* ***it is because they are strangers to the Archetype, the source of even the attraction they feel towards what is lovely here.*** *There are souls to whom earthly beauty is a leading to the memory of that in the higher realm and these love the earthly as an image;* ***those that have not attained to this memory do not understand what is happening within them, and take the image for the reality.*** *Once there is perfect self-control, it is no fault to enjoy the beauty of earth; where appreciation degenerates into carnality, there is sin."*

[Bold emphasis mine]

Here Plotinus is exhibiting the same arrogance that the hive has always shown for humanity. It is only understanding the Divine that has any value, your humanness, your 'carnality' as a human living in a human world is a 'sin'. Although Plotinus had doctrinal disputes with the Gnostics, this one aspect of the human body being a tomb or unworthy in the shadow of the alleged

Divine shows that at least this far, their ideologies are in concert. He continues:

> *"**Pure Love seeks the beauty alone,** whether there is Reminiscence or not; but there are those that feel, also, a desire of such immortality as lies within mortal reach; and these are seeking Beauty in their demand for perpetuity, the desire of the eternal; Nature teaches them to sow the seed and to beget in beauty, to sow towards eternity, but in beauty through their own kinship with the beautiful. And indeed* ***the eternal is of the one stock with the beautiful, the Eternal-Nature is the first shaping of beauty and makes beautiful all that rises from it.***"
>
> [Bold emphasis mine]

This whole passage has relevance, but what should be noted is the association of 'Pure Love' with the Eternal and the beautiful all being one thing. Here Plotinus is laying the foundation for what is to come in later passages. Moving forward a few paragraphs, we finally start to get at the crux of the matter when Plotinus tells us:

> *Now we have to consider* ***Love, the God****.*
>
> *The existence of such a being is no demand of the ordinary man, merely; it is supported by*

> *Theologians (Orphic teachers) and, over and over again, by Plato to whom* ***Eros is child of Aphrodite****, minister of beautiful children,* ***inciter of human souls towards the supernal beauty or quickener of an already existing impulse thither****.*
>
> [Bold emphasis mine]

Now we arrive at the fact of God being Love. We also get informed that Eros (love) the offspring of Aphrodite (Ninhursag) serves as the 'igniter of human souls' from 'an already existing impulse' to join with this God called Love. Is this starting to get interesting yet? I am going to let Plotinus continue with his explanations about Aphrodite and Eros:

> *"The matter seems to demand some discussion of Aphrodite since in any case Eros is described as being either her son or in some association with her.* ***Who then is Aphrodite, and in what sense is Love either her child or born with her or in some way both her child and her birthfellow?***
>
> *To us* ***Aphrodite is twofold****;* ***there is the heavenly Aphrodite,*** *daughter of Ouranos or Heaven: and there is the other the daughter of Zeus and Dione, this is the Aphrodite who presides over earthly unions;* ***the higher was not born of a mother*** *and has no part in marriages, for in Heaven there is no marrying.*

> ***The Heavenly Aphrodite****, daughter of Kronos (Saturn) who* ***is no other than the Intellectual Principle must be the Soul at its divinest:*** *unmingled as the immediate emanation of the unmingled; remaining ever Above, as neither desirous nor capable of descending to this sphere, never having developed the downward tendency, a divine Hypostasis essentially aloof, so unreservedly an Authentic Being as to have no part with Matter and therefore* ***mythically 'the unmothered' justly called not Celestial Spirit but God,*** *as knowing no admixture, gathered cleanly within itself.*
>
> *Any nature springing directly from the Intellectual Principle must be itself also a clean thing: it will derive a resistance of its own from its nearness to the Highest, for all its tendency, no less than its fixity, centres upon* ***its author whose power is certainly sufficient to maintain it Above****.*
>
> [Bold italics mine]

Despite the obfuscation and syncretism with the Greek belief in their gods, this passage is highly informative. It instructs us of the Heavenly Aphrodite who is above the concerns and interface with the material world. It also states that Aphrodite is the same as the Intellectual Principle, which is another one of those allusions to the hive collective and its source intelligence. We are told that the 'higher' Aphrodite was not born of a mother, and all this represents the Soul at it's finest. In all these cases, the word soul should be equated with the virus cells, whether referenced to as the Divine Oneness or the individual cells within their infected human hosts. Plotinus continues:

> *"Soul then could never fall from its sphere;* ***it is closer held to the divine Mind than the very sun could hold the light it gives forth to radiate about it, an outpouring from itself held firmly to it, still.***
>
> *But following upon Kronos or, if you will, upon Heaven (Ouranos), the father of Kronos* ***the Soul directs its Act towards him and holds closely to him and in that love brings forth the Eros through whom it continues to look towards him.*** *This Act of the Soul has produced an Hypostasis, a Real-Being;* ***and the mother and this Hypostasis her offspring, noble Love gaze together upon Divine Mind. Love, thus, is ever intent upon that other loveliness, and exists to be the medium between desire and that object of desire.*** *It is the eye of the desirer;* ***by its power what loves is enabled to see the loved thing****. But it is first; before it becomes the vehicle of vision, it is itself filled with the sight; it is first, therefore, and not even in the same order for desire attains to vision* ***only through the efficacy of Love, while Love, in its***

***own Act, harvests the spectacle of beauty playing immediately above it.***

[Bold emphasis mine]

With the highlighted and underlined passages, we are seeing that Love is this connector between the hive inner soul and the cosmic collective, that the goddess is the intercessor or 'mother' over this process. With the information in hand presented in this book, you should be able to read through the philosophical allusions and the mysticism to perceive the hive and Ninhursag in exactly the relationship I have laid out. With the code key to unravel the mystical mystery, then even what Plotinus shares can be seen through, despite the philosophical and mystical religious allusions. Plotinus proceeds in section 3 of this treatise to instruct us:

*"That* ***Love is a Hypostasis (a 'Person'), a Real-Being sprung from a Real-Being lower than the parent*** *but authentically existent is beyond doubt.*

*For the* ***parent-Soul*** *was a Real-Being sprung directly from the Act of the Hypostasis that ranks before it: it had life; it was a constituent in the Real-Being of all that authentically is in the Real-Being* ***which looks, rapt, towards the very Highest.*** *"*

[Bold emphasis mine]

What this passage seeks to tell us is that Love is a real person, what Plotinus refers to as a Hypostasis. This is indicative of the fact that Love is a created thing, it is not a naturally occurring thing, thus a platform from which the virus could replicate itself. Although the reader may still be in doubt about all this hive stuff being connected with the Divine propagator of this virus, in a passage a bit further along in the treatise, Plotinus informs us:

> *"The mental state will be designated as Love, like the Hypostasis, though it is no more than a particular act directed towards a particular object;* ***but it must not be confused with the Absolute Love, the Divine Being. The Eros that belongs to the supernal Soul must be of one temper with it; it must itself look aloft as being of the household of that Soul, dependent upon that Soul, its very offspring;*** *and therefore caring for nothing but the contemplation of the Gods.*
>
> *Once that Soul* ***which is the primal source of light*** *to the heavens is recognized as an Hypostasis standing distinct and aloof, it must be admitted that* ***Love too is distinct and aloof****. To describe the Soul as 'celestial' is not to question its separateness (or immateriality); our own best* ***we conceive as inside ourselves and yet something apart. So, we must think of this Love as***

***essentially resident where the unmingling Soul inhabits.***

*But besides this purest Soul, there must be also a* ***Soul of the All: at once there is another Love the eye with which this second Soul looks upwards like the supernal Eros engendered by force of desire****. **This Aphrodite, the secondary Soul, is of this Universe** not Soul unmingled alone, not Soul the Absolute giving birth, therefore,* ***to the Love concerned with the universal life;*** *no, this is the Love presiding over marriages; but it, also, has its touch of the upward desire; and, in the degree of that striving, it stirs and leads upwards the souls of the young and every* ***soul with which it is incorporated*** *in so far as there is a natural tendency to* ***remembrance of the divine****. For every soul is striving towards The Good, even the mingling Soul and that of particular beings, for* ***each holds <u>directly from the divine Soul, and is its offspring.</u>***

[Bold emphasis mine]

In these passages we are being told even more directly that the unmingled soul within us is separate from us, which the hive virus ever was as a predatory infectious agent, and that this soul is the offspring, or shall we say replica in the same form as a replicated amoeba as the Divine Soul. It also shares the fact that the virus within us was dependent on its spawning 'father' which is indicative of the collectivist dependency of the overall hive infection. We are told that this Love is what *compels* us, through the virus vector, to seek the Divine, the Love of God, the ecstatic experience, and that this love is the inciter to drive us into all the traditions of hive supernaturalism. This Love is the prod that creates an inner, virus-driven desire to seek communion with the celestial All, or Good or Beauty, or whatever vernacular spin words they want to allude to the begetter of the virus with. Love is the dependency programmed into the virus to perpetuate itself.

In Section 4 on his treatise on Love, Plotinus continues:

> *Does each individual Soul, then, contain within itself such a Love in essence and substantial reality?*
>
> *Since not only the pure All-Soul but also that of the Universe contains such a Love, it would be difficult to explain why our personal Soul should not. It must be so, even, with all that has life.*
>
> ***This indwelling love is no other than the Spirit which, as we are told, walks with every being,*** *the affection dominant in each several nature.* ***It implants the characteristic desire;*** *the particular Soul, strained towards its own natural objects, brings forth its own Eros, the guiding spirit realizing its worth and the quality of its Being.*

*As the **All-Soul contains the Universal Love, so must the single Soul be allowed its own single Love: and as closely as the single Soul holds to the All-Soul, never cut off but embraced within it, the two together constituting one principle of life, so the single separate Love holds to the All-Love.** Similarly, the individual Love keeps with the individual Soul as that other, the great Love, goes with the All-Soul; and **the Love within the All permeates it throughout so that the one Love becomes many,** showing itself where it chooses at any moment of the Universe, taking definite shape in these its partial phases and revealing itself at its will."*

[Bold emphasis mine]

Now, we can adhere to and bow down to all the mystical mysteries over the generations of man that such writings have steered us toward, or we can gain some pragmatism and see all this swill for what it is, an infectious mind virus that spreads itself through love as the infection vector, which keeps humanity ever seeking the mystical experience and a misperceived union with the Divine and aching for the acknowledgement of love anywhere and any way we can find it. There is nothing divine about this tyranny. But to put my final stamp of validation to all this using Poltinus' words from a passage a little further along in his presentation, he tells us:

*"For one thing, the universe is described as a blissful god and as self-sufficing, while this 'Love' is confessedly neither divine nor self-sufficing* ***but in ceaseless need.***

*Again, this Cosmos is a compound of body and soul; but Aphrodite to Plato is the Soul itself, therefore* ***Aphrodite would necessarily be a constituent part of Eros, (not mother but) dominant member!*** *A man is the man's Soul; if the world is, similarly, the world's Soul, then* ***Aphrodite, the Soul, is identical with Love, the Cosmos! And why should this one spirit, Love, be the Universe to the exclusion of all the others, which certainly are sprung from the same Essential-Being? Our only escape would be to make the Cosmos a complex of Celestials****."*

[Bold emphasis mine]

And there you have it! Everything I have related in this book in a nutshell. Ninhursag the hermaphroditic Mother Goddess of Love as the 'dominant member' of the Celestial hive collective using these *needy*, cosmic love doctrines to make the Cosmos a fully conquered collective of Celestial hive cells. And we were told this almost 1800 years ago. This is the Great Work, this is the grand agenda and design for humanity at the hands of this infectious mind virus collective over which Ninhursag stands as chief cook and bottle washer, sanitizing and obfuscating this agenda hiding behind the mask of love and Divine devotion to its cause.

As Plotinus plainly reveals, it is this Divine Love replicated in every virus cell that leaves humans so astoundingly neurotic where love is concerned. Our species doesn't know a thing about real love. All we understand about love is this false replica of love passed down to our species through this rabid mind virus, ever needy, ever seeking communion with is spawning agent in the stars. The aches you may have felt about love are not your own, they are the yearnings of the virus to use as a prod against your very humanity to seek communion with this divine form of communism, where every cell is the same, just as every amoeba is the same. This is the cosmic New World Order, the sought-after illusion of mystical and supernatural seekers of humanity throughout the ages. This never-fulfilled needy love has controlled every emotion you have ever experienced as love, and it always leaves us wanting in the final tally. Falling in love is the thrill, staying in love is harder, and this is specifically because what we know as love is a cheap dime-store imitation of the real thing. It is a simulated emotion, glass instead of a genuine gemstone. Our species has settled for a cheap version of love because it is not real love, it is a fabrication of the hive virus itself.

In light of what I have shared in this chapter about love and the hive infection, then when we review religious doctrines such as 'Love thy neighbor as thyself', we can only see the hive mechanism as play, because the virus in your neighbor was exactly the same virus that resided in all of us. We have been blinded by love since our creation as a species. Once Ninhursag's virus cell joined the hive, the love doctrine permeated every religion and mystical tradition on the planet. We have been conned in the most detestable way possible, by using love as a weapon, and we all scream to love and be loved. Through love we are all begging for our continued cognitive enslavement. We are all slaves to love whether we want to admit this fact or not, and the concept of love that enslaves us is not even human love, but a fabrication of a predatory mind virus. Love *is* the virus vector.

# 28. Humanity's Door to Freedom

This volume is the latest in a series of expository books I have written on many of the subjects touched on in this work. This book is the culmination of all the work I have presented before, and it is the capstone that links all my other books together into a comprehensive and complete picture. Each book I wrote provided pieces of this massive global puzzle of human history that all link together in this volume. I have done my utmost to provide humanity with a new understanding of itself as a species and provide the tools through which we can understand ourselves as a planetary race of beings. Regardless of our external differences and racial distinctions, we are all still one human race. Unfortunately, most of us refuse to acknowledge this one single fact that could serve as a starting point for us to stop killing each other and stop the incessant emotional conflict that those who choose to control our species thrive upon to keep their small Aryan elite cadre in power. Divide and conquer has always been the rule, even though homogenization was always the ultimate agenda of the hive collective intelligence. I realize the cognitive dichotomy this presents, but I think the explanations provided in this book illustrate how seemingly opposing ideologies would eventually be strung together to create this homogenization.

Humanity is currently being manipulated through conflict and chaos. The mantra of multiculturalism and humanitarianism used by the Marxist Fabian ideologues and the Theosophical faux spirituality ideologies only works to create more chaos. While the Left is antagonizing the Right, the Theosophists are trying to walk between the two with their mystical spiritual beliefs to dupe humanity into buying the perennial philosophy doctrine, seeking to harmonize all the divergent mystical and religious beliefs elucidated in this book. One is the carrot and one is the stick. Fabian revolutionary Marxist tactics are escalating, and people are being sold false spiritual beliefs as the salve to cure these chaotic woes. One hand is seeking to wash the other, and humanity overall is only the meat in this ideological sandwich which controls all sides of the argument.

At the root of every point of conflict we will find religion or spirituality, even as the root of Atheism, for without supernatural religions to contradict, Atheism has no basis to exist. Whether one wants to admit it or not, Communism is a religion as well, only its god is the State, and the mystical philosopher Plato was a strong proponent of the State. You can't remove the mystical traditions from the Marxist statist religion, for all these things lead toward collectivism, which was pushed by the hive and Ninhursag once she joined the collective and then became dominant power within that hierarchy.

The hapiym hive prided itself on its changelessness and being changeless is nothing we should aspire to as a species thinking that is progress. It only leads to sameness and stagnancy. The changelessness of the hive collective should be about as appealing to us as the changelessness of an amoeba, yet this is all the hive had to sell its infected victims living lives in a material world. The only thing that ever gave the hive intelligence any kind of leg up was the stolen inventiveness of our species. It could create nothing of itself except more of the same, just like the amoeba. The perceptions its acolytes and proselytizers over the ages failed to recognize is that all the alleged Divine Wisdom was intellect and ideas stolen from the human race. The hive could never be more than what it was, a mimic and a thief of our consciousness and our individual human personalities.

The hapiym virus stole our very humanity from us and enchanted our minds with mystical yearnings, using love itself as a weapon against us, to keep us ever seeking the alleged Divine communion or the afterlife in an attempt to help us destroy ourselves as a species and become nothing more than walking meat-bags so stolen dead human personalities could perpetually re-inhabit our forms. The hive creator never realized that if it ever gained full control over the cosmos and destroyed the inventiveness of the human species' it inhabited, that it would have died off into the oblivion of its much-touted changelessness. It is only our humanity that provided the knowledge the hive accumulated. Without our species genius and inventiveness, the hive was nothing - it was always nothing except a delusionary facsimile that had convinced itself through its own over-inflated ego that it was something it never was or ever could be – a free and independent consciousness.

We are fortunate indeed that this predatory virus within us is dead and that it won't ever return. Unfortunately, our species is plagued with the residual symptoms this virus left behind with all its fears and insecurities. We all still carry its habits, but they can be overcome with diligence and fortitude. We *can* gain our cognitive freedom from the harnessing effects of this predatory infection. This is a psychological process, not a spiritual process, because spirit, as people perceive it to be in the first cognition world, is an illusion. As Plotinus so clearly pointed out in the last chapter, the oversoul and the individual soul were all the same thing, the virus infection itself.

Throughout our history humanity has always had the chance to stay on the road to advancement. We have had our instructors throughout the ages to show us the straight road to advancement, yet our species has been seduced at the off-ramp of mysticism where the neon signs blare at us, Feel Good! Divine Love! Ecstatic Experiences! Tickets to the Afterlife, No Waiting! Connect with the Divine Aliens! Ascend to the 5th Dimension! Find Love, Happiness and Eternal Bliss! For thousands of generations we have taken the bait in one form or another and the Divine off-ramp and its holy seductions have always been the lure to steer us from the path of genuine cognitive development. The off-ramp to the mystical is the road to stagnation and sameness, it only leads us to the changelessness of the hive intelligence and nowhere else. It is the dead-end road for humanity's true advancement and the lane to the off-ramp has been lined up for thousands of years, while the road to true cognitive advancement lies ahead with weeds growing through its surface from disuse.

With the information I have provided in all my works, humanity now has a chance to remove itself from the Divine quagmire of deception and ignore the seductive neon of the mystical off-ramp. The only question is whether humanity will take the straight road to never-ending cognitive adventure and discovery or stay bogged down in the traffic seeking the mystical and supernatural off-ramp to nowhere. Your personal choice resides with you. You can't change anyone else, for they are as responsible for freeing their minds as you are for freeing yours. None of us has the power to change another, we can only change ourselves. If you are ready for that change, then you at least have the option for change based on the information provided in this book by seeing through the mystical chicanery that has held our species hostage for far too long. This book is designed to show mysticism in all its false glory with the intent that those who read it can finally shed these beliefs and their ideologies of supernatural payoffs.

Pragmatism and truth are more valuable than all the supernatural promises in the world. Only pragmatism will show you the way out of the mystical corrals of deception. Only pragmatism will give you the strength to endure the psychological processes of ridding your mind of the hapiym virus habits. No one can do it for you. Only you can free yourself. It is my personal desire that everyone who reads this book takes that challenge to find their own cognitive freedom and transcend all the dependency on supernatural pipe dreams. You are now in possession of all the information you need to throw everything mystical into the trash where it belongs. Good luck with your personal process of cognitive housecleaning. You have the strength to do it as a human being, on your own, without supernatural guidance to show you the way. Pragmatism is the key and developing the stamina to push through the psychological deprogramming will bring you a freedom you have never known.

Everything that had to be said to utterly gut mysticism is presented in this volume. I have provided the keys to solving these ages old mysteries which our theologians and academics have agonized over through the ages. If these authorities spend half as much paper as they have in endlessly speculating on these matters and turn to reinterpreting the past and unraveling mysticism with honesty and pragmatism, then libraries can be filled with the truth rather than speculative philosophical meandering and academic guesswork.

Through the passages I presented by Plotinus it should be observed that certain intellectual elite have had inside knowledge on the hive assembly for ages. Although Plotinus put this information out through a form of speculative philosophy, he was still selling a product to other intellectuals whose details he knew on an intimate and personal basis. This same intellectual class of elite has been the guiding light in all mystical traditions, from the Gnostics to Plato to the Neoplatonists, to the Hermeticists and the Kabbalists, and threaded through the Perennial Philosophy into Theosophy and Marxist Statist religion.

Before closing this book, I have a certain amount of polemic I want to level at the academic world, and the control of media and publishing houses in particular. We have copyright infringement laws to prevent the theft of the work of others through plagiarism and counterfeiting one's work. In times past, before the turn of the 20th century, one was free to quote the work of another so long as proper accrediting was given to the source of the references. This meant that so long as the original author of a work was given credit for any passages cited in the work of another, there was no infringement, for due credit was being given to the original author. With the advent of creeping Marxism and the Fabian ownership and control of virtually all the publishing houses on the planet, particularly university presses, copyright laws have turned into a form of censorship, meaning you can't quote the works of others without permissions, which usually comes with high fees to quote.

Gone are the days where one could cite their authorities in their work without this kind of thievery and censorship of information for a price. This is one reason that I often allude to where I got support for my contentions without using direct quotes. To quote anything directly I have to rely on what lies in the public domain to avoid copyright infringement issues and potential lawsuits. Anything outside public domain falls under the new rules of copyright censorship where one often has to pay hundreds or thousands of dollars and have written permission before they can quote anything in their work, with or without originating credit being given as due acknowledgment as was the practice as little as a century ago.

Another form of censorship that keeps information out of the hands of the general public is price prohibitiveness, where books are priced so high as to be ridiculous. Academia is particularly notorious for this practice. I have seen books with no more than 200-250 pages with prices ranging from $200-$800 written by academics and published by university presses. This type of cost prohibition also contributes mightily to censorship of scholarly materials. In a world where copyright goes beyond protection to the level of using the laws as a weapon to hide the practices of censorship, it is little wonder that computer hackers take advantage of putting out cost prohibitive material despite the attempts of the Fabian controllers to strangle the fair exchange of information in the marketplace.

All these practices serve as tools to keep the population dumbed-down, and even if one does have the interest in research material, cost and copyright laws used as a weapon for censorship prevent the sharing of information so the public can educate itself. The elite have always done their damndest to sequester knowledge into their own intellectualist bailiwick. Contrary to what you may believe, this sequestering of knowledge into the hands of the few was also part of the hive's agenda.

Within *The Enneads*, Plotinus also related how the soul would seek to gravitate upwards to the Celestial, but there was little reason for the Celestial to descend into matter. In regard to this, a later passage in *Ennead* 3 on *Love*, he reports:

> *"On the first question: every Celestial born in the striving of the Soul towards the good and beautiful is an Eros; and all the souls within the Cosmos do engender this Celestial; but* ***other Spirit-Beings, equally born from the Soul of the All, but by other faculties of that Soul, have other functions: they are for the direct service of the All,*** *and administer particular things to the*

*purpose of the Universe entire. The Soul of the All must be adequate to all that is and therefore must* ***bring into being spirit powers serviceable not merely in one function but to its entire charge.***

*But what participation can the Celestials have in Matter, and in what Matter?*

*Certainly none in bodily Matter; that would make them simply living things of the order of sense. And if, even, they are to invest themselves in bodies of air or of fire,* ***their nature must have already been altered before they could have any contact with the corporeal.*** *The Pure does not mix, unmediated, with body though many think that the Celestial-Kind, of its very essence, comports a body aerial or of fire.*

*But (since this is not so)* ***why should one order of Celestial descend to body and another not?*** *The difference implies the existence of some cause or medium working upon such as thus descend. What would constitute such a medium?*

*We are forced to assume that* ***there is a Matter of the Intellectual Order, and that Beings partaking of it are thereby enabled to enter into the lower Matter, the corporeal.***

[Bold emphasis mine]

I shared in Chapter 23 the truth about the 'soul' of the Dalai Lama being the same hive cell that has kept reinserting itself into human children for the past 544 years. The foregoing passage from Plotinus tells us specifically that souls can descend from the hive into matter through what he called "a Matter of Intellectual Order". If you look at all these mystical traditions and mystery schools, they all tout the Wisdom of the Ages, and they have created numerous 'Orders' of secret societies. You have Freemasonic historians like Manly P. Hall who produced books and lectures about *The Secret Teachings of All Ages*, and how the intellect holds a central position in all these teachings. With this revelation by Plotinus and what I have shared in this book, there is a hive-created artificial barrier to the advancement of human consciousness that has been reserved to the Aryan intelligentsia throughout the ages. Although Plotinus presented what he knew in speculative philosophical form, he knew more than he was admitting. The same can be said of Manly P. Hall and every other intellectual mystical philosopher throughout the ages.

Through hive manipulation and so-called 'walk-in' hive cells, human knowledge has been sequestered into the hands of the intellectual elite whose goal has been to create the World Soul professed in these ancient Neoplatonist doctrines and is still being promoted through Theosophy today. We can interpret this World Soul to mean the hoped-for fulfillment of the hive's overall agenda to cognitively conquer our species. We also shouldn't lose sight of the fact that Ninhursag as Hecate was also considered the Mother of Angels and the Cosmic World Soul, whether she is referred to as Aphrodite in Plotinus' work or not.

As Plotinus reveals, these souls that descend from the Celestial hive oversoul, return into material form to further facilitate the agenda of the All. This is where all this malarkey about 'service to others' originates within the New Age doctrines and also serves as the foundation for Lucis Trust's World Goodwill organization, and what is called their World Servers.

The primary thrust of the Fabian Society in its early days was to take control of the university systems, for the concept was that if you could indoctrinate the future teachers, there would be a trickle-down effect into the classrooms of the lower grades in schools. By gaining control of the publishing houses that printed school curricula, the sanitization of history began in earnest and over the last eighty years our schools have been turned into ideological brainwashing mills, making each successive generation more ill-informed and uneducated, and more indoctrinated with Fabian Marxist and Theosophical feel-good doctrines, peddling docility and multiculturalism as a norm. The radical hippies from the 1960s have moved into professorships and have become the advocates of such ideologies as Transpersonal Psychology, Gender Studies and the Marxist brand of Secular Humanism. This has been particularly focused through what they call the Humanities in the universities, and as the Professor of Psychology, Jordan B. Peterson calls attention to in his lectures, the universities have become hotbeds for promoting Fabian Marxist revolutionary doctrines through Humanities studies.

Through the present generation we are seeing an increase in revolutionary ideologies preached from the pulpits of university classrooms, and the expansion of the Theosophical spiritual ideologies through such courses as Transpersonal Psychology and

Spiritual Psychology. The Marxist ideologies are blended seamlessly with Theosophy's alleged spiritual ideologies as the money and power of the global Lucis Trust monolith drives the hive's collectivist ideology inexorably forward. The richest alleged 'Capitalist' families on the face of this planet have worked in collusion with this agenda for at least a century, and the call for class warfare against the rich is only a false distraction, for the rich Capitalist elite intelligentsia have been in bed with the Fabian Society since shortly after its inception. For those who choose to contest this information, just look up *Socialism for Millionaires*, a pamphlet written by the Fabian Society member George Bernard Shaw in 1901. It is readily available with an easy internet search.

Through the hive's hidden agenda, served through the intellectualists, hive cells have recycled throughout the last 4,000 years of our history, whether one can accept this terrible truth or not. The evidence has been presented, what remains in question is how many people are willing to accept this truth and transcend all the lies and the psychological programming plugged into our species by the hive virus infection.

Just as the review board insisted on censoring the doctoral thesis of Dr. Hillman with his research into recreational drug use by the ancient philosophers in their quest for Divine communion with the All, intellectualist censorship is also at work through abuse of the copyright laws and cost prohibition. Through the university and academic control of the peer review system, this censorship is even more profound when most collegiate writers can't get any kind of acknowledgement to have their papers presented in accepted academic journals. This is particularly true of anyone whose research rocks the boat of conventional accepted academic norms which, in the Humanities, are all geared toward radical Fabian Marxist ideologies. Papers that support mystical practices and Leftist ideologies are going to be more apt to find their way into these academic publications and journals than those who seek to expose this tyranny. This is how academic intellectualism controls our culture through censorship and why the population spirals ever downward into ignorance and illiteracy, seeking to return rank and file human beings into intellectualist-controlled drones like the gods and priests of old.

Through the reliance on technology, our species is becoming dependent on technology, with cell phones and social networks keeping everyone locked into hive social mentality and making the majority of people so reliant on the need to interact socially with others that our technology is slowly becoming another tool for enslavement. With the push towards Transhumanism these same intellectuals are trying to ultimately remove our humanity from us by merging us with machines, raising the specter of turning humanity into nothing more than programmable cyborgs. The idea of merging humans with animals is almost a century old and was presented by the Fabian member, J. B. S. Haldane in his paper, *Daedalus, or, Science and the Future* in 1923. Merging humans with machines through technological Transhumanism is no different in that regard where removing us from being wholly human is concerned.

There is nothing taking place in our world today that is not part of the Great Work of Ninhursag's mystics throughout the ages. It is all interconnected, and at its root we find the hapiym hive virus collective intellect running affairs on this planet, not humanity. You are now armed with the information to see through this illusion and extricate your consciousness from the illusion. Do not fall prey to the nihilism that the facts offered in this book may bring about, for even that defeatist mentality is only a residual habit of the virus that seeks to keep us all roped into and subjugated to the herd socialist mentality. As a species, we are better than that. It's time humanity realizes its value and takes the straight road to cognitive advancement and removes itself from the quagmire of mystical and supernatural thinking. We will never be the deciders of our own destiny as a species if we do not make this choice.

# References

Meiners, Christoph - *The Outline of History of Mankind (1785)*

Gobineau, Arthur de - *Essay on the Inequality of the Human Races (1853)*

Le Bon, Gustave – *The Crowd (1895)*

Patai, Raphael – *The Hebrew Goddess (1968)*

Stanley, Thomas - *The Chaldaic Oracles (1661)*

Westcott, W. Wynn - *The Chaldæn Oracles of Zoroaster (1895)*

Faraone, Christphoper A.; Obbink, Dirk - *The Getty Hexameters: Poetry, Magic, and Mystery in Ancient Selinous (2013)*

Eliade, Mircea - *Shamanism: Archaic Techniques in Ecstasy (1946)*

Woodman, Marion; Dickson, Elinor - *Dancing in the Flames: The Dark Goddess in the Transformation of Consciousness (1996)*

Huxley, Aldous – *The Perennial Philosophy (1945)*

*Brave New World (1932)*

Robinson, James M. (Editor) – *The Nag Hammadi Library (1978)*

Noyce, John – *Hildegard von Bingen and Her Visions of the Divine Feminine (2013)*

Swedenborg, Emmnuel – *Spiritual Diary (1758)*

Sidis, Boris - *The Source and Aim of Human Progress (1919)*

Unknown - *Tibetan Book of the Dead*

Beall, Endall - *The Psychology of Becoming Human: Evolving Beyond Psychological Conditioning (2018)*

Rosinus, Johann - *Antiquitatum romanarum corpus absolutissimum (1585)*

Dorn, Gerhard - *Speculativae Philosophiae (1568?)*

Beall, Endall – *We Are Not Alone – Parts 1-3 (2015-2016)*

Pike, Albert – *Morals and Dogma (1872)*

Rosinus, Johann - *Antiquitatum romanarum corpus absolutissimum (1585)*

Dorn, Gerhard - *Speculativae philosophiae*

Kosnik, Darlene - *History's Vanquished Goddess ASHERAH: God's Wife: the Goddess Asherah, Wife of Yahweh. Archaeological & Historical Aspects of Syro-Palestinian ... Traditions, Macrocosmically Examined (2014)*

Müller, F, Max (Editor) – *The Sacred Books of the East, No. 39 (1891)*

Bailey, Alice – *The Externalization of the Hierarchy (1957)*

Kvanvig, Helge S. - *Primeval History – Babylonian, Biblical and Enochic (2011)*

Noyce, John - *History and Prophecies of the Divine Feminine (2009)*

Leadbetter, Charles W. – *Invisible Helpers (1915)*

Nilus, Sergei - *Protocols of the Learned Elders of Zion (1905)*

Hillman, D. C. A. - *The Chemical Muse: Drug Use and the Roots of Western Civilization (2008)*

Beall, Endall - *The Energetic War Against Humanity: The 6,000 Year War Against Human Cognitive Advancement (2016)*

Woodman, Marion; Dickson, Elinor - *Dancing in the Flames: The Dark Goddess and the Transformation of Consciousness (1996)*

MacKenna, Stephen (Translator) - *Plotinus: The Enneads (1930)*

Hall, Manly P. - *The Secret Teachings of All Ages (1928)*

## Articles/Papers


Frothingham, A.L. - *Babylonian Origin of Hermes the Snake God, and of the Caduceus (1916)*

Harkness, Deborah E. - *Alchemy and Eschatology: Exploring the Connections between John Dee and Isaac Newton (1999)*

Calame, Claude - *V. Ritual and Initiatory Itineraries toward the Afterlife: Time, Space, and Pragmatics in the Gold Lamellae* https://chs.harvard.edu/CHS/article/display/5807.v-ritual-and-initiatory-itineraries-toward-the-afterlife-time-space-and-pragmatics-in-the-gold-lamellae - *(Harvard University Center for Hellenic Studies)*

Beyer, Catherine – *Squaring the Circle (2017)*
https://www.thoughtco.com/squaring-the-circle-96039

*Eliphas Levi's Baphomet: The Goat of Mendes (2017)*
https://www.thoughtco.com/eliphas-levis-baphomet-goat-of-mendes-95993

Myrevteam - *Eugenics Education Chapter 4: Alice Bailey and Annie Besant (2017)*
https://steemit.com/women/@myrevteam/eugenics-education-chapter-4-alice-bailey-and-annie-besant

The Truth about the Fabian Society (2012)
https://fabiansociety.wordpress.com/2012/11/15/hello-world/

Two hundred "Six million Jews" allegations from 1900-1945
https://ia800406.us.archive.org/14/items/TwoHundredSixMillionJewsAllegationsFrom19001945/TwoHundredSixMillionJewsAllegationsFrom1900-1945.pdf

Steinfels, Peter: *Beliefs; Millennial fears in the year 1000: apocalypse then, apocalypse now and apocalypse forever* https://www.nytimes.com/1999/07/17/nyregion/beliefs-millennial-fears-year-1000-apocalypse-then-apocalypse-now-apocalypse.html

Council of the Gods (authorship unknown) https://ia902709.us.archive.org/9/items/pdfy-RpoJ_9GUQqwVwGYy/The%20Divine%20Council.pdf

Shaw, George Bernard – *Socialism for Millionaires (1901)* https://digital.library.lse.ac.uk/objects/lse:duf537zem

Haldane, J. B. S. - *Daedalus, or, Science and the Future (1923)* http://www.unife.it/letterefilosofia/lm.lingue/insegnamenti/letteratura-inglese-ii/programmi-anni-precedenti/programma-desame-2011-2012/J.%20B.%20S.%20Haldane-%20Daedalus-%20or-%20Science%20and%20the%20Future-%201923.pdf/view

## Wikipedia References

Sophia (wisdom)

Sophia (Gnosticism)

Gnosticism

Veil of Isis

Platonism in Islamic Philosophy

Pseudo-Dionysius the Areopagite

List of Christian Mystics

Hildegard of Bingen

Great Architect of the Universe

Isaac Newton's occult studies

Great Work

Viaticum

Alchemy

Great Hymn to Aten

Seven Rays

Saturnalia

Cult of the Supreme Being

Liberty Leading the People

Eris (mythology)

Seven Seals

Kriophoros

Aphroditus

Plato

School of Athens

Timaeus

Christian Cross

Yoni

Chymical Wedding of Christian Rosenkreutz

Monas Hieroglyphica

Ashera

Whore of Babylon

Conversion of Paul the Apostle

Queen Mother of the West

Chinese salvationist religions

Egalitarianism

Numen

Yin and Yang

Occult

Alice Bailey

Annie Besant

Kali

Tantra

Vedas

Black Magic

Theistic Satanism

Phoenix (mythology)

Allah as a Lunar deity

Qalb

History of Sufism

Sufism

Tawhid

Christian views on suicide

Martyrs of Córdoba

Bardo Thodol

1st Dalai Lama

Tara (Buddhism)

Succession of the 14th Dalai Lama

Hermetic Brotherhood of Light

Great White Brotherhood

Invisible College

Spiritism

Isra and Mi'raj

Dome of the Rock

Foundation Stone

Baetylus

Shalim

Herma

1905 Russian Revolution

Irgun

Lehi

Bar Kokhba revolt

Sabbatai Zevi

Shekinah

Protocols of the Learned Elders of Zion

Eugène Sue

Veneration for the dead

Ancestor veneration in China

Georgia Guidestones

Hermes

Damnatio memoriae

Curse Tablets

## Ancient Textual and Other References

***Lamentation over the Destruction of Sumer and Ur*** - *http://etcsl.orinst.ox.ac.uk/cgi-bin/etcsl.cgi?text=t.2.2.3#*

***Ur Lament*** –

*http://etcsl.orinst.ox.ac.uk/cgi-bin/etcsl.cgi?text=t.2.2.2&charenc=j#*

***The Epic of Gilgamesh*** - *http://www.jasoncolavito.com/epic-of-gilgamesh.html*

***Great Hymn to Aten*** –

*https://katherinestange.com/egypt/hymn2.htm*

***Lion-throned Goddesses of Western Asia*** –

*http://www.sourcememory.net/veleda/?p=278*

***Enki and Ninmah*** –

*http://etcsl.orinst.ox.ac.uk/cgi-bin/etcsl.cgi?text=t.1.1.2&charenc=j#*

***Atrahasis Epic*** –

*http://www.livius.org/sources/content/anet/104-106-the-epic-of-atrahasis/*

***Enki and the World Order*** –

*http://wsrp.usc.edu/information/REL499_2011/Enki%20and%20the%20World%20Order.pdf*

## Useful Videos on Youtube

Worth, Victor - *Israel's Neighbors – Orphism*

https://www.youtube.com/watch?v=2INVBVPnSzQ

*NT Celestial Marriage*

https://www.youtube.com/watch?v=KCc6XDqbyEM

*Israel's Neighbors – Fuxi and Nuwas*

https://www.youtube.com/watch?v=usgazwSZL8Q

# Suggested Reading List by Topic

*Note – Most of these books can be found in .pdf format and this list is only a preliminary starting point for further research for those with the desire to know.

## Religion

Ancient Egyptian Religion – Jaroslav Cerny (1951)
A Handbook of Egyptian Religion – Adolf Erman (1907)
Gods, Demons and Symbols of Ancient Mesopotamia – Jeremy Black and Anthony Green (1992)
Religious Texts from Ugarit – N. Wyatt (1998, reprinted 2002, 2006)
Prophecy in the Ancient Near East - Jonathan Stökl (2012)
Religion and Magic in Ancient Egypt – Rosalie David (2002)
A Study of Mithraism – Unknown (1949) (17 pgs)
Ancient Religions – Sarah Iles Johnston (2007)
Baalism in Canaanite Religion and Its Relation to Selected Old Testament Texts – Unknown (2016) (29 pgs)
Babylonian Liturgies – Stephen Langdon (1913)
Babylonian Origin of Hermes the Snake God – A.L. Frothingham (1916)
Babylonian Religion and Mythology – L.W. King (1903)
Religions of Rome – Mary Beard, John North, Simon Price (1996)
Bel, The Christ of Ancient Times – Hugo Radau (1908)
Bestiality and Religion – Richard L. Matteoli (Date unknown, 16 pgs)
Late Traces of the Cults of Cybele and Attis: The Origins of the Kurenti and of the Pinewood
Marriage - Slavko Ciglenečki (Date unknown – 11 pgs)
Cybele and Her Cult in Rome – Krishni Burns (Date unknown – 5 pgs)
Demeter Mystery Cult – Yasmine Maher (2013) (12 pgs)
Development of Religion and Thought in Ancient Egypt – James Henry Breasted (1912)
Did God Have a Wife? - William G. Dever (2005)
Egyptian Book of the Dead - P. Le Page Renouf Translator (1904)

Papyrus of Ani - Egyptian Book of the Dead – E.A Wallis Budge Translator (Date unknown)
Fables of Ancient Israel Now Being Dissected – The Barnes Review (May 2007) (13 pgs)
Dictionary of Gods and Goddesses – Michael Jordan (1993, 2004)
Old Testament Theology Vol. 3: Israel's Life - John Goldingay (2009)
Greece and Babylon: A Comparative Sketch of Mesopotamian, Anatolian and Hellenic Religions – Lewis R. Farnell (1911)
Greek and Canaanite Mythologies: Zeus, Baal, and their Rivals - Carolina López-Ruiz (2014) (10 pgs)
Lectures on the Origin and Growth of Religion of the Ancient Babylonians – A.H. Sayce (1898)
Light on the Old Testament from Babel – Albert T. Clay (1907)
The Metroac Cult: Foreign or Roman? - Cathryn Caveney (2016) (59 pgs)
The Early History of God: Yahweh and the Other Deities in Ancient Israel – Mark S. Smith (1990)
Mystery and Secrecy in the Nag Hammadi Collection and Other Ancient Literature: Ideas and Practices – Essay Compilation (2012)
The Oriental Religions in Roman Paganism - Franz Cumont (1911)
Osiris and the Egyptian Resurrection – A.E. Wallis Budge (1911)
Pagan Monotheism in Late Antiquity – Edited by Polymnia Athanassiadi & Michael Frede (1999)
Thoth: The Hermes of Egypt – Patrick Boylan (1922)
The Pyramid Texts – Translated by Samuel A.B Mercer (1952)
Religion and Power – Edited by Nicole Brisch (2008, 2012)
The Religion of Babylon and Assyria - Theophilus G. Pinches (Early 20th century publication)
Religion and Ritual in Ancient Egypt – Emily Teeter (2011)
The Religion of Babylonia and Assyria – Morris Jastrow, Jr. (1898)
Religions of Ancient China - Herbert A. Giles (2000) (23 pgs)
The Religions of Ancient Egypt and Babylonia – A.H. Sayce (1902)
Roman Gods: A Conceptual Approach - Michael Lipka (2009)
Ritual and Cult at Ugarit - Dennis Pardee (2002)
Rome's Religious History – Jason Davies (2004)

The Complete Gods and Goddesses of Ancient Egypt – Richard H, Wilkinson (2003)
The Great Empires of Prophecy, from Babylon to the Fall of Rome - Alonzo Trevier Jones (1898)
The Hittite State Cult of Tutelary Deities – Gregory McMahon (1991)
Horus in the Pyramid Texts – Thomas George Allen (1915) (73 pgs)
Hittite Prayers - Itamar Singer (2002)
A study of the similarities between Hinduism and Ancient Egyptian Religion - Charlotte Booth (2004) (11 pgs)
Astrology and Religion Among the Greeks and Romans – Franz Cumont (1912)
Death and Initiation in the Funerary Religion of Ancient Egypt – Jan Assman (1989) (25 pgs)
Asherah: Goddesses in Ugarit, Israel and the Old Testament - Tilde Binger (1997)
A Search for the Origins of Judaism: From Joshua to the Mishnah - Etienne Nodet (1992)
An Introduction to Ancient Iranian Religion: Readings from the Avesta and Achaemenid Inscriptions – William W. Malandra (1983)
Sex and Religion: A Cultural History – H. Bruce Stokes (1999) (8 pgs)
Women and Religion in Ancient Egypt – Barbara S. Lesko (1999) (37 pgs)
The two Creation Stories in Genesis – James S. Forrester-Brown (1920)
The Old Egyptian Faith – Colin Campbell (1920)
Seth: God of Confusion – H. Te Velde (1960)
The Sex Worship and Symbolism of Primitive Races – Sanger Brown II (1916)
Sex Worship: An Exposition of the Phallic Origin of Religion – Clifford Howard (1897)
Serpent Worship, and Other Essays – C. Staniland Wake (1888)
The Idea of the Holy – Rudolph Otto (1923, 1936)
Discourse on the Religion of Priapus – Richard Payne Knight (1865)
Hellenistic Religion: Demeter Religious Cult – Yasmine Maher (2013) (12 pgs)
Sinister Yogis – David Gordon White (2009)

Ancient Religions – Editor Sarah Iles Johnston (2007)
Aphrodite in Proclus' Theology - Tuomo Lankila (2009) (23 pgs)

## Mysticism

The Mystical Thought of Meister Eckhart – Bernard McGinn (2001)
The Changing Shape of Late Medieval Mysticism – Bernard McGinn (1996) (24 pge excerpt)
Mithraism: Freemasonry and the Ancient Mysteries – Bro H. L. Hayward (Date unknown 26 pgs)
Astral Magic in Babylon – Erica Reiner (1995)
Mysticism East and West – Rudolph Otto – (1932)
Secret Teachings of All Ages – Manly P, Hall (1928)
Mysticism and Logic and Other Essays – Bertrand Russel (1917, 1956)
Religious Ecstasy - Nils G. Holm (1982)
Hermes Trismegistus and the Origins of Gnosticism – Gilles Quispel (20 pgs) (1992)
The Secret Wisdom of Qabalah – J. F. C. Fuller (1937)
Plotinus on the Soul – Damian Calouri – (2015)
Plotinus: The Enneads – Translated by Stephen MacKenna (1930)
The Changing Shape of Late Medieval Mysticism – Bernard McGinn (1996) (24 pgs)
Mysticism and its Contexts – Phillip Almond (Unknown publication date) (10 pgs)
The Ancient Greek Oracles of the Dead - Daniel Ogden (2001) (31 pgs)
Ancient Greek Mysticism - Hannah M.G. Shapero (http://www.eocto.org/article/103)
Ancient Mystery Cults – Walter Burkert (1987)
Ancient Philosophy, Mystery and Magic – Peter Kingsley (1995)
Aion: Researches into the Phenomenology of Self – Carl Jung (1969)
The Red Book – Carl Jung (2009)

## Ancient History

Primeval History: Babylonian, Biblical, and Enochic – Helge S. Kvanvig (2011)

Selected Sumerian and Babylonian Texts – Henry Frederick Lutz (1919)
Sumerian Texts of Varied Contents – Edward Chiera (1934)
The Sumerians: Their History, Culture and Character – Samuel Noah Kramer (1963)
History Begins at Sumer – Samuel Noah Kramer (1956)
The History of Science and Ancient Mesopotamia - Francesca Rochberg (2014) (24 pgs)
History of Egypt, Chaldea, Syria, Babylonia and Assyria – G. Maspero (Public Domain)
The Hittites: Their Inscriptions and Their History – John Campbell (1890)
In Search of the Indo-Europeans: Language, Archaeology and Myth – J. P. Mallory (1989)
The Horse, The Wheel and Language – David W. Anthony (2007)
Ancient Israelite Literature in its Cultural Context – John H. Walton (1989)
The Jews Under Roman Rule – W. D. Morrison (1895)
Egypt, the Aegean and the Levant: Interconnections in the Second Millennium BC – Edited by W. Vivian Davies and Louise Schofield (1995)
Egypt's Making: The Origins of Ancient Egypt 5000-2000 BC – Michael Rice (1990, 2003)
Early Civilizations: Ancient Egypt in Context – Bruce G, Trigger (1993)
Ancient Records of Egypt (5 Vols) – James Henry Breasted (1906)
Egypt after the Pharaohs: 332 BC-AD 642 from Alexander to the Arab Conquest - Alan K Bowman (1986)
Handbook to Life in Ancient Mesopotamia - Stephen Bertman (2003)
Berossus and Genesis, Manetho and Exodus – Russell E. Gmirkin (2006)
Animal Spectacula of the Roman Empire – William Christopher Epplet (2001)
Ancient Mesopotamia – Tom Head (2015)
Ancient Israel: What Do We Know and How Do We Know It? - Lester L. Grabbe (2007)
Ancient Egyptian Ritual Practice – Carolyn Diane Routledge (2001)
History of Sinai – Lina Eckenstein (1920)

A History of Babylon: From the Foundation of the Monarchy to the Persian Conquest – Leonard W. King (1915)
Stories from Ancient Canaan - Edited and Translated by Michael D. Coogan and Mark S. Smith (2012)
Assyrian Rulers of the Third and Second Millennia BC (To 1115 BC) – A. Kirk Grayson (1987)
Ancient Persia: A Concise History of the Achaemenid Empire, 550–330 BCE – Matt Waters (2014)
The Symbolism of the Biblical World - Othmar Keel (1997)
Ancient Persia from 550 BC to 650 AD - Josef Wiesehöfer (1996)
Ancient Rome: From Romulus and Remus to the Visigoth Invasion – Britannica Publishing (2011)
Life in Ancient Egypt – Adolf Erman (1894)
Early History of Gof: Yahweh and the Other Deities in Ancinet Israel – Mark S. Smith (UNKN) (35 pgs)
Law and Order in Ancient Egypt – A. J. van Loon (2014)
Loyalty and Dissidence in Roman Egypt – Andrew Harker (2008)
The Most Ancient East: The Oriental Prelude to European History – V. Gordon Childe (1928)
The Prehistory of Asia Minor - Bleda S. Düring (2011)
Sex in Antiquity: Exploring Gender and Sexuality in the Ancient World - Edited by Mark Masterson, Nancy Sorkin Rabinowitz and James Robson (2015)
Sulla, the Elites and the Empire: A Study of Roman Policies in Italy and the Greek East - Federico Santangelo (2007)
Sumerian Business and Administrative Documents from the Earliest times to the Dynasty of Agade – George A. Barton (1915)
The Origin of the Indo-Iranians - Elena E. Kuz'mina (2007)
The Ancient History of the Egyptians, Carthaginians, Assyrians, Babylonians, Medes and Persians, Macedonians and Grecians – Mr. Rollin (1808)
The Archaeology of Mediterranean Prehistory - Edited by Emma Blake and A. Bernard Knapp 2005)
The History of Civilization: The Aryans – V. Gordon Childe (1926)
The Theory of Aryan Race and India: History and Politics - Romila Thapar (1996) (28 pges)
Biblical Peoples and Ethnicity – Ann E, Killibrew (2005)
The Queen Mother and the Cult in Ancient Israel – Susan Ackerman (1993) (18 pgs)

Adam, Eve, and the Devil - Marjo C.A. Korpel & Johannes C. de Moor (2014) (17 pgs)

## Mythology

The God Enki in Royal Sumerian Ideology and Mythology – Peeter Espak (2010)
Hittite Myths – Harry A, Hoffner, Jr. (1990)
Indian Myth and Legend – Donald A. McKenzie – (Public Domain)
Indian Serpent Lore or The Nagas in Hindu Legend and Art – J. Ph. Vogel (1926)
Sumerian Epic of Paradise – Stephen Langdon (1915)
Middle Eastern Mythology – S. H. Hooke (1963)
Myths of Babylon and Assyria – Donald A. McKenzie (1915)
The Mythology of All Races Vol 5: Semitic – Stephen Herbert Langdon (1931)
The Mythology of All Races Vol 12: Egyptian – Indo-Chinese – W. Max Müller, Sir James George Scott (1918)
The Mythology of All Races Vol 6: Indian – Iranian, A. Berriedale Keith, Albert J. Carnoy (1917)
Cybele and her Cult in Rome: National Embarrassment of Benevolent Savior – Krishni Burns (Unkown publish date) (5pgs)
Demeter Mystery Cult – Yasmine Maher (2013) (2 pgs)
A Portrait of Hecate - Patricia A. Marquardt (2018) (19 pgs)
Adonis Attis Osiris – J. G, Frazer (1907)
Ancient Goddesses: The Myths and the Evidence – Edited by Lucy Goodison and Christine Morris (1998)
Aryan Sun-myths: The Origin of Religions – Charles Morris (1889)
Asherah as an Israelite Goddess: Debunking the Cult Object Myth - David Malamud (2016) (27 pgs)
Asherah in the Hebrew Bible and Northwest Semitic Literature - John Day (1986) (25 pgs)
Baal and Yahweh in the Old Testament - Brian Paul Irwin (1999)

## Magic

Pyramid Texts of Unas – Translated by Faulkner, Piankoff and Speleer (Date unknown)

Ancient Egyptian Magical Texts – J. F. Borghouts (1978)
Ancient Egyptian Ritual Practices – Carolyn Diane Routledge (2001)
Astral Magic in Babylon – Erica Reiner (1995)
Studies on Astral Magic in Medieval Jewish Thought – Dov Schwartz (2005)
Astrology and Religion Among the Greeks and Romans – Franz Cumont (1912)
Babylonian Religion and Mythology - L. W. King (1903)
Magic in Ancient Egypt – Geraldine Pinch (1994)
Magic in the Ancient Greek World – Derek Collins (2008)
Ancient Magic and Divination in Ancient Mesopotamia - JoAnn Scurlock (2006)
The Witchcraft Series Maqlu – Tzvi Abusch (2015)

## Ancient Texts

Ancient Near Eastern Texts Relating to the Old Testament – Edited by James B. Pritchard (1950)
Eridu Lament
Enki and Ninmah
Enuma Anu Enlil tablets - Lorenzo Verderame (Chapter excerpt, date unknown, 6 pgs)
The Enuma Anu Enlil: A Panoramic View - Rumen Kolev (2007) (10 pgs)
The Ahhiyawa Texts - Gary Beckman, Trevor Bryce, Eric Cline (2011)
Epic of Atrahasis
Miscellaneous Babylonian Inscriptions – George A. Barton (1918)
Neo-Babylonian Texts in the Oriental Institute Collection – David B. Weisberg (2003)
Prophets and Prophecy in the Ancient Near East – Martti Nissinen (2003)
Code of Ur-Nammu – (4 pgs)
Lamentation Over the destruction of Ur – Samuel N, Kramer (1940)
Ancient Fragments of the Phoenician, Chaldean, Egyptian, Tyrian, Carthaginian, Indian, Persian and other Writers – Isaac Preston Cory (1822)

## Conspiracy

The Sabbatean Frankists – David Livingstone (2009)
The Sabbatean-Frankist Messianic Conspiracy Partially Exposed – Clifford Shack (Unknown Date)
The Protocols of the Learned Elders of Zion – Sergei Nilus (1903)
The Unseen Hand: An Introduction to the Conspiratorial View of History – A. Ralph Epperson (1982)
Fabian Freeway: High Road to Socialism in the USA – Rose L. Martin (1966) (Recommended)
Lies my Teacher Told Me – James W. Loewen (1995)
The Anglo American Establishment – Carroll Quigley (1981)

## The Evolution of Consciousness Series

**Book 1**

*A Philosophy for the Average Man: An Uncommon Solution to a World Without Common Sense by Endall Beall*

**Book 2**

*Willful Evolution: The Path to Advanced Cognitive Awareness and a Personal Shift in Consciousness by Endall Beall*

**Book 3**

*Demystifying the Mystical: Exposing Myths of the Mystical and the Supernatural by Providing Solutions to the Spirit Path and Human Evolution by Endall Beall*

**Book 4**

*Navigating into the Second Cognition: The Map for your journey into higher Conscious Awareness by Endall Beall*

**Book 5**

*The Energy Experience: Energy work for the Second Cognition by Mrs. Endall Beall*

**Book 6**

*We Are Not Alone – Part 1: Advancing Cognitive Awareness in an Interactive Universe by Endall Beall*

**Book 7**

*We Are Not Alone – Part 2: Advancing Cognitive Awareness through Historical Revelations - Endall Beall*

**Book 8**

*Advanced Teachings for the Second Cognition by Mrs. Endall Beall*

**Book 9**

*We Are Not Alone – Part 3: The Luciferian Agenda of the Mother Goddess by Endall Beall*

## Companion Volumes to The Evolution of Consciousness Series

*False Prophecies, Reassessing Buddha and the Call to the Second Cognition by Endall Beall*

*Operator's Manual for the True Spirit Warrior by Endall Beall*

*Spiritual Pragmatism: A Practical Approach to Spirit Work in a World Controlled by Ego by Endall Beall*

*Revamping Psychology: A Critique of Transpersonal Psychology Viewed From the Second Cognition by Endall Beall & Mrs. Endall Beall*

*The Common Sense Revolution: Creating Common Ground and Genuine Common Sense – Endall Beall and the Psoyca Crew*

# Second Cognition Series

## Book 1

*The New Paradigm Transcripts: Teachings for a New Tomorrow by Endall Beall & Doug Michael*

## Book 2

*Breaking the Chains of the First Cognition: Tools for Understanding the Path to the Second Cognition by Endall Beall & Doug Michael*

## Book 3

*PSOYCA – Road to the Second Cognition by Endall Beall & Doug Michael*

## Book 4

*The Energetic War Against Humanity: The 6,000 Year War Against Human Cognitive Advancement by Endall Beall*

## Book 5

*The Cognitive Illusion of History: How Humanity Has Been Controlled Through Selective and Biased Historical Reporting by Endall Beall & Doug Michael*

## Book 6

*The Second Cognition Toolbox: Requirements for Advancing Your Consciousness by Endall Beall*

## Book 7

*Firestarters: The Gemma and Endall Transcripts – by Endall Beall and Gemma Beall*

## Book 8

*No Trespassing: Creating a New World Based on Mutual Respect by Endall Beall*

## Book 9

*Psoyca Consciousness by Endall Beall*

## Companion Volumes to the Second Cognition Series

*Understanding Wisdom: A Treatise on Wisdom Viewed from the Second Cognition by Endall Beall*

*From Belief to Truth – From Truth to Wisdom by Endall Beall*

*The Psychology of Becoming Human: Evolving Beyond Psychological Conditioning by Endall Beall*

## Standalone Work: Available for free .pdf download at our website

*Clarifying the don Juan Teachings for the Second Cognition: A Pragmatic Reanalysis Without the Mystical Misdirection – by Endall Beall*

## Beyond Second Cognition Series

*Gutting Mysticism: Explaining the Roots of All Supernatural Belief by Endall Beall (2018)*

For questions or inquiries contact the authors at *http://demystifyingthemystical.com/#/*

Further work by these authors can be found at the Gemma Beall YouTube channel at

https://www.youtube.com/channel/UCN3VfiNrozRSUBiDIR8k9EA

Or through the Gemma Beall Patreon channel for subscriptions of $5 per month for access to 300 video presentation, and $15 per month for all the videos and an expanding number of educational podcasts, chapter reviews, blogs and an interactive comment forum.

https://www.patreon.com/GemmaBeall/

93564134R00303

Made in the USA
Lexington, KY
15 July 2018